Rich and Poor
in Grenoble,
1600–1814

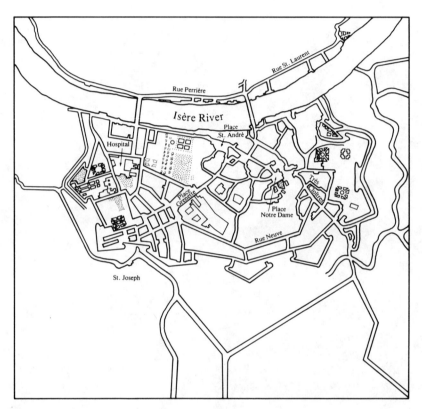

Grenoble, 1776

Rich and Poor
in Grenoble,
1600–1814

Kathryn Norberg

UNIVERSITY OF CALIFORNIA PRESS
Berkeley · Los Angeles · London

University of California Press
Berkeley and Los Angeles, California
University of California Press, Ltd.
London, England
© 1985 by
The Regents of the University of California
Printed in the United States of America

1 2 3 4 5 6 7 8 9

Library of Congress Cataloging in Publication Data

Norberg, Kathryn, 1948–
    Rich and poor in Grenoble, 1600–1814.

    Bibliography: p.
    Includes index.
    1. Grenoble (France)—Social conditions. 2. Charities—France—Grenoble—
History—17th century. 3. Poor—France—Grenoble—History—17th century. 4.
Charities—France—Grenoble—History—17th century. 5. Poor—France—Grenoble—
History—19th century. I. Title.
HN 438.G7N67 1985   305'.0944'99   84-16262
ISBN 0-520-05260-9

Contents

List of Illustrations   viii

List of Tables   ix

Preface   xi

Introduction   1

PART I: THE SEVENTEENTH CENTURY

1. Grenoble at the Beginning of the Seventeenth
   Century   11
2. Mothers to the Poor: The Confraternities of
   the Orphans and the Madelines   20
3. Great Works: The Company of the Holy
   Sacrament (1642–1662)   27
   The Company of Grenoble   28
   Crimes and Sins: Criminality in Seventeenth-
   Century Grenoble   40
   Attitudes toward the Poor in the Seventeenth Century   58
4. The Crusade for the Conversion of Souls: The
   Congregation for the Propagation of the
   Faith (1647–1685)   65

5. From Transgression to Misfortune: Poverty
   and Poor Relief in an Age of Transition
   (1680–1729)   81
   Charitable Activity between 1680 and 1729   82
   Deviance at the Turn of the Century   92
   Beggars and Paupers   100
6. Patterns of Charity: Testamentary Bequests
   (1620–1729)   113
   The Increase in Charitable Giving   117
   The Growth of Religious Giving   123
   Protestant and Catholic Testamentary Bequests   137
   Bequests to the Unconfined Poor   149

PART II: THE EIGHTEENTH CENTURY

7. Educating the Poor: The "Little" Schools
   (1707–1789)   159
8. The Hospital General in the Age of Light
   (1760–1789)   169
   New Problems and New Personnel   170
   The Hospital and Its Inmates   175
   The Poor Outside the Hospital   182
   Petitions from the Poor   192
   Illegitimacy and the Hospital   198
9. Vagrants and Criminals in the Eighteenth
   Century   216
   The King's Charity: The Dépôt de Mendicité   216
   Criminality in the Late Eighteenth Century   226
10. Patterns of Charity (1730–1789)   239
    Wills and Testaments   240
    Pamphlets and Essays   257
11. The Revolution (1789–1814)   267

Conclusion   295

Appendix A. Composition of the Sample of
   Wills: 1620–1729   305

Appendix B. Percentage of Testators Making
Bequests to the Hospital: Selected
Regression Results   306

Appendix C. Composition of the Eighteenth-
Century Sample of Testaments: 1730–1789   307

Notes   309

Archival Sources   343

Selected Bibliography   345

Index   353

Illustrations

Map
Grenoble, 1776   Frontispiece

Figures
1. Percentage of Testators Making Pious and Charitable
   Bequests   117
2. Homes of the Poor according to the Bread Distribution
   Lists of 1712–1722   184
3. Homes of the Poor according to the Bread Distribution
   Lists of 1771–1774   185

Tables

1. Percentage of Testators Making Charitable Bequests — 119
2. Percentage of Testators Who Made Charitable Bequests — 123
3. Percentage of Testators Who Made Pious Bequests — 125
4. Percentage of Testators Making Pious Bequests — 127
5. Percentage of Testators Who Made Pious Bequests — 132
6. Composition of Protestant and Catholic Samples — 139
7. Percentage of Protestants Who Gave to the Poor — 142
8. Percentage of Protestants Making Charitable Bequests — 143
9. Comparison of Average Protestant and Catholic Donations to Charity — 144
10. Percentage of Protestants Who Gave to the Consistory — 145
11. Selected Regression Coefficients — 155
12. Age of Hospital Inmates — 178
13. Family Status of Adult Hospital Inmates — 179
14. Percentage of Healthy and Sick Hospital Inmates according to Age — 180
15. Health of Inmates at the Time of Their Admission to Hospital — 182
16. Bread Recipients in the Early and Late Eighteenth Century — 186
17. Selected Occupations of Bread Recipients — 188
18. Heads of Household in the Capitations of 1735 and 1789 — 189
19. Percentage of Households in Each Category Which Were Impoverished — 190
20. Place of Seduction of Unwed Mothers — 202
21. Geographical Origins and Residences of Unwed Mothers — 203

22. Occupations of Unwed Mothers   204
23. Occupations of Unwed Fathers   205
24. Relationship between Unwed Mothers and Unwed Fathers   208
25. Father's Reaction to Lover's Unwed Pregnancy   212
26. Gender of the Inmates of the Dépôt   221
27. Origins of the Inmates Incarcerated in the Dépôt   222
28. Origins of Dépôt Inmates in the Late Eighteenth Century   223
29. Age of Individuals Arrested for Begging   225
30. Percentage of Urban Testaments Containing Bequests to the
    Hospital General   241
31. Percentage of Testaments Containing Charitable Bequests   242
32. Percentage of Testators Making Charitable Bequests   243
33. Percentage of Testaments Containing Pious Bequests   245
34. Percentage of Testaments Containing Pious Bequests and
    Size of Pious Bequests   246
35. Percentage of Pious Bequests in Testaments by Males Only   248
36. Percentage of Testaments Made by Men and Women
    Containing Pious Bequests   251
37. Percentage of Religious Bequests among Nobles,
    Magistrates, and Bourgeois   252
38. Percentage of Bequests to Peasants in Testaments   256
39. Comparison of the Recipients of Aid in 1793 with
    Recipients in 1771–1774   277
40. Hospital Inmates in 1790 and the Year VIII   293

Preface

This book began years ago as a paper for a graduate seminar at Yale University. At that time, it took the form of a short essay on attitudes toward the poor and constituted, I believed, a small contribution to the then popular history of "mentalities." Years have passed, and this project has undergone many transformations. It has grown in length and breadth, spawned new chapters and new tables, acquired new material and new interpretations. In short, it has become a very different study, larger in scope and greater in ambition. Three developments in social history prompted these changes. The first, the emergence of women's history, confirmed my interest in women and caused me to investigate topics like prostitution and illegitimacy. The second, the development of quantitative methods, allowed me to deal with large amounts of data and apply fairly sophisticated statistical tests to thousands of wills and testaments and scores of hospital records and lists of beggars. Finally, the prestige currently enjoyed by cultural anthropology convinced me that I should put aside my scruples about sparse data and attempt to analyze popular norms and values. Now, the views of the poor have their place next to the attitudes of the rich. Consequently, this project is no longer a study of elite ideas. It now makes, I hope, some small contribution to women's history, to the development of quantitative methods, and to our knowledge of popular customs and culture.

While writing this book, I incurred many debts. Professor R. R. Palmer guided this project through the dissertation stage; Professors John Merriman and J. H. Hexter also read the original thesis. Even a cursory examination of the book will reveal the debt I owe to two distinguished French historians, Michel Vovelle and Jean-Pierre Gutton. This book has greatly profited from their example and their criticism. Natalie Zemon Davis, Nancy Roelker, and Lynn Hunt also read the manuscript and brought their own unique critical faculties to bear upon it. A number of colleagues from the University of California helped me refine my argument. Robert Ritchie, Susannah Barrows, Ted and Jo Margadant, Paul Hansen, and Jeff Sawyer read a particularly rough draft. So too did Judith Hughes, who provided invaluable criticism when I most needed it. Karen Andrews typed the final manuscript. The Director of the University of California Press, Jim Clark, facilitated and accelerated the publication of this book.

It is traditional for historians to thank the archivists who provided the raw material for their work. My own debt in this regard is particularly great. Summer after summer and year after year, the Director of the Archives Départementales de l'Isère, Monsieur Vital Chomel, welcomed me to Grenoble and shared with me his expertise as archivist and historian. His excellent and efficient staff also helped enormously. Of course, archival work would not be possible without financial support. Grants from the Academic Senate of the University of California, San Diego, and the National Endowment for the Humanities funded my research. An Affirmative Action grant from the Regents of the University of California also allowed me to complete crucial archival work. Computer time was supplied in abundance by the University of California, San Diego. Without the unfailing patience of the consultants at the UCSD Computer Center, I could never have used it wisely. Finally, I owe the greatest thanks to my husband, Philip. He criticized the manuscript at every stage, proofread innumerable drafts, and most of all, listened to my incessant chatter. To him this book is dedicated.

Introduction

The subject of this book is the relationship between the rich and the poor at their point of closest contact in seventeenth- and eighteenth-century France—poor relief. Its purpose is not just to examine institutions and outline elite attitudes; nor is it merely to describe poverty and enumerate the forces that produced it. This study will address these topics, and it will deal with hospitals and workhouses, beggars and thieves, devout ladies and rich benefactors. But that is not its primary goal. The principal purpose of this book is to investigate poor relief, not for its own sake, but for what it can tell us about broader social conditions, about fundamental social and economic relations. Years ago, historians of English poor relief adopted a similar approach. J. H. Tawney and others used social welfare as a barometer of change and saw in innovations like the "new medicine for poverty" signs of England's journey toward capitalism and modernity. Obviously, Marx influenced some of these enquiries, but so too did Weber, for British historians were particularly quick to appreciate the impact of culture upon social relations. They did not ignore religion, and they scrutinized closely and at length the social assumptions inherent in Protestantism. The result was a body of literature in which poor relief functioned as a mirror of English society and illuminated the whole social landscape.

For a number of reasons, French historians have taken a slightly different approach. Writing years after British scholars, the French tended to be more "scientific," to marshal large amounts of data, and to specialize in only one aspect of the subject. Olwen Hufton, Richard Cobb, and their students examined the conditions that created poverty and painted vivid, insightful portraits of the poor themselves. Jean-Pierre Gutton and Cissie

1

Fairchilds focused on institutions and greatly increased our knowledge of formal relief. Attitudes toward the poor, on the other hand, remained the special preserve of yet another group of scholars, intellectual historians, in particular historians of the Enlightenment. Rich and poor, therefore, tended to be isolated from one another, dealt with in separate, specialized works. Even Jean-Pierre Gutton, who treated attitudes toward the poor and also the economic sources of poverty, confined each in separate, seemingly unrelated chapters. The relationship between the prosperous and the impoverished, between elite attitudes and material conditions, has thus remained unexamined and unclear.

So too has the connection between poor relief and other historical developments, be they social, economic, or cultural. Unlike their British predecessors, French scholars were reluctant to venture into what they apparently considered alien territory. They mentioned cultural movements, but they hesitated to explore them. Counter Reformation Catholicism, despite its importance, received scant attention, and "dechristianization" was evoked but not examined. They declined to consider the culture of the poor at all, deeming it the preserve of other specialists. As for economic trends, French scholars were not inclined to see changes in poor relief as manifestations of economic development. Perhaps their reluctance stemmed from the confusion which hangs over this field and still fuels bitter debate. But French historians were disinclined to talk about any change, be it economic, cultural, or institutional. Most operated within the context of the "old regime," a useful concept which accommodates sparse documentation, but which imposes a false homogeneity on over two hundred years of French history. Under these circumstances, relations between the rich and the poor could not serve as a barometer of social change or, for that matter, anything else. The history of poor relief could not function as a mirror of the rest of society, because it was too specialized, too static, and too self-contained to reflect anything but itself.

Consequently, despite a distinguished body of literature, some questions remain unanswered. Why did attitudes toward the poor change? In what ways did culture, in particular religion or the lack thereof, affect social attitudes? Why were the French more generous toward the poor at certain times and less at others? What forces lay behind qualitative changes in the ties between rich and poor? This study will try to answer these questions by adopting the broadest approach possible. It will bring the rich and the poor together again and place the judge beside the criminal, the benefactor next to the beggar. Institutions, attitudes, and economic conditions will all be dealt with, not just within the same covers, but within the same context, for the rich are incomprehensible without the poor, and vice versa. The poor, for example, shaped attitudes toward poverty: a rich man's notions about destitution varied according to whether he found a menacing vagabond or a helpless invalid before him. The rich also color our notions about the poor: the powerful and therefore the prosperous drew up the documents which tell us about poverty, and we must peel away the distortions imposed by the elites before we can arrive at an accurate understanding of the poor.

We must also take into account culture, that is, religion. Post-Tridentine Catholicism played in France a role similar to Puritanism in England. It dictated social attitudes and lent to institutions their sometimes peculiar shape. The compulsion to imprison all paupers in a workhouse, a peculiar notion but one central to seventeenth-century poor relief, is incomprehensible without reference to religion, in this case Catholicism. The time, effort, and money expended by elites upon such strange endeavors as the rehabilitation of prostitutes and the detection of fornicators makes no sense unless the Counter Reformation is taken into account. Poor relief lay in the hands of devout laymen and laywomen throughout much of the seventeenth and eighteenth centuries, and it cannot be considered apart from the spiritual revival that inspired these benefactors.

The culture of the rich must be examined, and so too must the culture—the values and habits—of the poor. Early modern men and women did not regard the impoverished solely as economic actors. In a beggar they saw not just a penniless individual, but a heathen who flouted the dictates of the Church and indulged in every sort of debauchery. Consequently, we too must examine the religion and morality of the poor and try to determine to what degree popular attitudes toward everything from fornication to the sacraments differed from elite norms. Of course, as historians never tire of remarking, the people of early modern Europe were "inarticulate," but that does not mean that they were mute. Historians can hear the voices of the people if they listen closely enough, if they consider documents which, on the surface, have little to do with popular culture. Judicial records, for example, provide considerable information on popular values in the form of lengthy depositions by casual witnesses. The people's views on prostitution, theft, vagabondage, and even the Church can be discerned from documents once used only to determine rates of crime.

Historians cannot overlook culture, nor should they ignore informal attempts at relief. Scholars of French social welfare have tended to focus solely upon large institutions, upon municipal hospitals-general or national *dépôts de mendicité*. They have done so, it seems, partly because official institutions produce plenty of documents, partly because of an unspoken assumption that only the State can provide significant aid. This assumption may well be true, but it is of little help when applied to a society where charity rather than public assistance was the norm. Much charity lay in the hands of small, religious associations—confraternities—which sponsored asylums and hospitals and tended to many of the sick and homeless. These confraternities were inspired by post-Tridentine Catholicism, but they were not tied to the Church. Devout laymen and pious laywomen created and staffed these organizations, and their efforts, though scattered and personal, were in many ways more typical of early modern France than the programs of the great institutions raised up by the government.

Furthermore, the financial support for both formal and informal organizations came from voluntary donations, principally deathbed bequests contained in last wills and testaments. Despite Michel Vovelle's pioneering work, historians of poor relief have been reluctant to examine wills. They have not investigated the numerous and varied bequests to the poor found in testaments, nor have they employed them to determine who gave to charity and why. This study, by contrast, will examine wills—some 5,000—and use them to chart the qualitative and quantitative evolution of charity. I will establish rates of charitable giving and explore the assumptions that inspired altruism. At the same time, I will compare legacies to the poor with bequests to the Church in order to examine the influence of post-Tridentine Catholicism or the effect of the Enlightenment on social attitudes. Wills allow us to measure the impact of cultural and social forces on attitudes toward the poor. No other document permits us to do so; no other covers such a long period of time. Last wills and testaments are not only valuable, they are indispensable.

If wills are such an enlightening source, it is because they are amenable to quantification, to advanced statistical techniques like multiple regression and tobit analysis. Of course, not all sources welcome quantification. Such an approach would be inappropriate and misleading when applied to judicial records. In the proper circumstances though, statistics do reveal changes that might otherwise go unnoticed. We need not assume, as does Jean-Pierre Gutton, that the poor did not change over the course of two hundred years. With even the simplest statistics, we can, for example, determine what caused illegitimacy and show how changes in the economy promoted growing bastardy. We can also compare bread-distribution rolls, registers of beggars, and lists of hospital inmates to determine how the incidence of poverty shifted over time and how certain groups became more vulnerable than others.

In other words, we can see how the poor changed and how attitudes toward poverty and institutions of poor relief changed with them. To facilitate this task, I have adopted a chronological organization which has the disadvantage of fragmenting the story of, say, a hospital, but has the benefit of bringing together diverse phenomena. The material conditions that created poverty, criminality, illegitimacy, popular culture, and popular religion can be considered at the same time as elite attitudes and charitable institutions. The interconnections then emerge, and the forces that made for changes in attitudes and institutions appear. Of course, notions about the poor and economic circumstances changed only slowly, particularly in old regime France. One must therefore take an extremely long period of time, and this study will deal with the whole period between 1600 and 1814. It will emphasize the seventeenth century because this period has been slighted by historians of poor relief, and it will carry the story of the rich and the poor up through the Revolution.

Such a wide chronological scope necessitates a narrow geographical focus, and so this study will deal with just one town, Grenoble. To claim that any city in early modern France was "typical" is foolhardy, but Grenoble certainly was not unusual. It was of average size—20,000 souls— and of average political and economic importance. Moreover, Grenoble experienced many of the events that historians generally regard as typical of the seventeenth and eighteenth centuries. In the seventeenth century, Grenoble was a relatively sleepy administrative center, dependent upon its sovereign courts and dominated by a local, landed elite. It knew conflict between Protestant and Catholic; it embraced the religious revival that we today call the Counter Reformation. In the eighteenth century, Grenoble, like the rest of Dauphiné, enjoyed an economic revival which brought industry to the town and produced an indigenous bourgeoisie enamored of Enlightenment ideas and enriched by commerce and industry. In 1788, conflict among the three estates erupted, and Grenoble rushed prematurely into the Revolution. Political turmoil plagued the city, and so too did economic dislocation aggravated by war. Gradually, the revolutionary ardor of the first years of the Revolution waned, and Grenoble sank back into conservatism and diffidence. Because it experienced those trends we associate with the seventeenth and eighteenth centuries, Grenoble provides a suitable "lens" through which to view the evolution of French social relations.

Grenoble also witnessed a considerable amount of activity in the area

that concerns us here—poor relief. In the first three quarters of the seventeenth century, responsibility for public assistance lay with private groups,
with lay religious associations, confraternities. Three groups were particularly active in Grenoble: a women's confraternity devoted to the care of
orphans and the rescue of prostitutes; the Company of the Holy Sacrament,
a secret organization which literally ran the city's largest purveyor of relief,
the Hospital General; and the Congregation for the Propagation of the
Faith, a self-proclaimed charity which devoted itself to the elimination of
spiritual poverty, that is, Protestantism. The first chapters of the book deal
with these confraternities and seek to establish through them the fundamental characteristics of seventeenth-century charity. These chapters examine the social composition, spirituality, and charitable activities of these
groups and contrast their special social vision with the reality of popular
culture in mid-seventeenth-century Grenoble. The criminal court records
provide the basis for this comparison, and the sins which obsessed the
rich—illegitimacy, prostitution, and blasphemy—receive special attention. Grenoble's benefactors, like their Protestant rivals in Puritan England,
sought to stamp out such manifestations of "disorder" but with less and
less enthusiasm after 1680. The fifth chapter examines the birth of a new,
more humane and less punitive vision of the poor and tries to establish its
causes. A diminution in crime did not lie behind the new attitude; nor did a
decrease in poverty. Criminal records show that violence increased, and
hospital records—registers of beggars and lists of bread recipients—demonstrate that poverty afflicted unprecedented numbers of Grenoblois. Still,
the years between 1680 and 1729 witnessed an outpouring of alms, a phenomenon more closely examined in the chapter on wills and testaments.
Here, the evolution of charitable giving and the dissemination of post-
Tridentine Catholicism is explored. Themes introduced earlier—the contrast between Protestant and Catholic, the disparities between elite and
popular culture, and the social impact of the Counter Reformation—are
reexamined, and the fundamental quality of seventeenth-century poor relief—seigneurialism—is reconfirmed.

The second part of the book seeks to define Enlightenment social attitudes and begins with a discussion of Grenoble's charity schools, a subject
which illustrates the transition from seventeenth- to eighteenth-century
charity. The focus then switches to the city's major institution of poor
relief, the Hospital General, which came under new leadership in the
eighteenth century and which adopted new, restrictive policies. Hospital
records—lists of bread recipients and registers of inmates—provide insight into the changing incidence of poverty. *Déclarations de grossesse*, or

unwed mothers' statements, also shed light on the causes of the Hospital's principal problem: a rise in illegitimacy. In the ninth chapter, popular habits and values come under closer scrutiny. The records of Grenoble's beggars' prison, or *dépôt de mendicité,* and its criminal court show that although geographic mobility and theft were increasing among the poor, violence was declining. This change in popular habits and values is explored in greater detail in the tenth chapter, which deals with eighteenth-century wills and testaments. These documents demonstrate that seigneurial charity and post-Tridentine Catholicism both lost their appeal in the late eighteenth century. The once rapid flow of testamentary bequests also slowed to a trickle. Only the aristocrats observed the traditional forms and clung to the old notions. Other Grenoblois struck out in new directions, directions best seen through the pamphlets and essays concerning poor relief written by rather average Grenoblois. This penultimate chapter summarizes the fundamental qualities of Enlightenment charity and argues that the new view of poverty led to a diminution of relief rather than an increase, as has commonly been assumed. The Revolution, however, ushered in a new set of circumstances, primarily political circumstances, that led to a renaissance of charitable activity. The last chapter covers the years between 1789 and 1814 and deals with all aspects of public assistance from voluntary charity to municipal relief programs.

This study seeks to understand why charity took different forms at different times and why it was more plentiful under some circumstances than under others. I will make comparisons, in particular comparisons between Protestant and Catholic, and between seventeenth- and eighteenth-century poor relief. But I do not mean to claim or even infer that one was somehow superior to another. Traditionally, historians of poor relief, whatever their country of specialty, have claimed that a society may be judged by the degree to which it provides for the disadvantaged. This study attempts no such judgments, for two reasons. First, all societies in the past failed to provide for the poor because all failed to eliminate poverty. I consider it axiomatic that no form of poor relief, Protestant or Catholic, seventeenth- or eighteenth-century, was efficient or sufficient to its task. Second, we have no standard by which to judge the past, for we have no superior knowledge and no successful formula for dealing with poverty. We ourselves have failed to do away with hunger and want, and our society will probably not fare very well at the hands of future generations. We should not celebrate without reservation those who come closest to our own ideas and institutions, as historians have been wont to do.

If the historian cannot judge, he can at least understand. This alone seems a tall order. The relations between rich and poor manifested themselves in numerous, seemingly endless ways: in the treatment meted out to an unwed mother, in the posture adopted before an insistent beggar, in the sentence handed down to a common thief, in the bread distributed to an ordinary pauper, and in the deathbed bequests made by an average citizen. Different cultures stimulated the social conscience in different ways, and various circumstances, not the least among them the poor themselves, produced various responses to poverty. To elucidate these relationships is a difficult task, but once performed it should illuminate the whole social landscape. The historian does not need to condemn or to justify seventeenth- and eighteenth-century French men and women; at best he can only hope to do them justice.

NOTE ON MONETARY AMOUNTS

To correct for inflation and devaluation, all monetary amounts cited in the text and in the tables have been converted to constant-value livres, using the decennial index of grain prices at the Grenoble market established by Henri Hauser in *Recherches et documents sur l'histoire des prix en France de 1500 à 1800,* pp. 370–371. The original monetary figures were divided by this index to yield livres tournois of constant value, with the 1730s as a base period. Other methods of dealing with inflation and devaluation (such as converting livres to their silver equivalent according to the tables in Natalis de Wailly, *Mémoire sur les variations de la livre tournois depuis le règne de St. Louis jusqu'à l'établissement de la monnaie décimale,* pp. 348–353) produced similar results. Consequently, neither devaluation nor inflation distorts the monetary data in the text.

PART ONE

The Seventeenth Century

Grenoble at the Beginning of the Seventeenth Century

On the nineteenth of October 1626, a solemn procession formed at the Hôtel de la Trésorie on the Place Saint André in Grenoble. Pageantry, even funerary, was rare in this small provincial capital nestled between the spectacular peaks of the Vercors, Belledonne, and Chartreuse mountains, so large crowds lined the streets in hope of catching a final glimpse of the person Stendhal considered "the last great man Dauphiné ever produced."[1] A week earlier, François de Bonne, duc de Lesdiguières and lieutenant-général of Dauphiné, had written his last codicil, naming as his universal heir his son-in-law, the duc de Créqui, and bestowing upon the mendicant orders and the hospital at Vizille several large and generous bequests. Then, dressed in the cowl of his Capuchin confessors and clutching a medal blessed by Saint Charles Borromeo, the old warrior received the holy viaticum and died quietly in his bed at the age of eighty-three.[2] His body was removed to the cathedral of Valence where it lay in state for several days, after which it was transported under escort to Grenoble. As the cortege moved across the plains of the Rhone valley, throngs of peasants crowded along the roadside to see the coffin of the mighty seigneur who had published *corvées* with the laconic postscript "come or burn."[3]

At Grenoble the procession brought together not only the relatives and retainers of Lesdiguières, but all of the city's notables. To the spectators, the cortege presented a lavish spectacle. To the historian, it provides a useful tableau of every aspect of Grenoble's life at the very beginning of the seventeenth century. Leading the procession were the provosts of Lesdiguières troops and behind them a swarm of notaries, lawyers, and advisers of various sorts who were a part of the duke's substantial household. After them came men of the Church. First, Grenoble's premier cleric, the bishop, accompanied by the canons of the cathedral, Notre Dame, and the canons of the collegiate church of Saint André. The regular clergy followed: Discalced Augustinians, Capuchins, Recollets, Minims, Sisters of Saint Clare, Cordeliers, Jacobins, and the canons regular of Saint Laurent. The religious formed a dark mass of hoods, which utterly obscured the handful of parish priests in attendance and aptly symbolized the dominance of the regulars in Grenoble's religious life.

Beside the corpse of Lesdiguières marched the most prestigious, most prosperous, and most respected citizens of the city—the magistrates of the sovereign courts, the Parlement of Dauphiné, and the Chambre des Comptes. First came the presidents of the Parlement, the highest ranking judges, then the counselors, the second most prestigious members of the court, and then finally the secretaries, *huissiers,* and lawyers who, though not a part of the bench, served it. Some guildsmen and the municipal officers followed, with a humble group bringing up the rear of the procession: two hundred paupers dressed in black cassocks and mantles, bearing torches emblazoned with the Lesdiguières coat of arms.[4]

Lesdiguière's funeral was exceptional in its ostentation; it would be years before Grenoble saw such magnificence again. But the funeral was typical in that like all such rituals it marked both a beginning and an ending, it pointed to the future and yet sealed the past. That October day, the Grenoblois honored not just the death of one man but the end of a whole era. Never again would a Dauphinois rise from obscurity—in Lesdiguières' case the complete obscurity of a notary's son—to occupy a position of such power and prestige. When Lesdiguières died, so too did a certain kind of warrior-noble, for the violent society which rewarded the condottiere's democratic virtues of cunning and brutality had also died. When Lesdiguières and his men seized the city for the Protestant cause on the night of November 24, 1590, the bloodshed and chaos we refer to as the Wars of Religion came to an end for Grenoble.[5] Tension between Protestant and Catholic remained, but when in 1622 Lesdiguières traded his Protestantism for Catholicism and the office of *connétable,* the highest military rank in the kingdom, it became clear that the Church of Rome had on its side the powers that be. The victory of Roman Catholicism was now only a matter of time.

So too was the triumph of the king of France. In the Middle Ages Dauphiné had been an independent kingdom with its own sovereign and its own laws. The transfer, or more properly the sale, of the province to the kings of France in 1349 failed to extinguish the Dauphinois' spirit of independence, and for centuries they clung to their provincial liberties. During the Wars of Religion, ties between Paris and Grenoble were all but broken, and Lesdiguières profited from the situation to make himself, in the words of Henri IV, the "viceroy of Dauphiné."[6] Louis XIII did not long tolerate these pretensions: when in 1622 he offered Lesdiguières the *connétablie*, the king received in return not just the Protestant's conscience but his province as well. Royal envoys would continue to clash with provincial authorities, and the Dauphinois would continue to invoke their provincial liberties until the end of the old regime, but in 1622 the region's fate was sealed: the long, often painful absorption of the refractory province into the kingdom of France had begun.[7]

The monarchy was not the only force that triumphed in the 1620s and 1630s. Since the mid-sixteenth century, Dauphiné's third estate and its nobility had been engaged in a political struggle known as the *procès des tailles*. The third estate had demanded that the property tax, the *taille*, be changed from personal to real, thus attenuating the fiscal privileges of the nobility. The third estate argued its case brilliantly and vigorously before the monarchy, but the kings of France always turned a deaf ear. Then suddenly, in 1634, Louis XIII granted the third estate's demands, but the victory was only illusory. The king also abolished the Estates of Dauphiné, depriving the third of its voice, increasing the powers of that bastion of nobility, the Parlement, and extending, not coincidentally, his own prerogatives. A long and bitter conflict came to an end, and the ascension of the judicial elite, which would come to dominate the province, had begun.[8]

The defeat of the third estate can be traced, at least in part, to the popular uprisings known as the *ligues* which erupted in Dauphiné in the years between 1578 and 1580. The first two estates shrewdly—although quite unjustly—identified the third with these bloody rebellions and succeeded in discrediting the commoners by invoking the specter of social chaos. The insurrections of 1578 had indeed been social warfare in the full sense of the term: these uprisings pitted the poor against the rich, and the weak against the powerful, and constituted the most serious threat to authority the province had ever seen. When the repression came, it was swift, violent, and definitive. There would be minor incidents of popular violence in the seventeenth century, but the target would be royal taxation, not society as a whole. Never again—at least until the summer of 1789—would the people rise up in defiance of all authority.[9]

When all of these conflicts, social, political, and religious, were brought to a peaceful resolution, the sixteenth century came to a close in Dauphiné. Lesdiguières was the child of these turbulent years and, in many ways, their symbol, so when the Grenoblois buried him they buried an epoch too. For Grenoble, the seventeenth century had begun, and all signs indicated that for the city the *grand siècle* would be grand indeed. When in 1590 Lesdiguières and his men gazed down upon the city from the heights of Saint-Martin-le-Vinoux, they saw nothing but a tiny town, safely enclosed in its old Roman walls, a little provincial capital seemingly destined for complete obscurity. At this point Grenoble could easily have taken the same path as her Savoyard neighbor, Chambéry, and remained nothing but a little administrative center with hardly more than 10,000 souls. Or she could have emulated nearby Vienne, which happily stagnated in its Roman splendor. But thanks to the peace secured in the late sixteenth century, and to the enterprising spirit of her inhabitants, Grenoble asserted her personality and began a long process of growth.[10]

Growth occurred, first of all, in the number of Grenoblois: in 1591 there were only 10,000 Grenoblois; by 1643 the number had increased to 14,000, and in 1685 it had swelled to 22,000.[11] Because of this growth Grenoble was always spilling outside of its walls. The city's two *faubourgs,* or suburbs, Très Cloîtres southeast of the city, and the Granges southwest of the town, spread out into the countryside, approaching the villages of Saint Martin d'Herès and Echirolles. Lesdiguières built new walls for the city in the early seventeenth century, and so did his son-in-law, the duc de Créqui, in 1639, but by the end of the century Grenoble was once again bursting out of its fortifications. When Vauban visited the city in 1692 he observed that "Grenoble is so packed that there is no space; . . . the city desperately needs enlargement and both the great and the small demand it with insistence."[12]

Behind this population growth lay economic growth. Situated at the convergence of the routes between Geneva and Provence, Lyon and the Midi, and Paris and Italy, Grenoble had access to a number of markets. Before 1600, however, she had failed to take advantage of this favorable geographic position and rarely sent her goods outside the Grésivaudan valley. In the seventeenth and eighteenth centuries though, Grenoble developed into a little manufacturing center specializing in textiles and leather goods. It was in the early 1600s that the city emerged as a producer of linen and wool; the populous quarters of Très Cloîtres and the Granges came to shelter large numbers of flax-combers and wool-carders, whose goods were sold throughout France.[13] Textiles—stocking weaving, silk spinning, and linen production—continued to play an important part in the Grenoble economy, but they were overshadowed in the eighteenth century by the industry that would make Grenoble's reputation, glove making. Before 1700 only a few glove-makers worked in Grenoble, and their products rarely sold outside the Grésivaudan valley. Then in the early eighteenth century the industry began to grow and continued to do so until the 1780s, when it came to occupy almost 6,000 Grenoblois and Grenobloises, and to send its prestigious product to markets as distant as Russia and America.[14] The success of Grenoble's glove-making industry reflected the general economic growth of Dauphiné in the eighteenth century. Though the city did not profit directly from such enterprises as the Allevard foundries or the Voiron textile manufactures, it did serve as a banking and financial center for such ventures and as the home of many of Dauphiné's wealthy commercial entrepreneurs.[15]

Though she enjoyed a certain reputation as a manufacturing city, Grenoble was best known in the old regime for her courts, for the law was her first and most important industry. At the beginning of the seventeenth century, the city could boast a Parlement, a Chambre des Comptes, a Bailliage, and a municipal court, the Justice, which attracted plaintiffs from all over the province. The most prestigious body in the city was the Parlement, which traced its origins back to 1337, when the dauphin Hubert II had created the Conseil Delphinale. After the transfer of Dauphiné to the French monarchy, Louis XI lifted the council to the rank of sovereign court and endowed it with the powers enjoyed by the other parlements in the kingdom.[16] In 1557 a special court was annexed to the Parlement, the Chambre de l' Edit, so called because it was the result of the king's edicts involving Protestantism. This court was empowered to hear all cases involving Protestants and was staffed by an equal number of Protestant and Catholic magistrates. Its jurisdiction extended beyond Dauphiné to include Burgundy and Provence, provinces that did not possess such biconfessional institutions.[17] Established at the time of the dauphins, the Cour or Chambre des Comptes was an integral part of the Parlement until March 1628, when Louis XIII made it an independent body in the fashion of the Parisian Cour des Comptes.[18]

No parvenu nobility of the robe, the magistrates who sat in these sovereign courts came from the oldest and most prestigious families in the province. As one Dauphinois remarked, "there is no other Parlement in France that possesses a larger number of officers of ancient and noble extraction than the Parlement of Dauphiné."[19] Many of the magistrates, like the Revels, the Chateauneufs, and the Allemans, had ancestors who served Louis XI in the Conseil Delphinal, and all had brothers and cousins who occupied the highest offices in the Church and the army. Well born, the magistrates were also well endowed, and in Grenoble as everywhere else in the old regime, wealth meant land. The magistrates lived in Grenoble, but they possessed enormous estates outside the city, holdings in the distant Oisans mountains or the closer Rhone valley. Each summer when the heat became too oppressive, the judges discarded their magistrates' robes and fled to their rural estates, where they donned another garb, that of the *grand seigneur.*[20]

Though the magistrates were the most important and the most prestigious members of the judiciary, they were not the most numerous. A host of lawyers, notaries, *huissiers,* secretaries, and other minor functionaries gravitated around the courts. They formed what contemporaries called the *basoche* and what one historian has referred to as the "bourgeoisie of the robe."[21] Neither birth nor wealth distinguished these Grenoblois, for most came from *roturier* families and few made fortunes. But by their sheer numbers alone the lawyers and secretaries imposed themselves upon Grenoble society: in the early eighteenth century the *basoche* constituted 16 percent of the total male population.[22]

Grenoble was not just a judicial center; it was also the home of a large and wealthy clergy and the seat of the Bishop of Grenoble, who administered a diocese that stretched from the Grésivaudan valley all the way into Savoy. The heart of Grenoble's ecclesiastical world was the bishop's palace near the Place Notre Dame and the cathedral, which housed twenty-two canons in its cloisters and employed twenty auxiliary priests. More modest was the priory of Saint Laurent on the other side of the Isère River, which was served by four canons and one parish priest.[23]

By their wealth and numbers, the clergy formed an important part of Grenoble society. At the beginning of the eighteenth century, the clerics, both regular and secular, comprised some six hundred souls, or 2.9 percent of the city's population. The Church was also quite prosperous. The chapter of Notre Dame, for instance, owned eleven houses in the city, several more in the *faubourgs,* and important estates in the countryside around Grenoble. More impressive was the fortune amassed by the Dominicans. They had managed to acquire all the houses around Grenoble's marketplace, the Place Grenette, fifteen homes on the fashionable Rue Neuve, and several more buildings in the *faubourgs.* All in all, the clergy owned 11.2 percent of the inhabited buildings in the city, a figure obviously disproportionate to the clerics' numbers.[24]

Still, Grenoble was a city lacking in religious institutions. Only three parish churches—Saint Laurent, Saint Hugues, and Saint André—served the city's 15,000 souls. Located in a densely populated quarter, Saint Hugues was nothing more than a tiny anteroom stuck on to the cathedral.

The canons who controlled the little parish church tended to neglect it, and by 1613 it had fallen into such disrepair that it threatened to collapse. Saint Laurent, too, was dilapidated, so dilapidated that the parish priest refused to say mass in it. The villain in this story of decay was the Wars of Religion. Grenoble had once possessed a fourth parish church, Saint Jean—Saint Joseph, but the building had been destroyed during the seige of 1560, and its ruins still stood undisturbed at the southwestern end of the city in the middle of the seventeenth century.[25]

The Church in Grenoble presented a picture of decadence and decay, but in the early 1600s there were signs of a religious revival: abruptly, the regular clergy began to multiply. From the twelfth to the fifteenth century, Grenoble had possessed only nine convents and monasteries; then in the years between 1600 and 1666, the number swelled to eighteen and then reached twenty-two in 1690. By 1700 Grenoble housed within its walls Recollets, Capuchins, Discalced Augustinians, Visitadines, Ursulines, Minims, Carmelites, Religieuses du Verbe Incarné, and Jesuits.[26] But all these orders catered mainly to the rich; the impoverished still went unbaptized and unconfessed.

The poor were hungry for spiritual nourishment, but then they were desperate for terrestrial nourishment too. At the beginning of the seventeenth century, Grenoble's institutions of public welfare were in disarray. A hundred years before, the city government had reformed the network of hospices and leprosariums bequeathed to the city by the Middle Ages.[27] The consuls, the municipal officials, had begun by seizing ecclesiastical properties and uniting them under the supervision of a lay body, the Bureau des Pauvres. A poor tax provided the money, and an increase in begging the inspiration, and behind the consuls' scheme was one goal: the abolition of begging through the confinement of all paupers in a workhouse, or *maison de force*. As early as 1519, the consuls decided to establish such an institution, but it would be many years before they succeeded.[28]

In the late sixteenth century, a series of plagues and famines disrupted the life of the city and the consuls' attempts at reform. What was needed was immediate relief, not reorganization, and as one plague and famine after another battered the city in the years between 1560 and 1600 the consuls' work gradually came undone.[29] Once peace and prosperity returned to the city, it was Lesdiguières who urged the Grenoblois to resume their work. In 1614 and again in 1619 he commanded the municipality to impose a poor rate on all Grenoblois and to transform the delapidated Hospital Notre Dame into a proper house of confinement. In 1620, officials did round up some paupers and throw them into the Hospital, but the building proved too small to contain all the city's indigents, and the Grenoblois were too stingy to pay for enlargement.[30]

Only after Lesdiguières' death did the city finally begin building the house of confinement it had so long desired and needed. Appropriately, the initiative came from Lesdiguières' son-in-law and heir, the duc de Créqui. In the spring of 1627, the duke assembled in his quarters a group of notables, primarily magistrates, and proposed that they found a Hospital General. The duke donated some of his own property in the northwestern part of the city for the site, and an equal amount of land was supplied by the municipal government. In April the duke and a group of notables visited the site and sketched out a general plan:

> It is necessary to construct four large *corps de logis* which will form a square: on the left and the right there will be the dormitories of the men and women; at the entry the kitchens, dispensary, laundry and other offices necessary to such an institution, along with the bureau of the administrators and the concierge's rooms. On the fourth side of the compound, opposite the entry will be constructed the chapel, and next to it the sacristy, the priests' quarters, the dormitory for the foundlings and the rooms of the nuns and all others who will serve the inmates.[31]

Such a plan was ambitious, very ambitious given the financial capabilities of the city. But the old solution—a poor rate—was discarded in favor of another means of financing, voluntary charity. The duc de Créqui made the first donation, 1,500 livres, and the clergy followed his example, giving 1,000 livres. The nobility pledged 6,000 livres, the Chambre des Comptes, 6,000 livres, and the Parlement an equivalent sum. Obviously, the magistrates dominated the list of subscribers, and some of them were unusually generous: on the average a counselor pledged 150 livres and a president 600 livres.[32]

In many ways, this enterprise recalled the reforms of the past; the legacy of the sixteenth century definitely served as the foundation of Grenoble's Hospital General. But there were new elements, too, among them a reliance upon purely voluntary donations. Henceforth, charity, in the true sense of the word, would act as the support of Grenoble's institutions of social welfare. Another innovation was the predominance of the magistrates. With the founding of the Hospital, the judges usurped the role played, up until then, by the municipal authorities, and the fact did not escape the consuls' notice. They parried by obstructing all charitable projects emanating from the Parlement and by lodging bitter and violent complaints at the court when the magistrates all but excluded the municipality from the administration of the new Hospital. The third estate, too, opposed the hegemony of the magistrates, albeit more subtly: the third simply refused to pay its part of the costs. But all this opposition had no effect: charity remained—and for over a century—the exclusive preserve of the judicial elite.[33]

Thus, of the Grenoblois who attended the Hospital groundbreaking in 1627, the great majority were judges, magistrates at the sovereign courts. But there were also a fair number of cassocks to be seen in the crowd that day. The magistrates had allowed the Bishop of Grenoble and his canons to play a small role in the founding of the Hospital, and the clerics' influence was cemented by the edict of 1635, which granted them permanent seats on the Hospital's governing board. In the sixteenth century, poor relief had been the business of laymen, and the pauper a primarily secular being. But as the first wave of the Counter Reformation swept over Grenoble, charity regained its spiritual quality and the pauper his religious significance. The plaque erected by the founders on the site of the Hospital spoke eloquently of the changes that had occurred and those that were to come:

For the sake of Jesus Christ, King of the Poor, and for the love of God and Heaven, the charity of the men and women of Grenoble has built this hospital to care for the bodies and the souls . . . of the poor.[34]

TWO

Mothers to the Poor: The Confraternities of the Orphans and the Madelines

On the afternoon of July 17, 1638, the people of Grenoble witnessed a strange spectacle: they saw twelve orphan children and twenty-four noble ladies marching together through the city streets. The odd procession passed by the cathedral and down the Rue Perrière to the western edge of the city and the Hospital General. There the Hospital directors greeted the group and ushered it into the institution's chapel, where the bishop himself said a special mass. After the ceremony, the ladies escorted the children into a wing of the Hospital which would now be their new home and which would henceforth be known as the Orphans hospice.[1] Two years later, another new charitable institution appeared in the city. In the spring of 1638, an asylum for repentant prostitutes called, appropriately, the Madeline hospice, opened its doors in the Saint Laurent quarter on the Rue Perrière.[2]

These institutions announced the beginning of a charitable revival in Grenoble. In the years to come, scores of new hospices would spring up, and a whole new set of ideas about poverty would emerge. The institutions created in 1638 were the first and freshest manifestations of this new spirit, so they deserve close scrutiny. They were also the first indication that a new kind of private organization—the confraternity—would eclipse the municipal government as a purveyor of relief. Confraternities, or small, religious associations for lay people, were to play, in the administering of charity, a role quite disproportionate to their size. They stood behind every major innovation in social welfare made in Grenoble between 1630 and 1690, and they seem to have had an equal importance in other French cities.

Students of religious and cultural history have recognized the importance of confraternities, but historians of social welfare have generally overlooked them.[3] They seem to suffer from the assumption that only public authorities and large institutions provide poor relief. Such was not the case in the old regime in general or in the seventeenth century in particular. Furthermore, to overlook the confraternities is to overlook the very essence of seventeenth-century poor relief and to misunderstand its guiding principles. For seventeenth-century Frenchmen, public welfare and private beneficence were indistinguishable, and charity was as much a personal as a social obligation. In principle, close ties bound benefactor and pauper, and these ties were not well expressed by large institutions, though the Hospital General came very close to doing so. Seventeenth-century Frenchmen preferred the "artificial families," as Gabriel Le Bras once called the confraternities, and the history of poor relief in the seventeenth century is largely their story.[4]

If historians have overlooked these associations in general, they have utterly ignored one type of confraternity in particular—the womens' confraternity.[5] Two of Grenoble's hospices, the Madelines and the Orphans, owed their existence to associations established by women solely for women. The Madeline confraternity, for instance, was the creation of two of the most prestigious ladies in the province, the baronne d'Uriage and the wife of the "first president" of the Parlement, Madame du Faure. These two women decided to form an organization which would promote the spiritual development of its members through common devotions and good works, and they quickly found a supporter in the duchesse de Lesdiguières, widow of the famous *connétable*. Other women joined the organization, a Jesuit confessor was attached to the group, and the bishop gave the fledgling confraternity his blessing.[6]

Next the ladies turned to the charitable side of their venture: the creation of an asylum where prostitutes could be confined—either by choice or by the order of the civil authorities—and transformed into models of Christian virtue. The idea was hardly novel; similar institutions existed in other cities in France. But the ladies' project encountered resistance because one of these institutions had occasioned scandal. In Paris, the administrators of the capital's asylum for prostitutes had become a bit over-zealous and had taken to imprisoning perfectly respectable women.[7] Some Grenoblois aware of these abuses "found it inappropriate," the ladies tell us, "that free women should be forced to enter a sort of cloister and assume the bridle of Christ in order to shake off that of sin." The Sisters of the Madeline, however, soon convinced their critics of the confraternity's moderation, and the Madeline hospice opened in 1640.[8] Three years later, the ladies invited the nuns of the Visitation to assume the internal administration of the asylum, but the noblewomen remained intimately associated with their good work: they still retained ultimate authority in all matters, laid down the rules to be observed in the house, canvassed each Easter for funds, and regularly visited the inmates, joining them in their devotions.

The ladies of Grenoble's other female confraternity, the Orphans, had a more difficult time establishing their organization and its hospice. While visiting in Toulouse, Madame de la Croix de Chevrières, niece of the bishop and wife of the comte de Saint Jullien, met a group of women who belonged to a confraternity and sponsored an orphans' asylum. She decided to form such a group in Grenoble, and when she returned to the city she shared her plan with several young friends. At this point, the ladies made an unfortunate decision: they resolved "to maintain the strictest secrecy until the company was firmly established." The mystery in which they cloaked their project only served to alarm their relatives, disturb their husbands, and arouse all kinds of suspicions. Some people thought the young women witches who flew up chimneys and passed through windows and who met each Saturday for a Black Sabbath. Others found their secret gatherings simply ridiculous. The ladies became the butt of a "cruel joke," something very much like a charivari. Each Saturday, when they were on their way to the weekly meeting, "young men" accompanied them with catcalls, insults, and "a general clamor." This "raucous youth" even forced lackeys to shout insulting remarks about the women in public places throughout the city. In the face of such ridicule, the ladies wisely abandoned their vow of secrecy. They asked the bishop for his official blessing, which he granted after an almoner had been attached to the group, and in 1635 they purchased the wing of the Hospital General which was to serve as their hospice.[9]

In July of 1636, when the little procession opened the new hospice, the ladies of the Orphans could look back on their faltering origins with some irony. They had grown into a respected organization which had no difficulty attracting new members. In fact, during the period for which we possess records—1636 through 1702—sixty-six of the most prestigious women in the city joined the now flourishing association. Recruitment was particularly brisk in the years just following the confraternity's birth and again in the months just after the Fronde. On both occasions, the groups's membership doubled.[10]

According to the confraternity statutes, any woman of good morals and sincere piety, regardless of age, marital status, or social background, could join the Orphans. In reality, however, members came almost exclusively from the city's political and social elite. Of the sixty-six members during the years 1636 to 1702, more than half were of noble birth: 18 percent hailed from the nobility of the sword, while 56 percent were the wives and daughters of magistrates. Descending the social scale, only 16 percent belonged to the *basoche,* or petty officialdom, and a mere 9 percent came from bourgeois or *rentier* families.

The elite nature of the confraternity is not too surprising; it reflects the social composition of the Bureau of the Hospital General and similar male-dominated charities. In fact, 16 percent of the women had husbands who sat on the Hospital board. What is surprising is that these women had living husbands at all. Since Brantôme, it has been commonly assumed that in the France of the old regime only widows played any active role outside the home.[11] But only 18 percent of the Sisters of the Orphans confraternity were widowed at the time of their admission. The rest— with one exception—were married and probably had both lively husbands and young children, for the ladies themselves were, surprisingly enough, very young. Of the women whose age we can determine, most were under thirty. Madame de la Croix de Chevrières, the founder of the confraternity, was only twenty years old.

Piety and a common desire for "spiritual perfection" brought these young women together. The goal of the Orphans confraternity, the statutes explained, "was the consecration of the heart to God," and this consecration was to be achieved through a number of special devotions and spiritual exercises. Some of these devotions the ladies performed together: they met each week to discuss one another's spiritual progress, and they frequently attended special masses in the confraternity's chapel on the Rue Perrière. Other devotions were to be performed in private: the statutes required each lady to say a certain number of litanies each day and read some religious book for at least one hour each evening.[12]

More than prayers and readings lay along the road to Christian perfection; the statutes of the confraternity also obliged the ladies to perform certain charitable duties. "Always bear in mind," the ladies were instructed, "that you are responsible for the orphans of the hospice and must provide them with all kinds of blessings, both spiritual and material." So that the ladies might know just what "blessings" the orphans required, the Sisters of the confraternity had to visit their asylum frequently, at least once every two weeks. Some Sisters went far beyond these duties. Madame de Chissé not only provided the orphans with wine and bread, she also sewed their dresses with her own hands and groomed them "with great respect, for she considered them the daughters of the Mother of God." Other Sisters supplemented their work at the Orphans asylum with visits to the city's prisons or membership in either the Madeline or the Propagation of the Faith confraternity. The ladies also expressed their Christian charity in less formal, less institutionalized acts of beneficence. According to the biography written by the confraternity after her death, Anne de la Croix de Chevrières always maintained in her home a pauper child "in honor of our Lord and his Mother," and she frequently nursed the sick in villages near her rural estates. Claude de Chissé carried charity a step further: she "fed as many as thirty paupers at her table and took such delight in bandaging their cancers and other disgusting, suppurating sores that she literally washed these ulcers with her tears, so much she loved serving Jesus Christ through his paupers."[13]

The particular vision of poverty which inspired all these good works was most clearly revealed each Easter, when the ladies performed the ritual "washing of the feet." At noon on Good Friday, the ladies gathered in the Orphans hospital, and two assistants, "remembering the fervor and emotion with which Saint Peter and Saint John went to prepare the Last Supper," gathered the objects essential to the rite: a table spread with a white cloth, a crucifix covered with a veil, several candles, two basins filled with warm water and aromatic herbs, and several chairs for the children. Then, "performing the same actions to the same purpose" as Jesus at the Last Supper, the Sisters washed the feet of twelve of the orphans. When they had finished, the Sisters each kissed the paupers' feet and then knelt before the crucifix.

Clearly, a highly spiritualized vision of the poor was emerging and displacing the more secular view characteristic of the sixteenth century. Once again, the quest for salvation began with good works: the ladies received a dispensation of sixty days each time they performed the ritual "washing." Once again the pauper possessed a significance which transcended his worldly identity: he embodied the humility and suffering of Jesus, he was the image of Christ. In fact, at the ritual "washing of the feet" the poor ceased to be people at all: they were sacred objects, utensils like the crucifix and the candles, necessary to the ceremony but not its focus.

Obviously, this view of the poor bears a certain resemblance to the medieval conception of poverty. But the similarity is only superficial, for the seventeenth-century ladies of the Orphans and Madeline confraternities had a much more complex, much more contradictory social vision than their ancestors. They attributed to the poor certain virtues, but they also saw in them a host of vices. They believed that a prostitute could be sanctified, but only after she had gone through a long and hard process of contrition, for the fallen woman had to be "cleansed of the filth and sin which is attached to her soul." The poor might be the poor of Christ, but they belonged to the Devil too. Even the little orphans, the "children of the Mother of God," were, in the words of the ladies, "disgusting," "dirty," and depraved.[14]

Why then did these honorable women, the wives and mothers of lofty magistrates, rub shoulders with these vessels of sin? Because contact with the orphans and prostitutes allowed a Sister to mortify her own flesh and thereby master it. Each time she approached a depraved orphan or a corrupt prostitute, the Sister herself moved one step closer to heaven. She saved her own soul, but she did not ignore the salvation of her charges. As their statutes instructed them, the ladies had to concern themselves with the orphans' spiritual welfare too. Charity for the ladies had one, overriding goal: "the glorification of God through the perfect conversion of souls."

This conversion was to be accomplished by confinement in a spiritually pure hospice and unbending discipline. The Sisters of the Madeline wanted to remove their charges "from all objects and occasions which might act as traps"; they wanted to establish "a refuge from the tyranny of the world." The Madeline hospice was therefore an asylum in the true sense of the word, but it was not without its penal aspects. The inmates who were "rebellious in spirit or obstinate" received "grievous and exemplary punishment, such as imprisonment, bloody whipping, and fasting on bread and water." Those who were less stubborn were subjected to strict discipline and constant supervision. "The spirit of hell," the ladies of the Madeline explained, "puts disorder into all things; the spirit of God, however, arranges all things and disposes of them in an admirable fashion." Consequently, every minute of the inmates' day was prescribed and ordered.[15]

A new word—"order"—which was to have a long career had entered the vocabulary of charity, and another too made its appearance—"instruction." Along with discipline, the ladies employed a second means of conversion, education. At first they employed lay governesses as teachers in their asylum, but these young women did not live up to the ladies' demanding standards. In 1664 the Sisters of Saint Joseph, an order specially trained in teaching, assumed the internal administration of the hospice. Although considerably more experienced than the orphans, the prostitutes of the Madeline asylum also received instruction. Three times a week, the prostitutes met with the superior of the house, who taught them the fundamentals of the Catholic faith, who dispensed to them, in the words of the ladies, "the pure milk of solid, spiritual instruction."[16]

Thus, the ladies provided their charges with food, clothing, instruction, and moral support. They acted, in other words, "like perfect mothers to the poor." The expression appears over and over again in the confraternities' records, and the metaphor was, in fact, singularly appropriate. In the hospice, the women performed just those functions they performed in their own homes. In their own households, the ladies "worked as hard as possible for the salvation of their families"; in the hospice, they tried to save the poor. At home, the ladies had to see that "every member of the household was well instructed in all matters Christians should know"; at the asylum, they provided the same instruction to the poor. Within their families, the ladies cared for the young and sick; in their charity work, they also attended to the young—the orphans—and the spiritually sick—the prostitutes. The Sisters "acted in the quality of mothers," and even the hardened prostitutes of the Madeline were told "to consider the ladies as their mothers and accord them all the respect and obedience due to real mothers."[17]

A new social posture was emerging. For the first time, we can see the outlines of the peculiar paternalism which inspired seventeenth-century charity and measure the gulf which separated this form of beneficence from its medieval predecessor. Still, the novelty, even the modernity of charity in the seventeenth century is only partially revealed in the ladies' good works. Because they were women, the Sisters of the Madelines and Orphans could not meddle in affairs deemed "political," so their charity remained limited, modest, and discreet. Their male colleagues, of course, labored under no such constraints, and the men's confraternities made the full implications of the ladies' posture clear. To take the full measure of seventeenth-century charity, we must abandon the gentle "good works" of the Sisters of the Madelines and Orphans for the more ambitious (and nefarious) "great works" of a men's confraternity, the Company of the Holy Sacrament.

THREE

Great Works: The Company of the Holy Sacrament (1642–1662)

While the ladies of the Madelines and Orphans dispensed charity inside their hospices, another group of benefactors was quietly, but persistently, at work through the city. These gentlemen did not limit their charity to a hospital; it spilled out into the streets and penetrated right into the homes of the poor. These gentlemen did not perform mere "good works"; they effected, in their own words, something more sweeping, "great works." Here, in their ambitious efforts we can confront seventeenth-century charity at its fullest. We can establish the contours, only glimpsed among the retiring ladies, of beneficence in the age of the Counter Reformation and untangle the contradictory impulses that led to the house of confinement. We can appreciate the fundamental militancy and the essential modernity of this seemingly spiritual, traditional form of beneficence and analyze the social ethic that underlay it. Most important, we can also confront the poor themselves and scrutinize, as did these intrusive benefactors, their intimate behavior and their cherished values. For these men, unlike the gentle ladies of the Madelines and Orphans, admitted of no restrictions and observed no limitations, save one: secrecy. Ironically, this most militant of charitable organizations was also the most discreet. It was a branch of the infamous secret society, the Company of the Holy Sacrament.

The Company was born in Paris in 1627 and its father was a devout nobleman, Henri de Levis, duc de Ventadour. The duke wanted to form an organization that would "honor God and serve one's neighbor," and other equally aristocratic, equally devout Parisian gentlemen soon joined him.[1] In many ways, the new Company of the Holy Sacrament was like any other confraternity, but the Company had one singular quality—it was clandestine. "Experience," the founders explained in their statutes, "shows that éclat is the ruin of good works and vainglory the destruction of merit."[2] Secrecy allowed the Company to undertake more than simple good works; covertly it could pursue that more ambitious form of charity, "great works."

Among these works were the abolition of begging, the confinement of the poor, the extirpation of the Protestant heresy, and the general revival of Catholicism throughout France. Clearly, these projects were of more than local importance, and the Company needed auxiliaries in the provinces to achieve its goals. Therefore, the Parisians established fifty-six daughter houses, modeled on the original group and loosely tied to it, in cities throughout the kingdom. For thirty-four years, the Parisian Company and its daughters pursued "great works" with considerable energy, some success, and complete secrecy. Then, in 1661 a number of disgruntled Brothers of Jansenist sympathies revealed the existence of the group to the royal authorities. Mazarin found the Company more than just a little suspect and immediately ordered its suppression. Correspondence between the mother house and the provincial companies ceased, and the Brothers of the Holy Sacrament went underground and then apparently disappeared in 1666.

It was not until 1865, when a Benedictine monk stumbled upon a manuscript in the Bibliothèque Nationale, that the Company of the Holy Sacrament was rediscovered. The document, entitled, *Les Annales de la Compagnie du Saint-Sacrement,* turned out to be the work of a member of the Parisian Company, René de Voyer d'Argenson, and a complete history of the activities of the Parisian group from its birth to its suppression. The revelations contained in the *Annales* immediately sparked a small controversy, one which owed more to the anticlericalism of the late nineteenth century than to dispassionate inquiry. The most important contribution to this dispute was a book by the Protestant theologian Raoul Allier, a book whose title subsequently became the Company's epithet— *La Cabale des dévots.*[3]

THE COMPANY OF GRENOBLE

The first indication that Grenoble possessed a branch of the cabal appeared in Allier's book. Several months before its publication, Allier had received a letter from the archivist of the Isère, Auguste Prudhomme, describing a very unusual document. While rooting around in some old papers stored at the Château de Meffray near Grenoble, Prudhomme had unearthed a register which he correctly identified as the work of the Holy Sacrament.[4] This register, entitled *Rôle des communions et des visites des pauvres,* is nothing less than the minutes of the Company's weekly meetings. Only three other cities—Tours, Lyon, and Limoges—possess similar registers, and the Tours document is only fragmentary.[5] Ironically, the Grenoble register allows us to reconstruct the life of this covert organization more completely than we can that of many open, officially sanctioned groups. Thanks to the Brothers' indiscretion, we can learn all the Company's secrets, from its origins and social composition to the broader issues of the Brothers' charitable vision and its social consequences.[6]

However, one part of the Company's activities still remains hidden: the first ten years of its existence. The Grenoble register opens with the meeting of January 3, 1652, but there is ample indication that the Company had already been in operation for over a decade. As early as 1640, the correspondence between the Marseille and Parisian groups indicates that the Provençal Brothers considered Grenoble ripe for a Company: one of the Marseillais who visited the town reported that "there is no city on earth where the establishment of the Company is more necessary than here."[7] Two years later, the Marseille Company had achieved its goal: a branch of the Holy Sacrament was firmly implanted in Grenoble, and the Parisian group congratulated the Marseillais on a "good work that will do much good with the grace of God."[8] But many obstacles remained: a Marseille Brother who visited Grenoble several years later bitterly observed that "the Brothers here are very eager to work for this important endeavor, for they consider it the most noble and elevated in Christianity, but few persons here are so zealous, to the great regret of these good men."[9]

These "good men" were made up of fourteen clerics and sixteen laymen. The high percentage of clerics—almost half—is notable; but even more striking is the status of these clerics. Six of the ecclesiastical members of the Company were canons at the prestigious Grenoble Cathedral, and the eight others occupied equally elevated positions. Typical of these ecclesiastical Brothers was Gaspard Laurent de Boffin, who held the lucrative position of prior at Croysil in distant Brittany as well as several benefices in Dauphiné. Most of these clerics boasted a similar collection of canonicates, benefices, priories, and confessorships at stylish convents, which provided them with more than spiritual blessing. One of the cathedral canons, M. de la Baulme, received annually from his benefices no less than 1,000 livres, and he was one of the poorest clerics. Two other

Brothers were more fortunate: they possessed the most lucrative benefices in the province—Saint-Robert and Vif.[10] Well born, well placed, and most important, well beneficed, the ecclesiastical contingent in the Company hardly represented a cross section of Grenoble's clerical society; it was, on the contrary, the elite.

The lay Brothers of the Holy Sacrament were no less distinguished. Two members, Alexandre Berenger de Gûa, seigneur de Vif, and Alphonse Ferrand de Saint-Ferjus, were gentlemen, sons of the provincal *noblesse d' épée* and former soldiers themselves. The rest of the lay Brothers served at the city's sovereign courts, giving the Company the air of a judicial enclave. Far from being simple functionaries, the Brothers occupied the most powerful and prestigious positions at the court. The Company could boast three presidents: Antoine du Faure, Jean de la Croix de Chevrières, and Gabriel Prunier de Saint-André, baron de Bochaine. Six other members, including the youngest Brother, François Grimaud, who was only twenty-two years old when he joined the Company, served at the Parlement in the capacity of *conseillers.* The Chambre des Comptes claimed two other Brothers, one of whom, Jean Louis Ponnat de Garcin de Combes, held the office of *doyen.* An *avocat-général,* Pierre de Galles, and one member of the *finance,* the *receveur-général* Pierre Gigou, completed the judicial contingent within the Holy Sacrament.[11]

The quality which characterized all the Brothers, whether lay or cleric, gentleman or judge, was nobility. Every member, without exception, belonged by birth to the second estate, but there were differences in the distinction and age of this nobility. Of the twenty-six families from whom the Brothers descended, twelve were of "ancient nobility," that is, nobility predating the dauphins, and nine were of more recent nobility, or nobility dating from the time of Louis XI. After these very old noble families came four families who had received their titles during the latter part of the sixteenth century, and five other relative parvenus whose privileges reached back no farther than the previous generation. Despite these differences, there is no indication that the Company was troubled by the hostility between *noblesse de robe* and *noblesse d'épée,* or old and new nobility, that some historians have described.[12] In fact, Brothers of old and new nobility were frequently related by ties of marriage and even blood.[13]

They were also united by a deep and demanding commitment to Catholicism. Like the sister confraternities, the Company of the Holy Sacrament required that its members perform certain spiritual duties. They had to say or attend votive masses when a Parisian Brother died, take a general communion when the Host was desecrated anywhere in France, say special prayers if the king fell ill or began squabbling with the pope, and go to mass daily during Holy Week.[14] All this made for an exacting spiritual schedule, especially for the ecclesiastical Brothers who officiated at these devotions. But no duty prescribed by the Company was more demanding and time-consuming than the organization's principal activity—charity.

Every week, the Brothers gathered together to determine how the poor might best be served. Usually, their discussions centered around the weekly "visit," a tour of the city made by two Brothers for the purpose of ferreting out paupers. These Brothers would visit the homes of the impoverished, listen to their grievances, estimate their needs, and then report their findings to the weekly meeting. There, the assembled company would debate the merits of each case and decide what kind of action should be taken. At the close of the meeting, each member made a voluntary donation, usually about two livres apiece, for the support of the Company's charitable efforts.

To a certain degree, these efforts fulfilled the classic, biblical definition of charity. The Company assisted widows and orphans, clothed the naked, fed the starving, reconciled enemies, and buried paupers.[15] Because these good works frequently took the form of alms distributed directly to the needy, the Brothers' charity bears a superficial resemblance to traditional, indiscriminate casual almsgiving. But there was nothing casual or indiscriminate about the Brothers. They always distinguished between the deserving and the undeserving poor, for they did not give alms to every pauper and did not hesitate to abandon those who were ungrateful or unruly. The Brothers were also methodical in their charity, inscribing the purpose and amount of each gift in their register and devising a complicated system of *billets,* or cards, to assure the swift delivery of relief. Their search for an efficient and effective form of relief led them to contemplate all sorts of schemes, such as the creation of a central depository for old garments, which would facilitate the distribution of clothing to the poor. This notion they borrowed from the Company of Le Puy, and they were not afraid to champion new ideas.[16] Indeed, the Company was an enthusiastic supporter of the seventeenth century's great innovation in charity—confinement.

Like devout men and women throughout France, the Grenoble Brothers believed that the confining of the poor in workhouses or hospitals would eliminate begging, and they made confinement the centerpiece of their charitable program. They discussed the project at almost every meeting and resolved to effect its speedy realization, but numerous obstacles lay in their path: the Hospital General, which would house the poor, had never been completed; its internal administration was chaotic and wasteful; the consuls, who feared that their grasp on the Hospital was weakening, opposed all innovations; the municipal treasury was literally empty.[17] The Company could not tackle these problems itself, for it was a secret organization. Consequently, it acted more discreetly, infiltrating, for example, the governing board of the Hospital General. In 1642 only two Brothers—Perrot and Guillaumières—served on the governing Bureau of the Hospital, but within nine years the Company had successfully packed the body. In 1651 five of the seven directors who regularly attended Bureau meetings were members of the Company, and over the next ten years five other Brothers joined the Bureau, of whom one, M. Lambert, was named rector of the Hospital.[18] Through these Brothers, the Company did not simply control the administration of the Hospital: it was the administration. Consequently, the Brothers could "use the borrowed name of the Messrs. Directors of the Hospital" without the slightest difficulty.

The Company also used other institutions, in particular the municipal court, the Justice of Grenoble, and the sovereign court, the Parlement. The Brothers alerted the prosecuting attorney at the Justice to any species of disorder within his jurisdiction and persuaded him to pursue malefactors of all sorts. The Company had even more direct influence at the Parlement, for most of the lay Brothers served there and they easily convinced their like-minded colleagues to issue edicts that bore the imprint of the Company. The ecclesiastical Brothers too had influence in high places, and they tried to persuade the indolent bishop, Etienne Scarron, to publish ecclesiastical ordinances which advanced the Company's schemes. Even the single most important political figure in the city, the duc de Lesdiguières, son-in-law of the late *connétable,* did not escape the Company's subtle but persistent lobbying effort.[19]

The Company brought a powerful set of connections to its good works, but it did not always meet with success. The Brothers did manage, after two years of intense lobbying, to bring a religious order, the Brothers of Charity, to the Hospital General to administer the men's wards. But they failed in their principal endeavor, the confining of the poor. The central problem was, of course, financing, and the Brothers had a novel solution: the imposition of a tax on all animals brought to the city for slaughter. The Brothers were extremely enthusiastic about this modern, "rational" means of support for public assistance, but most Grenoblois were not. The city consuls and the municipal assembly, the Three Orders, adamantly opposed the new tax, and they were joined by such disparate groups as the religious orders and local Protestants. The Brothers used all their influence to persuade the municipal government and taxed themselves informally. Finally, in 1662 the city agreed to assign the revenues from a tax on meat to the Hospital General.[20] Still, the "great confinement" of the poor did not occur. The revenue acquired by the Hospital was sufficient to make repairs and feed the poor already interned in the Hospital, but it was inadequate to complete construction or incarcerate additional paupers.

The crusade for confinement was a lonely, disappointing struggle in which the Brothers' only arm was their persuasive powers. We can get some idea of the arguments they used when they attempted to sway their fellow citizens, by looking at a pamphlet entitled *Le Projet charitable* published in 1657 under the Company's aegis. Of course, the Company did not sign the tract itself: it "borrowed" the name of the directors of the Hospital General. But the Brothers were clearly behind the pamphlet, for they discussed it frequently before its appearance and probably paid for its publication.[21]

The *Projet charitable* began with a very traditional celebration of casual almsgiving. "When one gives coins to a pauper," the Brothers told their fellow citizens, "one is God to that pauper and he in turn is God to you, for he opens the gates of Heaven to your soul." Confining the poor would only open these gates wider, for "if all the alms given in the streets and churches were assembled together and employed with order, this would make a very considerable sum" and the poor would be better served. If such spiritual notions failed to appeal to some Grenoblois, the Brothers had other arguments too, arguments, one senses, closer to their own, true feelings. "Charity and religion alone," the Brothers explained, "do not dictate the confining of the poor; so too do our convenience, even our own conservation." "Who," the Brothers asked, "does not feel revulsion and disgust at the importunity of these beggars, who corner [the rich] in the streets, churches, even in their homes, who use ridiculous artifices to excite compassion and pity," but who only evoke, in the rich, "embarrassment and horror."[22]

Locking up the beggars in a workhouse would put an end to this particular horror, and it would provide other benefits as well. The number of vagabonds would diminish when there was no casual almsgiving to attract them to the city. Epidemic disease would decline when the poor "who carry popular diseases about with them" were confined. Most important of all, the idleness, "ignorance, and vice so common among these people" would be eliminated as soon as they found "occupation and instruction" in the Hospital General. There, the Brothers explained, "each pauper would be given an occupation and forced to toil" until his innate laziness was expunged. There each inmate would receive "instruction . . . in the Christian virtues" until he renounced sin. Consequently, the Grenoblois who supported the Company's scheme for confinement contributed to a "holy design," for he helped to extinguish the pauper's "crime and sin," his vice.[23] This word appears over and over again in the *Projet charitable*, but it was the Toulousain Company of the Holy Sacrament which explained its full meaning to the devout:

They [the poor] live outside the Church, in blasphemy and against God. . . . They never hear the holy mass and never pray to God. . . . The beggars who live here and there in the city, and some for more than ten years, despoil their hosts and make them weak by their vice and libertinage. The poor contract a marriage with a threepence and a ring, and they dissolve the union without any other ceremony than by breaking the ring and returning the threepence. . . . I do believe that in giving alms one does more harm than good, because it seems to me that one thereby maintains a network of weaklings, tavern haunters, fornicators, villains, robbers, and thieves, in short, a network of vice.[24]

Clearly, the Brothers of the Holy Sacrament, like the Sisters of the Madelines or Orphans, saw in the poor not Christ but the Devil himself. For the Brothers, "crime and sin" always accompanied poverty, but they were not necessarily its causes. The Brothers' daily, intimate contact with the poor forced them to recognize that impoverishment stemmed from misfortune, from disease, accident, or economic depression. The Brothers could even be quite astute in their analysis of the sources of poverty, attributing it to a slowing of commerce on the Isère or a general scarcity of small coins.[25] Because they recognized the causes of poverty, the Brothers could apply the appropriate remedies, helping a bankrupt cobbler set up his shop again or providing a young prostitute with an apprenticeship so that she might earn her living honorably. But the sources of poverty and its material alleviation interested the Brothers much less than its consequences and its spiritual remedy. "Crime and sin" were the Brothers' main target, and they swore that "as we provide for the corporal, so too shall we provide, with more cause, for the spiritual."[26] Spiritual assistance always took precedence over material aid. Before the Company gave the young prostitute an apprenticeship, it admonished her to make a general confession and cleanse her soul of sin. When the Company gave a poor man in Saint Laurent a pair of shoes, it was not to warm his feet, but to see that he could get to mass.[27]

Getting the pauper to church was only half of the problem; once he was there the Company expected him to behave in a decent, reverent manner. Such was not, the Brothers complained, the custom in Grenoble, where the congregation regularly ignored the priest, failed to kneel when the Host was elevated, flirted "scandalously," and kept up such a din of chatter that the mass was inaudible.[28] Such impiety annoyed the Brothers, but the abuses of the sacrament which they detected among the popular classes distressed them even more. To the Company's dismay, the Grenoblois either delayed the baptism of children or failed to baptize them at all. Extreme unction too occasioned abuses, according to the Company, for the Grenoblois failed to understand that if one received the Holy Viaticum and then escaped death, one was not supposed to continue living as before, blaspheming, fornicating, and denying the efficacy of the sacraments. Marriage led to a particularly serious abuse. The Grenoblois would consummate their marriages in the evening and not go to church until the next morning, and this, the Brothers remarked, constituted a "mortal sin." No abuses, however, enraged the Brothers as much as the profanation of the very object of their devotion—the Eucharist. The Company complained of the theft of hosts, an indication that the Grenoblois, like many of their contemporaries, probably attributed magical, curative powers to the wafer.[29] The Grenoblois certainly misunderstood the official doctrine of the Church concerning the Eucharist: a young girl at Saint Hugues would take the Host, pace three times around the church, and then place it at the foot of the altar, a maneuver which she considered quite orthodox.[30]

Ignorance clearly lay behind some of these abuses, and the Company responded by funding the printing of catechisms and enjoining missionaries to "instruct the poor." The Brothers found it even easier to deal with indecent behavior in at least one church: they hired a Swiss guard to act as a beadle at Notre Dame. But the blasphemy and outright irreligiosity that the Company witnessed among the poor posed a more serious challenge. What could the Brothers do about the apprentice surgeons who "assembled and blasphemed the Holy Name of God"? or a certain Molard who was in the habit of shouting curses each evening from his home in the Tour Perche? Or how could they deal with a man who lived scandalously with his servant and had a child by her, yet boasted of this achievement and even claimed that fornication was condoned by the scriptures?[31]

The Brothers knew the cause of such impiety: a corrupt and negligent Church. They complained of priests who failed to say mass, who allowed their churches to fall into ruin, and who neglected to administer extreme unction to dying parishioners.[32] Vainly, the Company begged the Bishop of Grenoble, Pierre Scarron, to make a diocesan visit and to take matters in hand, but the indolent cleric allowed the most scandalous abuses to persist, among them violations of the vow of celibacy. To the great scandal of the Company, clerics maintained concubines and consorted with prostitutes in taverns. The Brothers frequently denounced the "licentious, ungoverned" life of one Des Henry, a stipendiary priest at Notre Dame, but they were powerless to contain his "extravagances." They pointed to a priest from nearby Mercuze who had dared to baptize his own child by a concubine, and they denounced a cleric who had run off to Geneva with a young woman, presumably to convert to Protestantism.[33]

The situation was no better among the regular clergy and the canons of Grenoble's two collegiate churches. A Cordelier taught astrology, a Provençale Minime openly prostituted herself, the Visitadines and the Recollets squabbled over testamentary bequests, and the canons of Notre Dame and Saint André engaged in a seemingly pointless quarrel over precedence, which sometimes erupted into violence on public occasions.[34] The canons of Notre Dame were responsible for an annual event that truly galled the Company. These clerics happened to own most of the vineyards around Grenoble, and each year, after the grape harvest, they sold their wine in a cabaret located right inside the cathedral, under the vaults of the cloister. There the Grenoblois, both lay and ecclesiastic, happily besported themselves, drinking, gambling, fornicating, and blaspheming.[35]

This was adding insult to injury as far as the Company was concerned. Not only did the canons defile their own ecclesiastical state, they also encouraged one of the Grenoblois' worst habits, the frequenting of taverns and inns. In these dens of iniquity, all sorts of behavior "scandalous" to the Company occurred: drunkards were heard to blaspheme the Holy Name of God, violent brawls broke out at all hours, and worse still, meat was regularly consumed on Fridays and during Lent. One Friday a Brother had even seen a spit of meat "roasting in full public view" right outside the Trois Dauphins, Grenoble's most respectable inn. Moreover, the city's drinking establishments usually served customers on feast days and Sundays during mass, thereby encouraging rowdiness and blasphemy when decorum and reverence would have been more appropriate.[36]

The Brothers quickly obtained from the Parlement an edict prohibiting this practice, for nothing enraged them so much as the intrusion of the secular into the sacred. They complained that the market outside Notre Dame frequently spilled over into the church, and the noise of street vendors sometimes drowned out the mass. They persuaded the judicial authorities to prohibit tightrope walkers and marionette shows during Lent, and they railed against the popular festivals that mixed too liberally the sacred and the ribald. They denounced, for instance, a special celebration held each year at the Minims of the Plain on Easter Sunday. "On this holiest of days," the Brothers complained, "one can see carts going back and forth bringing the wherewithal to set up cabarets" right outside the convent. The observance of patron saints' days in villages near Grenoble also occasioned "scandals." These *vogues* and *brelans,* as they were called, attracted many people and consisted of a brief mass followed by a great deal more drinking and dancing, sometimes in the parish cemetery, sometimes in the church itself.[37]

The Brothers struggled to keep holy places pure of such "debauchery," and they had their work cut out for them when it came to one source of pollution—prostitutes. According to the Company, whores plied their trade near all the churches and convents in the city, from the doorway of the Recollets to the cathedral itself. In fact, the Brothers saw prostitutes everywhere, in the Rue Neuve, on the quays of the Isère, in the Saint Laurent quarter and the Très Cloîtres suburb. The vineyards and fields outside the city gates provided a more discreet setting for assignations, and one Brother, the canon de Croysil, was himself solicited by two young prostitutes as he strolled near the Porte de Bonne.[38]

The Brothers could hardly step out of their homes without bumping into harlots, and they attributed this embarrassing situation to the sinister machinations of the *maquerelles,* or procuresses. These women—for they were always women—befriended unsuspecting girls and then prostituted them for their own profit. Some of these bawds were superficially respectable, the wives of artisans and the widows of honest laborers. All, the Company believed, were constantly in search of fresh girls, preferably ones who were young, alone, and impoverished. A beautiful widow or a penniless orphan was easy prey for the procuresses, and no child was too young for the greedy bawds. The Company seriously worried that children as young as fifteen or even ten years of age might fall into the clutches of these flesh peddlers.[39] The Brothers had to save these young souls, so they provided money to the impoverished, apprenticeships to the unskilled, shelter with a trustworthy family to the homeless, and immediate asylum in the Orphans hospice to the truly threatened. When all this failed, the Company still did not give up. It was only too happy to help contrite prostitutes renounce sin and start a new life. The Brothers showered money on their repentant madelines, some of whom repented three or four times. They found jobs for some and apprenticeships for others and paid for those whose families lived outside Grenoble to return to their parents. If these maneuvers failed to convert the prostitute, the Brothers had a final, sure solution—marriage. Nothing pleased the Brothers more than seeing one of their madelines placed under the protection—and authority—of a man, and they gladly constituted dowries or found mates for their protégées.[40]

Marriage would have eliminated another vice—concubinage. In Grenoble, the Company found a few artisans, usually cobblers, tailors, or members of other lesser trades, cohabiting with their servant girls.[41] In rural Dauphiné, around Froges, Venon, Bresson, and Domène, the Company unearthed a veritable host of couples living in sin. Two of these illicit unions involved gentlemen: one rural noble satisfied his sexual needs with a twelve-year-old girl whom he had purchased from her mother; another rural noble had fathered a child by his own illegitimate daughter born of his aging concubine.[42] If rural Dauphiné provided the Company with so many illicit unions, it may well be because the Brothers found it easier to detect cohabiting couples in small, country villages. The Brothers had to rely upon gossip and hearsay, and in a city like Grenoble, with a high rate of immigration, unmarried couples might easily have gone unnoticed.

Another sin on the Brothers' agenda was even harder to detect—pregnancy outside marriage. Unwed mothers, the Brothers believed, regularly concealed their pregnancies, not so much out of shame, but out of a desire to "destroy their fruit," that is, to abort the fetus. "This has already occurred several times," the Brothers maintained, and they pointed to a woman who was condemned by the Parlement for just such a concealment.[43] Obviously, the Brothers had trouble flushing out these women, but when they did, they applied one of two remedies: money, which they believed would prevent an abortion, or marriage, either to the woman's seducer or to some other, willing soul. The Company also had the Parlement publish an edict condemning women who concealed their pregnancies, and they implored local priests to force unwed mothers in their parishes to make public their pregnancies by making a formal *déclaration de grossesse* before a magistrate.[44]

Often, unwanted pregnancies ended in the abandonment of the child instead of abortion. The Company complained of infants left in churches, at the Hospital General, and on the doorsteps of Grenoble's most prestigious homes. Even a member of the Company, Monsieur de Saint Robert, found a child on his threshold one morning, which raised the ugly suspicion that he or a member of his household had fathered the infant. Apparently, wronged women often deposited their babies before the homes of their seducers: a girl left a child on the doorstep of the *avocat-général* of the Parlement, for she had been seduced by one of his servants.[45] In such cases, the Company swore to uncover the guilty party, that is, the mother, but it was virtually helpless before the flood of abandoned children.

The Company and perhaps the courts were equally impotent before the violence of the popular classes. The Company register describes shootings, stabbings, drunken brawls, bloody feuds, and unprovoked outbursts of violence. Persons unknown drowned a poor girl in the Isère, six soldiers raped an artisan's wife, and "valets and vagabonds roamed the streets at night attacking women and girls at random."[46] When an honest citizen ventured into Grenoble's streets he took his life in his hands. If he were lucky, he might escape injury or death; in any case, he was assaulted by a spectacle of teen-age prostitutes, licentious bawds, depraved priests, wailing foundlings, stumbling drunkards, and insolent, deformed beggars.

The "sins and crimes" of the popular classes were all too obvious to the Brothers of the Holy Sacrament, and the picture of Grenoble society that emerges from their register is one of depravity and lawlessness. In this light, the Brothers' obsessive concern with the moral regeneration of the poor seems understandable, even justified. But one hesitates to take their testimony, however vivid, at face value. The rich, whether in the seventeenth or the nineteenth century, have always enjoyed decrying the moral degeneracy of their social inferiors, and on this basis alone one is tempted to discount at least part of the Company's testimony. But how much? The Brothers were not, as the reader has undoubtedly suspected already, unprejudiced observers, but they had the great virtue of being among the only observers of the poor. The Company's register is one of the few accounts we possess of the habits and values of the average Grenoblois in the seventeenth century, and its very rarity makes it extremely persuasive.

Still, nagging doubts persist. To what degree was the Brothers' picture of poverty skewed by their own, special obsessions? Just how criminal and just how sinful were the popular classes? Did their values and norms truly differ from those of the elite? Were the Brothers actually wrestling with a sinister, alien force? In order to appreciate fully the social vision of the Company of the Holy Sacrament, we must temporarily leave the Brothers. We must turn to the objects of their peculiar charity, the poor, and scrutinize their criminal behavior more closely from a more impartial perspective, that of the judicial records.

CRIMES AND SINS: CRIMINALITY IN
SEVENTEENTH-CENTURY GRENOBLE

The records most likely to provide information on the poor come from the judical body most frequently "used" by the Brothers of the Holy Sacrament—the Justice of Grenoble. The Company often tried to sway the presiding magistrate and his prosecuting attorney, or *procureur,* because this municipal court had jurisdiction over almost all infractions committed within the city, in particular those of interest to the Brothers of the Holy Sacrament. The Justice prosecuted prostitutes, policed taverns and markets, settled violent disputes, dealt with blasphemy, concubinage, and illegitimacy, and even heard serious felony cases like armed robbery, murder, and rape.[47] Only the most privileged criminals with the honor of being prosecuted by the Bailliage or the Parlement escaped the Justice, so it is here, among the Justice records, that one is likely to encounter the criminal and sinful poor of whom the Brothers of the Holy Sacrament complained. Unfortunately, the Justice archives are scant and incomplete before 1670.[48] And they pose the same difficulties as any other set of criminal records: they provide information, not on all the crimes committed within the city, but only on those that came to court. Certain offenses, rape and prostitution for example, are almost always underreported. Other crimes might go unrecorded because the plaintiff was reluctant to deal with the judicial machinery. This problem is aggravated in the case of the Justice, for that court, like all others in the old regime, was a profit-making venture. The officials of the Justice, among them the *procureur,* or prosecuting attorney, expected to make money from defendants and therefore had little incentive to indict impoverished criminals. Worse yet, many Grenoblois might have been loath to bring a complaint to the court, for if they lost, they would be saddled with substantial court costs.[49] Of course, if they won, they had the pleasure of dishonoring an enemy publicly and ruining him financially to boot. Consequently, the Grenoblois' desire to wreak vengeance upon those who robbed or assaulted them did offset their reluctance to go to court. And the judges' fear of vagabonds frequently triumphed over their desire to make money. Still, a rigorous quantitative analysis of the Justice records would be misleading. The structure of old regime justice makes the precise measurement of the incidence of crime impossible. Figures will be offered here, but they are meant as general indicators and no more. A qualitative approach, however, is rewarding, even indispensable. Criminal records may not tell us how much crime there was, but they do tell us a great deal about crime.

The interrogation of defendants provides precise information as to the age, residence, profession, and motives of defendants and plaintiffs. The complaints filed by private citizens allow us to determine what the average Grenoblois, as opposed to the wealthy Brothers of the Holy Sacrament, considered criminal behavior. The testimony of witnesses, common people drawn by sheer chance into the proceedings, is perhaps the most precious of all: these depositions allow us to hear voices usually muted in seventeenth-century sources, those of the poor.[50]

We can also contrast the reality of crime in Grenoble with the picture of a sordid, pervasive deviance painted by the Brothers of the Holy Sacrament. On one point, the Brothers' views were distinctly misleading: despite one's expectations, the Grenoblois were not thieves. Thievery accounts for less than 10 percent of the more than a hundred cases brought before the Justice between 1674 and 1688, even though opportunities for theft were certainly not lacking.[51] Thieves could easily remove flour from unattended mills, utensils from remote farmsteads, and clocks from shops of artisans. Anyone, it seems, could march into the homes of the city's wealthiest magistrates: a twenty-two-year-old woman had no difficulty entering a counselor's house one Sunday while the family was at mass and stealing a mirror, some jewels, and two turkeys.[52] The wealthiest Grenoblois were not, by Parisian standards, very rich, but what they did possess lay in full view and largely unattended. No police force patrolled the city, and no banks kept the Grenoblois' possessions hidden from inquisitive eyes. Only a lock, easily picked, stood between a thief and a rich man's silver or a poor servant girl's clothes. Domestics, of course, were supposed to watch over their master's goods, but servants were often negligent, and it was just as easy—if not easier—for them to steal than to guard those possessions.

Theft by domestics and other kinds of stealing entailed hair-raising penalties: whipping, branding, banishment, and sometimes death. But it is unlikely that these punishments, however brutal, account for the small percentage of thefts we find in the Justice archives. Rather, it is probable that many instances of stealing never came before the court and that many Grenoblois failed to report theft. After all, nothing encouraged the citizen who had been robbed to run to the magistrates. The court had no effective police force and no means of tracking down thieves. Conflicting jurisdictions meant that criminals could easily slip out of the city and through the net of courts, so if a victim did not already know the thief's identity, he was unlikely ever to find it out.[53] A clockmaker whose shop was robbed of some extremely valuable merchandise reported the theft to the court, but despite all of his trouble, he never saw his clocks or his thieves again. Small wonder that six months earlier when he had been robbed of equally valuable goods, he had not bothered to go to court.[54]

Most of the Grenoblois probably followed suit and dealt with thievery informally. Often they took matters into their own hands. When a young girl selling flowers at the Place Saint André was robbed, her brothers pursued the thief, retrieved the flowers, and then beat the miscreant senseless. When a young boy filched wood from a pile outside a shop, the shopkeeper's clerks followed him home, repossessed the wood, and then vented their wrath on his father.[55] Such vigilantism had the advantage of being quicker, cheaper, and more effective than recourse to the courts. In addition, the victim actually got his possessions back. Consequently, when a Grenoblois was robbed, his first reaction was to take off after the thief—not to run to the courts. Only under special circumstances would he call upon the magistrates for assistance. For example, when an officer at the local Post Office suspected his domestic of stealing, he did not appeal to the Justice. Rather, he inquired as to the whereabouts of her strongbox, opened it, and repossessed his goods. Only because he was unusually fastidious and felt he needed a court order to break the strongbox lock, did he go to the court.[56]

Domestics of course were a special case: they, like apprentices and journeymen, formed a part of their master's household, and this special status seems to account for the rarity of domestic theft in the Justice records. Certainly, the opportunity to steal presented itself every day to every domestic and every apprentice. A few must have surrendered now and then to temptation. But these thefts never made it to court, for a kind of taboo prevented masters from prosecuting their dependents publicly. When the Company of the Holy Sacrament learned of a terrible blasphemer, it decided, rather uncharacteristically, not to inform the Justice. The blasphemer was, it seems, a domestic of one of the Brothers, and this Brother, Monsieur de Croysil, explained that he could not take his own servant to court.[57] If honor prevented a master from prosecuting his dependents publicly, nothing deterred him from disciplining them privately. Upon discovering a theft, many masters probably beat their dependents senseless and left it at that. Such was the case of a master tailor who suspected that one of his journeymen was filching cloth: he beat him "until the blood ran." We know of this incident only because the master was a Protestant and the journeyman a recent convert to Catholicism with powerful devout allies who supplied him with moral and financial support.[58]

Most domestics and journeymen had neither the funds nor the inclination to sue their masters. Other Grenoblois, though, did not hesitate to go to court when falsely accused of theft. There were many such people, for the Grenoblois who dealt personally with criminals often made mistakes. The victim of one such misunderstanding was César Luya, an *archer* for the Justice. One morning he went to a shop near the Place Saint André, and when he left, the merchant's domestic followed him. She asked him to return to the shop, where the merchant's wife accused him of stealing a pair of stockings. A crowd gathered and watched while the merchant's wife searched Luya's pockets in vain, but she remained convinced of his guilt. To exonerate himself, Luya took off his socks and waved them about so that anyone could see they were not the stockings in question. By this time the merchant himself had arrived, and he promised Luya that he would someday receive a thrashing for the supposed theft. Luya responded by filing a criminal complaint which demanded "an exemplary and terrible punishment for this outrageous and damaging insult."[59]

This case certainly demonstrates the perils of vigilantism, but it also suggests that theft, while rarely reported, was also rarely committed. Luya did not take the accusation of stealing lightly; he clearly feared that his reputation would be ruined, that he would be dishonored, perhaps even shunned by his neighbors. Popular values may well have diverged at many points from the norms of the elite, the principles of the Company of the Holy Sacrament. But when it came to theft, the average Grenoblois, even the most impoverished, shared the Brothers' horror and distaste. When a Grenoblois was robbed, all the neighbors sprang to his aid. When a stolen good was found on a public thoroughfare, it was conscientiously returned, whatever its value. Theft was taboo, and the insults of "thief" and "banished one" (banishment being a common penalty for stealing) were the most potent weapons in the Grenoblois' rich repertoire of curses and insults.[60]

Popular strictures against theft probably kept stealing to a minimum, and so too did the city's merchants and secondhand dealers, its putative fences. The receiving of stolen goods carried penalties as heavy as that for theft, and most Grenoblois were unwilling to risk prosecution. If a thief were caught, it was usually at the crucial moment when he tried to sell his booty. Marie Civet, the twenty-two-year-old who helped herself to the contents of a counselor's home one Sunday morning, came to grief when she tried to sell his turkey to a secondhand-clothes dealer, for the dealer alerted the authorities. As the value of the goods went up so too did the likelihood of being apprehended. Pierre Maugiron, a tailor, made the mistake of trying to sell some stolen silverplate to a master goldsmith: the goldsmith showed the silver to his fellow smiths, "as was [their] custom," and one of them quickly recognized his own "mark" and they reported the theft.[61]

In this case, the guild structure worked against the criminal and probably discouraged theft. Of course, the criminal records tell us nothing about the dishonest merchant; he, and his client the thief, escaped detection. So too did those who could sell their ill-gotten goods outside the city. Mobility conferred virtual immunity from prosecution, for the drifter easily eluded the law. Perhaps this explains why vagabonds, so feared by the Company and its contemporaries, appear so rarely in the Justice records. Only one incident involves transients: in 1679 seven boys filched an altar cloth from the Jacobins and other items from the homes of private citizens. These were hardly awe-inspiring characters: none was more than sixteen years of age, almost all came from rural communities adjacent to Grenoble, and most claimed to have no other profession than begging. The one exception was Maurice Cadon, a native of Chambéry, who called himself a domestic. He had come to Grenoble in search of a position, but, having been afflicted with rickets, failed and so took to petty thievery.[62]

These transients appear quite pathetic, and the Company's fear of them rather unjustified. But the Brothers were not alone, for the vagabonds struck terror into the hearts of all the Grenoblois and justifiably. Grenoble was, quite literally, at the vagrants' mercy. None of the forces that tended to frustrate theft affected drifters, and the courts were powerless to apprehend them. An outcast could steal or even kill with impunity. The only murder case to come before the Justice in the years between 1674 and 1688 involved two former soldiers, vagabonds by definition, who had ambushed a man, killed him, and then taken to the hills, never to be seen again.[63] The Grenoblois lived in fear of such crimes and with reason. At night, the city was so dark that witnesses claimed to see nothing. When the rich left their homes after sunset, they were always accompanied by a battalion of torch-bearing valets. As for the average, hard-working Grenoblois, he just stayed indoors. Only one crime in all the cases brought before the Justice occurred after nine in the evening, at which time, the witnesses testified, the city was so quiet that the footsteps of the criminals could be heard streets away.[64]

The Grenoblois may have been terrified of vagabonds, but they actually had more to fear from their next-door neighbors. The Company of the Holy Sacrament was absolutely correct when it portrayed the average Grenoblois as violent and volatile. Most of the cases brought to the Justice concerned the violence wreaked by one respectable Grenoblois upon another. The city's residents exchanged blows regularly and on the slightest pretext: a butcher's wife stoned a client whose dog had filched some tripe, a cook's apprentice ambushed an unsuspecting law clerk in the Grand Rue, and two customers at a mercer's shop traded blows over a piece of thread. A litany of insults usually preceded these incidents, but the Grenoblois did not stop at verbal threats or friendly fisticuffs—they meant business. The surgeons' reports filed with complaints show that the Grenoblois struck with bottles, tools, stones, and fists, pulled hair, and even bit one another.[65] If no one was seriously hurt in these altercations, it was not because the Grenoblois lacked the will; rather, they did not possess the weapons, either firearms or swords, to do one another in.

The eager participants in these fights were often neighbors, frequently former friends, sometimes business associates, and always Grenoblois either by birth or adoption. But they were not relatives. Unlike modern urban dwellers, the Grenoblois contained tensions within the family, and the city witnessed, at least publicly, little domestic violence.[66] Rather than fight each other, family members preferred to fight together, brother helping sister, husband siding with wife. Even women participated in these altercations. Marguerite Françon, for example, attacked another woman and then called in her two sisters and a servant to help. Women precipitated many quarrels, and received their fair share of blows. Gallantry did not prevent a man from striking a woman; on the contrary, the Grenoblois did not hesitate to beat, kick, or drown females, especially if they were widowed or unmarried—that is, without male protectors.[67]

In these and other disputes, the males were of no particular social class or occupation. Soldiers started fights; apprentices and journeymen from all sorts of trades joined in; day laborers and stevedores jumped into the fray; and law clerks and commercial clerks wielded their fists, all with equal frequency and ferocity. Literate and illiterate, skilled and unskilled, prosperous and impoverished—they all came together in the brawl. What these disparate groups and individuals had in common was their age: they were males between the years of sixteen and thirty. That these young men caused most of the violence in the city is, of course, far from surprising. In almost all societies—urban or rural, preindustrial or modern—adolescent males, or "youths" (as the Company called them), bear a disproportionate responsibility for violent crime.[68]

The youths were a volatile group, and contributing to their volatility was wine. The Brothers of the Holy Sacrament were right: the tavern was the scene of "crime and sin," especially violent crime. Under the influence of alcohol, minor disputes suddenly became bloody brawls. A young Protestant nobleman, for example, peacefully ate his supper in a tavern, drank a bottle of wine, and then went berserk when he suspected that the innkeeper had overcharged him. The unexpected could occur in the cabaret, and those who entered as friends might well part enemies. A farm laborer and some glove-workers went to play cards in an inn near the Porte de Bonne. They gambled, drank a great deal of wine, ate a supper of cheese, and then left. As they walked down the street their friendly roughhousing abruptly flared into violence, and three young men were seriously injured.[69]

Wine may account for these quarrels, but it is more difficult to explain other outbursts of violence that litter the Justice records. Historians surveying the seemingly gratuitous bloodshed in seventeenth-century France have concluded, not unlike the Company, that its inhabitants were "volatile" and lived in a "climate of violence."[70] With their hair-trigger tempers and their quick fists, the Grenoblois certainly seem "volatile," but it is by no means clear that they were pathologically or even peculiarly so. In this regard, the criminal records hide as much as they reveal. The nature of the criminal process in the old regime tended to obscure the motives and grievances of the participants in quarrels. The defendant, if he had assaulted the plaintiff before, had no interest in revealing this fact to the court. The plaintiff, if he had truly provoked the assault, certainly would not explain this to the judge. The judge himself was interested only in the incident reported and never questioned the participants, as would a modern jurist, about their motives. In addition, most of these quarrels were settled out of court after the initial complaint, so the judicial process never ran its full course. Consequently, violence which appears unprovoked and gratuitous to the historian, may well have had a long, bitter history.

Most likely this history turned upon a point of honor, for despite the Company's protestations to the contrary, the Grenoblois had a strict sense of personal and familial rectitude. When a doctor's son attacked an unsuspecting merchant, the young man explained, rather cryptically, that the merchant had spread rumors about members of his family and "impugned their honor." Similarly, when a spur-maker tracked a potmaker to an inn and then beat him senseless, the spur-maker excused his actions by claiming the man had slandered him and his wife.[71] Just what constituted slander and honor in this society is not easy to tell. Certainly, a man's honor was bound up with the sexual behavior of his wife. If she bore a child by another man, as did the wife of a poor lye-maker, he could expect to receive his share of insults and contemptuous asides. In such cases, "a man's honor required that he discipline his wife," as a boatman explained in a petition to have his errant spouse imprisoned in the Hospital General.[72] Female misconduct, however, rarely occasioned outright violence; more often it was insinuations about a man's behavior in the marketplace that caused fists to fly. When a woman implied that a flax-comber "put his foot on the scales," the flax-comber attacked her. When a clockmaker accused a customer of theft, the customer beat him sense-less. And when an innkeeper's wife spread rumors about a clerk which caused him to lose his job, the clerk ambushed and beat her son. In this particular case, a neighbor tried to stop the fight, but was hauled away by onlookers who believed the clerk "should be able to avenge his honor."[73]

The Grenoblois had a prickly sense of honor and with reason: a man's reputation could be undone overnight and with disastrous consequences. Rumors flew through the city, and the witnesses who testified in court, where hearsay was admitted as evidence, had no difficulty in supplying gossip about people they had never met. Newcomers would seem to be immune to such rumors, but in fact they were among the most vulnerable, for those who did not have an established reputation had, as far as the Grenoblois were concerned, a bad reputation. When a neighbor put it about that a new inn harbored prostitutes, the innkeeper sued: he was new to town and such malicious gossip could, he explained, ruin his business.[74] Under these circumstances, it is not surprising that the Grenoblois responded with violence to insults, real or imagined. Their livelihood depended upon a good reputation, and an artisan, laborer, or domestic in bad repute would not find work. No insult, however farfetched, could be ignored, for it would certainly not go unnoticed or unrepeated: a permanent, attentive audience assisted at the events of a Grenoblois' life—his neighbors. They listened through doors, peeped through keyholes, eaves-dropped on conversations, and committed every detail of a person's life to memory. In court, a Grenoblois could count on his neighbors to reveal this information. This nosiness, though, did not always work to his disadvantage: neighbors testified that a woman was not a prostitute, because they had seen everyone who entered her room and none were male. Similarly, a neighbor saved a woman from her husband's blows when she heard noise next door and rushed in "as a good neighbor should."[75] The Grenoblois may have lived in a "climate of violence," where they had to fear their neighbor's words as much as his blows, but they also inhabited a city in which mutual aid and neighborliness were commonplace. Affection existed alongside hostility, and both probably stemmed from the same close-knit, communal life.

Women in particular experienced both extremes of their neighbors' affection or scorn. A woman's reputation could be undone even faster than a man's, and if one woman was saved from her husband's blows, another was condemned as a prostitute because of a neighbor's idle gossip. In cases involving prostitution, the Justice relied heavily on neighbors' observations, and such cases did not lack in the years between 1674 and 1688. Several women were brought before the court on charges of selling themselves or other women, and these cases, particularly those prosecuted in 1688, tell us a great deal about a profession that literally obsessed the Brothers of the Holy Sacrament. Unlike most accused prostitutes, the women charged with procuring did not simply deny all charges: they accused other women and in the process painted a vivid, sometimes lurid, picture of their trade.[76] Consequently, we can learn just who became a prostitute and, in a few cases, just who bought her services.

What we cannot learn is how many prostitutes actually plied their trade in the city. The Company of the Holy Sacrament believed that Grenoble swarmed with harlots. The Justice, however, prosecuted only a dozen, but how many whores eluded its grasp? Those who were brought before the court were extremely young women, girls actually. Claire Prié, the most loquacious of the defendants, was sixteen, and the two Fonteville sisters were fifteen and sixteen when they went to court. All had begun their careers early, at fourteen years of age, and all would most likely retire early, around twenty, when they might turn to procuring. Therefore the prostitute was, by definition, a teen-age prostitute. To us, this suggests that the clients possessed some peculiar tastes, but it is more likely that they had a tremendous fear of venereal disease. Claire Prié described how one client inspected her nude body for signs of disease before sleeping with her, and the quality of the young girls most often vaunted by the procuresses was their "freshness," that is, their freedom from disease.[77]

Youth provided the client with some guarantee against infection, but it also meant that the procuresses had a constant need for fresh flesh. Where did they find these young women? A few of the prostitutes resided in Grenoble, as did the Fonteville sisters. One procuress, a master writer's wife, claimed to have recruited her harlots among her husband's pupils. Most of the prostitutes, however, hailed from outside the city, from the area surrounding Romans and Saint Marcellin near the Rhone valley. A procuring team of mother and daughter made regular trips to this area, the mother searching out the girls and then bringing them to Grenoble, the daughter lodging the teen-agers when they arrived. Once in the city, these highly mobile young girls continued their peregrinations, moving from one house to another and changing procuresses frequently. Claire Prié, whose brief career we can follow rather closely, came to Grenoble from Romans with a procuress and then lodged in four different neighborhoods during the two weeks she plied her trade in the city.[78]

Obviously, no one quarter housed all the city's prostitutes. The Brothers of the Holy Sacrament did indeed, as they claimed, see harlots on every street corner. According to their own testimony, the prostitutes worked out of rooms in the Rue Neuve, the Rue Saint Jacques, the Rue Saint Laurent, and the Place Grenette. Nor did the Brothers err when they claimed that harlots sullied Grenoble's most holy places. Prostitutes usually met their clients in the lower court of the Recollets, before the Augustinian monastery, and in the garden of the Jesuits. Grenoble's taverns and *académies de tabac* were also places of assignation. The owner of one *académie* prostituted three girls in a closet in her establishment, and prostitution was so common in inns and cabarets that any woman seen in such a place was immediately assumed to be a harlot. The summer months saw this activity move outside the city, to the cabarets near the Porte de Bonne and the Porte de France. Claire Prié testified that she met "an old gentleman" in a tavern outside the Porte de France and frequented the cabarets near the Porte de Bonne disguised as a boy. Having supped, the prostitutes and their clients adjourned to the nearby vineyards and fields where they could pursue their pastoral frolics discreetly, but not without being observed by passersby.[79]

The prostitutes and procuresses were everywhere, as the Company of the Holy Sacrament maintained, but the Company need not have feared that young girls would be spirited away from their families to a life of sin. Generally, procuresses did not approach young girls; instead they contacted their mothers. Claire Prié was "sold" to a procuress by her mother, and so too was Marguerite Arcenay. Often, procuresses prostituted their own daughters, and mother-daughter teams, like the Rossets who worked out of a room on the Rue Saint Jacques, were extremely common. Indeed, veritable dynasties of procuresses and prostitutes grew up in the city. La Saulnier, a former prostitute turned procuress, worked with her mother, La Motte, who had also given up prostitution for procuring. Louise Fonteville prostituted her daughter, Anne Noyelle, who in turn sold her younger sisters. Prostitution, like every other profession in the old regime, was a family affair.[80]

It was also an entirely female affair. Only three male pimps appear in the Justice records, and they were all amateurs thrust by chance and only temporarily into the profession.[81] The real professionals, the procuresses, were all women, and their gender probably facilitated their activity. A man and a girl together on the city streets might raise eyebrows; an old woman and a teen-age girl, on the contrary, were a common sight and could be taken for an honest widow and her daughter. In fact, many of the procuresses were widows. Catherine Salleman was the widow of a carter, and Marguerite Rosset, also a widow, worked as a *lingère,* which allowed her to tell the neighbors that the men they saw entering her room had come to pick up their linen. The married women among the procuresses, though not numerous, also profited from a superficial respectability: their husbands belonged to honest trades, such as master writer and nail-maker, and to all appearances they were the wives of hardworking artisans.[82]

Each procuress had a "cover," but it is unlikely that the Grenoblois were fooled. They were too intrusive and too indiscreet to be taken in by mere appearances. Catherine Froment and her daughters certainly did not escape the vigilant eyes of their neighbors, not even in the privacy of their rented room. Their next-door neighbor, a weaver, observed them through a crack in the wall and saw them "barefoot" and "in bed," cavorting with a client.[83] Most Grenoblois did not have such a convenient peephole, but they did not need one to find out what the widow next door was up to: neighborhood gossip would keep them well informed. Many witnesses at prostitution trials testified that they learned of a procuress's traffic from "rumors" which "everybody in the quarter knew." Sometimes this knowledge was not only public, it was official. The Rossets, for example, were twice the subject of criminal complaints, and two other bawds had actually been convicted of procuring years before. One of the two, La Lanteriau, had a particularly long and notorious career. Throughout the 1650s she had preoccupied the Company, and then, in 1661, she had been convicted, publicly whipped, and banished from the city, only to return a few years later to resume her activities.[84]

The Grenoblois certainly knew that prostitutes were living in their midst; but they did not like the fact. The reaction of the weaver who spied on the Froment women is instructive: far from ignoring what he had seen, the weaver beat on the Froment's door and then tried, unsuccessfully, to break it down. Later that evening, as the weaver's wife testified, the Froments came to the weaver's room and begged him, on bended knees, not to reveal what he had seen to the other neighbors.[85] The prostitutes feared their fellow citizens and with reason. It is likely that the neighbors informed the authorities of the prostitutes' activities, that is, turned them in.[86] Neighbors never hesitated to testify against prostitutes, and they enthusiastically elaborated, for the magistrates, the inconveniences that the prostitute's commerce had caused them. The average Grenoblois, like the Company of the Holy Sacrament, abhorred prostitution, and the curse that came most frequently to his lips in the heat of anger was "whore" or "pimp."

It is hard to measure the true depth of this hatred of prostitutes. The Grenoblois tended to deal with whores just as they dealt with thieves, informally and violently. Witnesses at prostitution trials frequently commented that the whore in question had previously been "chased out of the Rue du Boeuf," "removed from the Rue Saint Laurent," or "banished from other parts of the city." Since the authorities did not undertake these evictions, it was the Grenoblois who did, and it is possible that the young men of the city were entrusted with this task. When a woman accused another of prostituting herself, she added that "the youths will take care of you." When a merchant wanted a prostitute out of his neighborhood, he told his son to "serve these whores well and with your friends drive them out of the quarter." When some men broke into the room of two prostitutes and threw all their possessions into the street, witnesses claimed that the assailants were "young men." The authorities did nothing to discourage these raids: several nights later some municipal officers arrived at the whores' room and did exactly the same thing. As was common in early modern France, the young men of Grenoble acted as the city's conscience and disciplined those, including prostitutes, who flaunted prevailing norms.[87]

The youths' role in policing harlots presents an apparent paradox: the young men may have persecuted whores, but they were also, one would assume, their best customers. This is not altogether clear. The prostitutes did occasionally mention their clients in court depositions, but they rarely indicated their age. Rather, they identified them by profession as "a huissier," "a notary" or "a gentleman." These cryptic references suggested that the prostitutes' clientele were fairly well-heeled. The sums of money that changed hands were in any case considerable: "a louis d'or," "a pistolle," or "an écu," all sums that represented weeks of a workingman's labor. Neighbors too testified that "gentlemen" were seen entering the prostitutes' rooms, but they may have made such statements in order to incriminate the whore. The appearance of a gentleman at the door of an impoverished widow was no common sight in Grenoble; it constituted near-certain proof that unwholesome commerce went on within. Also, the prostitutes brought before the Justice may have represented the very elite of the trade. Older women, working out of taverns and *académies de tabac,* may have catered to a more plebian crowd, for the three such prostitutes indicted by the Justice serviced, according to neighbors, the city's journeymen butchers. In any event, prostitutes probably performed a function appreciated, if not condoned, by the Grenoblois: in a city with a large number of unmarried law clerks and soldiers, the prostitutes kept these youths out of the skirts of honorable women.[88]

Or did they? The Brothers of the Holy Sacrament thought that illicit love was as common in Grenoble as venal love, so common that it was tacitly condoned in some milieux. The Grenoblois certainly did make love outside marriage: the illegitimate births recorded in the city's parish registers testify to the fact. But the rate of illegitimacy was very low, only 2 percent in the 1680s, when reliable parish data becomes available.[89] This figure may be misleading, for, as we shall see, some unwed mothers baptized their children as legitimate, and others may have failed to baptize them at all.[90] In any case, we can determine the nature, if not the frequency, of illicit unions thanks to a document contained in the Justice archives—the *déclaration de grossesse.* As its name indicates, the *déclaration* was a verbal statement made before a magistrate by an unwed mother, which contained the mother's age, profession, birthplace, and residence, as well as similar information about the putative father.[91] Sometimes these declarations take us right to the scene of the seduction and reveal all sorts of information about illicit unions. But for all their detail, the declarations must be approached with caution. Only a verbal oath prevented the harried mother from reshaping events to suit her own purposes, and although this tendency to misrepresent seems to have varied over time and with attitudes toward illegitimacy, it is always possible that the declarations contain something other than the truth. In addition, declarations are relatively rare until the 1690s. Did most of the declarations simply disappear along with so many other documents in the judicial archives? Or did seventeenth-century Grenobloises, as the Company of the Holy Sacrament believed, fail to declare their illegitimate pregnancies despite royal edicts and parlementary decrees?[92] Whatever the cause, only fifty-odd declarations have survived from the years 1669 through 1689. This number is too small to permit a rigorous statistical analysis, but it does allow us, as does no other document, to lift the veil of secrecy covering one of the Grenoblois' most common "sins."

Of the illicit unions described in the declarations, about half began as ordinary, honest courtships. Then fate intervened, and the marriage was postponed, often indefinitely, even if the arrival of the offpsring could not be. Gabrielle Pillaud, for example, had already had the bans published in her parish when she discovered she was pregnant. She had promised her suitor, a journeyman baker, twenty louis d'or, and he would not take her to the altar until he had his money well in hand. As in this case, it was usually financial concerns that prevented a wedding, and not just the groom was subject to them. Dimanche Bally, a twenty-four-year-old domestic, had been courted by a valet who was extremely eager to marry her. Her parents, however, objected that the young man "had no fortune" and refused to allow her to wed, even though she was eight months pregnant. A disadvantageous marriage was, it seems, as disastrous as an unwed pregnancy, and even the mother could allow economic concerns to stand in the way of a wedding. Marie Dupré, a bourgeoise of Saint Marcellin, had accepted the proposal and the embraces of a certain Antoine Josserand. Though eight months pregnant, she did not want to marry him, for his father had failed to bestow upon him a sufficient financial settlement.[93] These aborted unions tell us a great deal about the harsh, economic realities of marriage in the seventeenth century, and they suggest that sex traditionally formed a part of courtship. Because we have no rates of bridal pregnancy, though, we cannot know just how many Grenobloise went to the altar pregnant nor how common sex was during courtship.

In any case, premarital sex did not account for all the pregnancies described in the declarations, for only half of the unwed mothers claimed to have yielded to a promise of marriage. The other half made no such excuse, either because they had not received an offer of marriage or because they could not reasonably expect the court to believe such a story. In both instances, it is possible that the putative father was either already married or of such a socially superior class that marriage was, to the seventeenth-century mind, quite unthinkable. The declarations do not give, unfortunately, the father's marital status, but they do provide information about his social standing and his relationship with the mother. In those cases where marriage was not offered, the fathers were artisans, prosperous peasants, members of the legal profession, or rural nobles. Almost all were the mother's employer or her employer's son. As for the young women, they were, as the reader may have already guessed, domestics serving their master's home.

Did these illicit unions constitute, as the Brothers of the Holy Sacrament feared, a form of concubinage? It is hard to tell. Unlike similar documents elsewhere in France, the Grenoble declarations give no indication as to the length of these unions. Some do enumerate the children already produced by these couples: a pregnant Madeline Mesle said she had presented her employer with a child two years before, and Anne Pajon had given birth to her master's infant five years earlier. These are clearly long-term relationships, but we can only guess the duration of other illicit unions. In any case, the girl's pregnancy did not necessarily bring to an end either her employment or her relationship with her employer. Far from firing the girl, many masters would keep her in the house until just before she delivered and then send her, at their expense, to another community for her confinement. Once the child was born, it would be whisked off to a wet nurse, and the servant girl would return to her master's house and, one assumes, his bed. Michelle Amaret, for instance, told the judge that her employer had paid her way to Grenoble, given her money for her confinement and a wet nurse, then supplied her with return fare to his home in Savoy.[94]

Such peregrinations were designed to hide the illicit affair, but it is unlikely that most of these gentlemen succeeded in fooling those around them, especially their wives. These were men of substance with established households, so we can assume that many were married, and one wonders how their spouses reacted to the presence of a concubine, acknowledged or unacknowledged, in the house. In only one case do we know the wife's response: Louise Naud, a servant girl, frequently slept with her employer when his wife was home, and one night he even invited Louise to crawl into bed with him and his wife. Louise was taken aback, but the wife explained that she had "nothing more to fear than if she had been her own sister." Most wives probably lacked such understanding, but it hardly mattered, since the husbands kept their servant-concubine anyway.[95] Concubinage was, as the Brothers of the Holy Sacrament claimed, an established, if somewhat hidden, tradition in Dauphiné, especially rural Dauphiné. Rural notables had been producing bastards for so long that by the seventeenth century their illegitimate offspring were making declarations and giving birth to bastards themselves. Rural gentlemen even went so far as to buy a young girl specifically for their sexual satisfaction. A procuress matter-of-factly proposed to Claire Prié that she sell herself to a gentleman who was looking for a young girl to maintain in his home. When seduction or money failed, seventeenth-century men did not hesitate to use violence, and nearly 20 percent of the unwed fathers literally forced themselves upon women.[96]

Most seventeenth-century males, it seems, considered all socially inferior women to be at their disposal sexually. The nonchalance with which they bedded servants and peasants suggests that such behavior was regarded as their right and was tolerated as an unfortunate fact-of-life. This does not mean that the Grenoblois, unlike the Brothers of the Holy Sacrament, condoned illicit sex, at least not as far as the woman involved was concerned. The woman who gave birth outside marriage ran a terrible risk. At best, she would fall into poverty in a city that as yet had no facilities for dealing with single mothers; at worst, she would sink into the world of prostitution. The distance between illicit sex and venal sex was small. Marie Babasset, a mere seventeen years old, was seduced by her employer and then prostituted by him. Antoinette Bertier, a widow, also drifted from illicit love to prostitution. During her marriage she began an affair with a carpenter, and after her husband's death she lived with the same man as his wife. The carpenter abandoned her, and she was then recruited by a procuress, "the Dame Moulhet who ruined girls and counterfeited money in a barn near Chambéry." There Antoinette Bertier was sold to a number of men, among them a gentleman with whom she was locked in a room for two days. Even the suspicion of an illicit union was sufficient to plunge an honest woman into the half-lit world of prostitution. Marguerite Francisque, age twenty, was working as a glove seamstress when a young man paid her court. She repulsed his advances and he put it about that she was a whore. Hearing that she was a prostitute, her landlord threw her out, and then her troubles really began. Twice she was locked up in the Tour Dauphine, and twice she escaped only to find that no one would lodge or employ her. Finally, she fell into the hands of a glove-maker who raped her and then dressed her as a boy and prostituted her in the taverns of the city.[97]

A man who had an illicit affair had no such fate to fear. Indeed, he could even be proud of his achievement. Barthelémy Fournier, a secretary to a *trésorier de France,* deflowered a poor serving girl on the banks of the Isère and later boasted about the matter in every cabaret in Grenoble.[98] This sort of locker-room talk is certainly not unique to the seventeenth century, but it points to the fact that for men, unlike women, no shame or even embarrassment followed an illicit union. The worst that a man had to fear was a lawsuit, and this could be easily avoided with a little compromise. The law clerk Guillaume Boys had impregnated his employer's servant girl, and she threatened to take him to court. But, "in order to terminate this affair and avoid costly court proceedings," Guillaume agreed to take charge of the infant and pay the girl a mere forty-five livres in damages. At worst, the man might be forced to assume responsibility for the child, that is, pay for its wet-nursing in the countryside. For a man of moderate means, this was not a heavy burden, and given the mortality rate of children at wet nurse, it was not likely to be a lengthy one. Consequently, many fathers in the seventeenth century rather cheerfully took charge of their illegitimate offspring; indeed, about half of the men named in the declarations had already agreed to assume financial responsibility for their bastards.[99]

The court by its policies encouraged them to do so, for if they did not, the judges would pursue them vigorously and without delay. At the very making of the declaration, the court intervened to force the putative father to recognize his responsibilities, even though this was neither the purpose nor the normal function of a *déclaration de grossesse*. In principle, the declaration was supposed to prevent a woman from aborting her fetus, and it constituted a safeguard (in an era of high infant mortality) against the accusation of infanticide.[100] In the hands of Grenoble's magistrates, however, the declaration took on very broad coercive powers: the magistrates usually appended a summons to the declaration, which required the putative father to "appear before the court and answer with his own mouth the charges brought before him." Often the Justice went even further: it issued an immediate warrant for the man's arrest. Barthelémy Fournier, who had boasted of deflowering a servant girl, was thrown into Grenoble's prisons, and Jean Coyet, who had seduced one of his master's domestics, was locked up with no further ado. The court was most likely to take such extreme measures when the girl in question was young, virginal, of a certain social standing, and most important of all, when she had been deceived by a promise of marriage. When the nineteen-year-old daughter of a lawyer found herself pregnant by her fiancé, she easily obtained a writ from the court preventing her seducer from leaving the province and all but forcing him to marry her. A certain class interest motivated the court in such cases, but the Justice was not above rushing to the aid of an impoverished, aging, none-too-pure domestic. When a pregnant thirty-eight-year-old domestic from Burgundy was abandoned one afternoon on the Rue Saint Laurent by her common-law husband, the court issued a warrant for his arrest and had him seized in Domène, where he had fled.[101]

The court was obviously on the woman's side, and this attitude contrasted with the prevailing view in Grenoble. Popular values condemned the woman and arrogated to her family, that is, her male relatives, the exclusive right to discipline her. The court, on the other hand, considered the woman a victim and bestowed upon her sweeping, even terrible, powers of retribution. In this regard, the court's attitude resembled that of the Company of the Holy Sacrament, and its actions probably signal the diffusion of the Company's views among the Grenoble elite. Like the Company, the court abhorred illicit sex, but it never persecuted or prosecuted the woman involved. Even in cases of prostitution, it was not the prostitute who was whipped and chased from the city, but the procuress. Of course, this indulgence had its limits: the prostitute was usually confined in the Madeline asylum or the Tour Dauphine. And naturally, the prostitutes' clients suffered no penalties at all. Had the court decided to pursue the men who frequented prostitutes, the results would have been highly embarrassing, for many were clerics.

The Company of the Holy Sacrament had reason to suspect the city's clergymen of consorting with prostitutes and other forms of misconduct. Priests and canons figured prominently among the prostitutes' clients, and Claire Prié, the most forthright of the harlots, claimed to have been taken "to a priest near Notre Dame who lifted [her] skirts and tried to have [her] from behind."[102] This sodomite cleric was probably none other than the stipendiary priest of Notre Dame who had so concerned the Company in the early 1660s, Father Des Henrys. Older but certainly no wiser, Des Henry was still causing trouble, for he appeared almost regularly in the judicial archives. In 1679 he was suspected of pimping and of selling girls in a sordid *académie de tabac*. In 1680 he himself brought criminal charges against a man who had slandered him in a tavern and called him to his face "a pimp and procurer for the canon Sautereau and others." That Des Henrys should not have been in the tavern in the first place seems not to have occurred to him or to many other of the city's clerics. Clergymen appear quite frequently among the witnesses to barroom brawls, and sometimes they even participated in these drunken fights.[103]

Did this spectacle of priestly misconduct shake the Grenoblois' faith? The criminal records are not the best place to look for information on popular religiosity, but there are a few examples of people's impiety. In 1676 a poor vagabond woman, a former prostitute by her own admission, was arrested for snipping material off the skirts of women during mass. At her trial, the judges informed her that this constituted a sacrilege, to which she replied that she was starving. In 1674 the Justice brought charges against merchants who kept their shops open on Sundays and during mass. These violations were so numerous that virtually every merchant in the city, in particular the butchers, was fined. In 1676 a more shocking event occurred. A group of cobblers and tailors were drinking in a local tavern, when someone suggested they toast the patron saints of their professions, Saint Crespin and Saint Luce. One of the cobblers then pointed out that this was appropriate, for Saint Luce was the pimp of

Saint Crespin. He was fined one hundred livres and instructed to give a third of this money to the chapel of Saint Crespin at Notre Dame and a third to the altar of Saint Luce in the Jacobins.[104]

Was the Company of the Holy Sacrament correct when it condemned the Grenoblois for their impiety and irreligiosity? These few examples refute as much as they sustain the Company's vision. After all, a society in which religion makes its way into the tavern is not necessarily irreligious, and some of the cobblers and tailors present at the blasphemy must have been shocked because the incident was reported to the Justice. As for the poor woman who tailored ladies' trains, she simply failed to understand that the demands of piety outweighed those of the stomach. And Claire Prié, the most perverse of all the city's prostitutes, was shocked when Des Henry tried to have intercourse with her, not because he attempted to sodomize her, but because he was a priest. The Brothers of the Company of the Holy Sacrament were acute observers of men, but sometimes their perspective may well have been skewed.

ATTITUDES TOWARD THE POOR
IN THE SEVENTEENTH CENTURY

Having examined the people of Grenoble from the perspective of the Justice, what can we say about the vision of the Company of the Holy Sacrament? Did the Brothers' view of the lower orders correspond to reality or was it subtly and unconsciously distorted by prejudice and bias? At first glance, one major omission, a real blind spot, stands out: if the Brothers were able to see sin and vice among the poor, they were incapable of recognizing it among the rich. On only two occasions did the Company focus upon deviance among the wealthy, and in one case the sin simply was too extraordinary to be overlooked. A rural gentleman had fathered a child by his own illegitimate daughter, a combination of illicit sex and incest which even the Company could not ignore.[105] But what about the other "scandals," to use the Company's vocabulary, which riddled Grenoble's elite? What about the elite men described in the *déclarations de grossesse* who fathered children by their serving girls? Or the "gentlemen" enumerated in the Justice records who frequented prostitutes? The Company either refused to acknowledge these sins or was incapable of seeing them, just as it was blind to the impiety that reigned among some members of the city's aristocracy. Grenoble possessed a small, but erudite, libertine circle whose members, like the Brothers themselves, came from the highest reaches of the sovereign court and the nobility.[106] Given their common origins, it is hard to believe that the Brothers were unaware of these aristocratic free thinkers, but they mention them only once and then in the most veiled terms. Certain "blasphemies," a Brother reported, were committed at the table of the comte de Roure, and though the precise nature of these blasphemies was never specified, it is likely that they were more cynical and dangerous than the rather innocent lapses of poorer Catholics. Did the Brothers react in their habitual manner and set in motion the machinery of the courts? No, they resolved to "leave the matter"—that is, ignore it.[107] Such inconsistency smacks of hypocrisy, but it stemmed, not from bigotry, but from sheer disbelief. The Brothers suffered from a case of social myopia so severe that they simply could not see "sin and vice" among their social equals.

By the same token, the Brothers could see nothing but sin and crime among the poor. The portrait of lawlessness and corruption they paint bears no resemblance to the real Grenoble of the seventeenth century. As the Justice records reveal, this was a society in which murder was unknown and theft extremely rare. Violence did break out in the city streets, but it was never deadly. Vagabonds did break into the Grenoblois' homes, but they were pathetic creatures, few in number and loathed by rich and poor alike. Fornicators did drop their illegitimate offspring on doorsteps, but the rate of illegitimacy in the city was relatively low. In short, this was an orderly society, and the "weaklings, tavern haunters, fornicators, villains and thieves" which the Brothers complained about were only a mirage. Even the humblest day laborer or seamstress who lived on the edge of poverty adhered to a set of values and norms which were not, in truth, that different from those of the Company of the Holy Sacrament. This was especially true in regard to sexual behavior. The average Grenoblois, like the Brothers, abhorred illicit unions, and the average citizen, like the lofty Company, condemned prostitution.

But we should not exaggerate these similarities, for there were important differences between the attitudes of the Grenoblois and the Company of the Holy Sacrament even in the area of sexual behavior. The Company, for instance, saw in the prostitute not a criminal but a victim of human frailty; in her repentance they detected not sin but something almost sacred, the triumph of man over the evils of the flesh. Consequently, the Brothers persecuted the procuress and not the prostitute, and they encouraged their wives and sisters to partake of the madelines' penance by joining the Madelines confraternity. Here, the Grenoblois definitely parted company with the Brothers. The average artisan had no intention of allowing his women to rub shoulders with harlots, and he certainly saw nothing sacred in prostitutes, just feminine corruption and deviance. In this regard, the ethic of the common Grenoblois was much more rigorous than that of the Company, but it was considerably more lax when it came to the prostitutes' clients. On the whole, popular beliefs spared the man involved in venal and illicit love. Opprobrium fell only upon the mother of an illegitimate child, not upon the father, who was subject to a different set of norms. For the Brothers, on the other hand, sin knew no distinction according to gender: man and woman alike sinned when they surrendered to the evils of the flesh, and neither could escape punishment, whether in this world or the next. Despite superficial similarities, the Company did have an ethic radically different from that of the average Grenoblois. The Brothers, unlike their fellow citizens, equated sexuality with sin and preached virtues of discipline and self-restraint to all, male and female alike.

The Company wanted to impose a new set of values and a new type of behavior upon the Grenoblois and not just in the domain of sexuality. For the Brothers, illicit sex was merely one example of the Grenoblois' pervasive and pernicious "disorder." This word had a peculiar resonance for the Company, and it appears on virtually every page of the Company register. Its meaning also goes far beyond the sexual. If a man with a concubine lived in "disorder," so too did an artisan who worked on Sundays, or a beggar who demanded alms during mass. What all these Grenoblois shared, in the eyes of the Company, was a lack of discipline, or "order," which had to be remedied by persuasion or force. If the cobbler refused to observe the Sabbath and put down his work, the Company would alert the courts. If the beggar persisted in his begging, he would be locked up in a workhouse and subjected to an endless regimen of labor that would teach him the virtues of work. Discipline would replace "disorderliness," if the Brothers of the Company had their way, and the Grenoblois would forsake their old ways for a new self-restraint, whether in the bedroom or the boutique.

In the Church, too, disorderliness would have to disappear. The Company often described the Grenoblois as irreverent and irreligious, and at first glance they were undoubtedly right. Upon closer inspection, however, it seems they were quite mistaken, for the Grenoblois did have a religion; it was just not the religion of the Brothers. In fact, the average citizen lived in a constant and close familiarity with the sacred. When he celebrated, it was on a saint's day; when he joined a journeymen's association, it was to the accompaniment of a semireligious ritual; when he wanted to gossip, he went to mass. Life and religion were not yet separated, and it was this very blend of the sacred and secular that enraged the

Brothers. They interpreted familiarity as contempt and vowed to purge popular festivals of their earthy elements and banish "indecent" behavior from the churches. This concern for proper decorum sometimes bordered on the picayune. The Brothers spent hours worrying that the priests might dispense the Host in short robes rather than the appropriate long ones, and they wasted a great deal of time trying to prevent the Grenoblois from urinating in a passageway adjacent to the Cordeliers. Given the sorry state of the city's clergy, one wonders if these projects really merited the Brothers' attention.[108] But the fact that they lavished so much time on them indicates just how ambitious their crusade for the conversion of souls was. Whenever and wherever the Company found disorder, they rooted it out. The Brothers wanted to do more than just convert souls, they wanted to change behavior in this world.

The Company's charity was essentially militant. The Brothers never denied the efficacy of good works for their own souls; they were simply more interested in the souls of the poor. The Company's crusade was also, to borrow a phrase from historians of Protestant poor relief, "secular and progressive."[109] The Brothers focused upon this world, not the next, and they sought to foist upon the poor a new, rather grim, social ethic. In fact, the Company's good works resemble nothing so much as Protestant social policies. In the past, historians have tended to stress the difference between the two confessions, but of late they have come to emphasize the similarities instead. Certainly, the Company of the Holy Sacrament shared many goals with Protestant benefactors, in particular the English Puritans. Like their contemporaries across the Channel, the Brothers sought to suppress popular sports and amusements, to instill a harsh, unbending self-discipline, and to replace traditional, casual almsgiving with a more "rational" system of poor relief centered around the workhouse.[110] In addition, the Brothers, like the Puritan reformers of charity, were primarily laymen. French historians have tended to view the Counter Reformation as a struggle between an enlightened Church and an ignorant, reluctant laity. They underestimate the importance of lay people and overlook the contribution of lay groups, like the Brothers of the Holy Sacrament, to the Catholic reform.[111] The vanguard of Catholic renewal came, as the Brothers of the Holy Sacrament demonstrate, not from the Church hierarchy alone, but from the very heart of French society, from the elite of the court and the nobility.

Consequently, the Counter Reformation in Grenoble was a struggle between two segments of society. Because the Brothers' crusade was so wide-ranging, encompassing everything from public festivals to intimate behavior, and because its values were so foreign to popular impulses, the Company's good works look a lot like a concerted attack on popular culture as a whole. From this vantage point, the Company's crusade was but part of a larger assault on traditional values and habits which Peter Burke believes occurred throughout western Europe in the sixteenth and seventeenth centuries.[112] Still, this was not just the victory of Lent over Carnival; it was also the triumph of one class over another. One could even go so far as to describe the Company's crusade as a cultural variant of the class warfare described by Boris Porchnev in a controversial study of seventeenth-century French uprisings.[113] The magistrates and nobles who came together at the Company to destroy popular culture certainly bore a distinct resemblance to the magistrates and nobles, the *front du classe,* as Porchnev called it, who combined to defeat the popular rebels. If the Brothers' oppression was less bloody, it was no less far-reaching in its consequences: if the Company succeeded, it would obtain a victory over popular rebelliousness which no amount of violence could achieve.

And yet more than sheer hostility characterized the Company's stance vis-à-vis the pauper. In his heated debate with Porchnev, Roland Mousnier stressed that vertical ties and mutual dependencies still characterized French society in the seventeenth century, and the Brothers of the Holy Sacrament, for all their rhetoric about the sins of the poor, did in fact maintain ties, sometimes close, personal, enduring ties with paupers. After all, the Brothers dealt with each pauper individually. They knew his name and a bit of his family history, and they did not hesitate to rub shoulders with a syphilitic cobbler, a teen-age prostitute, or a beggar. The Brothers gladly haunted taverns and inns, visited sick wards of hospitals, walked the streets of unsavory quarters, and even marched right into the homes of the poor. The Company was anything but squeamish, and the members had a positive appetite for personal contact with the poor—all of which would seem to contradict the Brothers' professed loathing for the impoverished and their enthusiastic support of confinement. But the contradiction is mainly illusory. Ever since Michel Foucault's influential book on madness in the classical age, historians have tended to speak of confinement in terms of exclusion.[114] The monarchy probably did want to rid itself of the sight and insubordination of the poor, but devout groups, like the Company, saw confinement in a different light. For them, the workhouse was not a prison but a place of asylum, a "refuge," as they frequently remarked. Here the pauper would be sheltered from the "evils of the age," from the temptations which assailed every Christian. If the pauper, unlike other souls, had to be incarcerated, it was because he was more vulnerable, more likely to fall victim to the machinations of the Devil.

Was the pauper the Devil's victim or his agent? The Company seems to have maintained both propositions with little conscious difficulty. At one moment, the Brothers would bemoan the fate of the city's porters whose labors left them disabled at an early age; the very next, they would condemn the excesses of these same porters and attribute all their hardships, especially their illness, to debauchery.[115] The Company's attitude toward the poor was contradictory, even confused, but all the ambiguity disappeared as soon as the Brothers entered into a relationship with an individual pauper. Then, hostility gave way to complete solicitude, and the Brothers were indulgent to the point of foolishness. They remained, for instance, utterly faithful to the prostitutes they assisted, even though these women were given to considerable backsliding. When a prostitute suddenly reappeared on the streets after the Company had given her a rather large sum of money to "repent," the Brothers did not chastise her. They rationalized her failings, chalking them up to the return of the troops or bad times, and they only redoubled their alms. The Company's indulgence toward the poor sometimes brought it into conflict with the more rigorous municipal authorities. The consuls refused to admit a pregnant girl to the Hospital because she had stolen some linen from the institution. The Brothers intervened and used their influence to have her accepted. The consuls wanted to prosecute another girl who had exposed her child, but the Brothers used all their connections to see that the charges against this former inmate of the Hospital were dropped.[116] In both cases, the women were among the Company's clients, "their" paupers, and the Brothers were extremely protective of their protégées, even the most "sinful." When in 1663 a crowd stoned one of the Company's prostitutes, La Grande Jeanne, as she was banished from the city, the Brothers swore to seek revenge, and they called upon all their connections to punish the malefactors.[117]

The irony here is that the Brothers may well have reported La Grande Jeanne to the Justice in the first place. They deplored her death, which they had never intended, but they had also contributed to it indirectly. Such ironies abound in the Company's history, for the Brothers' stance vis-à-vis the poor was riddled with seeming contradictions and apparent inconsistencies. In one breath, the Brothers would describe the poor as "devils" and attribute to them a host of fictitious vices; in the next, they would call them the poor of Christ and praise their supposed humility and frailty, also products of the Brothers' fervid imagination. One day the Brothers might persecute a prostitute; the next they would try to get her released from prison. The Brothers condemned in the most vehement of terms all sorts of sins; but they were always ready to help a sinner. The attitude which allowed the brothers to pursue these contradictory forms of behavior was paternalism. Located somewhere between Porchnev's crude class warfare and Mousnier's nostalgic seigneurial beneficence, the Brothers' posture in regard to the poor was like that of a stern, even cruel, but loving father.[118] Like a good father, the Company provided protection to its charges, albeit protective custody in a prison-like *maison de force.* Like a stern patriarch, the Brothers punished their paupers when necessary, but never abandoned them, however scandalous their behavior. Like responsible heads of household, the Brothers' relationships with the impoverished were also personal, obligatory, total, and ambivalent. The Parisian Company had been the first to draw this analogy between fatherly love and charitable duty: the statutes of the original Company instructed all members to extend the benefits of spiritual charity, not only to their immediate households, but to their children and servants, and to their more distant dependents, the poor.[119] The Brothers of Grenoble apparently accepted the analogy. They adopted a domestic metaphor and referred to themselves, when they sat on the Board of the Hospital General, as "the fathers of the poor."[120]

Modern notions about fatherly love should not obscure the sinister implications of this seemingly benign formula. As "fathers of the poor," the Brothers were obliged to help the impoverished, but they were also licensed to abuse them in the most cruel manner. The darker side of the Company's paternalism is most evident in the one area of the Company's activity we have yet to explore: the campaign to eradicate the Protestant "heresy." This was a crusade in which the Brothers had long been active, and almost all belonged to the organization that spearheaded the persecution of Protestants in Grenoble, the Congregation for the Propagation of the Faith. In 1663 the monarchy temporarily disbanded this organization, for it detected in it a "dangerous, devout cabal." The Brothers of the Holy Sacrament drew the logical conclusion: the monarchy had meant to abolish the Company itself. Consequently, the Brothers vowed to observe a stricter secrecy, but we cannot know if their discretion saved the Company. In 1666 the Company register abruptly comes to a halt. Perhaps the Brothers continued to meet as usual or, more likely, just regrouped within the revived Congregation for the Propagation of the Faith. There, the spirit of the Company would survive, and the sinister dimensions of its good works would be most fully revealed.

FOUR

The Crusade for the Conversion of Souls: The Congregation for the Propagation of the Faith (1647–1685)

Several years after the revocation of the Edict of Nantes, a Protestant minister from the Cévennes told a fellow believer:

> I never travel through the dioceses of Vienne, Grenoble, Embrun, or Gap. They say that in all of these episcopal cities there are Protestant children confined in convents, but the largest number is by all accounts in Grenoble. They assure me that in Grenoble, in the convent called the Propagation, there are five or six hundred children from all over the province. Frequently, the *archers* employed by this convent descend the Drôme, cross the plains and carry innocent Protestant children back to Grenoble.[1]

The institution described by the minister was indeed the Maison de la Propagation, a small building located near Grenoble's city walls. But the minister was partially mistaken: this was not a convent but a hospice, a charitable institution like the Hospital General or the Orphans asylum. This was yet another example of the charitable revival that was sweeping Grenoble, and an unusually instructive one. Here the fundamental qualities of charity in the age of the Counter Reformation—militancy and modernity—were manifested with particular clarity. Here the social roots of seventeenth-century beneficence—paternalism and seigneurialism—were revealed in a striking fashion. For here, unlike the modest Orphans or secretive Holy Sacrament, the contradictions inherent in seventeenth-century charity—its violence and cruelty—were displayed for all to see. The minister was not entirely ill-informed: this "charitable" institution was dangerous, a branch of that notorious agent of religious persecution, the Propagation of the Faith.

This sinister organization began modestly enough in 1632 at the Capuchin monastery in Paris. A monk, the père Hyacinthe, decided to found a confraternity "to work incessantly for the conversion of all heretics" and "to assist and instruct all new converts."[2] A number of devout lay men and women soon joined the Capuchin, and by 1632 the little Congregation had received both episcopal approval and the promise of substantial royal subsidies. Over the next forty years, similar "sister" Congregations sprang up throughout the provinces in cities like Rouen, Sedan, Marseille, Aix-en-Provence, Lyon, Montpellier, and La Rochelle and in the villages of the Cévennes.[3] Among the first of these was the Congregation of Grenoble, established in 1647 and recognized by the episcopal authorities three years later. Soon the Grenoblois proved to be more than precocious: by 1660 they had firmly established themselves as the model for all subsequent Congregations and had even won a national notoriety that outstripped that of the Parisian motherhouse.

The reason for this fame was the Grenoblois' extraordinary enthusiasm and effectiveness, as well as a flair for public relations. By 1670 the Grenoblois had arranged the suppression of Grenoble's biconfessional court, the Chambre de l'Édit, the destruction of scores of Protestant churches, including the Grenoble Temple, and the exclusion of Protestants from several professions and all municipal offices.[4] To broadcast these triumphs to the world and especially to a monarchy that the Propagandists considered too sluggish in the persecution of "heresy," the Grenoble Propagandists maintained in Paris a kind of lobbyist, the abbé de Musi. The genial abbé periodically issued reports on the Congregation's progress, kept the Assembly of the Clergy well informed of the triumphs of the Grenoblois, and cultivated the king's confessor.[5] For their part, the Propagandists kept up the tempo of persecution: they had Protestant ministers banished and at least two executed, imprisoned scores of Protestants, kidnapped Protestant children, in short, did everything in their power to deserve the epithet history has given them—"the terror of heresy."[6]

How could such an organization possibly be considered charitable? Historians have called the Propagation many things, but "charitable" is not among them. Michelet summed up the activities of the Grenoblois and their sister Congregations by evoking "the cries of desolate mothers that reached to the heavens."[7] Another historian concluded that the patrons of the Parisian Congregation, "Vincent de Paul, Bossuet, Fenelon, Louis XIV and Madame de Maintenon, would with the triumph of civil society, be liable to imprisonment under articles 324 and 123 of the Penal Code."[8] But contemporaries—and among them some of the most learned and cultivated souls of the age—celebrated the triumphs of the Propagation of Grenoble and called its efforts, of all things, charity. The famous preacher Bourdaloue praised the Grenoblois and pointed out that they knew how to "attract the heretic with the odor of charity."[9] Bossuet, in a letter to the administrators of a hospice like the Maison de la Propagation, insisted that "charity must inspire us to find a way of forcing them [heretics] to come" back into the Church.[10] Even the Propagandists, who hounded and harassed Protestants with such delight, casually referred to their activities as "assistance" and charity.[11]

Obviously, seventeenth-century Frenchmen had a rather strange definition of charity if it could be stretched to include the "terror of heresy." And it is precisely this peculiar, contradictory notion of charity—not the history of the Protestant persecution—that forms the subject of this chapter. That contemporaries referred to the Propagation as a "charitable" organization reveals a great deal about contemporary notions of social beneficence and the impulses that inspired it.

It is not hard to understand why most Grenoblois assumed that the Propagation of the Faith was just another charitable organization. In a town with several such groups, appearances would have led anyone to the same conclusion. The only visible signs of the group, a chapel and a hospice, would have immediately qualified the Congregation as "charitable" in most minds, particularly those familiar with similar establishments maintained by the Madeline and Orphans confraternities. In addition, the Congregation proclaimed itself to be a confraternity, a type of organization that, by tradition, devoted itself to good works. According to the Congregation's statutes, the "Brothers" and "Sisters" had a number of duties and mutual obligations, just like the rather mundane Penitents. The members of the Congregation were required to perform certain spiritual duties together, to attend each other's requiem mass, to walk in "Brothers'" and "Sisters'" funeral processions, and to pray for one another.[12] None of this was particularly unusual: the ladies of the Madeline and Orphans and even the directors of the Hospital General observed similar rules.

Had these similarities been incapable of bestowing on the Propagation a "charitable" reputation, the Congregation's membership alone would have sufficed. Not only were the Propagandists drawn from the same elite—a primarily judicial elite—that filled the ranks of orthodox charitable groups, they were frequently the same people. Of the thirty-odd men and women who joined the Propagation from 1647 to 1690, most of the women belonged to the Orphans or the Madelines confraternity and sometimes both; of the "Brothers," nine served as directors of the Hospital General and several belonged to the secret Company of the Holy Sacrament.[13] Typical of the Propagandists was the ubiquitous Madame de Revel, who was simultaneously cofounder of the Madeline, virtual dictator of the Orphans, principal administrator of both groups' hospices, head of the female Propagandists, and for a time, sole financial support of the Hospital General. Naturally, the Congregation profited from these connections. The "Sisters" often placed their protégés in the Hospital General for medical treatment or in the Orphans for advanced schooling; and in 1686, when the Maison de la Propagation was full, they foisted hundreds of children off on the Hospital. Sometimes the Orphans and the Hospital returned the favor. In fact, so intermingled were the affairs of the Propagation and Grenoble's other charitable institutions that the Protestants (who certainly should have known better) often mistook the Orphans or the Hospital for the Propagation.[14]

Another element in the Propagation's activities contributed to this confusion. The Propagandists, like the ladies of the Orphans or the directors of the Hospital General, concerned themselves with the young, the sick, the hungry, the homeless, in short, the poor. Dauphinois Protestantism certainly offered to the Propagandists a selection of "heretics" from every social class; but the Propagandists chose to concentrate on poor "heretics" for two reasons.[15] To begin with, royal measures affecting Protestants aimed primarily at the rich. From 1661 to 1684, the monarchy attempted to eliminate "heresy" by excluding Protestants from positions of power and influence, by denying them access to the honors, privileges, and especially offices granted by the king to his loyal and worthy subjects. Obviously, such measures affected only those with offices or privileges to lose and left to auxiliary groups, like the Propagation, the task of bringing the poor back to the Church. Second, the Propagation faithfully observed the social conventions prescribed by a hierarchical society. At no time during its fifty-year career did the Congregation disturb the wealthy Protestant magistrates or nobles who lived in and around Grenoble. Indeed, these prestigious "heretics" are mentioned in the records of the Congregation only in connection with their domestics, who were frequently the unwilling recipients of the Congregation's attentions.[16] Protestant domestics could be harassed, but not their masters. Like the Company of the Holy Sacrament, the Propagandists of the Faith recognized "sin," in this case Protestantism, only among the poor.

For these reasons, the Congregation, in the words of one historian, "generally deployed its most vigilant and active persecutions against the poor."[17] Contemporaries also noticed this tendency, and the famous Protestant Jurieu dismissed the Propagandists' accomplishments with the haughty remark that "their converts come only from the *lie du peuple.*"[18] Poverty did indeed characterize the Propagation's converts, but it was a particular kind of poverty, rural poverty. If these new Catholics were poor, it was because they came from rural areas, from remote villages like Besse, Mens, Bourdeaux, or Tréminis, where misery was the common lot and starvation a constant companion. And if most of these converts were peasants, it was because the great majority of Dauphinois Protestants lived in rural areas. Besides a small community in Grenoble (3.5 percent of the total population), all of upper Dauphiné's Protestants inhabited the barren regions of the Oisans, Trièves, and Piedmontese mountain ranges.[19] The geography of Dauphinois Protestantism alone would have assured the Propagation of a large number of peasant converts, but in addition the Propagandists concentrated most of their energies on rural Protestantism.[20] They knew that if converts were to be made, it would be here, in the remote valleys of southwestern Dauphiné.

The Propagandists were attracted to rural Dauphiné for tactical reasons too. Bishop Etienne Le Camus believed that "it would be easier to conquer the country than the capital," and the Propagandists poured the better part of their energies and resources into a relentless and (to their surprise) protracted campaign against rural Protestantism. Through a network of local contacts—usually village priests or local seigneurs—the Propagandists received information from all over the province and successfully manipulated the affairs of even the most remote Dauphinois communities. From their headquarters on the Rue Saint Jacques, they deposed village notaries, intervened in family disputes, manipulated local tribunals, and kept a close watch on Protestant ministers from Pont-en-Royans to Chateau-Dauphin. As for the heretics in their midst, the Grenoble Consistory, the Propagandists left them in relative peace. The war on heresy took on the contours of a conflict between town and country.

In this long struggle, one episode is particularly important: the Congregation's attempts to convert the valleys of Pragelas and Queyras. The Propagandists found this area a particularly suitable (if not to say challenging) terrain upon which to wage the war against heresy. For here was one of the most remote and stubbornly heretical areas in France. Actually, neither the Pragelas nor the Queyras valley was part of France at all: both belonged to an area that the Dauphinois called "the mountains beyond the mountains," a region near the Italian border that is now known in French as the Vaudois valleys and in English as the Waldensian valleys.

Before 1630 this region was a part of Savoy, but the Vaudois were no more Savoyard than French. They were quite simply Vaudois, members of a community that had its own language, customs, political institutions, and religion. They also had a long and bloody tradition of resistance. Since the fourteenth century, the Vaudois had been "heretics," Waldensians, and neither popes nor monarchs had been able to subjugate these rebellious *montagnards*. Hidden in their valleys between peaks that rose up to three thousand meters, the Vaudois were a politically independent and culturally distinct unit at the very heart of Europe.[21]

When they resolved to convert the Vaudois, the Propagandists were well aware that they were venturing into foreign territory inhabited by a race even stranger, even more deviant than urban poor who shocked the Brothers of the Holy Sacrament. One of the Propagandist's pamphlets went so far as to compare the Vaudois to the Chinese and to remark that these *montagnards* were as much in need of conversion as the Persians. After all, the Propagandists noted, the Catholic mass had not been heard in these valleys for over four hundred years, and in that time the Vaudois had become "the most stubborn and impudent of heretics." "This race is incorrigible," swore one of the Propagandists; "nothing can exceed the insolence and fiery passion of these heretics."[22] Impudence and incorrigibility—these qualities seem to have horrified the devout Propagandists as much as "heresy"; the sin of disobedience seems to have been as grave as the sin of disbelief. Being wealthy seigneurs themselves, the magistrates of the Congregation instantly detected the source of this impudence: "in this valley there is not a single noble house, not one seigneur, spiritual or temporal; this makes the people proud and defiant, despite their poverty, so that all of the inhabitants of this valley consider themselves independent." Men without masters, ignorant of the values of a hierarchical society, the Vaudois, in the words of the Congregation, "had to be humiliated."[23] Clearly, there was more at issue in the Pragelas than differences of theology.

The social concerns in the Propagandists' Vaudois crusade were evident from the outset. In 1657, when the prince de Conti, who had endowed a Jesuit mission in the valleys, asked the Propagandists to join him in his crusade, the Propagandists responded in a most significant way: they began to set up royal officials throughout the "terres sans seigneur." First of all, they bought the offices of *châtelain* from the royal government and then gave them to the first Vaudois to convert. Later, they increased the number of officers, purchasing offices of notaries, secretaries, and so forth, always giving them away to those Vaudois whom they could persuade to convert.[24]

Unfortunately, the Vaudois proved somewhat reluctant to embrace the True Faith, and those who did, had cause to regret it. In this tight-knit community, spiritual defections were frowned upon, and the first convert—and *châtelain*—was nearly beaten to death by his own brothers.[25] Another new Catholic "was subjected to strange persecutions, such as preventing him from drawing water at the village stream or baking his bread in the communal oven," and yet another new convert suffered a more dramatic fate. One Captain Croyzat, an unbalanced fellow according to some accounts, had defied the whole community and converted to Catholicism. Adding insult to injury, he built a private chapel in the very center of the Pragelas valley. Reprisals came swiftly; one night while the captain was praying before his new altar, the chapel mysteriously caught fire and the new convert perished in the flames.[26]

None too surprisingly, conversions were exceedingly rare in the Pragelas. After twenty years, the Propagandists could boast of only a handful. The Vaudois crusade seemed doomed to failure when, in 1676, the Congregation discovered a new device, money. A few coins distributed before the mass, the missionaries noticed, greatly increased the enthusiasm and receptivity of the impoverished Vaudois. With larger sums, how many errant souls might be enticed back into the bosom of the Church? The Propagandists opened their purses, appealed to the king for money, and the infamous "traffic in souls," as the Protestants would call it, was under way.[27]

The first monetary distributions took place in the spring of 1676 and immediately proved both successful and economical. For only ten livres, a whole family would convert, and some individuals would abjure their faith for as little as a few pennies. As in any transaction, the price paid depended on the goods offered. The Propagandists and the Jesuit missionaries preferred big families and were known to go as high as a hundred francs for particularly large ones.[28] But generally, they tried to keep prices down, an effort that was thwarted by their competitor, the Protestant Consistory. A missionary reported that he had to distribute large sums of money because "the ministers and elders circulate unceasingly through these hamlets, assembling their people, catechizing them, and making distributions to those in need; and as soon as they know that someone may convert they immediately give him something and promise him more."[29] In some places, such distributions were made at the door of the local Temple, in imitation of similar rites performed at Catholic churches in the valley.[30]

Stiff competition did not prevent the Propagandists from making spectacular gains. Only a few months after the first distributions, the Propagandists began receiving returns on their investment: sixty souls in June 1676, one hundred in July—the True Faith was clearly triumphing after years of defeat. By February 1677 the Propagandists could point to over eight hundred Protestants returned to the Church; later the figure would climb to an amazing four thousand. Such success did not long go unnoticed: in 1677 Paul Pellisson, a convert himself and administrator of the Caisse des Conversions, praised the Grenoble Congregation in a circular letter to the bishops of France and suggested that the new "method" be employed throughout France. Eventually, it was, with the monarchy supplying most of the money.[31]

Significantly, the monarchy chose to refer to its subsidies as "sacred alms" or even "holy dew." These coy euphemisms did not fool Protestants like Bayle and Jurieu: they called the "traffic in souls" just what it was, a new form of simony.[32] But most French Catholics, including austere Christians like Grenoble's Bishop Etienne Le Camus and Antoine Arnaud, believed that the distributions made by the monarchy and the Propagandists were, in fact, charity. According to Arnaud, just as it was charity to give money to a repentant prostitute so that she might abandon sin, so it was charity to give "alms" to a Protestant so that he might "not be retained by fear of impoverishment in a religion that he knew would lead only to his Eternal Damnation."[33] As strange as the argument now sounds, in the seventeenth century it had many adherents. Most French Catholics sincerely believed that the "heretics stayed in their heresy" only because they feared the social ostracism and economic hardship that conversion might bring. From this perspective, the Propagandists' monetary distributions did, in fact, look like conventional almsgiving, but the perspective was skewed. The "traffic in souls," like all the Propagandists' "good works," was based on a profound misunderstanding of the Protestants and their religion.

The monarchy shared the Propagandists' distorted vision, but it did not share their illusions about the "commerce in souls." Charity was not the monarchy's goal. Louvois made this abundantly clear to a new convert who asked for assistance: "The King's benefactions," replied the minister tartly, "are not for those who have converted; they are only for those who might convert."[34] Nor did the king necessarily regard the Vaudois crusade as a purely spiritual mission. Although barren and unproductive, the Vaudois valleys were of considerable importance to the warrior king, for they lay at the base of the mountain passes that connected France with Savoy, Switzerland, and ultimately Italy. La gloire and military security dictated that these rebellious valleys be absorbed into the French dominions, and Catholicization was one means of achieving this goal. In this process, the Propagandists acted unwittingly as the king's agents. They facilitated political assimilation by establishing royal officials in these valleys and supporting the intendant's claims to virtually absolute authority. They contributed to cultural absorption by transferring the focus of communal life from autonomous, local Protestant churches to Catholic parishes controlled by the bishopric of Grenoble.[35] Whether the Propagandists knew it or not, the conversion of the Pragelas involved more than the elimination of heresy: it also entailed the obliteration of the cultural identity of the Vaudois community and its absorption into the larger cultural and political unit of France.

Once again, the contribution of Counter Reformation Catholicism to the modernizing of French society is apparent. In the hands of the Propagandists, just as in those of the Brothers of the Holy Sacrament, this spirituality became a powerful cultural movement, sweeping before it traditional values and institutions and replacing them with new, more "progressive" alternatives. Nowhere was this process more obvious than in the Pragelas, for nowhere was it more radical. Here Catholicization meant the elimination of village independence, both cultural and political, and the community's absorption into the kingdom of France, under the direct authority of the central government. In quick succession the Propagandists dragged the reluctant Vaudois through a number of changes that were proceeding slowly elsewhere: the reduction of regional differences and privileges, the destruction of village independence, and the concentration of all political power in the hands of the monarch. In short, from their remote corner of France, the Propagandists made a small contribution to the political and cultural integration of the French state.

If these developments proceeded more swiftly in the Vaudois than elsewhere, they also provoked more resistance. In 1682 the Vaudois chose exile over the destruction of their community, and many Vaudois—as high as 33 percent of some villages—sought refuge among their Protestant brethren in the Swiss cantons.[36] The king was enraged and ordered the quartering of troops in the Vaudois, with the bloody consequences that usually followed the appearance of the feared *dragons*. Hundreds of Vaudois were tortured and maimed, scores were murdered, and all to the accompaniment of the praise and thanksgiving of devout Catholics throughout Dauphiné. "The Protestants were completely humbled at the sight of so many troops," reported one of the missionaries in the Pragelas; "those who previously spurned the Fathers now implore their protection from the soldiers." Even the moderate Bishop Le Camus delighted in the

forced conversions and reported happily that "12,000 Protestants converted in the Pragelas in one week." The Propagandists joined the chorus
of praise and regarded the bloody incident with particular satisfaction
because, fifteen years before, they had advised the king that such violent
methods would be highly effective.[37]

The bloody finale to the mission in the Pragelas brings us back to our
central question: why did contemporaries call this "charity"? The debate surrounding the "commerce in souls" has already shed some light
on the problem, but to pursue it further we must turn from ambitious
projects like the Vaudois crusade to the Congregation's more routine efforts. According to its statutes, the Congregation's goal was twofold: "to
convert all heretics" and "to assist and instruct" all those Protestants
who rejoined the Church, the "new converts" or "N.C." Though less dramatic than the Propagandists' rural crusades, this latter mission was more
time-consuming and more recognizably charitable.

Leafing through the Propagation's records, one finds, surprisingly
enough, that the "terror of heresy" spent most of its time doing just about
what other charitable groups did: dispensing alms, distributing food and
clothing, and providing medical assistance. The Propagation's first meeting set the tone: the Brothers and Sisters spent the afternoon of March 17,
1649, discussing the case of a recent convert, an old man from La Mure,
who was on the verge of starvation. The Congregation appointed one of
its members, a landowner in the area, to watch over the fellow and supply
him with grain. Over the next fifty years, the Propagation made hundreds
of similar benefactions, most of them to homeless, penniless new converts. To anyone who requested it, the Propagandists generously provided
temporary housing and food, and usually much more. The Propagandists
went beyond temporary assistance and tried to supply their protégés with
a permanent means of support. Young men and women were placed as
domestics in the homes of wealthy Grenoblois, lawyers were admitted to
the city's courts and artisans to its guilds, and several families were supplied with shops and boutiques, even houses. On the surface at least, this
frenetic activity differed from the good works of orthodox charitable
groups in only one aspect, its excessive generosity.[38]

Nor was there anything particulary unusual about the other part of the
Congregation's program, "instruction." Like the ladies of the Orphans,
the Propagandists tried to supply primary education to the young along
with material assistance. They established "little" schools in many rural
parishes and supplied money and books—both sacred and secular—to
schools already in operation.[39] Spiritual education—that is, instruction

in the fundamentals of the Catholic faith—was the Congregation's primary concern; but it was by no means its only goal. In its school, the Maison de la Propagation, the Congregation emphasized "reading and writing" and maintained a battalion of schoolmasters and mistresses to teach the children. Nor was the Maison curriculum limited to purely academic or religious subjects: the girls in the Maison learned to spin lace "so that when they left the house they could earn their living with their own hands." Vocational training may have been the professed goal of this activity, but work, for the Propagandists, as for most of their contemporaries, had a value in and of itself. In the Maison, all inmates had to work, spinning, weaving, or cleaning, for at least five hours a day, and the rules of the house stipulated that "no lazy or idle young person will be tolerated."[40] Apparently, industry was among the Catholic virtues that every true convert had to acquire.

This emphasis on work may sound familiar: the Brothers of the Holy Sacrament also tried to cultivate the values of discipline and industry at the Hospital General, and by much the same means, a regimen of work and devotion. In fact, so similar were the two institutions that if a pauper from the Hospital had been dropped into the Maison de la Propagation, he probably would not have noticed much difference between the two houses. Nor would he have doubted for an instant that he was in another "charitable" institution. Charity in seventeenth-century Grenoble, whether at the hands of the directors of the Hospital General or the zealots of the Propagation, always led to the same place, the house of confinement.

For all seventeenth-century Frenchmen—not just the Grenoblois—confinement was something of a panacea, a cure for all of society's ills from prostitution to chronic impoverishment. A certain mystique surrounded the *maison de force,* but the mystique does not explain why the Propagandists chose to apply this social remedy to a religious problem. The explanation, oddly enough, lies not in the Propagandists' notions about Protestantism, but in their contemporaries' equally peculiar ideas about social deviance. As far as the ladies of the Madelines or the directors of the Hospital General were concerned, there were no social problems, only cases of spiritual disorder. Prostitution, begging, illegitimacy, unemployment—in short, all forms of social deviance—were just manifestations of the same condition, spiritual corruption, and they all had to be attacked at the root, the soul. Consequently, the Propagandists and orthodox charitable institutions all faced the same enemy; and if they adopted the same solution, confinement, it was because they also pursued the same goal, the conversion of souls.

No wonder contemporaries considered the Propagation a charitable organization. It shared its goals, methods, and spirit with such orthodox, indisputably charitable groups as the Madelines, the Orphans, and the Hospital General. Still, one problem remains: how could contemporaries label the violent side of the Propagandists' good works—the abduction and incarceration of hundreds of children, the imprisonment of many adults and the exile of others—"charity"? How did they reconcile beneficence with force?

As for the Propagandists, quite easily: they had to resort to violence because they were at war, locked in combat with a desperate, unprincipled enemy who would go to any length to preserve his "heresy." Like the Brothers of the Holy Sacrament, the Propagandists tended to exaggerate the corruption and the strength of their enemy. To believe the Congregation, Dauphinois Protestants were capable of the most horrid atrocities, in particular those involving children, and regularly perpetrated the most shocking crimes: a Protestant nobleman kept a young convert in chains, a Reformed woman shackled and mutilated her own daughter because the little convert refused to go to the Temple, and scores of anonymous heretics ripped young children from their mothers' arms.[41] No one was safe, at least in the Propagandists' eyes, from the threat of "heresy," not even the isolated inmates of the Maison de la Propagation. Protestantism was like a disease (the king himself favored the metaphor) which could infect even the most stalwart, but tended to afflict the weak.[42] So insidious, so omnipotent was this mysterious force, that the Propagandists actually feared for the safety of the whole province: "At any moment," warned the Propagandists, "the whole province might fall under their [the Protestants'] yoke, as events everyday testify."[43]

With these fears for a background, the Propagandists' charitable pretensions begin to take on some substance. However violent their means, the Propagandists' goal was an essentially beneficent one, protection. Where we see only force and coercion, they saw a desperate attempt to save the weak from the worst of all possible fates, eternal damnation. The Maison de la Propagation exemplified this vision, for it was an institution which to us seems very much like a prison, but which to the Propagandists represented a place of asylum where the unusually vulnerable, children, could find peace and security. Even the most outrageous of the Propagandists' "good works"—the kidnappings—formed a kind of spiritual rescue mission. For example, in 1661 the Propagandists learned that the Protestants of Loriol had convinced an ignorant young Catholic to join the forces of "heresy." The Congregation asked the local seigneur to tempt the young man into his château, from whence the Congregation's agents spirited the young man away to a more spiritually secure environment.[44]

This incident displays all the contradictions inherent in the Propagandists' good works and points to the ethic that allowed them to resolve these inconsistencies—paternalism. The Propagandists treated their charges, like the young man from Loriol, harshly, even violently. But they did so, the Propagandists would have been quick to add, for their own good. The Congregation considered "their" charges victims. If the new converts had to be incarcerated, it was because they, like children, needed protection. And like children, they could sometimes misbehave. "Rebelliousness" was one quality that the Propagandists absolutely would not tolerate, even in "their" converts.[45] The little Catholic who defied his masters was likely to find himself out on the streets, and his name stricken from the Congregation's records, if a sound thrashing could not overcome his stubbornness. Considering their generosity, the Propagandists asked very little of their protégés; but they did insist upon absolute submission to authority, or, as they called it, gratitude.

But if a new convert was willing to pay the Propagandists due respect, he would invariably receive, like a dutiful child, generous assistance and unwavering support. One has only to think of the boutiques, the workshops, jobs, even houses casually distributed by the Propagandists to gauge the depth of their generosity and concern. Moreover, this was a particularly intense and effective kind of concern, for it was the product of a personal knowledge of each individual and his needs. The Propagandists never regarded their protégés as a faceless mass; they knew each new convert personally, always called him by name, and displayed an amazing capacity to remember even the smallest detail of his personal history. So intimate, so strong was the bond between donor and recipient that once the Propagandists took someone "into the arms of the Congregation" they remained faithful to him even to his death. For example, in 1701 the Propagandists received a letter from Paris telling them that "one of their converts"—a former inmate of the Maison—had been arrested for begging in the capital. The Propagandists immediately had the pauper freed and sent back to Grenoble; appropriately, he ended his days working in the very hospice where he had been raised.[46]

In this final episode, we can find all the elements that made the Propagandists' charity paternalistic: generosity to a fault, a taste for intensely personal relationships, a sympathetic almost condescending attitude toward the poor, an emphasis on mutual obligations, and a steadfast sense of duty. This beneficent side of the Propagandists' charity should not, however, obscure its more sinister elements. Paternalism conferred upon the Propagandists heavy responsibilities, but it also gave them incredible authority, authority to manipulate not just men's lives but their souls as well. Where did this sense of deep obligation and extraordinary license originate? One might well wonder why the Propagandists felt compelled to save the Protestant and licensed to harass him. Their actions were probably rooted in a deep sense of Christian community. Like their contemporaries throughout Europe, the Propagandists believed that the salvation of each individual was tied to the salvation of the community as a whole.[47] The fate of each soul hinged upon the overall righteousness of the community, and no one could afford to ignore his neighbor's corruption. Consequently, the stain of Protestantism could not be tolerated, for it threatened the salvation of every Christian, including the Propagandists. Just as the Brothers of the Holy Sacrament could not abide a prostitute in their midst, so too the Propagandists could not endure a Protestant in the province.

The Propagandists shared this intolerance with most of their contemporaries; but this cannot explain why the Congregation's actions took such unusual and peculiar forms. Not every Catholic felt compelled to convert distant villages, and few Christians thought it their duty to assume responsibility for hundreds of Protestant children. The Propagandists undertook obligations assigned, not to all good Catholics, but to every responsible seigneur. The Propagandists, seigneurs after all in their own right, simply extended their rule beyond their own domains. They took in hundreds of Protestant children because tradition and common law assigned to every seigneur *haut justicier* responsibility for all illegitimate children, and the Protestant children were, by definition, illegitimate, for their parents' unions had not been consecrated in Catholic churches.[48] Here the Propagandists were simply acting as responsible lords, and in the Pragelas their actions were even more clearly seigneurial. They exercised all the prerogatives of a seigneur, setting up seigneurial officials and courts, and acted as a kind of collective lord. Indeed, in all their good works, the Propagandists enforced the seigneur's ultimate privilege—that of determining his dependents' religion.

It is one of the ironies of the Propagandists' crusade that though it sprung from traditional sources, it also made war on traditional values and institutions. Like the Brothers of the Holy Sacrament, the Propagandists wanted to change this world and to convert, not just the soul, but the man as well. They tried to stamp out all popular disorder and disobedience, of which Protestantism was but one species, and in the Pragelas they succeeded in replacing ancient, communal organizations with the institutions of the king of France. Nowhere is the fundamentally militant and "progressive" nature of seventeenth-century charity more evident than during the campaign for souls. In their distaste for disorder, the Propagandists joined the Brothers of the Holy Sacrament in a crusade, not just against Protestantism, but against popular culture as a whole. And, in the end, the triumph of the Company and of the Congregation would inevitably lead to their demise.

The death of the Propagation was considerably accelerated by the king, who in 1685 decided to apply the final remedy to the Protestant problem, the revocation of the Edict of Nantes. Deprived of its raison d'être, "heresy," the Congregation began to decline: members lost interest, meetings became more and more infrequent until in 1694 only a handful of female Propagandists remained. The Maison de la Propagation was still in operation on the eve of the Revolution, but it had degenerated into little more than a shabby pension for young ladies of good but impoverished families.[49]

Ironically, the revocation had a beneficial effect upon Grenoble's major charitable institution, the Hospital General. In 1686 the king assigned to the hospitals of Embrun, Gap, and Grenoble the property of the now defunct Protestant consistories. Although it would take the directors of the Grenoble Hospital over twenty years to recover all of this property, the king's gesture placed the Hospital on a sound financial basis for the first time in its history.[50] Subsequently, the Hospital was completed in 1700, and the dream of Grenoble's benefactors for over a hundred years—the confinement of the city's paupers—was finally realized in 1712.

The revocation of the Edict of Nantes contributed to the development of Grenoble's charitable institutions in a more subtle but more significant way as well: it accelerated the dissemination of a renewed Catholicism. In the long run, the persecution of the Protestants probably did contribute, as some historians have suggested, to a certain disillusionment and a decline in piety; but in the last decades of the seventeenth century it seems to have had the opposite effect. A sudden outpouring of popular piety followed the revocation, and whole new social groups suddenly joined the forces of the Counter Reformation. The causes of this religious renewal remain obscure: some people probably joined the war on heresy for less than spiritual reasons, in the hope of political or economic advancement at the expense of a persecuted minority. Others may simply have been impressed by the spectacle of the Counter Reformation at its most militant and its most triumphant. In any case, this silent process was illustrated by a brief but significant incident, casually reported in the records of the Congregation. In 1680 a crowd of women, "artisans" and "merchants" according to the patrician ladies of the Congregation, gathered outside the Maison de la Propagation and asked to join the Propagation. The ladies of the Propagation obliged and admitted the women to the Congregation; of course, they did not allow these "femmes du peuple" to attend meetings or vote.[51] Still, the incident is significant: never before had anyone from outside Grenoble's elite either participated or even volunteered to participate in the city's charitable projects. The social complexion of the Counter Reformation was changing and with it the fortunes of Grenoble's institutions of poor relief. The stage was set for the achievements of the turn of the century, for the great charitable surge of the years between 1680 and 1730.

FIVE

From Transgression to Misfortune: Poverty and Poor Relief in an Age of Transition (1680–1729)

On August 25, 1712, an event occurred in Grenoble which marked an important transition. It began on the Place Grenette where an unspecified number of paupers dined before the assembled inhabitants of the city. After eating, the paupers formed a line and marched through the streets to the Hospital General. There they exchanged their rags for new clothes in a gesture symbolic of their transformation from free individuals to inmates of the Hospital General. Finally, the gates of the *maison de force* closed behind them, presumably forever, for this pageant signaled the culmination of an era, the final realization of the great confinement.[1] For the poor, the procession marked an ominous transition; they exchanged freedom for incarceration when they changed their clothes. For the rich, on the other hand, the pageant signified a kind of liberation; they exchanged old ideas for new when they finally succeeded in confining the poor. Now, they could bury old bogeys and abandon familiar palliatives. With confinement behind them, they could search for new solutions and anticipate novel attitudes. Henceforth, the poor would indeed be cloaked in new garments, for as the Hospital directors performed old gestures they contemplated new ideas.

The procession of 1712 was just a tangible symbol of the profound changes sweeping Grenoble in the years between 1680 and 1729. At the turn of the century, new conditions produced new attitudes toward poverty, and most of the ideas usually associated with the Enlightenment first appeared at this time. Jean-Pierre Gutton has pointed to the importance of these years and remarked that they formed the most fertile and fruitful in the history of old regime poor relief. Grenoble certainly bears out his contention, for this period witnessed a transition from old points of view to new attitudes toward the poor. The second generation of pious Grenoblois still drew inspiration from post-Tridentine Catholicism, but they ceased to show any interest in converting the poor. The Grenoblois still pursued confinement, but once they had achieved it, they quickly became disillusioned and looked for new solutions. They still maintained close, personal ties with the poor, but they also displayed a more system-atic, even bureaucratic approach to relief. They still worried over the crimes and sins of the poor, but they learned to forgive transgression. They continued to abhor begging, but they accepted the beggar. In short, the Grenoblois of the years between 1680 and 1729 abandoned the puni-tive stance of their predecessors. They developed a more humane attitude toward poverty in response to changes among the poor, changes which we can delineate with precision, thanks to the detailed bread-lists and regis-ters of beggars left by the benefactors of the turn of the century. These unusually informative documents, in conjunction with the judicial re-cords, indicate that the poor, like the rich, underwent a change in values and habits. Crime and sin became less common among them, and in re-sponse the elite adopted a more benign view of their social inferiors. The rich also extended poor relief to unprecedented numbers of paupers. For the Grenoblois not only adopted new attitudes, they also created a host of new charitable endeavors and increased the services offered by existing institutions.

CHARITABLE ACTIVITY BETWEEN 1680 AND 1729

This intense charitable activity occurred at a time of unprecedented hard-ship. Plague, famine, and flood lashed the city over and over again in the years between 1680 and 1729. Repeated bad harvests created extensive misery, which culminated in the disastrous winter of 1708–1709 when prices for wheat and rye reached an all-time high. As grain prices rose, wages fell, and industry suffered from the financial debacle of the Law Crisis while commerce came to a literal halt during the Provençal plague of 1720. Many workers were thrown out of work, and in 1708 conditions were so severe that over half the domestics in Grenoble were turned out of doors. In 1711 the Isère suddenly left its banks and engulfed the Saint Laurent quarter, leaving hundreds of poor families homeless. To these horrors was added, in 1692 and 1702, yet another scourge, that of war.[2] Dauphiné's neighbor, the kingdom of Savoy, declared war on France, and

Grenoble suffered the high taxes, quartering of troops, epidemic disease, and general disorder and depredation which the army always brought with it.

Never before had so many Grenoblois been so impoverished, and the elite responded with a veritable flurry of charitable activity. Between 1680 and 1729, the Grenoblois created a number of new institutions, the first of which was the Filles de Service hospice. Gaspard de Boffin, prior of Croysil and a zealous member of both the Company of the Holy Sacrament and the Propagation of the Faith, gave 3,500 livres to endow a hospice devoted to the care of young girls bound for domestic service.[3] In 1672 the Filles de Service opened its doors to a dozen inmates, and it was joined shortly thereafter by another hospice for girls, the Presentation. One Mlle Raysson, renowed for her piety but otherwise quite obscure, took to sheltering girls in a house on the Rue Saint Claire. In 1720 the Bishop of Grenoble conferred letters patent upon this arrangement, which allowed Mlle Raysson to receive donations and solicit testamentary bequests on behalf of her young charges.[4] Older Grenoblois too received attention: in 1699 the bishop, in conjunction with a number of pious laymen, established a charitable pawnshop, the Prêt Charitable, which made interest-free loans to the poor.[5] Later, magistrates and lawyers from the Parlement attached to this institution a Bureau de l'Aide Judiciaire which provided free legal counsel to the needy.[6] Perhaps the most ambitious of these fledgling charities was the hospital of the Providence. Begun in 1676 by a group of five devout laywomen guided by the abbé Lestellet, the Providence was a hospital in the true sense of the word. Its purpose was the care of the sick native to Grenoble, and with the help of voluntary donations, it provided shelter and medical care in a house on the Rue Chenoise.[7]

New projects and fresh initiatives were also undertaken at the Hospital General. Throughout the 1680s and 1690s, the directors considered enlarging the Hospital and extending the services it offered. They talked of establishing a special ward for the incurably ill and considered creating a refuge for diseased prostitutes. Most of all, they wanted to complete the Hospital, which lacked at least one building foreseen in the original plans. Hard times, however, forced them to delay this construction. As the economic climate worsened the Hospital was saddled with an increasingly large number of paupers. The meeting of daily expenses became problematic. In addition, as a large landowner, the Hospital saw its revenues diminish while the price it paid for goods, especially bread, increased. Under these circumstances, it is surprising that the directors were able to realize any of their plans, but realize them they did. In 1712 the directors took over the Tour Dauphine and built a refectory inside the Hospital. In 1724 they annexed the building of the old Bon Pasteur hospice and designated a ward of the Hospital for repentant prostitutes. Finally, in 1726 the building which the Hospital had lacked for so long was finished, and the Hospital assumed the dimensions intended by its founders.[8]

As one might guess, this activity was sustained by a rising tide of alms and charitable donations. The dimensions of this increase are hard to measure precisely, for the account books of the Hospital and the other independent charities are so fragmentary or inconsistent as to be useless. Luckily, the ladies of the Providence hospital were more conscientious in their bookkeeping. They kept a detailed, week-by-week account of the alms and donations they received between 1679 and 1697, and from these records a distinct upward trend in charitable giving emerges. In 1680, for example, the Grenoblois dropped 1,607 livres into the almsbox outside the Providence; twelve years later the same box yielded 3,000 livres. Donations, that is, gifts by living persons as opposed to casual alms or testamentary bequests, also increased and even more dramatically. The Providence received a paltry 829 livres in 1680, but in 1694 the Grenoblois opened their purses and gave the institution over 4,000 livres. An increase in the number and the average size of donations occurred, and as a result the Providence's income doubled in the years between 1680 and 1693.[9] To appreciate the true dimensions of this growth in charitable giving, we must compare the generosity of the Grenoblois of the late seventeenth century with that of their ancestors. Here again, the data are fragmentary, but a few figures do exist which make for an impressive contrast. Between 1631 and 1634 the Hospital received 1,703 livres in gifts, bequests, and donations; in 1692—in only one year—the Providence received twice that amount in donations alone. In 1652 the Grenoblois gave their Hospital a mere 306 livres; forty years later they gave the Providence 2,722 livres, almost ten times that amount.[10]

Who were these generous benefactors? In some cases, we cannot know, for, beginning in the 1690s, anonymous donations became increasingly popular. Most Grenoblois, however, continued to take credit for their altruism, and the most generous of these were the magistrates. The president Alloy, for instance, gave the Hospital the fabulous sum of 10,000 livres, and the marquis de Valbonnais almost matched his munificence with a gift of 9,000 livres. The sovereign courts had certainly not abandoned the Hospital General, which was to a large degree their own creation. At the end of the century, though, a new type of benefactor appeared who was neither as wealthy nor as well born as the magistrates. Men like Antoine Benoit, a simple lawyer, or Balthazard Dou, an even simpler notary, began making donations to the Hospital. Even lowly parish priests, like the curé Dufour of Saint Louis parish, bequeathed their estates to the Hospital.[11]

The emergence of this new type of benefactor coincided with the appearance of a new kind of director at the Hospital General. In principle, the composition of the governing board of the Hospital, the Bureau de la Direction, was established by royal letters patent in 1699, but in practice the Bureau appointed directors at will, and some honorary members did not attend meetings.[12] Among those who took their duties seriously were the canons of Grenoble's two collegiate churches. Of course, a few of these clerics had always taken an interest in poor relief, but now the canons on the board were positively legion. Next to them sat another group of men in soutanes, the parish priests. Before the first years of the eighteenth century, one looks in vain in the Hospital records for even the slightest trace of the parish clergy. Then, in 1700, the curés of Saint Laurent, Saint Hugues, and Saint Louis parishes begin to appear consistently in the minutes of the weekly Bureau meetings. The assiduity of these curés must be attributed, at least in part, to the reforms of the dynamic Bishop of Grenoble, Le Camus, who rendered an indolent and ignorant clergy more learned and energetic. Therefore, it is none too surprising that the imposing Le Camus personally asserted his influence on the Bureau. Every week, when he was not visiting his diocese, Le Camus was present at the Bureau meetings, and when he was absent his associate, Monsieur Canel, a *conseiller-clerc* at the Parlement, represented his wishes. In his own right, Monsieur Canel was a tireless supporter of good works, and his long career, almost fifty years, as a director of the Hospital earned for him the reputation of a saint among Grenoble's common people.[13]

While Canel and other clerics were extending their powers at the Hospital, another group of religious, the Sisters of Saint Joseph, assumed the internal administration of the Providence hospital, joining the Brothers of Charity and the Sisters of Saint Martha in nursing the city's sick.[14] The clerics seem to have been advancing on all fronts. Still, it would be incorrect to conclude that a reclericalization of poor relief had occurred, and with it a return to the status quo ante of the Middle Ages. Laymen and women continued to dominate the governing boards of the Hospital General and the Providence, and the religious who served in these institutions had no voice over their general administration. Indeed, the regular orders signified, not clericalization, but professionalization of medical care. In the old regime, trained nurses with some knowledge of drugs and bandages were, by definition, members of religious orders. When the directors and directresses called upon these religious, they were not trying to strengthen the role of the Church in poor relief; rather, they were trying to provide the poor with the best available medical care.

It is harder to assess the impact of another new actor at the Hospital— the intendant. Before the end of the seventeenth century, the monarchy's envoys had been only temporary visitors in Grenoble, and they had rarely exerted any influence over poor relief. Then, in the 1690s, the intendants began to play an important role in the life of the city and in the administration of public assistance. They began to settle disputes over the composition of the Hospital Bureau, and they facilitated the liquidation of the Protestant consistories whose funds now belonged to the Hospital. More important, the intendants started to acquire royal "gifts" for the Hospital when its financial needs were most acute.[15] Royal intervention in poor relief culminated in the ordinance of 1724, which sought to abolish begging from the kingdom of France by incarcerating all beggars at the king's expense. In Grenoble, the intendant Fontanieu agreed to pay the Hospital General six sous per day for each adult beggar it locked up. In addition, the king promised to provide funds for the completion of the Hospital's buildings.[16]

Citing these activities, one historian has concluded that a "humanitarian" spirit came to characterize royal policy in the last years of Louis XIV's reign.[17] It would be tempting to agree: certainly the monarchy had never before displayed such interest in the poor and homeless. Still, these "humanitarian tendencies" were ephemeral, intermittent flashes of beneficence that could vanish as soon as they appeared. Royal gifts to the Hospital came only sporadically and only in emergencies. The grants did not provide and were not intended to provide a permanent source of financial support. Sometimes these grants did not materialize at all, as the execution of the ordinance of 1724 illustrates. At first the monarchy was conscientious in its payment of the promised subsidy for interned beggars. Then, in about 1730 the subsidies began to arrive more slowly at the Hospital, and finally they ceased altogether. By 1735 the monarchy owed the Hospital 91,000 livres, and the directors faced a grave financial crisis. The intendant appealed to the controller-general on their behalf, but the only response he received was that "the funds have now been effected by the king to another use," that is, war.[18] The king, it appears, was not always generous, and sometimes he was very demanding. In 1691, when

Louis XIV was about to embark on the war of the Second Coalition, he created a new set of officers, the *jurés et crieurs,* funeral undertakers, and "asked" the Hospital to purchase the positions for thousands of livres.[19] In this instance, the monarchy was not granting a subsidy; it was asking for one.

Nor were the monarchy's motives entirely altruistic. The ordinance of 1724 was clearly repressive in intent; and provisions that were made for the succoring of the poor came from local hospitals, not the king.[20] Also, it is hard to believe that royal officials did not consider the possibility of social unrest when they granted money to the Hospital. Usually these gifts came in years of high grain prices when the intendant considered the situation in the city volatile. The true motives of the monarchy are best illustrated by the creation of the *lieutenants de police* in 1699. Grenoble, like many towns in France, received one of these officers, and the new lieutenant was invested with relatively broad powers. In particular, he sat on the Bureau of the Hospital and enjoyed the right, conferred upon no other, to incarcerate a pauper without delay and on his word alone.[21]

When the lieutenant of police first appeared at the Bureau he caused a minor uproar. The directors absolutely refused to seat the interloper, partly out of wounded pride—they had not selected him—and partly out of sheer snobbery. Whatever his official attributes, the new lieutenant was, after all, nothing but a notary's son. Of course, he was not the first: a few professional men, lawyers, doctors, and notaries, had always sat on the Hospital Bureau because the Hospital simply could not care for the sick or keep its books without them. Although these men were nominally directors, they were in fact treated like hired help. They rarely attended meetings, and when they did, they said nothing. Then, in the early 1700s the directors swallowed their pride and admitted more unpedigreed but skilled Grenoblois. Lawyer Boliat, merchant Guérin, and apothecary Bozonnat took up places on the Bureau; they were more assertive and more conscientious than their predecessors. Lawyers in particular began to multiply because the Hospital found itself embroiled in a considerable amount of litigation in the years between 1690 and 1730. Even merchants became directors, and their appearance signified not only a decline in the Bureau's snobbery but a rise in the fortunes of a certain group of Grenoblois. Directors were expected to "loan" money to the Hospital in times of need and leave substantial bequests to the institution at their death. Now merchants, lawyers, and even notaries, like Balthazard Dou, could marshal the funds necessary to fulfill these obligations.[22]

Eventually Balthazard Dou and his kind would be the salvation of the

Hospital, but for the moment their activity was not that important. For every notary on the Bureau there were still a half-dozen counselors; for every merchant, a first president of the Parlement whose word carried more weight than that of hundreds of merchants. Charity was, as forty years before, the prerogative of the magistrates and nobles, of the city's seigneurial elite. And the goals of this charity remained (at least superficially) faithful to the same pattern. The directors of the Hospital still considered begging their major problem and confinement the miraculous solution. In 1680 M. Canel reopened the issue and reminded the directors "that it is has been a long time since we talked about confining the poor in order to spare the people of this city the inconvenience they receive from insolent beggars."[23] Lesdiguières could have made this statement, and like Lesdiguières, the directors failed, which is hardly surprising given the Grenoblois' history of aborted and incomplete "confinements."

What is surprising is that thirty-two years later, in 1712, the directors finally did succeed. This time they had the help of an expert, a Jesuit missionary named Père Guévarre who had organized hospitals in cities throughout the Midi.[24] The secret of Guévarre's success was his method, what contemporaries called the "capuchine" method because it was based on almsgiving. Before appealing to the Grenoblois for donations, the Jesuit preached for three weeks at the cathedral, explaining to the Grenoblois "the necessity of such an institution [a house of confinement] and the advantages that every inhabitant would receive from it."[25] Then Guévarre and the directors canvassed the city for gifts of furniture and linen. A cart circulated through the city streets collecting tables and sheets, and although we have no description of the event, it probably differed very little from a similar collection, made several weeks later in Chambéry, which was described by Guévarre himself as

a miracle which even surpassed my own expectations. You would have thought that the city was being sacked; twenty carts did nothing but haul from morning until night and still gifts arrived at the Hospital in such quantity that if it had continued, I would have been forced, like Moses in the desert, to command them to bring no more.[26]

After the furniture had been installed in the Hospital and the linen washed and mended by a group of devout noblewomen, the directors organized another collection. This time they appealed for food, and the Grenoblois, rich and poor, magistrates, cobblers, and flax-spinners alike, brought hundreds of pounds of bread, meat, oil, and wine to the Hospital.[27] All this activity culminated in the procession of August 27 when the directors of the Hospital led the paupers into the Hospital General.[28]

Anticipating this event by a few weeks, Guévarre had distributed on his arrival a pamphlet entitled *La Mendicité abolie dans la ville de Grenoble par l'Hôpital-Général*. The author was Guévarre himself: he had written the treatise in 1696 and had then employed it in his missions throughout southern France.[29] The purpose was purely rhetorical: the format, a series of objections and rebuttals, was designed to lead the reader to the conclusion that confining the poor was the most holy and useful of endeavors. The Grenoblois were both impressed—years later they still came to the Hospital to read the pamphlet—and persuaded.[30] Though the words were Guévarre's, the arguments in the *Mendicité abolie* seemed to reflect the hopes and fears of the Grenoblois, the aspirations and concerns that brought them together with the poor on the Place Grenette that August afternoon.

On the surface at least, these concerns seemed to be identical to those of the original founders of the Hospital General. In the *Mendicité abolie*, begging was presented as the major problem; confinement was still the only solution. Casual almsgiving was condemned as self-defeating; the house of confinement was praised as highly effective. Then Guévarre went beyond the mundane issue of efficiency to consider the "higher" purposes of the Hospital: "the spiritual advantages," he emphasized, "that the pauper derives from these establishments is more considerable" than the other advantages.[31] Here Guévarre sounded as if he were speaking for the Brothers of the Holy Sacrament or the ladies of the Orphans. This was the same spiritual paternalism that we have encountered before, a paternalism that had by no means died out among the Grenoblois. In 1713 the directors of the Hospital General reaffirmed that "the spiritual regeneration of the pauper" was still their goal, and several years later the founders of Notre Dame de Refuge protested, much like the ladies of the Madelines sixty years earlier, that it was their mission "to wrench from the clutches of Satan those who might ... otherwise go to Eternal Perdition."[32] In short, the goal of charity was still, in the words of a supporter of the Filles de Service, "the conversion of souls," and religious instruction and devotional exercises continued to occupy an important place in the new charitable institutions.[33] Even at the Providence, Grenoble's first hospital in the true sense of the word, the sick had to make a general confession within twenty-four hours of their admission or be thrown back out on the street, however grave their afflictions.[34]

Not that the inmates of Grenoble's hospitals were to spend their days in leisurely contemplation of the divine mysteries. They were to be set to work, forced to do hard and unproductive labor, just like the inmates of the Holy Sacrament's imaginary hospital. In fact, the Company's vision finally came true in October 1712, when the directors of the Hospital General contracted with a Romans merchant to establish "manufactures" inside the Hospital.[35] Significantly, although the intricacies of the arrangements were narrated in some detail in the Hospital records, the kind of goods to be manufactured was never mentioned. It was the work that was important, not the product. And well it should be, for, as Guévarre stated quite plainly, "a criminal laziness is the source of all their [the pauper's] vices."[36] By virtue of discipline and plain work, this "vice" might be extinguished.

Unfortunately, "idleness" was not the pauper's only vice. According to Guévarre, the poor were also "insolent," "importunate," "proud," and they even dared "to curse the directors of the Hospital General." It is hard to imagine any sin worse than this last one, but Guévarre had not finished his catalog of the pauper's transgressions. "Lying, perjury, and blasphemy are their familiars; complaints, quarrels and insults, drunkenness and impiety are all too frequent among them." The rhetoric with its pious outrage is worthy of the Brothers of the Holy Sacrament, and Guévarre embellished upon it. "They are the paupers of the Demon," he stated emphatically, "the enemies of good order, *fainéants*, liars, drunkards and braggarts who know no other language than that of the Devil their father." The poor were the instruments of the Devil, and why? Simply because they were poor. The equation between poverty and sin had never been stated with more ferocity.[37]

But just when we think that we are still in the mental universe of the Brothers of the Holy Sacrament, Guévarre introduces a new element. Besides the hellish pauper with whom we are so familiar, there was, according to Guévarre, another kind of pauper, the "true" pauper. "You must distinguish between the paupers of the Devil," he warned the benefactors, "and the poor of Jesus Christ." These poor souls seem to be the opposite of the demonic poor. They were "patient, humble, modest and content with the state in which Divine Providence had placed them." At first, it seems that we are dealing with a very old category of poor, the *pauvres honteux*, the impoverished gentlemen and gentlewomen whose discretion and "shame" had always made their poverty more palatable to the rich. But this is not the case, for these "true" paupers committed the indiscretion of begging. They too gathered in the streets and churches crying for alms, not out of "criminal indolence" like the "false poor," but out of an "unfortunate necessity."[38] This last comment represented a subtle but nonetheless terribly significant break with the past. Suddenly, sin was not always the companion of poverty, and misery, not vice alone, could be the legitimate focus of the benefactors' charitable vision.

We are now on the threshold of a new attitude toward poverty, a more secular, more economic perception of the pauper. Alongside familiar notions and old habits of mind, we see a new set of ideas emerging, if only gradually. The founders of the Presentation, just like their forerunners, the Sisters of the Orphans, considered the salvation of young souls their task. But the benefactors of the Presentation gave no less importance to their purely economic mission, vocational training. And they no longer saw a little sinner in every one of their charges: they attributed the "miserable state" of many of their young girls to no more than the "ignorance and poverty of their parents."[39]

The creation of the Prêt Charitable, the charitable pawnshop, represented a more decisive break with the past. The founders of this institution also believed that the pauper was not intrinsically evil, just a victim of his poverty. They were so convinced of the truth of this notion that they virtually eliminated religion from their charitable program. At the Prêt Charitable, the pauper received his money, a few "good words"—an exhortation to frequent the sacraments—and then left. The old formula of the Holy Sacrament—spiritual assistance before material relief—seems to have been reversed. Feeding people, not saving souls, was the goal of the Prêt Charitable, and the founders had been moved by sheer human misery, not blasphemy, promiscuity, or impiety, to create the institution. As they explained in their statutes:

Several people, knowing of the great abuses which are committed in this city by loans at 30 percent or 40 percent a year, decided that it would be very useful to the public to bring a halt to the cause of so much misery. We saw that the pauper who receives only a quarter or at most one-third of the value of his pledge when he borrows gets nothing in the end; the huge amounts of interest absorb in one or two years the whole value of the pledge: this is what occasioned the establishment of the Prêt Charitable.[40]

Comparing this calm analysis to the effusions of the Brothers of the Holy Sacrament, we can see just how radical was the change that had occurred. The loathsome beggar had disappeared; in his place emerged a more sympathetic and secular analysis of the causes of impoverishment. Paradoxically, the experience of the ordinance of 1724 reinforced this new tendency and led the Hospital directors away from their old obsession, the suppression of begging, and their old panacea, confinement. Disillusionment with confinement was bound to follow in the wake of the ordinance of 1724: it was a dismal failure. Even the monarchy admitted as much in 1730 and responded characteristically by reissuing the same decree. The directors of the Hospital who had enforced the ordinance with vigor and honesty also conceded that it had not had the intended effects. The Hospital was saddled with hundreds of beggars and cursed with huge debts, yet begging persisted in the province. But the ordinance had had important, if unforeseen, consequences. Having confronted the beggar, the directors altered their view of him. The beggars who were incarcerated in the Hospital were not dangerous criminals and vagabonds. They were, according to the directors, "poor amputees, old men and women, those with incurable diseases, young children whose parents are too poor to feed them, foundlings and pathetic mad men and women." Despite the Hospital's dire financial condition, the directors refused to turn these beggars out onto the streets, but not out of fear. "Compassion," they told the controller-general, prevented them from abandoning these hapless creatures.[41]

Here was a new stance in regard to poverty: the Hospital directors may well have regarded their charges with pity in the past, but never with compassion. A more humane, less punitive attitude had emerged and with it a new vision of charity's goals and mission. What was the source of this new attitude? Louis Pérouas has attributed it, in the diocese of La Rochelle, to a decline in Jansenism and a rise in optimism. In Grenoble, however, the elites were probably less optimistic and certainly more Jansenist in the years between 1680 and 1730 than ever before.[42] No spiritual change among the elite can account for the new social vision. The explanation must lie elsewhere, not among the rich, but among the poor themselves. Grenoble's elite may have seen the poor differently because the poor were different. The second generation of devout benefactors may have abandoned the old rhetoric of sin and vice because it no longer applied. In short, changes among the poor may have precipitated changes in attitudes toward the poor. In order to test this hypothesis we must turn from Grenoble's benefactors to the objects of their altruism, the impoverished. We must determine who became a beggar and why, who depended on the Hospital for bread and under what circumstances. And we must establish in what ways these individuals differed from the poor of three decades before. First, however, we must examine that aspect of the poor which literally obsessed the Brothers of the Holy Sacrament but hardly concerned the second generation of pious Grenoblois—criminality.

DEVIANCE AT THE TURN OF THE CENTURY

One would assume that crime decreased in the years between 1680 and 1729, prompting the rich to adopt a more benign view of the poor. The equation between growing compassion among the rich and waning crime among the poor—be it violent assault, theft, or illicit sex—seems obvious, straightforward, even simple. But in fact it was not so simple, for the criminal archives, the records of the Justice of Grenoble, suggest that an increase, not a decrease, in crime occurred. Of course, criminal records are poor indicators of quantitative trends, and the evidence they supply is mainly impressionistic. But the change which occurred in the years between 1680 and 1729 was one of quality as much as of quantity. Crime did not just increase; it became markedly more violent, and even the simplest infractions involved bloodshed. The barroom brawl, for example, now became a deadly affair. In 1695 two soldiers got into a scuffle, and before the fight was over, one had lost his nose and two fingers and the other his life. In 1710 a ridiculous quarrel between two law clerks ended at midnight in the darkened streets around the Place Grenette. Both clerks had raised a band of retainers, and in the ensuing skirmish, several were wounded and one killed. Sometimes these fights were, as in the past, precipitated by insults, both real and imagined; sometimes they were caused by disputes over debt. But always they were more bloody than before. At the same time, thievery, which had been virtually unknown in the past, increased from 10 percent of the cases brought before the Justice to over 25 percent. Here too bloodshed occurred.[43] In 1695 one Adret, described as a foreigner in the records, slit the throat of a Grenoblois under the stone bridge after having robbed him. In 1710 a certain Mathieu was convicted of armed robbery, murder, and arson.[44] Instances of assault also increased, as did rape, to an alarming degree. In 1701 four thieves stopped one Philiberte Mermin outside Grenoble. When they discovered that she had no money, they stuffed a handkerchief in her mouth and raped her "each in turn." They then took all her clothes and left her naked on the highway. In 1693 four anonymous soldiers attacked a domestic on the road to Laval, and in the same year three cavalrymen raped and beat two other servant girls just outside the city gates. Suddenly, life had become dangerous in Grenoble. For the first time the city knew a real "climate of violence."[45]

What caused this apparent increase in crime? The terrible economic crisis which afflicted Grenoble in these years and reduced many Grenoblois to hunger and want comes to mind immediately. While it is hard to see any relationship between rape and impoverishment, it is possible that theft was dictated by need. In a few cases, out-of-work laborers and unemployed domestics filched foodstuffs, but the majority of Grenoble's thieves aimed at more valuable, inedible items, like linen and tools. Moreover, sheer impoverishment was not the most striking characteristic of Grenoble's thieves. Mobility was the quality that they all shared. All were described in the criminal records as "strangers," transients, or only temporary residents in the city. A Lyonnais, for example, robbed another Lyonnais in an inn, and three soldiers from the army of Italy stole at gunpoint all the worldly goods of a baker. Mobility encouraged theft, for the transient was all but impervious to the forces that discouraged it.[46]

Behind this movement of individuals stood the event which, more than any other, contributed to the rise in crime—the war. The notion may seem old-fashioned, but it is nonetheless true: war meant an influx of troops and that in turn signified hardship, violence, and worst of all, real danger. By their very presence, the soldiers created the opportunity for theft and the means of bloodshed. Traveling officers and army provisioners constituted easy prey for thieves, and they, more than any other group, suffered from the wave of theft. Armed men in the city streets forced the Grenoblois to take up weapons themselves, and the barroom brawl, previously a relatively harmless affair, became deadly. Now, law clerks and simple day laborers wielded swords and pulled knives, and conflict between locals and soldiers spilled into the streets where armed bands lurked at night. An already volatile population of young men was swollen by a huge contingent of equally violent, equally young males—soldiers—and this latter group, as the reader may already have noticed, provided Grenoble with most of its criminals. Soldiers stole, robbed at gunpoint, ambushed at night, brawled in taverns, and, especially, raped on the highways.

So ferocious, so violent were the men at arms that their mere presence terrified the Grenoblois. In 1711 a card inspector named Maugier appealed to the Justice for protection: two soldiers were following him in order, he assumed, to kill him. The subsequent court proceedings showed that Maugier's assumptions were unfounded, but his impulses were absolutely justified. The soldiers were dangerous, and no one—not even the respectable bourgeois or tradesmen—escaped their violence. In 1710 two soldiers broke into the apartment of a bourgeois and held him and his neighbors hostage while they drank and threatened to slit their throats. Only several livres provided by a frightened surgeon released the Grenoblois from their ordeal, for money was usually the object of these nocturnal forays. Extortion, it appears, was the soldiers' specialty, and they regularly harassed even the most respectable citizens. They also threatened tradesmen, stalked young women, and tormented any female found out of doors after sunset. The war rendered everyday life in Grenoble absolutely terrifying; the Grenoblois had more cause than ever before to fear for his life and his property.[47]

What he did not have to fear was the poor. Elite attitudes toward impoverishment were little affected by the increase in crime because the poor themselves had little to do with the wave of violence. Aside from a couple of vagabonds, described as deserters or former soldiers, the impoverished rarely appeared as criminals in the court records. More often they occupied the position of victim, a role which they shared with the rich and one which the elite could not have failed to notice. Just as the poor ceased to monopolize the world of crime, crime dropped out of the lexicon of the rich.

Did "sin" follow the same path for the same reason? The Company of the Holy Sacrament had been more obsessed by the sexual infractions of the poor than by their criminal activities. The Brothers could not pour enough vitriol on the evil procuress or the depraved fornicator. As far as prostitution is concerned, the criminal records of the years between 1680 and 1729 are as silent as the second generation of benefactors: the bawds and streetwalkers disappear. But not literally, for in a city swarming with troops, procuresses and prostitutes must have plied their trade, and the criminal records do provide indirect proof of their existence. In 1701 a band of law clerks attacked two servant girls under the impression that they were prostitutes. The clerks explained, in court, that the girls "had no candles and prostitutes are the only women out of doors at night."[48] Apparently, prostitutes were a common sight in Grenoble's darkened streets, but the new generation of pious Grenoblois was little troubled. They, like the judges of the Justice, probably accepted the women's presence as an unfortunate, but necessary, consequence of war.

The rich were resigned to venal love and, it appears, to illicit love as well. Illegitimacy, far from diminishing in this period, was, like crime, on the rise. Between 1680 and 1689, only 179 bastards were baptized in Grenoble's parishes; in the decade 1690–1699, the number rose to 333 and then grew to 641 in the years between 1730 and 1739. The rate of illegitimacy, that is, the ratio of illicit to legitimate births, provides a better measure. Between 1680 and 1684, the rate of illegitimacy in Grenoble was a relatively low 2.54 percent. By 1695–1699, the rate had risen to 5.19 percent, and it then increased to 7.33 percent between 1725 and 1729.[49] The Grenoble elite, at least the directors of the Hospital, were not unaware of this rise in illicit love, for the Hospital suddenly found itself saddled with a host of infants. Before the 1690s, the Hospital had maintained a few foundlings and illegitimate children in the homes of nurses in the Grésivaudan valley. By 1735 it was supporting 850 children and had incurred for their maintenance a debt of 20,080 livres. One director candidly admitted that the infants accounted for the institution's grave financial difficulties.[50]

The circumstances which produced so many unwanted babies are revealed in the *déclarations de grossesse* made by the mothers of these unfortunate infants. More numerous than in the past, the 760 declarations appear, at first, to reveal little that is new.[51] The typical unwed mother was still, as before, a native of an adjacent village, who migrated to Grenoble to serve as a domestic and then fell prey to a false promise of marriage.[52] It seems, as one might suspect, that no major changes in illegitimacy occurred in the decade between the 1680s and the 1690s. But when one turns to the unwed fathers of the years between 1690 and 1729, important and striking variations begin to appear.

The unwed fathers of the turn of the century were, it emerges, much better traveled than their predecessors. In the 1680s, only 25 percent of the men named in the declarations resided outside Grenoble; by 1719 this rate had risen to 63 percent. These were not innocent peasants whose pastoral loves ended up in the Grenoble records. These were seasoned travelers, who came from places like Burgundy and Provence, for the percentage of illegitimate fathers hailing from outside Dauphiné rose from 8 percent in the years prior to 1680 to over 20 percent in the period 1680–1729. These footloose males suffice to explain the 5 percent increase in illegitimacy which occurred at the end of the century. After all, a hasty marriage cannot save an infant from bastardy and a mother from dishonor if the father is far away.

The force behind this mobility is not hard to detect: the war. Many of the unwed fathers were soldiers, and the hostilities created conditions under which familiarity was easy and a rise in illegitimacy all but inevitable. Catherine Bit, for example, was a twenty-eight-year-old domestic serving in the home of a Grenoble wigmaker when, in 1699, troops were billeted upon the house. Bit had to share her room with two soldiers, and one night while she was sleeping, "one of them threw himself upon her and had carnal knowledge of her." When soldiers were in the house, mischief occurred, as Anne Guine, a domestic at an inn where troops were quartered, feared. Guine begged her mistress not to leave her alone with the soldiers, but her mistress ignored these pleas, and nine months later Guine gave birth to a child. The war not only brought soldiers to Grenoble; it installed them right in the bedroom. Blessedly, the quartering of troops was only intermittent in Grenoble, but when the soldiers left, their places were taken by other men no less tied to the war effort. Provisioners, muleteers, and tax collectors who supported the war effort passed constantly through the city, and they too contributed to the rise in illegitimacy. A muleteer impregnated An-

toinette Micaud, and a commissioner of provisions seduced Jeanne Villard.
Like the proverbial traveling salesmen, these individuals were highly mobile, and they left broken hearts and unwanted children in their wake. And
it was the war which created these men (or at least their livelihood) and so
produced a rise in illegitimacy. But the war also promoted bastardy in
other, less defined ways, as the story of Marianne Dardoux illustrates. Dardoux was a native of Avignon, but left the city in 1706 to find her brother,
who had absconded with the family fortune and joined the army. She traced
him to Briançon where she had the misfortune to meet a sieur Pouchet,
inspector of His Majesty's military hospitals. Pouchet courted Dardoux and
then abandoned her, pregnant and penniless, in the streets of Grenoble. It
was not just mobile young men who produced bastards, but mobile young
women too.[53]

The war stimulated mobility and created, along with a wave of crime, a
flood of bastards. The Grenoblois were well aware of the problem: the
directors of the Hospital General attributed the increase in illegitimacy to
the war and remarked that soldiers were the fathers of most of the infants.[54] Circumstances, not sin, caused illegitimacy; the new generation of
benefactors were more forgiving and more resigned than their predecessors. They did not try, as did the Company of the Holy Sacrament, to
uncover illicit unions or marry off unwed mothers. Scandal did not trouble
them, but the welfare of the unwanted infant did. At the end of the century,
the directors calmly accepted every child deposited on their doorstep or
presented by his mother, with no questions and no remonstrations. The
child, not the parents, became the object of the benefactors' concern.

This does not mean that the Grenoblois spared the unwed father or condoned his irresponsibility. Their concern for the welfare of the child and the
financial well-being of the Hospital General dictated that the rigorous judicial measures of the previous decade be continued and even enlarged. The
Justice still conferred upon the unwed mother sweeping powers. Judges still
attached arrest warrants to *déclarations de grossesse* and continued to require men who had abandoned their pregnant mistresses to appear before
the court. In 1705, these sweeping powers were further enlarged when the
financially pressed Hospital acquired an edict from the Parlement. This
edict permitted any woman, once armed with a writ from the Justice, to
return to the place of her seduction and deposit her bastard upon the doorstep of her seducer, who then became subject to the penalties incurred by
those who exposed infants. The Justice proved rather generous with these
writs, and curious scenes often ensued. When a woman accompanied by

the officers of the court tried to deposit the illegitimate offspring of one Paradis upon his doorstep in Barraux, Paradis, his new wife, and his mother-in-law hurled insults at the officers and refused to take in the child. Threats were exchanged for several hours and then the officers withdrew with the child for fear that he would freeze to death.[55]

Paradis' refusal to claim his bastard was unusual only in its ferocity. Most fathers were equally reluctant but more discreet, for the unwed fathers of the years between 1690 and 1729 were different from their forebears. Instead of boasting of their achievement, they now sought, sometimes at considerable expense, to hide it. To this end, they persuaded or coerced their lovers into making false declarations, whose errors were subsequently revealed in a second, correct declaration.[56] For example, in 1700 one Claudine Pascal made a false declaration in Vizille in which she identified, quite wrongly, the father of her child as an itinerant laborer. A few months later she was apprehended in Grenoble in the act of exposing her child before the Recollets and brought before the Justice. There, she made a second declaration and admitted that her employer, one Ennemond Bonjard, had fathered her child and persuaded her to make a false declaration. Financial concerns may have motivated some unwed fathers; they may have employed subterfuge in order to escape the expense of a child. But not Bonjard. He, like many unwed fathers, cared more for his reputation than his pocketbook, for he was willing to go to considerable expense to conceal his illicit paternity. Bonjard paid his lover's voyage to Vizille, housed and fed her while there, provided a midwife for her confinement and a nurse for her child, and then settled a sum of money upon her. Many other fathers did the same, and Bonjard's maneuver would have succeeded had Pascal not retrieved her infant from the nurse and spent all the money, leaving her destitute and with no choice but to expose the baby.[57]

Other fathers were somewhat more successful in concealing their illicit paternity. About a quarter of the fathers whose reactions we know chose to compromise and settle some money upon the expectant mother even before the declaration was made.[58] These informal settlements are mentioned in the declarations, and they had the advantage of avoiding widespread scandal and the kind of scenes occasioned by the edict of 1705. They did not, however, spare the father financially. Although the exact sum of money exchanged is not mentioned in the declaration, it is unlikely that even the most naive unwed mother would allow the father to get off with a mere token payment. Other fathers risked even greater expense: about a quarter stood their ground and fought the mother's accusations in court. This could be a very costly maneuver, for if the father failed in court, he faced, not only the expense of maintaining the mother and child, but the excessively high costs which any court procedure would entail. Apparently, no price was too high to maintain a good reputation.

Of course, the most effective means of saving face was to get rid of the source of embarrassment, to abort the unwanted fetus. In the years between 1690 and 1729, one encounters for the first time in the declarations mention of abortifacients. One learns, for example, that a lawyer tried to persuade a linen seamstress, one Jeanne Buisson, to take a "powder which had cost him six livres" and which was supposed to get rid of her baby. Another lawyer persuaded Marie Terraz, a domestic, to take "remedies" ("a red powder and a blue stone"), which she, out of fear, refused. A glove seamstress, Marguerite Gray, obliged her apothecary lover and ingested a whole series of powders until the apothecary's professional knowledge had been exhausted.[59]

These cases indicate that quite a change in attitudes had occurred. It was the man, not the woman, who proposed abortion, and the father, not the mother, who wanted the declaration falsified and his identity hidden. Shame, previously limited to the unwed mother, now infected the father too; the disgrace formerly reserved for the woman in an illicit union now extended to the man as well.[60] The well established, lawyers and apothecaries, were probably the most anxious to preserve their reputations, but even humble men could worry about their honor and react with near panic when they heard of their lover's predicament. One weaver promised to throw his mistress down the stairs if she told the neighbors of their affair, and a common soldier threatened to run his lover through with a sword if she revealed his name.[61] Public censure now awaited the unwed father, and his predicament pointed to a more rigorous sexual morality among the popular classes.

The second generation of devout Grenoblois must have been aware of this shift in popular values. They must have realized that popular opinion no longer condoned illicit sex and that common values no longer tolerated male debauchery. The Grenoblois had moved a step closer to the elite, and the rise in illegitimacy in no way contradicts this alteration in norms.[62] Even the most pious admitted that circumstances, not corrupt morals, produced bastards, and they buried the old rhetoric of sin. Now, the pious could leave the policing of sexuality to the community, and they could switch their focus from the illicit union to the fruit of that union, the infant. With a change in popular values, elite views could change too. That old bogey of the Company of the Holy Sacrament—unsanctioned sex—could vanish, and a more humane and forgiving attitude could emerge.

BEGGARS AND PAUPERS

If crime and sin loomed less large in the mental world of the elite, so too did that other bogey of the past—the beggar. The years between 1680 and 1729 witnessed distinct, dramatic changes in attitudes toward the poor, both errant and domiciled, and the programs of the Hospital General accelerated and reflected these changes. The charitable efforts of the turn of the century altered views and none more so than the administration of the royal ordinance against beggars issued in 1724. The initiative did come from the monarchy, but there was nothing in the ordinance to displease or disconcert the Grenoble elite. Were it not for the ordinance's lack of religious content, the Brothers of the Holy Sacrament could have written it, and the directors of the Hospital General had long dreamed of incarcerating the city's beggars. Consequently, the Grenoblois approached the ordinance with enthusiasm and enforced it honestly and seriously, unlike some of their counterparts elsewhere in the kingdom. Once they had agreed with the intendant upon the amount of money to be supplied by the monarchy, the directors increased to six the number of *archers,* the Hospital employees who arrested the beggars, and in October 1724 the confinement began.[63]

Ten years later though, the Hospital directors' enthusiasm had distinctly waned. Genuine disappointment with the monarchy and a vague disillusionment with the whole notion of confinement had replaced the fervor of 1724. The directors now had a different vision of the Hospital's mission and a new view of the beggar himself. Certainly, the criminal vagabond still haunted their nightmares, but the directors now placed beside him another kind of mendicant. The experience of the ordinance of 1724 had changed the Hospital. It had plunged the institution into debt because the monarchy had failed to provide the promised subsidies, and it had brought the directors face to face with the beggars who had long been the focus of their efforts. The confrontation altered their views, so it is worthwhile determining just whom they encountered. Fortunately, the monarchy required that each hospital keep a record of the beggars incarcerated. The name, origin, age, physical description, and sometimes the profession of each beggar was to be recorded, and we possess this information for most of the period from 1724 to 1735. Only the data for the year 1731 and the months of June through March of 1726 are lacking, so we can put faces on the previously faceless beggars.[64]

First, however, we must consider their numbers. The Hospital directors told the monarchy that they had incarcerated 708 mendicants; we have no reason to disbelieve them.[65] Seven hundred and eight represents a substantial number; neither the smaller hospital at Saint Etienne nor the comparably sized institution at Aix-en-Provence confined so many beggars.[66] Does this mean that begging was more common and the beggars more numerous in Dauphiné than in adjacent provinces? Not necessarily, for these figures measure the energy of the *archers* who arrested the beggars as much as the number of beggars themselves. Still, it seems safe to say that the economic crises of the 1720s created considerable hardship and prompted many Dauphinois to take to the road with their hands open. Whether begging was more widespread in these years than before, we cannot say, but it does seem that the directors were right: begging constituted a serious and common problem.

The Hospital directors were also correct when they maintained that most of the mendicants in the city were "strangers," outsiders not resident in the city. Only 26.7 percent of the beggars whose origins we know came from Grenoble, and most of these were incarcerated in 1724. By 1730 only 12 percent of the mendicants lived in the city. Begging thus constituted, not too surprisingly, a tramping trade. Beggars were, almost by definition, vagrants, but most did not hail from regions far removed from Grenoble. Only 14 percent of the mendicants arrested came from far-flung areas like Spain, Italy, or the Parisian basin, and these beggars constituted a peculiar, almost archaic, group. Several, like Joachim Sarcuitaa, a forty-eight-year-old man on his way from Italy to his native Spain, considered themselves "pilgrims," and one mendicant listed his profession as that of hermit.[67] The average beggar, by contrast, was neither a holy man nor a foreigner in the true sense of the word: he was either a native Dauphinois or a resident of nearby Savoy. Forty percent of the beggars came from within the confines of Dauphiné, and the communities along the Grésivaudan valley, which attached Grenoble to Savoy, provided the largest contingent. Surprisingly enough, very few beggars hailed from the high mountainous regions of the province, from the Oisans or the Briançonnais. Nor did the more densely populated Rhone valley supply many mendicants. The explanation of this curious distinction probably lies in the impoverishment of the province and the geographical location of Grenoble. No major thoroughfares crossed in the city; only the Savoyards and the inhabitants of the Grésivaudan valley had to cross the town to reach the more fertile and more prosperous Rhone valley. As the figures on begging demonstrate, people did not migrate to Dauphiné, they left it. The rate of recidivism—the number of beggars arrested more than once by the *archers*—was so low as to indicate that most mendicants did not tarry in the city. It was not their final destination, just a stopping place on the way to the more prosperous regions to the west.

Consequently, these were not the rootless vagabonds imagined by the Grenoblois, but their fellow provincials for whom begging was probably an expedient and travel a novelty. Most were males; only 33 percent of those arrested for begging were women. But few were of an age to do harm to anyone. At first, it seems that all age groups were represented among the beggars; 30 percent were between one and twenty years of age, another 30 percent were between twenty-one and forty-five, and 40 percent were forty-five years or older. But this distribution probably does not reflect the normal age distribution in Grenoble or rural Dauphiné. Though we lack a precise breakdown of the population by age, it is likely that the very old and the very young are overrepresented among the beggars. Certainly, the very old were much too common among the beggars, for 21 percent were more than sixty-one years of age. Some, like one Joseph, who begged in a hut in La Tronche, or the weaver Guillaume Mode, were very old indeed: eighty and seventy-eight, respectively.[68] Others were extremely young: the beggar François Chrétiene was a mere ten years old. Many were actually less than fifteen years old, and the presence of these children among the mendicants tends to shock modern sensibilities. However, the juvenile beggar was an extremely common sight in the old regime, and what bands of beggars there were, were usually made up of families—parents and children or a group of siblings who begged together.[69] Occasionally, a child like François Chrétiene would be found wandering the streets alone, demanding alms. Chrétiene, like several other juvenile beggars, had been abandoned by his parents; he knew neither where they were nor, for that matter, where he was.

Little François Chrétiene certainly posed no threat to the community, nor did a considerable number of the other beggars, for many were disabled. Eighty-three percent of the mendicants did not suffer from any physical ailment, but this number is deceptive, since the healthy juveniles among the beggars skew the figures. Once the children are removed, the true dimensions of disability appear. One-third of the adult males suffered from some form of illness or impairment. Of the beggars between twenty-one and forty-five, 20 percent had lost a limb, and among the older men 17 percent were described as "infirm." The rest were blind or insane, like Justine Paroissan, a twenty-three-year-old native of Grenoble, who was also mentally retarded.[70]

The disabled probably did not—because they could not—work, so begging was their only means of support. The juvenile beggars too probably exercised no trade, so it is not entirely surprising that no occupation is given for most of the mendicants. Of those whose occupation is listed, their trades run the gamut from fairly elevated to quite humble. A couple of priests, traditional vagrants despite the laws of the Church, a few itinerant merchants, a surgeon, and several bourgeois who had come to Grenoble under strained circumstances appear among the beggars. So too do weavers and the very humble flax-carders. The single largest contingent among the beggars were the unskilled, the *journaliers, manouvriers,* and *gagne-deniers,* who accounted for almost a quarter of the mendicants. Surprisingly, agricultural laborers constituted only 6 percent of the beggars, but this does not mean that the majority exercised urban or even semiurban professions. Weaving and flax combing constituted the traditional winter occupations of Dauphinois peasants, and the fact that these rural dwellers chose to identify themselves by their hibernial professions may well indicate that they were looking for work in just these occupations.[71]

Whether flax-comber or day laborer, the average beggar bore little resemblance to the professional vagabond so frequently evoked in the seventeenth century. In fact, only fourteen individuals, all former soldiers or deserters, came even close to this menacing figure or to his companion, the false beggar who used subterfuge to excite compassion.[72] Most of the mendicants arrested between 1724 and 1735 simply did not and could not prey upon society.[73] They were, on the contrary, its victims—first of abandonment: like Marguerite Camasault, the wife of a schoolmaster from Chabeuil, who, when eight months pregnant, had taken to the road in search of her errant husband; like Catherine La Rue who was seduced by a soldier and abandoned to a life of begging with her infant child. Other beggars were the victims of old age, extreme youth, or disability. Like Jean Blanc, a thirty-year-old native of La Mure who had been a mason's hod carrier until he dislocated his arm, many of the mendicants begged because they could no longer do anything else. Finally, the beggars had fallen prey to unemployment. By their own admission, many of the mendicants had taken to the road in search of work. Like two women from near Perpignan who had come to Grenoble to find a place as domestics, they hoped to find in the world outside their own communities the employment that eluded them at home. In the meantime they begged, but only temporarily until a job materialized.[74]

At this point, the distinction between the domiciled poor and the itinerant beggar becomes unclear. In fact, with some variation in gender and residence, the mendicants arrested by the *archers* were identical to the paupers chosen by the directors to enter the Hospital.[75] Both groups knew disability and disease; both were characterized by old age and extreme youth; all suffered from hunger and want. Small wonder then that the Hospital directors themselves came to confuse the two groups and that, for the first time, they extended to the beggars the "compassion" formerly reserved for the "deserving poor."[76] The ordinance of 1724 may have done little to abolish begging, but it did partially dispel the old phantom of the criminal vagabond. The directors approached the intinerant poor in a new spirit, just as they brought a new vision to another group of paupers, those who depended, quite literally, on the Hospital General for their daily bread.

If anything altered the Hospital directors' views of the poor it was the distribution of bread to paupers domiciled in Grenoble. This sort of relief had long been one of the services provided by the Hospital, but in the years between 1712 and 1722 these distributions were greatly increased and also systematized. The directors kept a large, two-volume register in which they laboriously noted the name, profession, birth date and place, occupation, illness, and number of dependents of every pauper. Such orderly procedures signaled the emergence of a new bureaucratic spirit at the Hospital, a spirit which would have quite a future. But the old taste for intimacy with the poor had not yet died, and in this time of transition, the directors still rubbed shoulders with the impoverished. They entered their homes, inspected their furniture, peeked into their closets, and questioned them about their habits. Thanks to the directors' lack of discretion, we possess an unusually rich document which could not have been produced before or after and which provides a wealth of information about the poor. For example, we learn that in 1712 one Ennemond Molard, a native of Grenoble, forty-nine years of age and a glove-maker, lived on the second floor of a house on the Rue Saint Laurent with his wife, Elizabeth Cheminande, and their six children, who ranged in age from nine months to eighteen years. Madame Molard supplemented the family income by making playing cards for her card-maker brothers, and usually the two eldest daughters helped her. Recently, however, both had come down with the "cold humors" and could not work. Nor could Madame Molard work for long: she was three months pregnant. This growing family lived in one room and possessed "one bed, fairly well garnished, two old armoires with some linen inside, two tables and several upholstered chairs." When the directors returned for another inspection a year later, little had changed. In 1719, however, Madame Molard returned the bread card to the Hospital, explaining that two of the children had died and the family no longer needed assistance.[77]

There is nothing particularly unusual about this sad anecdote; many Grenoblois suffered the Molards' fate. But, in a historical sense, this story and the hundreds like it in the register were almost unique. Few cities, including Aix-en-Provence and Lyon, possess such abundant data on the respectable poor before very late in the eighteenth century.[78] Few documents allow us to follow the fortunes of individual paupers for almost a decade, the years between 1712 and 1721. But, for all its value, this document presents one problem which should be underscored immediately. If the register allows us to see the poor, it only permits us to see them through the Hospital directors' eyes. We encounter only those paupers deemed worthy of aid, and the directors had very definite ideas about who was eligible. According to their own pronouncements, the directors were to assist only those born and domiciled in Grenoble, and they had to exclude anyone able-bodied enough to work or arrogant enough to beg. In addition, these bread distributions were meant to be temporary, a short-lived palliative designed to tide a family over a difficult period, not a permanent source of relief. Still, the directors often dispensed bread to the same families for years on end, and they did not hesitate to break their other rules as well. Apparently, they did so quite often, because too many Grenoblois were on aid for these strictures to have been applied with rigor. According to a sample of half of the households listed in the register, 1,360 families received bread between 1712 and 1721. Since the average family size among the poor was 4, we can estimate that 5,440 individuals received assistance, a figure that jibes with the directors' own assessment of their efforts. In other words, in a town with a stable population of some 20,000 individuals, something like one-fifth of the city needed and received help.[79]

Where did these poor souls live? There were clearly pockets of misery in the city: 34 percent of the families who received bread lived on the right bank of the Isère, in the sordid and insalubrious Saint Laurent parish, along the Rues Saint Laurent and Perrière, and on the *montée de Chalemont*, which scaled the mountain abutting the quarter. The suburb of Très Cloîtres, populated by flax-workers, housed some 10 percent of the poor, and the Rue du Boeuf, which as its name indicates, was home to the leatherworkers, contained some 7 percent of the families assisted. But no true ghetto existed in Grenoble. The poor lived throughout the city, right next to the rich—or more precisely on the floors above them—even in the chic quarters like the Rue Neuve, where wealthy magistrates maintained elegant *hôtels particuliers*.[80]

Though they resided in Grenoble, most of the poor had not been born there. Over 46 percent of the heads of household assisted by the Hospital came from outside the city, from the nearby communities of the Grési-vaudan valley near the Savoy border, or from the villages of the Char-treuse mountain range or the Rhone valley. These were not, however, re-cent immigrants. Most had been domiciled in the city for ten years and many for more than twenty. They had been a part of the wave of immigra-tion experienced by Grenoble in the seventeenth century, and it was not because they were born outside Grenoble and were unfamiliar with city ways that they found themselves dependent on the Hospital.

If they were in need, it was sometimes because they were born female. Only 42.8 percent of the recipients of the Hospital's bread were male, whereas over 57 percent were female. The contrast was even more marked among the unwed: single men accounted for only 4 percent of the recipi-ents, whereas unmarried women constituted 18 percent. Women seem to have been at greater risk of falling into impoverishment, but we should not make too much of these figures. In preindustrial cities like Grenoble, women almost always outnumbered men, so it was not surprising that they constituted a higher percentage of the poor. In addition, the single women we encounter in the Hospital's register suffered from the same problems as single men. Few of these women were domestics; most were seamstresses and spinners, who like their male counterparts occasionally lacked work or fell ill. Once the crisis had passed, they could, like Mar-guerite Broquères, a thirty-year-old embroiderer from Marseille, return their bread card to the Hospital, for their wages, though very small, were sufficient to maintain one person.[81] It was only when a woman married, had children, and lost her husband that she truly faced the prospect of permanent and severe immiserization.

Of all Grenoblois, widows were those most likely to find themselves dependent on the generosity of the Hospital. They constituted 34 per-cent of the recipients of bread, and they had more than fate to blame for their predicament. Several husbands, like the thirty-four-year-old weaver Jean Arnaud, simply vanished, leaving their wives and children to face starvation alone.[82] Occasionally, a wandering husband would rematerialize, as did Jean Arnaud five years after his sudden departure, and this fortuitous event would precipitate the return of the bread card and what must have been an awkward reunion. But few women were snatched out of poverty so abruptly. When Marie Sybille, a thirty-year-old glove seamstress was abandoned by her weaver husband, she found herself out of work and nursing a five-month-old infant. When the Hospital directors investigated one year later, the situation had only gotten worse: Marie now had another child, born seven months after her husband's mysterious disappearance.[83]

Marie Sybille was not impoverished because her husband's departure broke up a working team. Contrary to what historians have long believed, most poor women did not work in tandem with their husbands or help them in their trades. This was probably true at a higher level of society, among the skilled artisans, but it was not the case among the great majority of Grenoblois, among those who occasionally found themselves on the welfare roles. The family may well have been the principal unit of production in the old regime, but not every family was a unit of production. Most wives had an occupation quite separate and distinct from their husbands' and the wife of an unskilled laborer or journeyman cobbler probably contributed to the family economy by spinning, glove sewing, or taking in laundry. Sometimes women worked outside the home, selling fruit, cakes, or coal on the street or running errands. And widowed or not, all women worked, for it was only when she was nursing an infant that a woman abandoned—if only partially—her labor. Often, the Hospital paid for the child to be sent to a country wet nurse, but even this lightening of a widow's burden was of little assistance. Marie Sybille, for example, was not destitute just because she was nursing a child. Rather, she was impoverished because her tiny wages as a glove seamstress were insufficient to support more than one person. Alone, a woman could make a go of it; with a child, she was doomed to impoverishment.

In any household, young children were a burden. They did contribute to the family economy by working, but generally not before the age of fourteen or fifteen. None of the children described by the Hospital directors as "sewing gloves," "making cards," or "spinning" were less than fourteen years of age, and most were quite a bit older. In the old regime, child labor was actually teen-age labor, and the real disaster was to have a number of children too young to take in work. Such was the case with Claude Brandin, a thirty-six-year-old tailor who, despite good health and his wife's wages as a glove seamstress, could not support his six children, aged three months to eight years.[84] Most young couples must have found themselves in such a position at some time or another, which explains the popularity of mercenary wet nursing and the common practice of dumping children with an obliging uncle in the countryside, where they could be put to work at an early age. But Brandin was also a bit of an exception: only 21 percent of the households listed in the bread-distribution register had more than three children. The ferocious infant and child mortality of the old regime kept families small, and the death of an infant was often a blessing. When Marguerite Bouzère, a widowed seamstress with five children, brought her bread card back to the directors in 1714, she explained that she no longer needed it, that her two youngest children had died the previous month.[85] Under such circumstances, old-regime parents' supposed indifference to their offsprings' demise may well be comprehensible.

Partly because of this high infant mortality, and partly because of the Hospital's policies, few infants were among the individuals receiving bread. Generally, the directors dispatched needy infants to country wet nurses, and these infants do not appear in this particular register. Nor were many old people given bread, for they were usually placed in the Hospital General. Most of the recipients of bread were in the prime of life, between the ages of thirty and forty-five, but one does have a sense that old age struck early in the old regime. Men and women of no more than fifty years of age were described as "infirm," too debilitated to work because of crippling arthritis or painful rheumatism. Young or old, the working people of Grenoble had disease as a constant companion: over 50 percent of those who received aid were described as ill, a rate that is surprisingly high given that the Hospital General and the Providence hospital dealt with most sick people. But the laboring poor of the bread lists did not suffer from the same diseases that afflicted the inmates of the Hospital or the Providence. Here there were no mysterious humors or congenital defects, but rather the fruits of a hazardous working life. Sixty-five percent of those labeled sick by the directors had debilities which stemmed from their occupations. Among men, amputations, twisted and broken limbs, and hernias were common, whereas women, who had more sedentary occupations, suffered from bad eyesight and lung disease. Work, whether it was hard manual labor or just glove sewing, was dangerous.

If all the laboring poor risked disease or permanent injury on the job, it was not because they all had the same occupation. On the contrary, the bread recipients exercised a variety of trades, everything from priest to printer. Women's occupations, such as glove seamstress, flax-spinner, stocking-knitter, or washerwoman, do bulk large on the list of occupations, but women were the principal recipients of bread. Among the men, all sorts of trades were practiced, but there was some concentration in the professions of cobbler, chair-carrier, tailor, wool- and flax-comber, and day laborer. Despite their variety, all these trades had one thing in common: they were not a part of the luxury trades considered by historians most vulnerable to sudden shifts in style or market. These were semi-industrial, unskilled professions, which nonetheless knew sudden and unexpected periods of unemployment and low wages.

This brings us to the causes of impoverishment, the forces that reduced a respectable laborer and his family to the bread of the Hospital. Some of these causes were universal and eternal, to be found at just about any time or place. Disease or some personal catastrophe could reduce a laboring family to hunger, and sometimes they struck all at once, as in the case of Georges Giraud, a forty-six-year-old flax-weaver who, within a month, had his right arm amputated and forty *aulnes* of cloth stolen, and could not find work.[86] Most often, however, the causes of poverty were periodic crises, or in the parlance of French historians, "mauvaise conjoncture," bad economic circumstances that reduced work to a trickle and working men to the bread of the Hospital. Even though they exercised common, unskilled trades, these laborers were no less vulnerable than their skilled neighbors to fluctuations in the provincial or even national market. The plague in Provence in 1720 reduced trade on the Rhone and the Isère and threw many laborers out of work. Similarly, the financial debacle of the Law crisis brought on widespread unemployment.[87] Because they were consumers as well as producers, working families also suffered during the bad harvests which punctuated the last years of the seventeenth and the first two decades of the eighteenth century. Everyone suffered during the horrible year of 1709, but this was only the most notorious year in three decades of general immiserization. Periodic crises were played out against the backdrop of a long-term depression in the manufacturing sector, which sent prices down by 50 percent and wages with them. In short, the laboring poor suffered from occasional unemployment and chronic low wages.[88]

Nevertheless, many were able to bounce back after these crises. One year a family was on the verge of starvation; the next year the wife turned in the bread card or the family was struck from the register. Even Georges Giraud, the weaver who lost both an arm and his cloth in one month, was, by 1720, hard at work, with five looms and a number of employees. Similarly, another weaver, Claude Terrant, recovered from dropsy and bought five looms, thanks to the death of two children.[89] Though in greater destitution in 1712, the nail-maker Philippe Guisson had recovered sufficiently by 1720 to give his daughter a substantial dowry of 400 livres.[90] These were what Jean-Pierre Gutton has described as the "conjonctural poor," those who knew occasional bad times but still got back on their feet once the crisis had passed.[91] But so frequent and so grave were the crises of the late seventeenth and early eighteenth centuries that some workers never recovered. They found themselves falling into the "structural poor," the chronically and permanently impoverished who, year after year, in both good times and bad, depended on the Hospital for their bread. "Ruined since 1709," "begging since the failure of the bank notes"—such notations appeared too frequently in the register of the bread recipients to leave any doubt as to the unprecedented severity of the years between 1712 and 1722 for many working people.

Indeed, not just working people were vulnerable to hunger and misery; so severe and so frequent were the crises of the last years of Louis XIV's reign that previously immune social groups suddenly found themselves plunged into permanent distress. Poverty reached up into the bourgeoisie, the legal professions, even the nobility. People like Marguerite Odoz de Boniot, descendant of one of the most prestigious and ancient noble families in the province, found herself destitute and living off "secret alms."[92] Similarly, Demoiselle Marie Fine, widow of a *greffier,* possessed of land in the Granges and Fontaine as well as two houses in town, had to depend on the Hospital General because creditors had seized all her assets.[93] Debt was often at the root of these disasters, and a spouse's death could precipitate a rash of foreclosures. But not just widows faced the prospect of begging and disgrace. The sieur Antoine Brun, bourgeois of Grenoble, was forced to seek alms for his family at the homes of wealthy citizens because all his lands were in the hands of creditors.[94] These *déclassés* were not the "shameful poor" who had long led a mysterious and discreet existence in the city. The Hospital General left their assistance to the *bureaux de charité* in each parish and devoted itself to more "serious" impoverishment. But in the last years of Louis XIV's reign, the immiserization of previously invulnerable groups had become a serious problem. Suddenly, bourgeois, lawyers, and nobles dropped from the "shameful poor," down beyond the laboring poor, into the lowest level of poverty and degradation. How the directors must have shuddered when they described Demoiselle Barbe Begue, the wife of François Berlioz, a clerk, who was so impoverished that her daughter had taken to a life of "debauchery" or prostitution.[95]

No wonder the Hospital directors altered their view of the poor; they had a new pauper before their eyes. Even though a lack of documents prevents us from measuring precisely the dimensions of this change, it does seem that poverty was more widespread in the last years of Louis XIV's reign than ever before. The beggars so often decried by the Brothers of the Holy Sacrament were no longer vagabonds or thieves: they were respectable, hardworking Grenoblois. Now the poor were Christian men and women forced by circumstance to depend on the Hospital General for aid. Indeed, they were even bourgeois and lawyers. Even the directors of the Hospital could not help but notice the difference, and this change in the incidence of poverty goes a long way toward explaining the shift in attitudes toward the poor which occurred between 1680 and 1729.

Not that the Hospital directors abandoned all the old notions surrounding poverty. They still held begging in absolute horror, even though they granted bread to many paupers who demanded alms quite publicly. No real contradiction, however, existed in this behavior, for the directors used the bread distributions to discourage the poor from begging. When Ennemond Francan, a forty-year-old spinner, was discovered asking for alms on the Place Grenette, he was stricken from the roles.[96] When blind Michel Betton and his wife were found demanding alms, they were first reprimanded, then threatened with the loss of the bread card, and finally deprived of it.[97] Like their predecessors at the Hospital General and the Brothers of the Holy Sacrament, the directors tried to extinguish the pauper's vices, be they begging, debauchery, or drunkenness. They made "good behavior" a precondition for receiving bread, and they admonished the gagne-denier Jean Colombe and his wife that if they did not cease "getting themselves drunk during Lent," they would lose their bread.[98] Similarly, they warned Clemence Reymond, a twenty-five-year-old glove seamstress with the habit of "frequenting the cabaret," to abandon the tavern or forfeit her bread.[99] For women "in danger" the directors, like the Brothers of the Holy Sacrament, had a special concern, and on more than one occasion they tried to remove young girls from situations in which they risked becoming streetwalkers. The impiety of the pauper concerned the directors, and on one occasion they forced a poor orphan to attend mass or give up his bread.[100]

This moral police recalls the efforts of the Holy Sacrament, but the poor had changed since the heyday of the Brothers. The arrogance and lack of deference the Company so often decried had, it seems, vanished. However much the poor may have resented the prying of the Hospital directors—and it is hard to imagine that they did not—they never expressed it. A surprisingly large number of bread recipients returned their cards voluntarily when they no longer needed them and even "thanked the directors for their generosity." In addition, although the directors were eager to wage the war against impiety among the poor, they rarely had occasion to use their arms. Only once did they remark that a pauper was "without conversion," and only infrequently did they have to force the poor to attend mass. Apparently, the campaign for the conversion of souls had achieved some success.

The gap between rich and poor had narrowed. Thanks in large part to the missionary efforts of seventeenth-century benefactors, the impoverished embraced new attitudes, new habits, and a new spirituality. As yet, we can only glimpse the dimensions of this cultural change among the poor; we shall have occasion to scrutinize it in detail shortly.[101] Still, we can see that patterns of criminality and popular sexual mores altered in the years between 1680 and 1729 and in ways that permitted the rich to exonerate the poor. No longer could the elite "blame" the impoverished for violence or accuse them of sexual libertinism. Now a more humane and more secular attitude could emerge. That it did so at a time of unprecedented hardship when poverty threatened previously invulnerable groups and impoverishment became, as much as it could in the old regime, a shared experience, is not surprising. That this same period witnessed such an outpouring of alms and good works is considerably more astonishing. We have examined the qualitative change in this period, but not the quantitative change: the tremendous increase in charitable activity. Another document, the last will and testament, allows us to do so with some precision. The will permits us to confront each benefactor personally, to scrutinize his motives, and to explain the growth in charitable activity which brought to a close the seventeenth century.

SIX

Patterns of Charity: Testamentary Bequests (1620–1729)

Sometime on the afternoon of April 16, 1685, François de la Croix de Chevrières, marquis of Ornacieu and president of the Parlement of Grenoble, sat down to dictate to his notary, maître Froment, his last will and testament. He did so, his will tells us, because "the hour of our death is uncertain and it is imprudent to leave the disposition of one's estate to the end of life and the pain and confusion that accompany a grave illness." Thus, "to avoid the conflicts which may arise over the division of the estate," and "while still in good health and full possession of [his] senses, will and faculties," the president set about providing for his heirs. First, however, he provided for himself, for the fate of his immortal soul.

For his grave, he chose the church of the Hospital General, and he instructed his heir to bury him "without the slightest pomp or display." He then asked that a thousand masses be said for the repose of his soul immediately after his death, either in the church of the Hospital or elsewhere. He also bequeathed 1,000 livres to the Hospital with the stipulation that a mass be said in his honor the first day of every month "in perpetuity." In addition, he left 100 livres apiece to the Augustinian, Carmelite, Capuchin, and Recollet monasteries, as well as the Saint Claire convent, so that these religious might take a general communion and attend a requiem for the benefit of his soul.

Having provided for his own salvation, the president now looked to that of the poor. To the Congregation for the Propagation of the Faith, he left 100 livres, and upon the inhabitants of the community of Marisolles, he bestowed the income from a tax, the *vingtaine du vin,* for the "establishment and maintenance of a schoolmaster so that the youth may be raised in the fear of God." In addition, he instructed his heir to distribute 200 livres to the poor of his other estates. Then the president bequeathed 100 livres to the urban needy, to be administered by the ladies de Barral, Canel, Thonard, and Virieu, directresses of the Providence hospital, and gave 100 livres to the Hôpital de la Charité, for the establishing of a bed, to which the president's heirs would be allowed to affix their coat of arms and "nominate" a sick pauper of their acquaintance from time to time.

At this point, the president turned to his immediate dependents. He left two years' wages to the domestics in his service at the time of his death, and 1,000 livres to his widowed mother. To his two sons, Gabriel and Jean, he left 21,000 livres to be paid on their twenty-fifth birthdays, and he did the same for any child who might be born in the future. Then the president named as his principal or "universal" heir and executrix his wife, Marguerite Vidaud de la Tour, with the provision that she turn the bulk of the estate over to her elder son at death. There followed a number of lengthy clauses of substitution designed to keep the Croix de Chevrières fortune within the family, no matter how many of the heirs died. Having foreseen every possible disaster, the president closed his will and signed it. The document was also signed by the witnesses: five clerks employed by the notary, the president's lawyer Dumolard in whose house the will was made, and finally by the notary Froment himself. Sometime later, Froment had one of his clerks copy the will into his *minutier,* a bound register containing copies of all the notary's transactions, where it is still to be found today, sandwiched in between hundreds of other notarial registers, in the Archives Départmentales of the Isère.[1]

Thus we have at our disposal a very personal document, created under rather intimate circumstances. But how much does it tell us about the author, the president de la Croix de Chevrières? What can we expect to learn from the thousands of documents like it that lie in the archives? Not much in the way of economic information. We know that the president could bequeath 21,000 livres to his heirs, a relatively substantial sum of money, but we have no indication as to the exact size or even composition of the president's estate, and few seventeenth-century wills were more loquacious. As a family document, the will is not quite so disappointing. The preamble and lengthy clauses of substitution reveal that the president was deeply concerned that the Croix de Chevrières fortune remain intact and in the family. But beyond this, we have little sense of the nature of the president's relations with his family or the value he placed on these relations. Not many seventeenth-century wills are more revealing, and some, which fail to specify the number of younger heirs or the size of bequests, are even less informative.

The president's will does tell us something about his attitudes toward death. We learn that he is concerned about his funeral and worried lest it be too ostentatious, a fact that is not without interest to historians of death. Indeed, Pierre Chaunu's analysis of the language of Parisian wills has demonstrated just how valuable this kind of document can be in constructing a history of attitudes toward death.[2] The president's will also provides considerable information concerning his religious sentiments. Though the president may not reveal his innermost thoughts or deepest metaphysical reflections—if he had any—he does indicate which devotions he favors and which religious houses he prefers. Such information can, in the hands of a brilliant historian like Michel Vovelle, reveal wholly new ways of looking at religious and cultural life, as his seminal work *Piété baroque et déchristianisation en Provence au XVIIIe siècle* so amply demonstrates.[3]

To the historian of death, the family, and religion, the president's will and documents like it have a great deal to offer. But fully a third of the document is devoted to another subject—charity. The charitable clauses, concerning donations to the Hospital General or to the poor of the president's estates, are among the lengthiest and the most detailed stipulations of his testament. Quantitatively, wills are irreplaceable: no other source permits us to determine the amount of charitable giving from the first years of the seventeenth century to the Revolution. Qualitatively, wills are equally invaluable: no other document allows us to confront the donor personally, to examine his motives and outline his particular vision of poverty. Through the thousands of bequests contained in the Grenoblois' testaments, we can establish the social contours of seventeenth-century charity and uncover its deeper meaning. At the same time, with the help of wills made by Protestants, we can contrast post-Tridentine and Reformed charity and arrive at a better understanding of both. Wills may not be, as Brian Pullan has argued, "the whole story," but they are certainly a very important part of it.[4]

However, wills and testaments have yet to receive the sustained attention of historians of French charity. This neglect results, most likely, from the problems which this source, for all its virtues, presents. First the sheer abundance of testaments—while a blessing—is also a curse. Wills can easily be found in the judicial records, but these documents concern only the elite of old regime society.[5] Consequently, the historian must turn to the notarial archives, to the registers, like the one in which the president's will can be found, which stand row upon row in the archives. For the years between 1620 and 1789, we have 1,731 such registers for the city of Grenoble, which contain approximately 500,000 acts, ranging from marriage contracts to land sales. Testaments represent only 2 percent of this output, but picking them out of this mass of paper would be extremely time-consuming, if not impossible. Therefore a sample had to be made. Registers from a wide variety of notaries were read, and a sample which conformed as closely as possible to the composition of Grenoble society was created (see Appendix A). The result was 5,012 wills which, given an estimated 10,000 wills in the archives, represented approximately 50 percent of the wills available.[6]

While sampling solves one problem, it also creates others. With any sample, one always wonders whether the results are real or are only artifacts of the sample. Changes in charitable giving which appear significant could merely reflect variations in the composition of the sample. Or they could be, sample or no, illusory, the result of an alteration in demographic patterns or the practices of the notaries, not an indication of new attitudes. Worse yet, such changes could, in reality, be nothing more than the product of sheer chance, a fluke. And even if a valid change in charitable giving can be demonstrated, which of the many variables affecting bequests—gender, class, residence, or literacy—accounts for this change? Which are the most important? and how does one separate the effects of two such closely linked phenomena as literacy and urbanity?

Fortunately, these problems can be partially solved by certain statistical techniques. Once the data in the wills have been rendered machine readable, cross tabulation can be used to determine general trends. Then multiple regression analysis and tobit analysis, both of which provide t-statistics, or measures of significance, can be used to test the validity of these trends.[7] Also, the coefficient which these techniques supply for each independent variable allows the historian to rank all the variables in order of importance and to disentangle the effects of linked variables, like literacy and urbanity. With these tools the historian can therefore avoid the pitfalls which a quantitative analysis of wills presents, and he can escape the pointless empiricism that often plagues this kind of study. Still, however sophisticated the statistical technique, it cannot reveal everything about charity. Social attitudes are a matter of quality, not just quantity, and it is not how much a testator believes but what he believes that counts.

THE INCREASE IN CHARITABLE GIVING

What patterns of charitable giving emerge from the data? A quick look at the percentage of Grenoblois making charitable bequests reveals an overall upward trend. The rate of charitable giving increased from 32 percent in the 1620s to 51 percent in the 1680s and then peaked at 66 percent in the 1690s (figure 1). A similar increase characterized giving to the Hospital General: in the 1620s only 13 percent of the Grenoblois gave to the *maison de force*, but by the 1690s 45 percent did so. After 1700 this upward trend slackens somewhat and a period of brief decline occurs (fig. 1). But these lower percentages do not mar the general impression of growing altruism, for they coincide with one of the worst periods in Dauphinois' economic history. In the years between 1680 and 1730, bad harvests and the Savoyard war disrupted agriculture and commerce and strained the Grenoblois' economic resources.[8] The Grenoblois apparently felt the pinch acutely, for our best available indicator of wealth—the dowries contained in wills—point to an abrupt and painful decline in incomes: the average Grenoblois, who in the 1660s could afford to give his daughter a dowry of 9,061 livres, could only manage, in the 1720s, to provide her with 2,224 livres.[9]

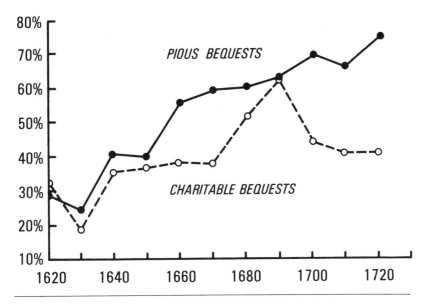

Figure 1.   Percentage of Testators Making Pious and Charitable Bequests

Diminished resources, not flagging altruism, created this slight decline, and not all Grenoblois were equally daunted by hard times. Some continued to make bequests, in fact larger bequests, for the size of the average gift to charity rose thoroughout this period. In the 1630s the average donation to charity was a mere 68 livres, but by 1670 this sum had climbed to 421 livres and then surpassed 600 livres in the 1720s.[10] The charitable impulse continued to grow among many Grenoblois, and those who bowed temporarily to economic circumstances failed to cloud the overall picture of increase. Regression analysis of the percentage of Grenoblois making charitable bequests reveals that a statistically significant increase in charitable giving occurred in the years between 1620 and 1729 (table 1). The increase is even greater if we consider only the giving to the Hospital General and to the other new institutions created in the period (Appendix B). In addition, tobit analysis, which has the virtue of combining both the percentage of gifts and the size of these gifts, confirms that, in the seventeenth century, more Grenoblois gave more money to charitable endeavors (table 1).

Is this increase real, does it reflect a true growth of altruism, or does it spring from other, extraneous sources? The aforementioned statistical techniques remove the possibility that fluctuations in the sample composition account for this increase, but it is not so easy to dismiss other factors, such as changes in the economy or in family sentiment. For instance, an increase in wealth might produce an increase in charitable giving, and prosperity could masquerade as altruism. This seems highly unlikely in seventeenth-century Dauphiné, for the economic disasters of the years 1680 through 1730 were only the climax of a long period of hardship.[11] Stagnation at best, if not outright decline, characterized the Dauphinois economy in the years between 1620 and 1679, and regression analysis of the size of dowries and bequests to family members confirms that no significant increase in wealth occurred during this period.[12] In addition, while family bequests were stagnating, charitable bequests were growing in size. When this relationship is expressed as a ratio, charitable giving, which amounted to only 1 percent of family bequests in the 1620s, grows to account for over 4 percent of the same bequests at the end of the period.

Though these percentages may seem small, they are significant and provide one of our best indicators of the Grenoblois' true altruism. In principle, a special, dialectical relationship always exists between charitable bequests and family legacies. When a testator considers leaving money to charity, he weighs his social duties against his family obligations and ponders whether to serve society at the expense of his heirs, who would

TABLE 1

PERCENTAGE OF TESTATORS MAKING CHARITABLE BEQUESTS:
SELECTED REGRESSION AND TOBIT RESULTS

Variables	Regression Coefficient	Tobit
Date	0.004 (1.84)	7.37 (11.54)
Nobles	0.337 (9.90)	761.99 (9.214)
Magistrates	0.496 (12.52)	1,216.69 (12.86)
Basoche	0.273 (8.47)	453.26 (5.38)
Bourgeois	0.325 (8.38)	543.89 (5.63)
Merchants	0.212 (6.29)	393.25 (4.41)
Plowmen	−0.079 (1.36)	−151.32 (−0.87)
Domestics	−0.036 (0.53)	−67.41 (−0.32)
Female	0.022 (1.10)	−25.84 (−0.50)
Literacy	0.065 (2.50)	185.69 (2.84)
Urban	−0.126 (0.47)	20.18 (0.295)

Note: Here both the regression analysis and tobit analysis are multivariate techniques: they both attempt to measure the separate effects that the various independent variables have upon the dependent variable. These are not, therefore, individual regressions. In our regression example, the dependent variable is zero for testators who did not make charitable bequests and one for those who did—in effect, it is the likelihood of making charitable bequests. In the tobit example the dependent variable is the actual amount of the bequest. In each case, the coefficients measure the size of the effect that a given independent variable has on the dependent variable: a negative coefficient means a negative effect, a large coefficient means a larger effect, etc. The regression and tobit coefficients are raw coefficients: they are not beta weights or weighted coefficients, and they therefore need not sum to one. The numbers in parentheses below the coefficients are t-statistics, which measure the statistical significance of the effect. If the t-statistic is larger than 1.96, then there is less than a 5 percent chance that the effect we have measured is merely a statistical fluke. If, on the other hand, the t-statistic is small, then the real effect is likely to be zero, and we can ignore the corresponding independent variable. Thus the date has a significant effect on the amount of a testator's charitable bequests (t = 11.54), but being female has no statistically significant effect (t = −0.50). As for the meaning of the various independent variables, the date is simply the year in which the will is drawn up, and the class variables from nobles to domestics are 1 for members of the corresponding classes and 0 otherwise. In other words, these class variables measure the effect of being a member of a given social class. The one group without an associated class variable, the arti-

otherwise receive all his estate. Consequently, family sentiment and obligations—that is, the number of heirs—should always inhibit charitable giving. But such was not, oddly enough, the case in seventeenth-century Grenoble, where testators seemed to ignore the claims of their immediate heirs. In fact, testators with three or more children—those with the heaviest family burdens—were just as likely as their less prolific neighbors to make charitable bequests.[13] Like the counselor Saléon, who regretted that his children were too numerous to receive legacies equal "to [his] affection and their merits" and then bestowed sizable bequests upon a number of charities, the Grenoblois did not always allow family duty to impinge upon social obligations.[14] Conversely, those with no children—bachelors, unmarried women, and some widows—showed little interest in helping the poor.[15] Family does not seem to have entered into the charitable equation in seventeenth-century Grenoble, at least not family in our sense of the word.

Gender and residence also failed to influence charitable giving. Pierre Chaunu, in his study of Parisian wills, found strong and marked contrasts between male and female testamentary behavior, but no such division existed in Grenoble. Women were just as likely as men to make charitable bequests, and vice versa. At the same time, city dwellers enjoyed no advantage over country folk in this regard (table 1). Both were equally likely to make charitable bequests, though urban testators naturally favored urban institutions, like the Hospital General, while country testators preferred rural, informal means of relief. Male or female, urban or rural, one factor, though, did predispose a testator to remember the poor in his will—literacy. Those who could sign their testaments were much more apt than their unlettered neighbors to make charitable bequests, and they were much more likely to prefer the Hospital General to older forms of relief (table 1 and Appendix B).

Literacy may have predisposed a testator toward charity, but it was his social group or occupation that truly determined his propensity to make charitable bequests.[16] If we look at the regression and tobit tables, we see immediately that the professions, from magistrate to domestic, have

---

sans, serves as the standard to which all other groups are compared. Similarly, the variable female is 1 for women and 0 otherwise; literacy is 1 for those who signed their wills; and urban is 1 for those who lived in Grenoble. These variables measure the effects of, respectively, gender, literacy, and residence within the city of Grenoble. The coefficients of additional variables—immigrant, family status, and sick, which measured the effects of being an immigrant to Grenoble, a single person, and an ill individual—were insignificant in both the regression and the tobit, and they have not been reported in the table. A constant term was also included in both procedures, but it too has been omitted from the table.

higher t-statistics, or measures of significance, than do the more general variables like literacy or gender (table 1). Occupation influenced altruism, and the single most charitable group in the city was the magistracy (the judges of the sovereign courts), followed by the nobles (titled country gentlemen and army officers), the *basoche* (lawyers and notaries), and so forth, on down the social scale. Because the magistrates were the wealthiest group in the city and the nobles the second most prosperous, this hierarchy of charity looks suspiciously like the city's hierarchy of wealth. But if we look above the t-statistics at the coefficients, which measure the differences between social groups, we find that income does not, in fact, correspond exactly to altruism. A more complex, intriguing picture emerges, for the disparities in charity among social groups do not match up with their differences in wealth. The nobles, for example, were almost as wealthy as their cousins the magistrates, and yet they fall far behind. The bourgeois, on the other hand, were by no means as prosperous as the nobles, and yet they nearly equal them in altruism. Clearly, income alone did not determine a particular group's propensity to make charitable bequests; other cultural forces were also at work.

In the case of the nobility, which lagged so far behind the magistracy, cultural differences must account for this relative lack of altruism. Linked by ties of blood and marriage to the magistrates and second only to them in wealth, the nobles differed in that they had a higher rate of illiteracy, particularly female nobles, and about one-third resided in villages outside Grenoble.[17] Isolated in their chateaux and lacking access to written culture, these country gentlemen, unlike their cousins the magistrates, probably had little occasion to learn of the new ideas about poverty, and they consequently showed little interest in the Hospital General or the Congregation for the Propagation of the Faith. Of course, great nobles did sit on the governing boards of these institutions, but they were the minority, the handful of barons and counts who were firmly ensconced in the highest reaches of the army, the monarchy, and the Church. These great nobles did have a rate of charitable giving—65 percent—which approached that of the magistrates, but the majority of nobles, the privileged but untitled noblemen who had little hope of reaching the highest ranks of the military or the Church, showed no such generosity. With a rate of charitable giving of only 33 percent, these nobles seem curiously isolated and cut off from a culture of which the altruistic magistrates were the primary stewards (table 2).

No such isolation characterized Grenoble's bourgeoisie in the old regime sense of the word, that is, the rentiers who resided in the city but lived off their rural estates. Though these bourgeois shared with the nobility similar kinds of income, they were by no means as wealthy. The average bourgeois could only afford to give his daughter a dowry a third the size of that bestowed by the average noble on his daughter, but this relative poverty did not prevent the rentiers from coming close to matching the nobles' generosity toward the poor. What accounts for this unexpected altruism? Unfortunately, we know very little about Grenoble's rentiers, but it does seem that the reasons were both social and cultural. Socially, the bourgeoisie may well have aspired to "live nobly," to enjoy the prestige of the nobility; their generosity may therefore indicate that they took the obligations of nobility as seriously as its prerogatives. They became, so to speak, more noble than the nobility. Culturally, however, the bourgeoisie was much more thoroughly integrated than the nobles into the life of the city. They participated in municipal government and served on the board of the Hospital General next to the magistrates, a fact which may have contributed greatly to their altruism.

The degree to which cultural factors influenced charitable giving is probably best illustrated by the *basoche,* that is, the lawyers, notaries, and *huissiers* who composed the bulk of the legal profession in Grenoble. These moderately wealthy, moderately prestigious men and their wives hardly saw their fortunes rise significantly in the seventeenth century; yet their rate of charitable giving soared. At the beginning of the period, barely 40 percent made any sort of charitable bequest, but after 1680, just when the Dauphinois economy was entering its bleakest period, the *basoche* opened its pocketbooks. The rate of charitable giving jumped to almost 70 percent and came close to equaling that of the magistracy (table 2).

What happened to the legal profession? If we include a new independent variable, religious giving, in the regression equation, we find that those who made gifts for spiritual purposes were also highly likely to leave money to charity.[18] A very strong link seems to exist between religious giving and charity, and this impression is confirmed if we look at the general evolution of religious bequests in the seventeenth century. Here, a familiar pattern of increase emerges: whereas only 30 percent of the Grenoblois left money for spiritual purposes in the 1620s, this rate rose by 1670 to 60 percent and then soared to 76 percent in the 1720s (table 3). When the rates of both religious and charitable giving are charted along the same axis, we find that both curves follow a similar path, that the increase in charity was complemented and to a certain degree preceded by a growth in religious giving (see figure 1). This suggests that the charitable renaissance of the seventeenth century was a function or at least a part of a larger religious revival. Grenoble's lawyers and notaries,

TABLE 2

PERCENTAGE OF TESTATORS WHO MADE CHARITABLE BEQUESTS

Decade	Nobles	Magi-strates	Basoche	Bour-geois	Merchants	Other	Total
1620–1629	33	86	44	46	28	17	32
	(9)	(7)	(34)	(13)	(29)	(87)	(179)
1630–1639	75	33	29	13	28	8	22
	(12)	(12)	(41)	(8)	(25)	(100)	(198)
1640–1649	41	88	48	29	22	20	37
	(29)	(24)	(33)	(14)	(32)	(138)	(270)
1650–1659	62	66	49	61	42	15	38
	(26)	(29)	(39)	(18)	(38)	(124)	(274)
1660–1669	54	76	51	44	48	16	43
	(46)	(34)	(35)	(16)	(23)	(77)	(232)
1670–1679	50	82	41	56	52	4	41
	(44)	(39)	(56)	(26)	(21)	(186)	(265)
1680–1689	54	82	69	61	55	20	55
	(46)	(39)	(49)	(36)	(29)	(55)	(254)
1690–1699	79	72	69	69	63	47	66
	(34)	(32)	(59)	(32)	(32)	(49)	(238)
1700–1709	61	74	51	55	43	18	44
	(33)	(27)	(69)	(20)	(46)	(77)	(272)
1710–1719	55	72	68	52	31	20	44
	(33)	(36)	(47)	(25)	(55)	(89)	(285)
1720–1729	66	80	45	33	33	16	41
	(41)	(40)	(66)	(3)	(58)	(97)	(305)
	58	75	52	53	39	18	42
	(353)	(319)	(528)	(210)	(388)	(974)	(2,272)

Note: Testators for whom no occupation is given and soldiers and peasants have been omitted from this table. The figures in parentheses are the absolute numbers of testators in each category.

like many of its other citizens, underwent a profound cultural change, a conversion to Counter Reformation Catholicism.

THE GROWTH OF RELIGIOUS GIVING

To assume that an increase in religious giving reflects a major spiritual upheaval is to make a big conceptual jump; before we take the leap, we must establish that this increase is in fact real, that it is the reflection of growing piety and not the product of some extraneous force like the notary. Almost all Grenoblois dictated their wills to a notary, and he did more than just transcribe their words. The notary prompted the testator, supplied the correct legal jargon, and even fashioned whole phrases in the will. If he dictated the form of the will, did he also determine its contents, that is, the religious bequests? Michel Vovelle in his study of Provençal wills found that measuring the notary's influence was vexing if not impossible; but regression analysis provides a solution to this problem.[19] If each notary imposed his personality upon his clients, then there should be distinct differences between wills made by different notaries. In fact, different notaries should account for disparities in charitable giving. However, when each notary in the sample is included among the independent variables, almost every notary is, unlike several of the other variables, insignificant.[20] Whoever or whatever prompted the Grenoblois to make religious bequests, it was not his notary.

On the other hand, the testator's state of health at the time he dictated his will may well have had some effect upon his decision to make religious bequests. The testator who knew death to be near, who was, as the wills tell us, "rotten with corporal sickness and lying on his deathbed," might have been more inclined than his healthy neighbor to think of God and the fate of his immortal soul. Such was not, however, the case in Grenoble, for when the testator's health is included among the independent variables in the regression equation, it is insignificant.[21] The healthy testator was just as likely as the sick one to make religious bequests.

If the testator's own health had no influence upon his religiosity, then perhaps the general demographic conditions surrounding him at the time he made his will did. One would expect a great catastrophe like a visitation of the plague to turn men's minds to God; indeed, in Marseille the plague of 1720 produced a sudden, dramatic upsurge in testamentary bequests. But the worst demographic disaster to strike seventeenth-century Grenoble, the bubonic plague of 1629, unleashed no such flood of alms (table 3). The Grenoblois faced this disaster with stoic calm and reacted, not with heightened piety, but with their usual indifference. Demographic accidents did not alter long-term conditions; they simply accentuated them.

If we can quickly dismiss the possibility that demographic circumstances affected religious giving, it is not so easy to deal with another possible source of distortion—attitudes toward death. Obviously, a testator's view of death and the afterlife, and the importance he placed upon his demise and the fate of his soul, affected the contents of his will. These views had a particularly important effect upon seventeenth-century testators' religious bequests, for fully 75 percent of these legacies were for masses, that is, services to be said for the redemption of the testator's soul

TABLE 3

PERCENTAGE OF TESTATORS WHO MADE PIOUS BEQUESTS

Decade	Nobles	Magi-strates	Basoche	Bour-geois	Merchants	Other	Total
1620–1629	44	86	47	38	21	21	30
	(9)	(7)	(34)	(13)	(29)	(87)	(179)
1630–1639	58	92	34	25	28	16	29
	(12)	(12)	(41)	(8)	(25)	(100)	(198)
1640–1649	69	88	42	43	34	35	44
	(29)	(24)	(33)	(14)	(32)	(138)	(270)
1650–1659	73	86	51	50	37	22	41
	(26)	(29)	(39)	(18)	(38)	(124)	(274)
1660–1669	67	97	86	81	57	37	64
	(46)	(34)	(35)	(16)	(23)	(78)	(232)
1670–1679	80	85	70	68	52	41	63
	(44)	(39)	(56)	(26)	(21)	(80)	(265)
1680–1689	72	85	69	61	69	35	62
	(46)	(39)	(49)	(36)	(29)	(55)	(254)
1690–1699	62	81	68	75	66	49	65
	(34)	(32)	(59)	(32)	(32)	(49)	(238)
1700–1709	70	81	71	75	78	58	70
	(33)	(27)	(69)	(20)	(46)	(77)	(272)
1710–1719	73	81	77	68	60	50	67
	(33)	(36)	(47)	(25)	(55)	(89)	(285)
1720–1729	75	90	83	100	74	68	76
	(41)	(40)	(66)	(3)	(58)	(97)	(305)
	70	86	65	63	55	39	57
	(353)	(319)	(528)	(210)	(388)	(974)	(2,272)

Note: Testators for whom no occupation is given and soldiers and peasants have been omitted from this table. The figures in parentheses are the absolute numbers of testators in each category.

and the reduction of its stay in purgatory. These bequests, therefore, indicate a belief in purgatory, and it could be argued that they reveal very little else. But such a narrow view fails to appreciate the true meaning of these legacies, for it fails to take into account the context in which they were made. When a testator left money for masses, he asserted, in the face of Protestantism, his own belief in the intercessory powers of the Church and the efficacy of both the mass and the clergy who administered it. These beliefs were central to post-Tridentine Catholicism, and if they are a part of a certain view of death, they also lie at the heart of a certain kind of piety. As Daniel Roche and Robert Chartier have revealed in their studies of the *artes moriendi*, the pious books which enjoined the faithful to live in the fear of death and prepare themselves well in advance for it, a way of death was, for seventeenth-century Catholics, also a way of life.[22]

When properly appreciated, testamentary bequests do tell us about the dissemination of post-Tridentine Catholicism, and it comes as no surprise that the literate were among the first supporters of this new spirituality. Resurgent Catholicism used the written word to spread its doctrines, and the literate were those able and apparently most willing to embrace the message. In this regard, the Catholic Reformation did not differ from its Protestant rival, but the two confessions part company when one considers where the Counter Reformation first took hold. As the regression tables show, urban and rural Dauphinois were equally likely to make religious bequests, and the Counter Reformation triumphed simultaneously in both city and country (table 4). This pattern of dissemination sets the Counter Reformation apart from all the other spiritual revivals of the medieval and early modern periods and points to two important, if not unique, characteristics of the movement: first, that the city was just as heathen as the countryside; second, that the Counter Reformation, in Dauphiné at least, did not constitute the triumph of the city over the country. A few historians have been tempted to regard early modern cultural movements, like the suppression of witch beliefs and the extension of Reformed Catholicism, as the imposition by the city of urbane, rational, and orderly values upon a fundamentally irrational and disorderly countryside.[23] Certainly, conflict between town and country existed in seventeenth-century Dauphiné, but it did not pervade the Counter Reformation. The values and beliefs promoted by resurgent Catholicism were rational and orderly, but they were the property, not of a place, as if that were possible, but of individuals, of a particular social group.

In Dauphiné, that group was the magistracy. The judges of the sovereign courts were the earliest and most faithful converts to the new spirituality. Their fidelity was manifested in a rate of religious giving which, from the very beginning of the period, rarely fell below 85 percent and often exceeded that figure (table 3). Not content to be mere believers, the magistrates became ardent apostles, working tirelessly and with only token assistance from the ecclesiastical authorities to spread the new spirituality. For more than fifty years before the arrival of the reforming bishop, Etienne Le Camus, the magistrates alone preached the new doctrine, and their crucial role in the formation of Grenoble Catholicism requires that we scrutinize more closely the spirituality revealed in their religious bequests.

TABLE 4

PERCENTAGE OF TESTATORS MAKING PIOUS BEQUESTS:
SELECTED REGRESSION RESULTS

Variables	Coefficients	t-Statistic
Date	0.02	12.24
Nobles	0.302	10.53
Magistrates	0.417	12.80
Basoche	0.243	9.16
Bourgeois	0.243	7.16
Merchants	0.187	6.95
Plowmen	0.014	0.36
Domestics	0.236	4.17
Female	0.052	3.12
Literacy	0.088	4.23
Urban	−0.002	0.08

Note: Regression coefficients for the variables immigrant, family status, and sick have been omitted from this table. For an explanation of the variables, see table 1.

Most of these bequests were for masses, for the judges, like all good Catholics, pondered the fate of their eternal souls with considerable apprehension. They did eschew the perpetual masses favored by their Provençal neighbors, though such an endless stream of services guaranteed that even the most sinful of souls would eventually be released from purgatory. But they still asked for many masses, fourteen hundred on the average, and stipulated that these be sung very soon after their death. Three days was invariably the limit placed upon this furious saying of masses, and the magistrates' haste points to their inner motives. In the early modern period, common wisdom had it that divine judgment occurred within three days after death, so the magistrates' bequests were designed to affect this solemn verdict.[24] Such an obsession with judgment, rather than punishment in purgatory, seems very appropriate to the magistrates: judging, after all, was their business.

To say the masses that would secure a favorable verdict, the magistrates called upon the specialists in such matters, the "four convents," as most testators referred to them, the friars of the Recollet, Capuchin, Augustinian, and Reformed Carmelite monasteries, who made of the liturgy of the dead their particular vocation. Many magistrates also asked for masses at the Visitadine convent or at the chic house of Saint Claire, and they certainly did not ignore the collegiate church of Saint

André, near the courts, or the cathedral, Notre Dame. Here were the loci
of judicial spiritual life, for more than occasional attendance at mass
linked the magistrates to these institutions. Some judges had served
these convents as advisers, many had made retreats inside these houses,
and several had children among the religious.[25] The connections established in life were often pursued by the magistrates in death: most chose
to be buried in Saint André or Notre Dame, either in an ancestral crypt
or near a favorite chapel.

Magistrates almost always bequeathed some money to the institutions
where they were to be interred, and occasionally they noted that these
legacies were to serve as a "burial fee," that is, compensation for funeral
expenses. These legacies raise the suspicion that many religious bequests
merely served to satisfy the seventeenth-century appetite for lavish funerals and that they were therefore actually secular in intent. Such
pseudo-religious bequests are easily discernible and few in number, for
the magistrates drew a clear distinction between bequests for masses and
bequests for funeral display, and they had nothing but disdain for the
latter. Like the counselor Jullien who instructed his heirs to suppress "all
superfluous funeral expenses which do my soul no good and have masses
said instead," the magistrates abhorred the "banks of candles surrounding the coffin," the "draperies and coats of arms which adorn the bier,"
the "swarms of priests," the "hoards of paupers," and especially the "incessant clanging of bells" which made for an impressive funeral.[26] They
branded such accouterments "worldly vanities," "superfluities," "ostentatious," "ridiculous," and "useless," and commanded their heirs to bury
them with "simplicity" and spend the money on masses. Sometimes one
must take these modest requests with a grain of salt: in one breath a testator would condemn all "funeral pomp" and then in the next ask that
twenty-four paupers dressed in black and bearing his family arms accompany his body to its grave.[27] But on the whole, the magistrates were quite
sincere and serious in their requests for "simplicity." Several first presidents asked that the eulogy which always accompanied the burial of such
a lofty magistrate be suppressed, many counselors requested that only
one priest attend their funeral, and at least one member of a judicial family ordered that he be buried in a cemetery "without a headstone or any
other mark of distinction just like the most impoverished inhabitant of
this town."[28]

This "ostentatious asceticism," as Pierre Chaunu has called it, tended
to flourish in the years between 1660 and 1710, only to disappear thereafter.[29] Testators may have ceased asking for "simple" funerals because bur-

ial practices on the whole became simpler. But the decline in bequests for masses among the magistrates which occurred at precisely the same time argues that something more was at work here. The decline was not enormous, from 90 percent in the 1660s to 75 percent at the beginning of the eighteenth century, nor did it persist for long. But it demands explanation because it coincided with an increase in bequests for masses among the rest of the population.[30] Coming as it did in the aftermath of the revocation, the magistrates' sudden disinterest in bequests for masses may have been produced by the sudden appearance of "new converts" in the sample. One would assume that these crypto-Protestants would eschew masses as ineffective or even offensive, and such was, in fact, the case with those formerly Protestant magistrates whom we can identify. But these "new converts" account for only five wills in the sample, and when they are removed, the decline in masses persists.[31] Of course, some "new converts" could have escaped notice, for few risked proclaiming their Protestantism, but they would not necessarily produce a decline in bequests for masses. Some, like Anne de la Gache, widow of a magistrate, thanked God for their conversion, whether sincerely or not, and then lavished huge sums of money on masses for the salvation of their souls.[32]

This decrease in bequests for masses must indicate a real change in the magistrates' sensibility, perhaps even a decline in piety. Were they the forerunners of the Enlightenment, the harbingers of dechristianization, or the vanguard of a "crisis of the European consciousness"? It seems not, for if we turn from bequests for masses alone to legacies for any spiritual purpose, the decline is not so great.[33] A shift, not a decline, in piety occurred, for those who abandoned the convents usually turned to other religious institutions, to the priests' seminary, to the Jesuit college, or to rural parish churches. Some shifted their patronage to charitable institutions which had a religious mission, like the Hospital General or the Propagation of the Faith, and as a consequence, charitable donations in this period exceeded, for the first time, bequests for masses.[34] Still, other magistrates made no religious bequests at all in their wills, but this does not mean that they were freethinkers or libertines: the devout baron de Valbonnays made only charitable gifts in his will, and a man as pious as Monsieur Canel failed to leave money for masses.[35] Perhaps most revealing are those magistrates who indicated in their wills that they had already seen to their "alms" and "prayers." For the second generation of devout Grenoblois salvation apparently no longer waited upon death, nor redemption on the prayers of friars.[36]

It is tempting to call this new sensibility "Jansenist," but the term cannot be applied with anything approaching rigor.[37] Once one leaves the well-documented realms of the Parisian elite, it is virtually impossible to determine just who was Jansenist. Rumor maintained that Grenoble's sovereign courts were infected with this heresy, but since contemporaries tended to brand as Jansenist anyone even remotely suspected of heterodoxy, their testimony must be taken with a grain of salt.[38] Moreover, wills provide only sparse and ambiguous evidence of Jansenism. A gift to the Oratorians might be construed as proof of Jansenism, and some magistrates made such bequests. But as reputedly Jansenist a judge as Monsieur Canel ignored the Oratorians in his will, and many of the magistrates who displayed the very sensibility we have described made substantial bequests to the Jansenists' archenemy, the Jesuits. What we are dealing with here is something much more general, but also more pervasive than Jansenism, and we should not, as so many historians have done, abuse the term. Suffice it to say that in the late seventeenth and early eighteenth centuries, Grenoble's magistrates embraced a new spirituality, which was still Christian and still Catholic, but more rigorous and austere than before.

Those who came closest to adopting the magistrates' new sensibility were the lawyers, notaries, and *huissiers,* who rubbed shoulders with them at the sovereign court. This group tended to mimic its social superiors' religious style, and by 1690 many lawyers were abandoning bequests for masses in favor of other religious legacies. In addition, the *basoche* was an early and enthusiastic convert to post-Tridentine Catholicism: by 1660 over 80 percent of the lawyers and notaries were making bequests for spiritual purposes in their wills. A roughly similar pattern of religiosity characterized Grenoble's bourgeois and merchants. These groups declined to follow the magistrates and lawyers into the new sensibility which emerged after 1670, but they did not hesitate to embrace Counter Reformation Catholicism around mid-century, at a time when the magistrates were still this spirituality's primary proponents (table 3).

One would expect the nobles to share the sensibility of their cousins at the sovereign courts, but such was not in fact the case. Few nobles arranged for prayers before death, and only one asked to be buried with simplicity. Austerity held no appeal for the nobility, who positively craved the banks of candles, hordes of paupers, and scores of priests that made for an elaborate funeral. One noble went so far as to request that thirty pounds of candles adorn his bier, and another commanded his heirs to spend no less than 1,400 livres on his funeral.[39] But more than a certain fondness for display separated the nobles from their cousins the judges. The nobles had a surprisingly low rate of religious giving, only 44 percent in the 1620s as opposed to 86 percent among the magistrates, and impiety was even more widespread among the rural nobility (table 3).

Not one of the rural nobles in our sample made bequests for spiritual purposes in the 1620s, and the rate had risen to only 33 percent by 1669.[40] As we saw in our discussion of the nobles' charitable habits, a cultural gulf separated the country gentlemen from the magistrates, and religion was not the only dissimilarity. The rural nobility had a surprisingly high rate of illiteracy, and country gentlemen were wont, as their wills reveal, to beget illegitimate children.[41] Only slowly did this situation change. It was not until 1700 that the country nobility achieved a rate of religious giving—60 percent—commensurate with its wealth and status. At the same time, illiteracy tended to diminish, particularly among women, and illegitimacy disappeared. The rural gentlemen either ceased fathering bastards, or suddenly became too ashamed to recognize them in their wills. In any event, a new set of values, as well as a new kind of belief, finally got hold of the rural nobles.[42]

Another sort of Dauphinois, the working men and women of Grenoble, experienced an even more dramatic conversion. Here it was not the first wave of the Counter Reformation, the early spiritual revival led by the magistrates, that prevailed. For almost the entire seventeenth century, the common people of Grenoble remained stubbornly indifferent to the missionary efforts of the magistrates. The rate of religious giving among master artisans rarely exceeded 40 percent, and the rate was even lower among journeymen and day laborers (table 5). No other Grenoblois were so little disposed to consider the fate of their immortal souls, and these figures are deceptively high. Just a small percentage of Grenoble's working people made wills, and those that did so were probably older, more literate, and more prosperous than the general working population. They were, therefore, more likely to make religious bequests than the intestate majority. Consequently, only the top of the iceberg is revealed by these figures; beneath lies impiety or indifference or a form of religiosity foreign to post-Tridentine Catholicism. It would be interesting to know which. Were the Grenoblois thoroughgoing materialists, like Carlo Ginzburg's Menocchio? Or old-fashioned, Rabelaisian Catholics like Natalie Davis' Lyonnais? Or were they, after the horrors of the Wars of Religion, just hostile and indifferent to all kinds of religion? For lack of evidence, we cannot say.

What we can analyze and describe with considerable precision is the timing of the working people's conversion to post-Tridentine Catholicism. The elite of the working world, the master artisans, led the way. Gradually,

TABLE 5

PERCENTAGE OF TESTATORS WHO MADE PIOUS BEQUESTS

Decade	Master Artisans	Workers	Plowmen	Domestics
1620–1629	26	17	13	25
	(35)	(40)	(8)	(4)
1630–1639	25	10	18	33
	(28)	(58)	(11)	(3)
1640–1649	34	29	36	73
	(38)	(75)	(14)	(11)
1650–1659	30	18	9	60
	(27)	(81)	(11)	(5)
1660–1669	48	،16	43	75
	(31)	(32)	(7)	(8)
1670–1679	62	25	25	57
	(29)	(24)	(20)	(7)
1680–1689	39	21	17	57
	(28)	(14)	(6)	(7)
1690–1699	45	25	25	50
	(33)	(10)	(4)	(2)
1700–1709	65	53	44	100
	(26)	(30)	(16)	(5)
1710–1719	60	56	52	50
	(35)	(25)	(21)	(8)
1720–1729	77	59	68	71
	(31)	(37)	(22)	(7)
	46	29	37	63
	(341)	(426)	(140)	(67)

Note: The figures in parentheses are the absolute numbers of testators in each category.

between 1620 and 1669, their rate of religious giving grew and then attained, in the 1670s, 62 percent (table 5). Thereafter a decline occurred, produced, most likely, by an influx of "new converts" into the sample in the wake of the revocation of the Edict of Nantes.[43] By 1700 the rate of religious giving had again attained 62 percent, and then rose in the 1730s to reach 77 percent. Here was one of the most spectacular conversions worked by the Counter Reformation, but the transformation of the journeymen and day laborers was equally impressive because it was more abrupt and unforeseen. For most of the seventeenth century, barely 30 percent—and sometimes fewer—of these workers saw to the fate of their immortal souls in their wills (table 5). Then suddenly, after 1700, the rate of religious giving jumped to over 55 percent. These were, of necessity, small bequests, no more than 10 livres on the average, but they are still highly significant. They

show that the pious elite's efforts bore fruit, that the majority of Grenoblois experienced some kind of conversion.

They did not, however, passively swallow the religion fed them by the
judicial and ecclesiastical elite. Some historians of popular religion and of
what the French call *mentalités* have unwittingly adopted the categories
used by contemporary elites and labeled popular spirituality either pious
or impious, orthodox or heterodox. On the whole, the impious have been
better served than the pious, for once a group gives signs of adherence to
authority, they are assumed to be "devout" and quickly dismissed. Popular spirituality was not, however, an exact reflection of elite beliefs, and
even a movement as determined as the Counter Reformation to impose
orthodoxy could not prevent the working people from altering Catholicism and shaping it to suit their needs and values. The master artisans of
Grenoble, for instance, diverged from the elite model in that they had a
marked preference for corporate forms of devotion, for confraternities in
particular. The more literate and prosperous masters, like the apothecaries and master bakers, drifted toward the Jesuit confraternities, the Congregations of the Bourgeois or of the Artisans which were, to a certain
degree, segregated according to income and status. The humbler master
cobblers and carpenters preferred the more democratic Penitents,
whether of Saint Laurent or Confalon. But all favored institutions that
tended to supplement or replicate the common spiritual life they knew
within their own guilds.[44]

The parish clergy were not, despite one's expectations, the principal
beneficiaries of the master artisans' generosity. The literature on the lower
clergy of the old regime usually stresses the close, even intimate relationship between the curé and his parishioners. In Grenoble, however, even
after the reform of the lower clergy by Bishop Le Camus, journeymen and
day laborers showed little inclination to remember the curé in their
wills.[45] The priest of Saint Jean–Saint Joseph was an exception, but his
popularity stemmed not from his personal qualities but from the location
of his church: Saint Jean–Saint Joseph was the only religious institution in
the populous quarter of the Granges where many working people lived.
Similarly, the Recollets received more bequests from laboring men and
women than any other regular house, but they too monopolized religious
life in a poor quarter, the Très Cloîtres, where many textile workers made
their homes.

The Recollets also offered a special kind of devotion—a confraternity. The journeymen and day laborers of Grenoble shared with the
master artisans a taste for communal forms of devotion, and most of

their bequests went to institutions like the Penitents of Saint Laurent, the Congregations of the Artisans or the Apprentices run by the Jesuits, or the mixed Rosary sodality sponsored by the Dominicans. This predilection for the confraternities reveals at once both the extent and the limits of the working people's acceptance of orthodox, elite Catholicism. While these bequests to confraternities confirm the workers' belief in certain rituals central to post-Tridentine Catholicism, they also reveal a pervasive, if vague, distrust of the clergymen who performed these rituals. Unlike any other group in the city, the working people did not entrust their posthumous services to a priest alone. They asked that their confraternal brothers, their peers, assist at their masses and lend their prayers to those of the clergy.

One group within the world of work stands apart from this tendency, indeed from all the impulses that characterized the laboring people of Grenoble—the domestics. Though they shared with the day laborers a precarious income (they were not paid for years on end) and a high rate of illiteracy, they moved in a separate sphere and developed a different spirituality. From the beginning of the seventeenth century to its end, the domestics were always more likely than their peers to make religious bequests, and they tended to favor prestigious institutions like the chic convent of Saint Claire (table 5). Culturally, the domestics had more in common with their employers than with their peers. The resemblance is even more striking when the domestics who served magistrates and nobles are separated from those who worked for commoner folk. The magistrates' servants had significantly higher rates of religious giving, which indicates that they absorbed with remarkable speed and thoroughness their employers' values.[46] Isolated from other working people, the domestics were something of an anomaly, proof once again that culture, not just income, determined testamentary bequests.

The best way to appreciate the influence of culture on the domestics is to compare their religiosity with that of the milieu from which they sprang, the milieu of the country *laboureurs,* or plowmen.[47] These relatively well-off peasants certainly did not provide their servant daughters with the piety we have noted: the plowmen, like the working people of Grenoble, were stubbornly indifferent to the Counter Reformation throughout most of the seventeenth century (table 5). Then suddenly after 1700, the plowmen, like the common city dwellers, began to make religious bequests in substantial numbers. Apparently, a massive conversion, of which we can only glimpse the outlines, occurred in rural Dauphiné, for the plowmen suddenly began to ask the parish priest to say masses for them and even more frequently requested that the local confraternity—a Holy Sacrament, Rosary, or Holy Spirit sodality—pray for the redemption of their souls.

The preference of many Dauphinois for confraternities and communal forms of devotion raises a general question about the nature of early modern Catholicism. Since Weber, historians have assumed that Catholicism perpetuated an archaic, medieval corporate ideal and frustrated the development of a more individualistic and therefore more "modern" social ethic. Catholicism was at odds with individualism and hence with the modern world. Ironically, testamentary bequests, which must be accounted among the quainter manifestations of Catholicism, suggest that the social consequences of post-Tridentine spirituality were not so simple or clear-cut. After all, when a testator left money for masses to be said for the good of his soul, he acted in a very self-seeking manner. He deprived those nearest to him, his family, of money that would otherwise be theirs, in order to promote his own personal good. This was individualism of the most radical sort. The Catholic testator tried with his religious bequests to do the impossible: he tried to take "it" with him.

But he also remembered to leave some of "it" behind, to provide not just for his own salvation, but for that of the Christian community as a whole. If Catholicism has been taxed for a lack of individualism, it has also received the opposite charge: it has been branded too selfish and too self-serving. Were bequests for masses the only kinds of spiritual legacies made by the Grenoblois, the charge would be justified. But these devout Catholics also left money for the construction of churches, the building of a seminary, and the establishing of primary schools. In other words, the Grenoblois sought to save, not just their own souls, but those of others as well. Bequests of this sort never outnumbered legacies for masses, but they did constitute one-third of religious gifts at the beginning of the period, when the magistrates virtually monopolized religious giving. Thereafter, they tended to decline as other social groups entered the pool of benefactors, but rose again after 1700 to constitute almost a quarter of all religious bequests.[48]

Among the most popular of such bequests were those that sought to rebuild and embellish the Church in a very literal sense. Gifts for the "ornamentation" of sanctuaries, that is, the purchasing of vestments, candles, and ciboria, were made by Grenoblois of all social groups. Both lofty magistrates, who could lavish thousands of livres on the parishes in their estates, and poor seamstresses, who had only the lace from their skirts to give, tried to increase the earthly splendor of the Church.[49] Some Grenoblois also chose to enhance its more transcendent glory, for they provided money for silver chalices and tabernacles so that the miracle of the Host could be celebrated with dignity and grandeur. This preoccupation with the Eucharist sprang from the very heart of post-Tridentine Catholicism. The Grenoble benefactors who professed "a very special respect and affection for the Very Holy Sacrament" partook of the "Christocentrism" and the emphasis on the sacraments which distinguished seventeenth-century French Catholicism from its medieval predecessors.[50]

The spirit of the Counter Reformation also pervaded another sort of bequest. The Catholic reformers sought to rebuild the church in Dauphiné, and they had to do so in a material way. Many parish churches had been allowed to fall into ruin, and a good many benefactors left funds for their repair. Usually these churches were rural churches, but the Grenoble parish of Saint Jean–Saint Joseph, which had been sacked during the Wars of Religion, also needed and received such legacies. Only rarely did the testator specify the exact use to which his legacy would be put; apparently, the damage to the church in question would be obvious. But one magistrate, the counselor Garnier, stipulated that his bequest be used "to close the cemetery wall so that neither man nor beast could profane such a holy place."[51] This bequest reveals that legacies for repairs had a moral as well as a material intention. The counselor Garnier sought to rebuild the Church, but he also wanted to change the parishioners' behavior, to force them to respect the separation of sacred and secular and adopt new attitudes and habits.

This goal was made explicit in another form of bequest: the endowment, usually established by magistrates, to support annual missions in rural areas. These revival-like events took place at Lent, or at other times when the weather was good, and consisted of two weeks of preaching by Capuchin monks or the religious of some other order. The goal was to awaken the parishioners' dormant faith and also to instruct the young. Many testators asked that the missionaries catechize the young or check on the curé's efforts in this regard.[52] Apparently, the shaping of young minds was extremely important to the Grenoblois, for quite a few legacies were for educational purposes. The Jesuit *collège* received many bequests, but it was primary education that truly interested the Grenoblois. Many benefactors, especially magistrates, left money for the establishing of primary schools for boys, and their wives supplemented their efforts by founding schools for girls.[53]

Rural areas were the principal recipients of these legacies for schools, but the Grenoblois did not ignore city children. The charity schools established by the Christian Brothers in Grenoble during the first half of the eighteenth century received many bequests, as did the older hospice of the Congregation for the Propagation of the Faith. The latter institution blended primary instruction with considerable amounts of religious indoctrination, and the benefactors approved of the mixture. Above all else, they wanted their students to learn, in the words of the president de la Croix de Chevrières, "to fear God," but that does not mean that they disparaged or disapproved of secular instruction. On the contrary, some benefactors specified that their schools must teach basic reading and writing, for these Grenoblois knew, as did the Catholic reformers, that literacy provided access to God's word.[54] In addition, the benefactors occasionally included vocational instruction in their legacies: to orphans raised at the Hospital General, they provided funds for apprenticeships in whatever trade the directors deemed appropriate.[55]

Such vocational bequests reveal not just the essentially militant nature of Catholic charity; they also point to its considerable social utility. Even religious legacies, the most otherworldly of all bequests, sought to glorify God by changing the moral and material conditions of this world. The charge of social uselessness, so often leveled against Catholicism, fails to appreciate just what every Grenoble benefactor knew: that the path to Heaven begins in this world, and so too does the work of the truly devout. Of course, the traditional criticism of Catholicism springs from an unflattering comparison with its rival, Protestantism. In recent years, however, interpretations of each confession have shifted radically, so that the contrast between Protestantism and Catholicism, as well as our view of each separately, is no longer so sharp. Pierre Chaunu and Jean Delumeau have reshaped our notions about the Counter Reformation, and Natalie Davis and Philip Benedict have recently provided us with whole new ways of thinking about the Protestant Reformation.[56] The time seems ripe to reconsider the similarities and the differences between the two confessions and to recast our interpretations of their respective social policies.

PROTESTANT AND CATHOLIC TESTAMENTARY BEQUESTS

Fortunately, Grenoble provides the material for such a comparison, for the city had, as we have seen, a small but stubborn Protestant minority. Conflict between the two confessions forced the Reformed community to develop its own separate and distinct system of poor relief. In principle, the Hospital General welcomed the sick and impoverished of all faiths, but by 1660 it had become something less than hospitable toward the Protestants.[57] The Reformed community was then thrown back on its own resources. It would be interesting, of course, to know just how it managed and administered the relief of its poor. Unfortunately, the relevant documents disappeared, along with the rest of the Consistory's papers, shortly after they were deposited at the Parlement in 1685. Only a catalog of these mysterious documents remains, but we can glean some information from it.[58] Apparently, the Consistory, like the Hospital General, frequently found itself embroiled in lengthy litigation, for most of the vanished documents were court records. The Consistory, which managed poor relief, maintained a *procureur des pauvres* to represent the interests of the poor and employed a *receveur des pauvres* to collect and disburse funds. And where did these funds come from? From the bequests that Protestant Grenoblois, like their Catholic neighbors, included in their last wills and testaments.

These Protestant wills are available and easily accessible. Despite their precarious situation, Protestants, like Catholics, went to a notary when they wanted to make a last will and testament. They usually chose a Protestant, either maître Blanc or maître Patras, but like their Catholic colleagues, these notaries kept registers, which have now made their way to the Departmental Archives. In addition, Protestants and Catholics had similar notarial habits. Wealthy Protestants, like prosperous Catholics, were more likely than their more unfortunate coreligionaries to visit the notary, and Protestant men were more apt than women to make a will. In fact, the percentage of men and women making wills was identical in the Catholic and Protestant samples, which suggests that a valid basis for comparison does indeed exist (table 6). Of course, not all social groups were equally represented in the two samples, but these differences are as informative as they are expected. They allow us, as nothing else does, to determine the social composition of seventeenth-century Grenoble Protestantism.

It is the enduring contours of an embattled community, not the initial social appeal of Protestantism, that is revealed by a comparison of Protestant and Catholic seventeenth-century wills. Royal policy and resurgent Catholicism have left their mark. The most underrepresented group in the Protestant sample—the magistrates—was also the most vulnerable to the king's policy of retracting his favors and excluding Protestants from office (table 6). The nobles, on the other hand, had little to gain from the king and therefore not much to lose. In Dauphiné as in the rest of southern France, the lesser country nobility, the *hobereaux* like Lesdiguières, con-

TABLE 6

COMPOSITION OF PROTESTANT AND CATHOLIC SAMPLES

Social Group	Protestant (%)	Catholic (%)	t-Statistic
Nobles	11.7 (39)	11.5	
Magistrates	3.9 (13)	10.4	10.62
Basoche	18.8 (63)	17.2	
Bourgeois	4.5 (15)	6.9	2.02
Merchants	20.1 (67)	12.6	3.55
Master artisans	21.3 (71)	11.1	4.44
Plowmen	1.2 (4)	4.6	5.22
Workers (artisans and day laborers)	5.1 (17)	13.8	7.15
Domestics	0.6 (2)	2.1	3.67
Soldiers	6.0 (20)	3.8	
Unknown	6.8 (23)	6.0	
	100.0 (334)		
Gender			
Male	61.4 (205)	61.0	
Female	38.6 (129)	39.0	
	100.0 (334)		

Note: The t-statistic measures the significance of the difference between Protestant and Catholic percentages. If the t-statistic is larger than 1.96, there is significant difference. The figures in parentheses are the absolute numbers of testators in each category.

stituted first the vanguard and then the mainstay of the Protestant movement. Nor should the contribution of their tenants, the peasantry, be underestimated. In this particular sample, peasants are distinctly underrepresented, but this relative absence reflects, not a loss of faith, but the distance that separated Grenoble from the Protestant strongholds of Dauphiné. These peasants did not come to Grenoble to make their wills, but they were still, as Bishop Le Camus remarked, his greatest "enemies" in Dauphiné.[59]

The relative absence of other groups from the Protestant sample is more revealing of the history of the Dauphinois Reform. Artisans constitute only a tiny portion of the Protestant sample, and unskilled day laborers are altogether absent (table 6). Of course, one would expect these low-income groups to be underrepresented in any sample of wills, for whether Catholic, Protestant, or indifferent, the laboring poor were always less likely than their social superiors to make a testament. But if one compares the Protestant and Catholic data sets, one finds that the laborers are inordinately and disproportionately scarce in the Protestant sample (table 6). Conversely, the workers' employers, the master artisans and merchants, constituted the two largest groups in the Protestant sample, and they dominate there to a degree they do not in the Catholic data set. These discrepancies suggest that the members of certain kinds of professions remained more faithful to the Reformation than did those of others, that the independent, self-employed merchants and master artisans found it easier than the dependent wage laborers to withstand the pressures brought to bear by the Catholic majority.

This impression is borne out if we scrutinize the artisans and master artisans more closely. Among the Protestants, representatives of the most exclusive professions, those that demanded the greatest skill and conferred the most wealth and independence, far outnumber the practitioners of lowlier trades: master apothecaries, surgeons, physicians, clockmakers, and goldsmiths predominate, while textile workers, the numerous but lowly flax-combers and -spinners, whose income and situation barely distinguished them from common wage laborers, appear hardly at all in the Protestant sample.[60] Skill, training, and independence apparently prevented apostasy, and this principle is underscored by the relative rarity among Protestants of domestics (table 6). These most dependent of workers probably shared with their Catholic counterparts an uncanny ability to absorb the values of their employers. Certainly, a young servant girl fresh from the countryside and isolated from the Protestant community was ill equipped to withstand the evangelizing efforts of her employers or of devout groups like the Propagation of the Faith. Perhaps many rural Protestant families were reluctant to thrust their children into such a situation and either refused to send them to Grenoble or placed them in the rare Protestant home. These fears would account for the rarity of Protestant domestics, but they also confirm our suspicions: the dependence inherent in domestic service could lead to apostasy, and it was therefore to be avoided at all costs.

If domestics were relatively underrepresented among Protestants, workers in the leather trades, especially glove-makers, were surprisingly prominent.[61] Glove making was a relatively new and unestablished profession in seventeenth-century Grenoble, but it was not the novelty of their trade that accounted for the glove-makers' Protestantism.[62] Rather it was their origins, for most came to Grenoble from Grasse, a glove-making center and Protestant stronghold. These workers brought their Protestantism with them to Grenoble; so too did many other members of the Reformed community, for over 50 percent of the Protestant testators claimed to have been born in other communities.[63] This high rate of migration, almost double that among Catholic testators, reflects, to a certain extent, the enduring vitality of Protestantism in rural Dauphiné and southeastern France. But it also points to the extreme mobility of the Protestant community, for 29 percent of the Protestant testators, as opposed to 17 percent of the Catholics, claimed, when they made their wills, to be residents of parishes outside Grenoble.[64] These were not peasants or vagabond laborers, but respectable merchants, artisans, or even nobles, who made their homes in the villages of the Trièves, the towns of Die and Romans, and even the far-flung cities of Provence and Switzerland. When death surprised them, they were in Grenoble, which explains why we have their wills. We can only guess how widely they had traveled before landing in the town. Perhaps royal persecution fed the Protestants' wanderlust, or maybe their espousal of skilled, highly mobile trades rendered them more likely than Catholics to take to the road. In any event, the Protestant community in Grenoble was made up—and not just at its fringes—of a shifting, well-traveled population.

Considering the mobility of the Protestant population in Grenoble, one would expect the Consistory to have had difficulty in creating a sense of Christian community and an attachment to local institutions and interests. But if the incidence of testamentary bequests to the Protestant poor is any indication, such was not in fact the case. In the 1620s, 70 percent of the wills made by Grenoble Protestants contained bequests of varying sizes to the Reformed poor (table 7). This rate did tend to decline, especially after the 1660s when royal persecution sapped the Protestant community of its solidarity and strength. But on the whole, the Protes-

TABLE 7

PERCENTAGE OF PROTESTANTS WHO GAVE TO THE POOR

Decade	Nobles & Magistrates	Basoche	Bour- geois	Merchants	Workers & Artisans	Unknown	Total
1620–1629	75	57	75	78	75	50	72
	(4)	(7)	(4)	(9)	(20)	(2)	(46)
1630–1639	100	100		100	58	33	72
	(3)	(2)	(0)	(5)	(12)	(3)	(25)
1640–1649	63	56	100	79	50	60	61
	(8)	(9)	(2)	(14)	(22)	(5)	(60)
1650–1659	63	75		59	70	20	63
	(16)	(20)	(0)	(17)	(20)	(5)	(78)
1660–1669	44	70	83	60	17	33	49
	(9)	(10)	(6)	(10)	(12)	(6)	(53)
1670–1679	38	42	33	60	63	100	53
	(8)	(12)	(3)	(10)	(19)	(2)	(54)
1680–1689	25	0		0	60		29
	(4)	(3)	(0)	(2)	(5)	(0)	(14)
	56	60	73	67	58	43	59
	(52)	(63)	(15)	(67)	(110)	(23)	(330)

Note: Peasants have been omitted from the table. The figures in parentheses are the absolute numbers of testators in each category.

tants' rate of charitable giving was astonishingly high: 59 percent as compared with a mere 39 percent rate of beneficence among Catholics during the same years.

These figures suggest that in the Protestant community charitable giving was not, as among Catholics, limited to the elite but spread up and down the social scale. Regression tables for Protestant giving confirm this suspicion. Here, no gulf separates noble from commoner, lawyers from magistrates. Only one group—the merchants—was more likely than other Protestants to make charitable bequests, and the difference is relatively small and only barely significant (table 8). The average size of these bequests did vary from one social group to another, and the elite, the magistrates and nobles, tended to be more generous than their social inferiors. But here too the differences are only slight by comparison with the enormous disparities that characterized the size of Catholic bequests. Nor did those traditionally disadvantaged groups—women and rural folk— prove less apt to remember the poor in their wills. Men and women were equally generous in their bequests, and country Protestants enjoyed a slight advantage over their city cousins. On the whole, all Protestants,

TABLE 8

PERCENTAGE OF PROTESTANTS MAKING CHARITABLE BEQUESTS:
SELECTED REGRESSION RESULTS

Variable	Coefficient	t-Statistic
Date	−0.003	2.38
Nobles & Magistrates	0.050	0.58
Basoche	0.078	0.98
Bourgeois	0.219	1.68
Merchants	0.162	2.31
Urban	−0.217	2.58
Female	0.044	0.76
Pious giving	−0.321	5.08

Amount of Protestant Gifts to the Poor:
Regression Results

Variable	Coefficient	t-Statistic
Date	−0.186	1.05
Nobles & Magistrates	29.61	3.01
Basoche	7.29	0.82
Bourgeois	2.29	0.15
Merchants	3.25	0.41
Urban	−12.88	1.95
Female	1.66	0.25
Pious giving	0.03	2.12

Note: Regression coefficients for the variables literacy and family status as well as the constant have been omitted. For an explanation of these variables, see table 1.

whatever their origin, gender, or place of residence, no matter how rich or poor, remembered to provide for the disadvantaged in their community.

Because everyone in the Reformed community made charitable bequests, Protestantism appears to have been very successful in stimulating the social conscience, more successful than its Catholic rival. But every Protestant also gave about the same amount, which suggests that no one gave too much. In fact, the average Protestant donation totaled 46 livres, whereas the average Catholic bequest for charitable purposes amounted to over 262 livres. A comparison of the size of gifts made by Protestants and Catholics of the same social group bears out this picture of Protestant inferiority. Only Protestant merchants exceeded their Catholic counterparts in generosity, and Reformed nobles, lawyers, and artisans lagged far behind (table 9). These differences could, of course, stem from inferior

TABLE 9

COMPARISON OF AVERAGE PROTESTANT AND CATHOLIC DONATIONS
TO CHARITY (IN LIVRES)

	Protestants	Catholics
Nobles & Magistrates	110.69	480.58
Basoche	49.66	112.27
Merchants	32.78	21.50
Master artisans	29.88	40.20
Overall average	46.34	262.57

Average Family Bequests 1620–1689

	Protestants	Catholics
Nobles	6,534	5,164
Basoche	1,222	3,668
Merchants	1,941	1,391
Master artisans	1,693	918

means, not lack of altruism. Considering the hardships experienced by Protestants, it would be surprising if they were not economically handicapped. The lack of data which plagues the study of Grenoble Protestantism as a whole makes any comparisons between Protestant and Catholic incomes difficult, and any conclusions are only tentative. Dowries, usually a good index of wealth, are not helpful here, for Protestant tended to marry Protestant, so the Reformed marriage market was separate and distinct from the Catholic marriage market. Any juxtaposition of Protestant and Catholic dowries would therefore be specious. Family bequests contained in wills provide a more solid basis for comparison, even though they are less common in Protestant wills than one would like. It seems clear from this source that, with the exception of Protestant lawyers, other members of the Reformed community—nobles, merchants, and artisans—enjoyed wealth equal to or even superior to that of their Catholic counterparts (table 9). That they were less generous with this wealth is perhaps best demonstrated by comparing the ratio of charitable bequests to all other family bequests among testators of the two confessions: whereas the ratio among Protestants never exceeded 2 percent in the whole seventeenth century, that among Catholics climbed to 4 percent at the height of the Counter Reformation.

Protestant bequests were not only smaller than Catholic legacies, they were also less varied. Aside from the Protestant poor, the only other recipient of the Protestants' altruism was their Church, the Consistory. Twenty-three percent of the Protestant testators made such bequests, and they tended to do so more frequently as the revocation of the Edict of Nantes approached and the destruction of the ministry seemed imminent (table 10). Usually these religious legacies outstripped charitable bequests in size: the average gift to the Consistory exceeded 200 livres, whereas the average bequest to the poor amounted to only 46 livres. Also, Protestant testators rarely included both kinds of bequests in their wills, opting for either one or the other. Consequently, charitable and religious giving were, as the regression tables show, negatively correlated, divorced from one another (table 8). Protestant charity, unlike Catholic altruism, was not bound to religion, which implies that quite different impulses and motives inspired it.

To define these differences precisely, we must consider not just what appears in Protestant bequests, but also what is omitted. The charitable

TABLE 10

PERCENTAGE OF PROTESTANTS WHO GAVE TO THE CONSISTORY

Decade	Nobles & Magistrates	Basoche	Bour- geois	Merchants	Workers & Artisans	Unknown	Total
1620–1629	0	29	25	11	10	0	13
	(4)	(7)	(4)	(9)	(20)	(2)	(46)
1630–1639	67	0		20	8	33	20
	(3)	(2)	(0)	(5)	(12)	(3)	(25)
1640–1649	38	22	0	21	23	0	21
	(8)	(9)	(2)	(14)	(22)	(5)	(60)
1650–1659	50	20		29	15	0	25
	(16)	(20)	(0)	(17)	(20)	(5)	(78)
1660–1669	33	20	33	50	25	17	30
	(9)	(10)	(6)	(10)	(12)	(6)	(53)
1670–1679	38	42	33	30	5	50	25
	(8)	(12)	(3)	(10)	(19)	(2)	(54)
1680–1689	50	33		0	0	0	21
	(4)	(3)	(0)	(2)	(5)	(0)	(14)
	40	25	27	27	14	13	23
	(52)	(63)	(15)	(67)	(110)	(23)	(330)

Note: Peasants have been omitted from the table. The figures in parentheses are the absolute numbers of testators in each category.

clauses in Protestant wills tended to be much shorter than those in Catholic wills: most Reformed benefactors simply assigned a sum of money to the Protestant poor and then hastily, without comment or explanation, proceeded to the division of their estates. Lacking the elaborate stipulations as to the beneficiaries of the bequest, and the complicated instructions as to its administration, these Protestant bequests seem terse, unvaried, formulaic, and stereotypical. Does this seeming impersonality indicate a deeper lack of concern for the fate of the bequest and its recipients? Perhaps, but it could also denote the Protestants' greater faith in their heirs. Isolated and persecuted, Protestants might well have retreated into their families and developed domestic ties much closer and more intimate than those of their Catholic neighbors. Such ties would have rendered complicated testamentary clauses unnecessary, but if Protestants enjoyed a warmer family life than Catholics, it is not evident in their wills.[65]

Whatever his sentiments toward his family, a Protestant testator may well have been less meticulous than his Catholic neighbors in framing his charitable bequests simply because he was less concerned about what happened after his demise. Protestant theology certainly encouraged a view of death very different from that of Catholic spirituality, for a Protestant achieved salvation through God's will alone. Nothing his heirs or anyone else did after his demise could affect Divine Judgment.[66] The kind of postmortem redemption offered to Catholics was unavailable to Protestants, but they still considered testamentary bequests appropriate and necessary, as the extremely high rate of charitable giving in Protestant wills testifies. Still, these legacies lack the urgency one senses in Catholic bequests. Protestants had little personal stake in their gifts, so they could afford to be parsimonious in both words and funds.

Of course, Protestants did not need to waste their time distributing alms to an array of hospices, asylums, and confraternities. Only the Consistory catered to their poor, and the simplicity of their bequests derives, to a certain extent, from the Protestants' forced reliance on this one institution. Still, a paucity of institutions does not explain the lack of individuality attributed by Protestant testators to the poor themselves. When Catholics sought to assist the impoverished, they approached them as prostitutes, prisoners, orphans, peasants, and so forth, never as a rather vague, disembodied mass called the "poor." Protestants, on the other hand, saw the unfortunate as an undifferentiated group whose only distinguishing feature was membership in the Protestant community. Catholics might reach outside their faith to assist the unfortunate of the rival confession, whether out of genuine altruism or crusading zeal, but Protestants never looked beyond their own community, never did more than make a quick, almost mechanical donation to the faceless "poor."

The absolute fidelity of Protestants to their "own" provides a clue to the impulses and motives behind the Protestants' maddeningly laconic charitable gifts. By limiting their alms to the Protestant poor, the Reformed testators made of a seemingly simple charitable gesture a powerful and brave affirmation of faith, for a gift to the Protestant poor confirmed, in the face of Protestant persecution, membership in and solidarity with the Reformed community. For a true believer, such a gesture would be absolutely required, which explains the Protestants' high rate of charitable giving, and it would not warrant the expenditure of vast sums of money, which accounts for the relatively small size of Protestant bequests. Nor would it prompt the testator to include elaborate stipulations in his bequest to assure the genuine relief of the poor or move him to focus on the impoverished in any specific way. The affirmation of the testator's continuing ties to the Reformed community was the principal purpose of Protestant bequests, and under the circumstances it was a courageous gesture.[67]

Though persecution certainly shaped the altruism of Grenoble's Protestants, it did not alter the assumptions that fueled Reformed charity in both good times and bad. In an article on a quite different city, Lyon, at a quite different time, the Protestant heyday between 1562 and 1572, Natalie Davis has outlined the basic qualities of the Protestant social vision and contrasted them to Catholic social views.[68] In her examination of the two confessions' concepts of the "urban body social," Professor Davis found that Catholicism constituted (to simplify a subtle and complex argument) a "helping religion," which, through rituals such as prayer for the dead and exorcism, encouraged the faithful to help one another achieve salvation. Protestants, on the other hand, vociferously denied the efficacy of such rites and proclaimed each true believer incapable of either giving or receiving spiritual aid. One hundred years later, these same qualities still characterized Catholic and Protestant social visions; indeed, they had become more pronounced. The whole purpose of Catholic charity was, as we have seen on numerous occasions, the conversion of men and women. Whether it took the form of building a hospital or making testamentary bequests, Catholic charity always expressed this desire to save souls. Grenoble's Protestants, on the other hand, never sought to save either themselves or anyone else through their charitable activities. No souls were at stake in Protestant beneficence, which accounts, perhaps, for its lack of urgency. A Protestant only aspired to strengthen the Reformed community symbolically by asserting his individual ties with the true faithful. A Grenoble Protestant could not, whether by his charity or anything else, actually save other souls, just—perhaps—his own. If Catholicism was the spirituality of "helping" others, then Protestantism was the religion of "self-help."

At this point, the reader may suspect that he is receiving old wine in new bottles. Certainly some of the elements of the traditional interpretation of Catholic and Protestant social policy are here: the individualism and secularism usually attributed to Protestantism, and the selfish other-worldliness often ascribed to Catholicism. These elements, however, must be properly construed and placed within context. Protestants might not have tried to save souls by their alms, but their charity was by no means "secular." They always made bequests within the context of the Protestant church, and they sought, if not to convert men, at least to maintain and perpetuate their church. Moreover, while Reformed theology did throw the believer back on his own resources and create a kind of spiritual "individualism," this does not mean that Catholics automatically lack such a quality. On the contrary, Catholics in their wills demonstrated the most radical, thoroughgoing kind of individualism. They gleefully deprived their heirs in order to purchase masses and make charitable bequests that would save their own souls. Selfish is certainly the only way to describe such behavior, for Catholic charity, however secular in nature, always carried with it the promise of spiritual benefit. But did this selfishness make the alms distributed by Catholics any less effective? As we have seen, Catholics usually went to greater lengths than Protestants in framing their charitable bequests so as to assure their correct and effective administration. Did the self-serving quality of Catholic charity render it any less welcome to the poor or any less abundant? Probably not, for the selfishness so often decried by historians, prompted Catholic benefactors to be more generous than Protestants in their bequests, and it therefore actually benefited the poor. In other words, Catholicism succeeded where other doctrines, both social and spiritual, failed: it tied self-interest to the general social good. If alms flowed so freely in Grenoble during the Counter Reformation, it may well have been because Catholics, unlike their more noble Protestant neighbors, were deeply and hopelessly selfish.

Although Catholicism proved fairly successful at stimulating the social conscience of believers, it would be premature and foolhardy to conclude that the Roman Church was somehow superior to its Protestant rival, or vice versa. Differences certainly existed between the two confessions, but so too did important similarities. Both Catholics and Protestants faced the same problem, endemic poverty, and both applied the same solution, voluntary donations and periodic distributions of food and money. Both confessions also had, to our knowledge, only limited success in relieving the hunger and disease that afflicted their less fortunate members. In other words, Protestants and Catholics operated within the same social and economic environment. They also fell heir to the same cultural heritage, the same traditions of mutual aid and seigneurial beneficence which antedated both confessions by many years. Because of this common legacy, many of the benefactions made by both groups resembled one another in both form and spirit. This was particularly true in rural areas where the relatively new institutions of the Protestant Consistory and the Hospital General had yet to displace more traditional forms of charity. When Protestant Paul de Durand set aside 60 livres to redeem the debts of the most impoverished families of Cornillon, he performed, along with Catholics, an ancient gesture. When Protestant Marc de Vulson left 100 livres to the poorest inhabitants of his estates, he perpetuated, as had his Catholic ancestors, a tradition of seigneurial beneficence. Such gifts had a decidedly rustic flavor, but city folk, whether Protestant or Catholic, who had ties to the country also made such bequests. When Judith Gard, a Protestant, left 29 livres to dower the poor Protestant girls of her hometown, she, like many other Grenoblois, eschewed the poor of the Hospital General in favor of the "free" poor, the urban or rural unconfined poor.[69]

BEQUESTS TO THE UNCONFINED POOR

In both Catholic and Protestant wills, these bequests to the "free" poor took a number of forms, but they can be divided into two broad categories: first, those that reinforced horizontal ties within the community and sprang from a sense of communal solidarity; second, those that strengthened vertical ties and confirmed the links between seigneur and peasant. In the first category, the bequest that one encounters the most frequently and consistently throughout the seventeenth century is the gift stipulating a distribution of alms. Usually these alms took the form of food—grain, bread, soup, wine, beans, or salt—which was to be served at the door of the testator's house "to whoever presented himself." Often the testator requested that this ritual occur on the day of his death or after his funeral, which indicates that such distributions formed a part of the funeral practices common in Dauphiné. But most testators stipulated no precise time for the distribution, and a few, like the noble Antoine du Frenet, who requested that rye be doled out annually for thirty years after his demise, placed the distribution long after death.[70] Were these gifts made in the hope of receiving the special, intercessory prayers of the poor for the redemption of the testator's soul? Perhaps, but no such explicit request is made in the wills. Several testators did ask that the distributions occur after the anniversary mass that marked the year following the testator's demise, which implies that the poor were expected to attend mass.[71] But such bequests were rare, and most distributions had little explicit religious content.

Occasionally, a testator, most likely a magistrate, would ask that the parish priest officiate and distribute money rather than the more traditional bread or salt. In such cases, it is hard to tell whether the testator prized the curé for his spiritual powers or for his intimate knowledge of the rural community. In any event, few testators made such bequests, either because they had little faith in the patently untrustworthy rural clergy or because they felt such distributions a strictly family duty. Most Dauphinois testators preferred to forego intermediaries and charge their heirs directly with these offerings, and they almost always chose, whatever their wealth, to offer food rather than cash. Consequently, these distributions resemble the funeral banquets which were still common in rural Dauphiné and other parts of France as late as the nineteenth century.[72] These banquets formed a part of the rites of passage surrounding death and served to reunite, in symbolic fashion, communities shattered by the loss of a member. A kinship may well exist between these village rituals and the bequests for distributions, for both were communal, secular, and rural. Because no priest, institution, or other "outsider" interfered, distributions remained a communal affair and had little manifest religious significance. At the same time, such distributions attracted primarily rural testators and not just the notables, the nobles and large landowners of the village. Merchants, artisans, even peasants ordered their heirs to serve a "supper" to the poor, thereby nourishing both the community's solidarity and its regret for the dead.[73]

The clothing, not the feeding, of the poor was the object of another kind of bequest, one which straddles both "vertical" and "horizontal" categories and admits of no easy interpretation. Several testators commanded their heirs to clothe a certain number of paupers, that is, give them cloth, usually black serge, leather shoes, felt hats, and sometimes candles. These gifts were loosely connected to funeral practices, for some testators specified that paupers thus clothed were to march in the funeral cortege and accompany the coffin to the cemetery. In these cases, the number of paupers assisted could vary widely: one testator asked that only four paupers accompany her coffin, but others requested as many as twelve, twenty-four, or thirty-three. Under such circumstances, these bequests look less like charity than like payment for services rendered; but such was not always or frequently the case. Toward the middle of the seventeenth century, gifts of clothing and shoes tended to become detached from funeral practices. Testators made such bequests to paupers who could not possibly have attended their funerals, for they lived far from the testators' place of burial. Gaspard de Ponnat, for example, had himself buried in Grenoble, but left money for the clothing of twelve paupers in distant Gresse and Beaurivières.[74] Merchant Thomas de Puissan was interred in his adopted home, Grenoble, but clothed paupers in his native village, Villard-Bonnot.[75] If not made in payment for attendance at the funeral, were these bequests given in return for the paupers' prayers? One testator did urge his heirs to instruct the poor, so clothed, to pray for the salvation of his soul, but no other testator mentioned prayers specifically.[76] Perhaps it was tacitly understood that those who were clothed would also pray; perhaps not. In any event, these bequests had a certain religious significance, for the number of paupers—twelve, thirteen, or thirty-three—usually recalled either the Apostles or the duration of Christ's life. Still, they seem to spring, not from the post-Tridentine spirituality with which we are familiar, but from an older type of Catholicism.

The archaic quality of these bequests to clothe the poor is suggested by a number of factors. First, such bequests were much more popular among rural than among urban testators. Second, even these country dwellers tended to abandon these bequests as the seventeenth century drew to a close and the Counter Reformation triumphed in rural Dauphiné.[77] Perhaps they acquired, along with post-Tridentine spirituality, their city cousins' taste for simple funerals. A few rural testators did ask, after 1690, for relatively austere funerals, and banished the hoards of paupers, priests, and crosses that had previously been prized.[78] Perhaps this decline in gifts to clothe the poor indicated the demise of an old vision of poverty. Maybe rural testators ceased to clothe the poor as Christ and his apostles because they now preferred to see paupers in a new dress, that of the "shameful" or even heathen poor. In any event, the message conveyed by these bequests before their complete demise was essentially ambiguous: on the one hand, these gifts pointed to the spiritual superiority of the poor of Christ; on the other hand, they manifested the social and economic superiority of the testator by a flashy display of wealth and generosity. It is hard to tell just how much money was involved in these bequests, but it was probably a considerable amount. Only the wealthiest members of the rural community, the nobles and prosperous merchants, made such bequests, and if they ceased to do so, it was probably because they chose to manifest their dominance in other ways.

The need of the dominant groups within Dauphinois society to display their generosity and to strengthen the ties binding their dependents to them certainly did not disappear with the seventeenth century. It just took different, less ambiguous forms. As the century wore on, the notables of rural society tended to abandon gifts in kind, whether of food or clothes, in favor of straight cash grants. This was particularly true of those whose connection with the rural poor was most tenuous, absentee landlords like Grenoble's bourgeois, nobles, lawyers, and especially magistrates. Great disparities in wealth clearly characterized this group: a lawyer like Guigues Bonnet could leave only 30 livres to the poor of Claix where he owned land, but a great magistrate, like the counselor Micha de Bursin, could lavish 1,000 livres on the poorest tenants of his estates at Chapeaucornu.[79] More than means, however, determined the size and distribution of these bequests. When the marquis de Valbonnays bestowed gifts of 2,000 livres on the peasants of his large and dispersed estates, he carefully distributed money to each area in proportion to the size of his holdings there.[80] The marquis' sense of responsibility points to the qualities that characterized all such bequests, large or small: they were personal, paternal, and deeply seigneurial.

That gifts from an absentee landlord could be personal may at first seem impossible. Certainly, Grenoble's lawyers and rentiers resided only infrequently on their rural properties, and the magistrates, who had extensive holdings, probably never set foot on all their far-flung estates. Still, despite these circumstances—or perhaps because of them—testators sought to make their bequests appear as personal and direct as possible. They did so by avoiding intermediaries, by eschewing the assistance of their stewards and judges, and by refusing the help of the local priest. It was to family members, to the heirs, that the task of choosing the recipients and distributing the alms fell. The marquis de Virieu, for instance, bequeathed a substantial sum of money to the judge of his estates, but entrusted to his heir the task of distributing hundreds of livres to needy peasants.[81] The marquis de Valbonnays requested that the "tenants of the longest standing and in whom signs of good conduct are coupled with slender means" receive 500 livres and then left the selection of these tenants, not to his steward, who would be most qualified, but to his wife.[82] By sidestepping the most obvious administrators of these bequests—the lord's agents and managers—and entrusting this task directly to his heirs, the landlord tried to bring his tenants closer to himself and to his family.

Not that the distance between the testator's immediate household and his more remote dependents was all that great. In almost all wills, whether dictated to a notary or written out by the testator himself, bequests to peasants came long after other charitable and religious gifts, but directly before those to domestic servants and relatives. Gifts for impoverished tenants sometimes mingled with legacies to lackeys and serving girls, and both were swiftly followed by bequests to direct descendants. So intertwined were these kinds of beneficence in the minds of some testators that they became confused. When Abel de Servien, magistrate and ambassador, made his will, he left a great deal of money to his maître d'hôtel and then 500 livres to the paupers of Claix, "in particular our more unfortunate relatives who must not be forgotten or treated with contempt."[83] To the seigneur, poor relatives, domestics, and rural tenants all formed part of his larger household, and he owed them all the same protection and assistance. In fact, this beneficence frequently took precisely the same form. Abel de Servien asked that his 500 livres be used to dower the poor girls of Claix, just as he might provide dowries to his servant girls, and Isabeau de Treffort, Baroness of Barry, apprenticed her lackeys in the same breath as she dowered poor girls.[84]

The paternal spirit of these bequests to the rural poor is obvious, but not all seigneurs acted out of pure, fatherly altruism. Two benefactors requested that their peasants kneel once they had received their alms and pray to their Heavenly Lord for the redemption of their earthly seigneur. Another asked that the interest paid her by her peasants be given to the poorest of these peasants; in effect, she robbed Peter to pay Paul.[85] Not all testators were as blatantly selfish as these, but that does not mean that they were any more effective in alleviating poverty, or less self-interested in their generosity. Even though bequests to peasants could run into thousands of livres, they certainly did not eliminate hunger or disease, for they were made only once and on an extraordinary occasion, the death of the seigneur. Such gifts supplied the peasants with little comfort, but they do provide us with a clue to the function and deeper meaning of these bequests.

The fact is that more than an outpouring of alms accompanied the seigneur's death. His demise also occasioned a host of events that were considerably less palatable to the peasantry. When the old lord died and a new one took his place, leases might be renegotiated, feudal charters combed for new exactions, and traditional death duties levied.[86] The equilibrium between lord and peasant (albeit an equilibrium always weighted in favor of the lord) was seriously disturbed, and the ties that bound tenant to seigneur were suddenly ambiguous and dangerously loose. Because the lord's relationship to his peasants was, by definition, personal, this relationship died with the lord and had to be renegotiated by his heirs. Consequently, it is not surprising that the lord picked this particular, tense moment to display in an ostentatious fashion seigneurial beneficence. Nor is it coincidental that he chose his heirs, who had to renew the seigneurial compact and often chose to redefine it to their own advantage, to distribute his largesse to the community. These bequests served to reestablish the equilibrium within the seigneurial relationship and often took quite explicitly seigneurial forms. Like the noble Jean de Boffin, seigneur of Avanson, Saone, and other places, who bequeathed to his peasants rights of usage in his forests, some lords made of seigneurial privileges the very coin of their bequests.[87] Such gifts tried to reaffirm the lord's paternalism and legitimize, if only in a symbolic fashion, seigneurial rule.

It might be objected that the foregoing discussion tends to overestimate the importance of seigneurialism and ignore the more modern forms of land tenure that certainly existed at the time. By the seventeenth century, a noble was often just a landlord, and a peasant just a tenant. But this does not mean that seigneurialism, especially in the form of traditional usage rights, had utterly disappeared from the Dauphinois countryside, or that other forms of dependency had not arisen to replace or reinforce it. Emmanuel Le Roy Ladurie's *Carnival of Romans* has made historians familiar with the phenomenon of rural indebtedness in sixteenth-century Dauphiné, and this problem certainly did not disappear with the resolution of the *procès des tailles*.[88] Long after 1622, peasants and rural communities still groaned under the weight of huge debts which were owed, more often than not, to the local seigneur. Under these circumstances, it is not surprising that many local seigneurs chose to demonstrate their benevolence by alleviating this burden. In their wills, quite a few suspended collection of interest on debts for a year, instructed their heirs to reduce the size of arrears, or canceled debts of less than 50 livres. One seigneur even obliterated a debt owed him for the loan of grain during a year of scarcity.[89] These bequests did little to relieve the peasantry's indebtedness, but they demonstrate that Dauphiné's lords, whatever their real relations with their peasants, considered such a display of paternal benevolence necessary and still took their seigneurial duties and obligations seriously.

In fact, Dauphiné's seigneurs tended to take their traditional duties more seriously as the seventeenth century wore on. The percentage of nobles and magistrates leaving bequests to rural tenants and dependents tended to rise steadily throughout the period, and so too did the size of average bequests.[90] What accounts for this heightened sense of seigneurial responsibility? The search for a definitive answer to this question would lead us far from Grenoble into the untilled fields of Dauphinois rural history. Suffice it to say, for the moment, that such an increase must signify a profound and far-reaching change in the attitudes and behavior of the Dauphinois landed elite, a change which may have been provoked by the social conflict that ended the sixteenth century and which may have contributed to the social truce that characterized the seventeenth. In any event, we can say with some assurance that the new sense of seigneurial responsibility was closely related to the progress of post-Tridentine spirituality among the elites. As statistical regression analysis shows, giving to the rural poor was closely correlated with giving to the new religious institutions (table 11). Some deep affinity must have existed between the old seigneurial ethic and the new post-Tridentine spirituality. They both, after all, had the same champions: the magistrates, nobles, and canons who staffed the Hospital, conspired in the Company of the Holy Sacrament, and gave most generously and consistently to religious institutions, also bestowed gifts upon their rural dependents. These devout Grenoblois were not just an urban elite. They were also a rural elite, a group of noble seigneurs who dominated the countryside as much as the city and regarded their inferiors in both spheres, it seems, with the same haughty paternalism.

In the city as in the countryside, the old seigneurial ethic inspired poor relief and permeated even the newest institutions of public assistance. If

TABLE 11

SELECTED REGRESSION COEFFICIENTS: GIFTS TO THE FREE POOR

Variables	Coefficients	t-Statistic
Date	0.129	2.05
Nobles	66.867	6.34
Magistrates	122.946	10.69
Basoche	19.778	2.05
Bourgeois	24.244	2.19
Merchants	3.688	1.20
Plowmen	−5.517	0.37
Domestics	−3.626	0.17
Females	−8.888	1.47
Urban	−1.820	0.60
Pious giving	0.027	5.85
Giving to Hospital	0.028	5.85

Note: Regression coefficients for the variables sick and family status and the constant have been omitted. For an explanation of variables, see table 1.

Ennemond de Sibut, a counselor at the Parlement, chose to dower the poor girls of his rural holdings, he did the same for those of his urban neighborhood.[91] When Jean Louis de Ponnat de Garcin left 1,000 livres for the dowering of poor girls from his rural estates at Combes and Seyssinet, he asked that an urban, adamantly post-Tridentine institution, the Congregation for the Propagation of the Faith, administer this bequest.[92] Apparently, even the new institutions of public assistance bore the marks of the old social ethic, and that monument to Counter Reformation Catholicism, the Hospital General, was no exception. Annually, it dowered poor girls and apprenticed poor boys with the funds provided by foundations established by magistrates, nobles, and high clerics. Sometimes the recipients of these alms were residents of the founders' estates.[93] Sometimes they were native Grenoblois. But always they were chosen by the founders' descendants, thereby preserving, even after death, the benefactors' ties with the poor. In form, substance, and even intent, these bequests were identical to those made by seigneurs to their peasants, and these legacies underscore the debt owed by the new view of the poor to an ancient social ethic.

Thus, when the president de la Croix de Chevrières, whom we began with, bestowed gifts on the Hospital General and the poor of his estates in 1685, he expressed not two different social views but just one. Though the recipients were different, the spirit of each gift was the same and the president blended the new with the old. He at once honored a new piety and performed an ancient gesture which his most distant ancestors might well have undertaken. About the president's descendants, however, we cannot speak with the same assurance. In the next century, the ties between past and present would be broken, and a new view of the relationship between rich and poor would emerge.

PART TWO

The Eighteenth Century

Educating the Poor: The "Little" Schools (1707–1789)

In 1707 a number of Grenoblois "distinguished by their piety and authority" assembled in the home of a prominent magistrate. They had come together in the spirit of charity to establish a school that would provide the very young and the very poor with a primary education. The gentlemen immediately proclaimed themselves the Bureau des Ecoles Charitables and decided to tax each member or "associate" twenty-five livres annually for the support of the new "good work." The Bureau also resolved to seek the assistance of an obscure Parisian cleric who had had some success running charity schools in the parish Saint Sulpice. Two members of the Bureau volunteered to write Jean-Baptiste de La Salle, and the little group adjourned for the evening. In only a few hours, the Grenoble "little" schools, which would remain open until the Revolution and provide hundreds of young paupers with a rudimentary education, had been born.[1]

Nothing about the event was particularly unusual. Other charities, the Prêt Charitable and the Providence, for instance, had been born in much the same fashion and with equal speed. Nor were the goals of the Bureau's "associates" particularly novel. Since the early seventeenth century, the Grenoblois had tried to instruct the poor in such venerable institutions as the Orphans and the Hospital General. In both form and spirit, the Bureau des Ecoles Charitables closely resembled several other charities, and it would not merit close scrutiny were it not for its longevity. The Bureau continued to function right up to the Revolution, and it consequently formed a bridge between turn-of-the-century attitudes toward the poor and Enlightenment conceptions of poverty.[2]

The links between seventeenth- and eighteenth-century attitudes toward the poor are unusually clear in the case of charity schools. Their history contains, as if in microcosm, all the old and the new features of poor relief in the Enlightenment, and it allows us to survey this new terrain from a particularly revealing perspective. For the philosophes, the instruction of the poor was a difficult, even painful issue. It brought into conflict their most cherished notions and their deepest, unspoken prejudices. It forced them to consider the poor in a clear, unsentimental light, and it consequently elicited different responses from different thinkers. Historians themselves have had difficulty characterizing the Enlightenment position on the instruction of the poor, and they have arrived at contradictory interpretations.[3] Luckily, the Grenoblois are considerably less complicated than their intellectual contemporaries, but for them too the educating of the impoverished constituted a kind of litmus test. It laid bare their tacit assumptions and exposed their newest impulses. No other charitable issue set them at such odds with their seventeenth-century ancestors or, in fact, with each other.

But the men who established the Bureau des Ecoles Charitables in 1707 still belonged to the relatively serene world of the late seventeenth century. Many, like Monsieur Canel and the canon Saléon, sat on the boards of the Hospital General or the Prêt Charitable, for the new Bureau closely resembled the old charities in its social composition. As usual, magistrates predominated, and they were accompanied by their brothers and cousins, the canons of Notre Dame and Saint André. Just as at the Hospital General, only a handful of lawyers and notaries disturbed the otherwise aristocratic atmosphere.[4]

Given its rather traditional composition, it is hardly surprising that the Bureau pursued equally traditional goals. Some of these were quite practical and down-to-earth. The "associates" boasted that their school "would rescue the poor from the perilous idleness where they are wont to languish without help."[5] "A love of work" would replace the little pauper's innate laziness, and a blind resignation would supplant his natural "disorderliness." In short, the Bureau's schools would produce docile, industrious little Grenoblois. But behind these patently social goals lay a higher purpose. As the Bureau explained, "to instruct is to lead others in the path of justice so that their souls might shine like stars for all eternity."[6] In the end, the "associates" had the same goal as their seventeenth-century predecessors—the conversion of souls.

To lead the little pauper down the road to salvation, the Bureau obtained the services of the order formed by Jean-Baptiste de La Salle, the

Christian Brothers.[7] The "associates" first issued an invitation in 1707, an invitation that stipulated that the ultimate authority in all matters concerning the schools would remain with the Bureau. But for a number of reasons, several years elapsed before any of the "sons" of de La Salle set foot in the city. By 1709, however, two Christian Brothers had opened a school on the right bank of the Isère in the Saint Laurent quarter. It was there, at the present number forty, that Jean-Baptiste de La Salle himself taught for several months in the years 1711 and 1713. The presence of the founder seems to have had a good effect on the fledgling institution, for in 1716 the Bureau decided to extend the benefits of charity schooling to the inhabitants of the left bank of the Isère. Three more Christian Brothers came to Grenoble and opened a second school in the parish Saint Hugues near the cathedral.[8] This school flourished, to such a degree that in 1730 the Brothers had to find more spacious quarters. They moved into the old seminary of Saint François de Sales, also in the parish Saint Hugues, but these new quarters soon proved unacceptable. In 1733, thanks to large bequests by two canons of Notre Dame, the Bureau purchased a very large house on the Rue Saint Laurent which the Brothers used as both schoolhouse and residence. About the same time, the "little" schools finally received official sanction: through the intervention of several prestigious magistrates, royal letters patent were bestowed upon the Grenoble charity schools in 1730.[9]

At this time the fortunes of the "little" schools reached something of a peak. From a miserable room in the parish Saint Laurent, the institution had grown to include four separate schools, two on the Rue Saint Laurent, one in the parish Saint Hugues, and one in the Hospital General. About 80 children attended each school, making some 320 students altogether, and the number soon increased.[10] In 1731 one Jeanne Reynier opened a school closely modeled on the Christian Brothers school in the parish Saint Laurent. This institution, staffed by two lay Sisters and supported by Mlle Reynier herself, catered exclusively to girls and sought to provide them with the same kind of instruction that their brothers were receiving down the street. At her death, Mlle Reynier signed over her estate to the institution and placed the school under the supervision of the curé of Saint Laurent.[11]

No account of life in the Grenoble "little" schools has come down to us, but we may safely assume that it followed the same pattern as life in any of the hundreds of other Christian Brothers' schools in France. At eight o'clock sharp the students filed into the classroom reciting the Veni Spiritus Sancti. Together they proclaimed that "it is to learn, to know and to serve God that I have come to school," and then they opened their books. Each lesson began with the proclamation "My Lord, I am going to say my lesson for the love of you; give it your blessing," and closed with the exclamation "May God be blessed forever!" In between, the students read from religious books, usually the catechism. Clearly, the emphasis was on religious learning.[12]

But the Brothers did not exclude secular instruction from their schools. On the contrary, the teaching of reading and writing occupied most of the school day, and the students spent virtually all of their time "saying lessons." Each child would in turn read aloud, and the schoolmaster would correct his mistakes, allowing the whole class to profit from each individual's errors. Jean-Baptiste de La Salle himself had devised this method, and it solved one of the problems facing the charity schoolmaster—the large size of his classes. Similarly, most elements in Lasallian pedagogy were designed to meet the difficulties inherent in charity education, but the disciplinary measures observed at Christian schools were inspired by rather different, social concerns. Order and silence reigned at all times, and the children never escaped the schoolmaster's watchful eye. He observed them constantly—even secretly—and policed their every move, so that they might develop those virtues so prized in the poor, obedience and discipline. To be sure, in their more socially elevated colleges, the Jesuits also enforced strict discipline, but here the similarity between the two pedagogies ended.[13] The Christian Brothers never adopted the Jesuit principle of "emulation," for de La Salle had expressly banished it from the "little" schools along with all sorts of prizes and contests. Such devices, he argued, formed a spur to vanity, a quality desirable in the rich, but inappropriate in the poor. The Christian Brothers, unlike the Jesuits, did not seek to form competitive, self-reliant men. They wanted to produce a quite different man: a cooperative, obedient, and above all else, subservient individual.[14]

Apparently, many Dauphinois shared the Christian Brothers' goal, for in the years after the establishment of the Grenoble schools, Christian schools were established in towns and villages throughout the province. In the 1730s the Brothers opened schools in Valence, Crest, Montélimar, Die, Saillans, and Mens-en-Trièves. This latter school is of particular interest, for it had a most dramatic and revealing history. Mens-en-Trièves was a Protestant stronghold, a most unpromising site for a "Christian" school. And the little institution was in fact foisted upon the reluctant Trièvois by the Parlement of Dauphiné. Never had the mission of the Brothers—the conversion of souls—been so explicit or so difficult. At first, the Trièvois adopted a passive stance: they refused to pay the Brothers' expenses. Then they moved to violent resistance. According to the parlementary commissioners sent to investigate the incident, the Brothers' students "constantly shook their fists at their masters in school and threatened to strike them." Outside the school, the children "hurled rocks against the windows and doors" and "insulted and assaulted the Christian Brothers when they walked down the street." The Parlement proved unable to stop these disturbances, but the Christian Brothers persevered for another twenty years.[15]

Less violent, but equally trying events awaited the Christian Brothers of Grenoble. In 1776 the house on the Rue Saint Laurent collapsed, killing several pupils but sparing the Brothers themselves. The Bureau issued a subscription in hope of collecting enough money to rebuild the house, but donations came in slowly.[16] For the first time in its existence, the Bureau had to appeal to the municipality for help, and the necessary money was provided by the consuls. The event was symptomatic. In the 1760s the Bureau's fortunes had begun to turn: donations shrank, the schools' income fell off, and by the 1770s it had virtually disappeared. During the good years of the 1730s, the "associates" had raised about 1,000 livres annually; in the 1770s, they had difficulty collecting 500 livres. "The zeal of the benefactors has cooled" protested the "associates," and the Bureau account books show that they were not indulging in idle complaining. In the decade 1730 to 1739, the Bureau had received over 9,012 livres. Between 1760 and 1769, it acquired only 6,645 livres, and in the 1770s it was just barely able to scrape together 4,537 livres.[17]

Subtle, but highly significant changes were also occurring in the social composition of the Bureau. A new breed of benefactors—men whose wealth derived from commerce and industry, not offices or land—began to infiltrate the formerly aristocratic Bureau. It is not uncommon to find the names of wealthy but hardly prestigious glove merchants like M. Bovier next to the names of first presidents and counselors in the 1780s subscription lists.[18] Négociants, men like M. Pascal, M. Dupuy, and M. Mounier, whose son would become famous during the Revolution, also figured prominently among the benefactors. So did industrialists like M. Devoise, entrepreneur of the canon foundry of Saint Gervais, and M. Bottut, owner of the Rives foundries. But most symptomatic of the changes occurring at the Bureau was a notice appended to the 1780 subscription, which informed the Grenoblois that they could leave their donations at the office of one Claude Périer. Périer, the son of an obscure merchant, had made a fortune in the cloth trade and used part of it to purchase, appropriately enough, the castle of Lesdiguières. Wealthy, dynamic, but definitely not aristocratic, Périer symbolized the new order at the Bureau. The aristocracy's monopoly of charity was coming to an end.[19]

So too were some of the goals that had animated charity for over a century. The Grenoble benefactors seem to have lost their religious fervor, their compulsion to save souls. They did not actually revoke their spiritual mission. They just mentioned it less and less often, indeed so infrequently that by the end of the century the desire "to make souls shine for all eternity" had disappeared from the Bureau's pamphlets. Not that the benefactors abandoned religion altogether. They continued to provide some religious instruction in their schools, but for new and quite different reasons. The spiritual benefits the pauper might receive no longer interested them. As far as they were concerned, religious instruction's only "utility" lay in its ability to form docile, obedient subjects.[20] As the "associates" boasted, the "little schools form good Christians and therefore good citizens."[21] Catholicism had lost its militancy and its spiritual significance. For the Bureau des Ecoles Charitables, it had become something close to "civil religion."

Some Grenoblois were willing to go even further. Some were willing to abandon spiritual instruction altogether, as a small controversy in the 1780s revealed. The curé of Saint Louis parish, M. Sadin, asked the municipality to dissolve the old Presentation charity so that he might open a charity school for girls on its premises. Several benefactors provided support, both financial and moral, but the governesses of the Presentation opposed the project. The consuls hesitated, and both the governesses and Sadin took the issue to the public by writing pamphlets explaining their respective positions. In his tract, Sadin told the Grenoblois that his school would provide religious instruction just like the Presentation, but then he added that "only a few minutes" a day would be devoted to the catechism. The governesses seized upon this remark and accused the curé, quite correctly, of ignoring the children's spiritual development. "We can see," wrote one governess, "the utility of a public school ... provided that religion is the basis," but at Sadin's school "the little children will not even learn that they have a father in Heaven." She summed up her argument with an exclamation: "If one devotes only a few minutes a day to the catechism, one can say with reason, what an education!"[22]

What an education indeed. If Sadin's curriculum allowed little time for spiritual instruction, it provided even less for the teaching of reading and writing. "Only a few minutes a day will be devoted to reading," stressed the curé, and in a manner which was almost apologetic. The tone may sound incongruous—the curé claimed that he was founding a school after all—but it was by no means unprecedented or uncommon. From the 1750s on, the Grenoblois approached the education of the poor with greater and greater reluctance. They came to spend more and more time in their pamphlets and public appeals refuting the "so-called supposed inconveniences" that stemmed from educating the poor.[23] Indeed, they wasted so many words defending their schools that one senses a certain uneasiness on their part. Finally, one "associate" simply dismissed the whole problem: the schools had to offer instruction, he explained, because there was no other way of persuading "the children's parents to send them to school."[24] By the 1780s the benefactors' feelings about educating the poor had become so ambivalent that they even denied the efficacy of their own institution. "The children who come out of our schools," one associate proclaimed, "are not very good at writing and even less skilled at spelling, which is only learned by long apprenticeship, so that these children know how to write only a few words and those only imperfectly."[25]

If not reading and writing, what should a pauper learn? The curé Sadin had the answer, and he responded without hesitation, "work." He even went so far as to call his new institution a "school for work." The idea was not, of course, entirely new. Seventeenth-century benefactors had also included hard, unremitting labor in their curricula, but the curé Sadin was not interested in work for its own sake, for the sheer discipline of it. It was not the lack of industry at the Presentation that enraged Sadin, but the lack of productivity. "All the children in the house and the governesses," he complained, "produce barely ten écus a month." Such an institution could not form productive laborers, but the curé's school would. There, no time would be wasted on religious or secular instruction. Work would begin promptly at six in the morning and continue, uninterrupted, until late at night. Under the supervision of several "schoolmistresses," the children would sew and embroider gloves and pay three sous a month for the privilege of doing so. "What could be more edifying," asked the curé, "than the spectacle of all these little children gathered together in two rooms, working in silence and with great industry and speed."[26]

Apparently, other Grenoblois agreed with Sadin, for they established institutions remarkably similar to his "school." In 1779 a merchant named Ducoin established a lace manufacture in the adjacent community of Sassenage. There he housed about a dozen girls between the ages of eight and sixteen, whom he had taken from the local beggars' prison, the *dépôt de mendicité*. The girls made lace or were, in Ducoin's terms, "worked and instructed."[27] Similarly, in the 1780s, Claude Périer considered creating a hardware manufacture and asked the municipal government for a small "charitable subsidy." The money, he argued, would allow him to employ pauper children between the ages of eight and twelve years and work them for over eighteen hours a day.[28]

Neither Ducoin or Périer went as far as Sadin. They did not call their ventures schools, but it is clear that work was still considered the appropriate "instruction" for a poor child. As such, the curriculum of the new school or workshop—for they were now indistinguishable—point to important, deep-seated changes in attitudes toward the poor. The old obsession with salvation of souls had vanished—quietly, almost imperceptibly, but entirely. The eighteenth-century benefactor felt no compulsion to inculcate religious values and no need to effect "perfect conversions." The cultural mission of seventeenth-century charity had disappeared, and the pauper now emerged as a purely economic actor.

This new view of the poor was fundamentally more benign than the old. The poor child was no longer a "vessel of sin" as he had been to the ladies of the Orphans. But he was not necessarily better off for his new identity. The eighteenth-century Grenoblois were still deeply distrustful of any attempt to educate the poor. Unlike their seventeenth-century predecessors who had foisted religious instruction upon one and all, the Grenoblois of the Enlightenment approached primary education of the poor with considerable misgiving. Why they did so is not altogether clear. Political and social anxieties, in any case, do not seem to have prompted their apprehensions: nothing in eighteenth-century Grenoble suggested that the poor, even if educated, would rise up and challenge the ruling elite. Rather, the Grenoblois' concerns were more practical and prosaic.

"Utility," to quote the Bureau des Ecoles Charitables, inspired their pedagogic efforts; work was the only curriculum they had to offer. The eighteenth-century Grenoblois wanted to produce, not good Catholics or even good subjects, but simply able, productive workers. Labor was the key, and the Grenoblois had a near mystical faith in its powers. It could extinguish poverty just as surely as Catholicism had once been believed to destroy idleness. Consequently, the rich now owed the able-bodied poor one thing and one thing only—work. In return, the impoverished owed the rich their labor. The utility of the scheme derived from the fact that both parties were enriched, if not equally, at least simultaneously. The Grenoblois believed that work ordered and perfected society and led to social harmony. To us, their "schools" may look like vocational training at best, exploitation at worst. But to them, such pedagogic efforts were charity of the highest order.

The Grenoblois probably came to regard their social obligations in this new light for a number of reasons, but a change in the incidence of poverty was not one of them. It is true that the Grenoblois directed most of their pedagogic efforts toward women, and as we shall shortly see, single women did suffer a progressive deterioration of their fortunes in the eighteenth century. The elite's rather sudden interest in the education of females, however, had less to do with changes in the poor than with changes in economic structure. In the eighteenth century, Grenoble experienced an economic renaissance along with the rest of Dauphiné. Formerly a rather sleepy administrative center dependent upon its law courts, Grenoble became in the eighteenth century a manufacturing city of considerable importance. Textile production contributed to Grenoble's new economic vocation, but its glory lay indisputably in its glove making. By 1787 Grenoble was producing 160,000 dozens of gloves annually and exporting them to countries as distant as Russia and England. More than 6,000 Grenoblois were employed in glove making, and most of these— 3,864—were women who sewed and embroidered the gloves.[29] Grenoble therefore needed a large, slightly skilled female work force, and the charity schools were designed to produce it. The needs of the city's merchant-manufacturers, as much as the needs of the poor, determined the curriculum of Grenoble's charity schools.

The schools' new function also reflected changes among the poor, important cultural changes. Beginning in the late seventeenth century and proceeding into the eighteenth, the habits and values of the laboring classes shifted and altered. The working Grenoblois embraced Counter Reformation Catholicism (or a variant thereof), and the charity schools were both an agent and a proof of this victory. With the support of pious benefactors, the Christian Brothers had inculcated the values of resurgent Catholicism and thereby, in a paradoxical fashion, rendered their own efforts obsolete. Late-eighteenth-century benefactors no longer insisted upon "saving" the poor, because the poor, quite simply, no longer needed saving.

This does not mean that the poor were the victims of elite benefactors and their hired schoolteachers. The laboring Grenoblois were accomplices in the process of acculturation, for no one forced them to send their children to the schools. They did so willingly and sometimes at considerable expense. Some of the pupils were adolescents, old enough to contribute to the family; their wages or labor were probably sorely missed. Occasionally, the instruction of a child constituted a genuine sacrifice. In the years between 1712 and 1722, the directors of the Hospital General noted that several bread recipients, among them impoverished widows, managed despite their destitution to send their sons to the primary schools or even the local *collège*.[30] The poor wanted their children to read and write, and the Bureau des Ecoles Charitables catered to this desire, but only reluctantly.[31] The Bureau did not willingly teach these skills; they included reading and writing in the curriculum only because working parents would not otherwise send their children to the schools. Was the laboring Grenoblois' hunger for literacy the product of the new culture imbued with Counter Reformation Catholicism and its values? If it was, the elite found itself in the difficult position of the sorcerer's apprentice: having created the monster, they now wanted to destroy it.

   In other areas of poor relief, the repudiation of seventeenth-century attitudes toward the poor was not so dramatic. Charity instruction was a particularly thorny issue for Enlightenment benefactors, and it evoked an unusually clear and novel response. When it came to the treatment of the poor as a whole, eighteenth-century Grenoblois were more comfortable with the legacy of the past. Although they did effect some changes in old institutions and did adopt some new ideas, these actions were not particularly radical. To judge the true dimensions of change in the Enlightenment, we must turn, therefore, away from the troublesome little charity schools to the largest insitution of poor relief in Grenoble—the Hospital General.

EIGHT

The Hospital General in the Age of Light: 1760–1789

Early on Good Friday 1786, the directors of the Hospital General sent twelve inmates out into the streets of Grenoble. The paupers were armed with alms boxes and instructed to stand in church doorways where, the directors hoped, they would "excite" the pity of the faithful and the altruism of the rich. For over one hundred and fifty years, the inmates of the Hospital had undertaken such collections, and although the Revolution was but three years away, the directors still upheld old forms. The old spirit, however, they found considerably more difficult to maintain. This Good Friday, for example, the inmates did indeed collect some coins, but they quickly repaired to the nearest cabaret to toast the Grenoblois' generosity. Once they had consumed the alms, they returned, unsteadily one imagines, to the churches, refilled their alms boxes and then stumbled back to the cabaret. The process was repeated until nightfall, when the inmates straggled back to the Hospital. The directors were embarrassed: unlike the processions and collections which had been a part of civic life for generations, this spectacle was comic, not edifying. But the directors were undaunted. They would uphold tradition, and the Lenten collection would continue, but in the future, only children would be used.[1]

Like the Lenten collection, the Hospital General was, in the late eighteenth century, superficially unchanged; the old forms were still intact. The Bureau of Direction still consisted of the directors established by letters patent in 1699. The services provided by the Hospital still fell into the broad categories of food, shelter, and medical care for the impoverished. Even the Hospital building had not been altered since the early eighteenth century. But beneath this facade of permanence, certain important changes had occurred. New men with new ideas had unseated the old, aristocratic directors. The sick and the very young had replaced the sturdy beggar within the Hospital, and without, women and children now received the bread once distributed to able-bodied family men. Changes in poverty—the growing hardship experienced by women, and the soaring illegitimacy produced by new social forces—prompted some of these changes, but to a certain degree all owed their existence to a problem amply symbolized by the Hospital building itself. The old *maison de force* was on the verge of collapse, its foundations sapped by neglect and a financial crisis of unprecedented dimensions. The Lenten collection of 1786 brought in no money, but this was not unusual. The Hospital's income, like its walls, was crumbling.

NEW PROBLEMS AND NEW PERSONNEL

In this respect, the Hospital General of Grenoble was no different from scores of other charitable establishments in late-eighteenth-century France. Royal officials at the time, and even some historians today, blame the administrators of these institutions for their insolvency. They point specifically to the directors' mismanagement as the source of the problem. The situation in Grenoble, however, was considerably more complex, for the finances of the Hospital were themselves complicated. The Hospital depended upon a number of sources for its income. First came the endowment, that is, the twenty rural estates given to the Hospital by charitable individuals in the late seventeenth and early eighteenth centuries. These estates produced income both from feudal dues and from the rent paid by the leaseholders who farmed the estates. While the feudal dues accounted for only a miniscule portion of the Hospital's income, the rent paid by the leaseholders produced a substantial sum of money— 25,000 livres in 1755. But this amount tended to diminish as the century wore on, for the Hospital was forced by its financial problems to sell some of the estates, first in 1714 and then again in the 1750s and the 1770s.[2]

These sales certainly did not help the Hospital's long-range financial prospects, but they did not do inordinate harm either. The Hospital relied heavily on its second major source of income, a group of municipal duties on grain and cattle sold at the market. Together with some lesser duties, these taxes, called the *octrois,* provided almost twice as much income as the Hospital's estates and considerably less annoyance. The octrois, as well as the Hospital's monopolies on funeral arranging and selling of meat during Lent, were farmed out to individuals for five years at a time, sparing the institution time and trouble. But, as economic optimism declined in the late eighteenth century, so too did the prices fetched by the octrois leases. In 1730 the Hospital negotiated a contract for the octrois which provided it with 35,000 livres annually; in 1785 it was able to obtain only 16,000 livres when inflation is taken into account.[3]

The Hospital's declining fortunes were directly tied to the succession of crises which rocked the Grenoble economy, and that of France as a whole, in the last years of the eighteenth century. Though five-year leases provided a measure of security, the Hospital was still extremely vulnerable to periodic subsistence crises which reduced the traffic in grain and all but halted the sale of meat, thereby affecting the institution's tax revenues. In short, the Hospital was in the unenviable position of losing money just when it needed money the most, when the numbers of the poor swelled and the price of grain to feed them soared. It is hard to see how the directors could have avoided financial difficulties under these circumstances, but of course their predecessors, the directors of the years between 1680 and 1729, had done so. They too had faced declining revenues and soaring prices, and they too had borrowed heavily. But they were always saved from insolvency by sheer luck and, more often, the generosity of the Grenoblois. Timely donations and substantial testamentary bequests had always allowed them to retire their debts rather quickly. In the late eighteenth century, however, this particular form of salvation ceased to materialize. The average donation by living persons declined from 14,566 livres annually in the 1740s to only 6,000 livres in the 1780s, and these donations were fewer and farther apart than in the past.[4] A short-term expedient became a long-term burden, and by 1763 the Hospital owed more than 200,000 livres to a variety of creditors. Most of this debt had been acquired in the 1740s and the 1750s, when the directors had yet to realize that the life-saving gifts would no longer appear. By the 1760s, however, the Grenoblois' stinginess was all too apparent. The directors of the subsequent years came to borrow more reluctantly and more prudently and took other measures to balance the institution's budget.[5]

The Hospital directors of the late eighteenth century actually dealt with the institution's financial difficulties with considerable acumen, and the fact is not surprising. They were a new breed of men, quite different from the magistrates who had previously dominated the Bureau. In principle, the magistrates of the Parlement still occupied a considerable number of seats on the Bureau by virtue of their position at the sovereign court and the letters patent of 1699. But in fact, fewer and fewer appeared at the Bureau's weekly meetings, and by the 1770s the magistrates had abandoned the institution which they had created to a new group of men, men well versed in financial affairs and aware of the perils of the marketplace, for that is where most of them made their living. Director Barthelon, for example, was a merchant and the head of Barthelon, Aillous et Compagnie, a banking concern. Monsieur Bottut, another director, was a part of the consortium that ran and owned the Rives iron foundries. He was also involved in the commercial ventures of the Dolle and Raby families, whose spectacular success in the West Indies trade had made them the envy of the province. Director Bovier, while nominally a lawyer, was also a glove merchant, and Director Prat owned a stocking factory near Briançon which employed seventy workers, a substantial number for the day. All of these men were obviously quite prosperous, but the wealthiest of them all was Claude Périer who, in deference to the nobility conferred by excessive wealth, was known as Périer-Milord. Périer's father, Jacques, had turned a modest cloth business near Voiron into an enormous enterprise and with the profits had purchased for his son the petty office of *référendaire dans la Chancellerie.* Though titled, Périer-Milord had not betrayed his origins and had expanded the family business to include exporting to the West Indies. He also purchased Lesdiguière's castle at Vizille, the most sumptuous chateau in the vicinity, and turned it into first a wallpaper factory and then a cotton-printing enterprise. Along with Milord, there sat on the Hospital bureau his business associates, Monsieur Dupy, Monsieur Pascal, and his cousin Périer-Lagrange.[6]

For a body that had once spurned a notary's son, the Bureau of the Hospital General was becoming very plebian. Beside wealthy industrialists and prosperous merchants, there sat less well endowed members of the liberal professions, like the engineer Renauldon and the lawyers Barthelémy d'Orbanne and Achard de Germane, two distinguished members of the Grenoble bar. The Hospital had always included such men among the directors because it needed their skills to carry on its work. Now, however, these professionals dominated the Bureau, and they were joined by a group whose rise was even more meteoric, the physicians. Ever since its creation, the Hospital had hired doctors to care for the sick, but in the late eighteenth century the physicians moved from the sick wards to the boardroom. This promotion reflects both the growing prestige of the medical profession and a new concern for good medical care in the Hospital. Of the physicians who played an important role at the Bureau, one stands out, the doctor Gagnon. In Grenoble he was known for his considerable learning as much as for his medical skill. Subsequent generations have not forgotten him either, for he played a prominent role in the memoirs of his even more celebrated grandson, Stendhal.

A new set of men had thus emerged to take charge of the Hospital. As always, the Church provided a large contingent of directors, but they too were a bit different from their predecessors. One was the curé Hélie, the priest of Saint Joseph parish who would become one of the leaders of the Dauphinois "revolt of the curés" during the early Revolution. Another was the curé Sadin whom we have already encountered in the guise of an educator.[7] There were also three nobles: the marquis de Viennois, the marquis de Barral de Rochechinard, first president of the Parlement, and the marquis de Barral de Montferrat, also a president, his son. For all their titles, the two Barrals really do not fit the traditional notion of an old-regime aristocrat. They certainly possessed grand estates, but they also owned the largest smelting and mining venture in the province, the foundries of Allevard. Here they revealed a concern for technical innovation which, while not always profitable, was certainly progressive.[8]

With the aristocratic but financially troubled Barrals, on the one hand, and the lowly but wealthy Périer clan, on the other, it is hard to see what these gentlemen had in common. But they shared certain interests, perhaps even a certain point of view, for most were among the founders of Grenoble's first public library, purchased in 1771 from the bishop's estate, and almost all belonged to the Académie Delphinale, the local learned society.[9] In other words, the directors were a part of Grenoble's intellectual elite, a small, provincial intelligentsia to be sure, but not an uninformed or isolated one. The directors did not ignore the intellectual fashions of their day; they were not immune to the new ideas which we now call the Enlightenment. Director Bovier, glove merchant, lawyer, and host to Rousseau, possessed a rather daring library even if Rousseau upon viewing it proclaimed "there are many lies here." There were also copies of *La Nouvelle Héloise, Emile,* and the *Contrat Social.* Bovier also wrote a pamphlet in defense of the disenfranchised "natives" of Geneva, and he contributed an article on glove making to Panckouke's *Encyclopédie méthodique.*[10] Doctor Gagnon was a student of all the philosophes, his grandson tells us, and he held Voltaire in such esteem that he kept a bust of the author on his mantel. It was here, under the gaze of Voltaire and the watchful eye of the young Stendhal, that the directors met informally to discuss books and ponder the "new ideas."[11]

The Revolution, which came prematurely to Grenoble in the summer of 1788, also revealed common bonds among the directors. All, including the aristocratic marquis de Barral, participated in the first stages of the Dauphinois revolt. When the representatives of the Three Orders of Grenoble met on June 14, 1788, and called for the convocation of the provincial Estates, many of the directors were present. One, Monsieur Périer, hosted a preliminary assembly at his chateau in Vizille, and almost all the directors were present.[12] There, the third estate was doubled for the first time, setting an important and revolutionary precedent. Some of the directors continued to play a role in the local events precipitated by the Revolution. Achard de Germane, like his more celebrated colleague Barnave, wrote a pamphlet defending provincial liberties, and the marquis de Barral became the head of the local militia and later mayor of the city. For many, however, the subsequent events led to disillusionment, and many of those who embraced the Revolution prematurely also tired of it quickly. Achard de Germane joined the emigrés in exile in 1793. The glove merchant Bovier was incarcerated for harboring a refractory priest. Even Doctor Gagnon retreated from the political scene, and Périer-Milord was only saved from serious difficulties during the Terror by several timely "patriotic gifts." Ironically, only the marquis de Barral navigated the storm of the Revolution with success. He became a leader in the local, radical Société Populaire and was named, during the Terror, "an honorary sans-culotte." Most of the directors, however, were more consistent (or less opportunistic) in their politics. Like their famous compatriots Barnave and Mounier, most of the directors were revolutionaries, but moderate ones, for whom the events after 1791 were too sweeping in their effects.[13]

What should we call these gentlemen who had so much in common and yet came from such diverse backgrounds? They certainly did not all share, as had their predecessors at the Bureau, ancient lineage, vast landed estates, and positions of power and prestige at the sovereign courts. Some were aristocrats, like the Barrals; others were fairly plebian, like Bovier and Gagnon. A few depended on industry and commerce, instead of land, for their living; the Barrals relied upon vast seigneurial estates but also a foundry for their wealth. All, however, took an interest in ideas, especially new ideas, and therefore formed a part of what Daniel Roche has called "the community of the Enlightenment."[14] The directors also shared certain general political assumptions, for they all participated actively in the early years of the Revolution. Should we therefore call them, as their compatriot Mounier probably would have, "the commons"?[15] Or should we adopt the formula favored by the more visionary Barnave when he talked about the early revolutionaries, "the bourgeois aristocracy"?[16] Whatever one chooses to call them, the directors of the years between 1760 and 1789 were men radically different from their predecessors, men whom one would expect to make great changes in the Hospital. And they did alter the institution in subtle but important ways.

THE HOSPITAL AND ITS INMATES

The directors in fact wanted to rebuild part of the Hospital from the ground up. The men's ward had deteriorated so badly in the years since its construction that the directors contemplated razing it to the ground and starting afresh. According to Director Rolland, an engineer, the floorboards of the men's ward were rotten, its walls perpetually humid, and the building as a whole "more apt to cause than to cure illness." Humidity in fact posed a problem for the Hospital as a whole; its seven wards, kitchen, laundry, and isolation cells, or *cachots,* were frequently under water. The Hospital's location on the banks of the Isère River made it extremely vulnerable to the floods that periodically afflicted the city, and in 1763 the directors simply resolved that henceforth the inmates would wear galoshes from October to April. There was little the directors could do to remedy the perpetual flooding, and equally little they could do to improve the men's ward. In 1782 they opened up a subscription to rebuild the ward, but the resulting funds were insufficient, so they had to content themselves with mere cosmetic improvements in the men's quarters.[17]

The Hospital directors also had a great deal of trouble dealing with the employees who actually cared for the inmates, the "demoiselles." These young women of genteel but impoverished birth were a constant source of annoyance and complaint. To the directors, they were unduly harsh or overly lenient in their treatment of the poor, incompetent in medical matters, and far from conscientious in their duties. In 1761 the directors tried to rectify the situation by imposing a new set of rules on the demoiselles. Apparently, this reform had little effect, for in 1781 the directors again drew up a set of regulations for the young women. This time they appointed a Superior from among the demoiselles and charged her with disciplining the other young women. She was to see to it that the demoiselles did not "pass the day in their room, reading and writing, while the inmates are utterly neglected." She was to prevent the young women from leaving the Hospital for long periods of time to run errands in town. And she was to ensure that the inmates "were never left to their own devices for hours on end." Apparently, the demoiselles were far from diligent, but even if they had been hardworking, the task of caring for all the inmates would have been nearly impossible. One demoiselle had charge of a ward of forty-five bedridden men and boys, many of whom were so debilitated by physical and mental disease that they required virtually constant care.[18]

Historians have imagined that life in a *maison de force* was regimented and disciplined. This was clearly the directors' dream, but given the non-chalance of the demoiselles, it was probably not the reality. Neglect, chaos, and squalor seems to have typified life in the Grenoble Hospital more than did order, and if the directors talked so much about discipline it was because there was so little of it. They complained in particular about thievery, which was, it seems, endemic. The inmates stole bread, they filched linen, and they even carried off the furniture and sold it in town.[19] Contrary to what one might assume, the inmates were not confined, and if the Hospital maintained a porter at the gate, it was primarily to search the inmates' pockets before they departed. And depart they frequently did. Every day a "commissioner" from each ward would go out into the city and purchase fruit, tobacco, and wine. Sometimes these errand-runners also placed bets on the lottery for the paupers. Given the ease with which a pauper could slip out of the institution, it comes as no surprise that those able to work did so for their own profit.[20] They sewed gloves and spun wool for merchants in town, not for the Hospital. Within the Hospital itself, inmates mixed freely, and the directors were particularly sensitive to "scandals" involving both sexes. A man who was caught conversing with a female inmate had to face a stay in the *cachots* and a diet of bread and water, a common punishment for minor offenses committed by inmates. The directors tended to refer to these incidents as "uprisings" and "rebellions." Such "rebellions" erupted, for example, when a stove was removed from the women's ward, when the paupers were given cow's head to eat, and when a masquerade was organized in the girls' ward for the Carnival of 1783.[21]

None of these events or the host of other "insolences" of which the directors complained could possibly qualify as rebellion, but they were, nonetheless, important and revealing, for they tended to become more frequent in the 1770s and 1780s. Were the inmates, in fact, more assertive and less deferential than in the past? Or were the directors just more sensitive to their petty infractions and more determined than their predecessors to impose order within the house? There is some truth in both explanations, but the bulk of the evidence points toward the latter interpretation, for most of the inmates were in no condition to pose a serious threat to the calm functioning of the Hospital.

The registers kept by the Hospital syndic reveal just how old and debilitated—and far from menacing—the Hospital inmates actually were. In principle, the syndic noted in his registers the name, date of entry, age, state of health, occupation, family status, and date of departure or death for everyone who entered the Hospital. In practice, however, the registers were kept only sporadically. Before 1770, registers exist only for the years 1724, 1731, 1761, and 1763. It was not until 1771 that recording procedures became more consistent and precise. Sometimes this poses problems: in 1741 the syndic included all the illegitimate and foundling children accepted by the Hospital even though these data were normally carried on a separate register. With the help of the computer this inconsistency and others can be rectified, so that a general profile of the Hospital inmates emerges. Of course these data have nothing to say about the incidence of poverty or disease in Grenoble as a whole. Those who entered the institution were, at least in principle, selected by the Hospital directors, so the Hospital population reflects the priorities of the directors themselves. Their notion of the Hospital's mission is reflected in the inmates' features, and the paupers' changing physiognomy points to changes in the institution's goals and functions.[22]

One thing which the directors could not and did not alter was the number of inmates sheltered by the institution. This was determined, to a large degree, by the capacity of the Hospital buildings, and since this capacity was not increased by the construction in the eighteenth century, neither was the size of the inmate population. About 350 to 400 individuals lived within the Hospital at any one time, though they tended toward the end of the century to leave more quickly, thereby making room for new inmates. Another seemingly permanent feature of the Hospital population was the ratio of males to females. The Hospital catered to more women than men, for when the infants are omitted, 44.6 percent of the population was male and 56 percent female. Age too remained fairly constant, with children between the ages of one and five years constituting 23.2 percent of the population and individuals over sixty-one years accounting for 20.2 percent (table 12). In other words, the Hospital catered to the very young and the very old.

Of the very young, most came to the Hospital involuntarily: they were either abandoned or warehoused by their parents. Most of the infants had been exposed, usually on a major thoroughfare, then brought to the Hospital, baptized, and given names, such as Joseph Vendredi Saint, for the day on which he was found, or Catherine Exposée, for obvious reasons. If the infant survived the next few days—and many did not—he or she was quickly shipped out to wet nurses in the countryside. Older children, those deposited by their parents at the Hospital, tended to reside there for longer periods of time while the directors tried to find employment for them in rural areas. Often, the relationship between these children and

TABLE 12

AGE OF HOSPITAL INMATES

Age	No.	Percent
0 to 5 years	349	23.2
6 to 12 years	224	15.0
13 to 20 years	246	16.4
21 to 30 years	140	9.4
31 to 45 years	111	7.4
46 to 60 years	125	8.4
60 and older	302	20.2
	1,497	100.0

Source: A.D. Isère, A.H.F. 13, 17, 18, 21, 22.

the Hospital became permanent, just as it did in the case of a foundling or an illegitimate infant. Only death or maturity broke the ties to the Hospital, and as a result most of the children contained in the Hospital registers were actually adolescents returning to the institution, as they would to a parent, when they were between jobs, out of work, or ill. André Lagrue, an orphan, entered and exited the Hospital four times in the space of two years, and Jean Dumirail, aged thirteen and the cast-off son of an artisan, spent most of 1772 waiting for the Hospital to find him a new employer in the countryside.[23]

The old people within the Hospital usually left it but once, at death, for they were not just aging individuals, they were aged even by modern standards. Vincent Cros, for example, entered the institution at seventy-two years, and his wife was admitted when she was over eighty. Because historians have recently taken an interest in the treatment of the aged, it would be nice to know if the Cros and other elderly inmates had living relatives, in particular children, who had callously dumped them in this sordid institution.[24] We may assume that about 38 percent did not, for they were adult women for whom no husband, living or dead, was listed in the register, and the syndic was very conscientious on this point (table 13). Having never married, these women probably did not have offspring to care for them. As for the rest of the inmates, widows and men, we cannot tell if they had or did not have children. On the one hand, at sixty years or more, most would have outlived their immediate descendants, given the life expectancy in the old regime. On the other, if they did possess living children, these were probably both unable and unwilling to support their

TABLE 13

FAMILY STATUS OF ADULT HOSPITAL INMATES

Family Status	No.	Percent
Married male	21	3.8
Married female	34	6.1
Widow	84	15.1
Single male	204	36.6
Single female	214	38.4
	557	100.0

Note: Children between the ages of 0 and 20 have been omitted.

Source: A.D. Isère, A.H.F. 13, 17, 18, 21, 22.

aged parents. The elderly inmates of the Hospital came from the most impoverished segments of Grenoble society. In their youth, they had labored as cobblers, spinners, flax-combers, weavers, and day laborers, the most precarious and ill-paid occupations. Their children were unlikely to have done much better, so they were probably no more able to feed and clothe their parents than they were to support all of their own children. And the elderly were just as dependent, just as helpless, as the unwanted children who also lived in the Hospital. The old inmates could no longer work, no longer feed or care for themselves because they were too debilitated, by age and disease, to do so.

Of the elderly inmates, only 10 percent were listed as healthy when they entered the institution, and the rate was not much higher—about 15 percent—among the other inmates when children and adolescents are excluded (table 14). All adults, who were the only individuals to reside in the institution for any amount of time, were sick, and they suffered from a variety of ailments, which are sometimes difficult to translate into modern terms. What does one make of "cold humors," "white fevers," or just rashes?[25] Medical terminology, like eighteenth-century medicine itself, was primitive and, by our standards, peculiar. But the cryptic vocabulary of the Hospital physicians had the virtue of being consistent over the long term and, in some instances, crude but comprehensible. Many of the ailments from which the inmates suffered were afflictions whose nature is unequivocal and which admitted of no cure, either in the eighteenth century or now. The inmates were blind, deaf and dumb, paralyzed or mentally retarded, minus a limb, or lacking their senses.[26] Some poor souls endured a combination of these scourges. Suzanne Belay, admitted in

TABLE 14

PERCENTAGE OF HEALTHY AND SICK HOSPITAL INMATES
ACCORDING TO AGE

Age	Healthy	Sick
0 to 5 years	99.7	0.3
6 to 12 years	78.6	21.4
13 to 20 years	67.1	32.9
21 to 30 years	26.3	73.8
31 to 45 years	15.4	84.6
45 to 60 years	17.5	82.6
61 and older	10.3	89.7
N = 1,374		

Source: A.D. Isère, A.H.F. 13, 17, 18, 21, 22.

1763 at age fifty-four, suffered from "occasional madness" and wore a wooden leg. Marie, a "child of the house," was mentally retarded, was "malformed," and had "hemorrhages." Neither of these women suffered from a disease that would kill her, but both were so incapacitated that they were unable to work or care for themselves. Indeed, many of the inmates were bedridden, whether from paralysis, severe retardation, or old age. Not all of these permanently incapacitated were old: Antoine Chion, thirteen, was so severely retarded that he could not get out of bed or walk. Neither could Marie Marthe, an imbecile who had spent her entire life in the Hospital General. For the bedridden, the Hospital reserved two of its seven wards, which gives one some idea of just how helpless and how dependent many of the inmates were.[27]

Because these individuals did not suffer from diseases that would kill them, at least immediately, many spent extremely long periods of time in the Hospital. About 52 percent of the inmates spent more than one year in the Hospital, and 13.5 percent passed more than nine years there. Some lingered even longer. Geneviève Sybilly, for example, had spent forty-five of her seventy-three years in the institution, and an imbecile, Louise Jordan, had been there since her fifth birthday forty-eight years before.[28] In other words, the Hospital provided long-term care for the chronically ill, who were unable to care for themselves and whose families were incapable of coping with the demands of a permanently bedridden individual. The Hospital was thus a kind of repository for the detritus of society, for those who were old, weak, and useless, and whom no one else would take in. Under these circumstances, the suggestion made frequently in the late eighteenth century—that the hospitals be closed down and their inmates dispersed—looks unrealistic and unfeeling.[29] The reformers believed that the sick would receive better care at home in the bosom of their families with the help of visiting physicians. But the inmates of the Hospital of Grenoble had no homes and no families either. Instead of an occasional visit from a physician, they needed full-time custodial care, and it is hard to believe that most laboring families had the resources to provide it. One wonders what would have happened to the imbeciles, the paralytic old, and the demented young, had the reformers triumphed and the Hospital closed its doors.

Whatever their effects, the reformers' proposals had been prompted by humanitarian concerns, by the conviction that the *maisons de force* were unwholesome, insalubrious institutions, where disease was propagated rather than cured. In this regard, the reformers were absolutely correct: many of the inmates who entered the Grenoble Hospital also died there. The institution was unhealthy and apparently became more deadly with each passing year. Whereas 20 percent of the inmates died in the early part of the century, 40 percent expired in the Hospital in 1791.[30] This figure is alarming, but it is also deceptive. The number of those who actually contracted disease inside the Hospital was declining. In 1700, 24 percent of the inmates who were healthy at the time of their admission subsequently died; by 1781 this rate had dropped to only 6 percent.[31] It was the inmates, not the Hospital, who were becoming more unhealthy. While the percentage of inmates who entered in sound health declined sharply, those with contagious diseases, with various fevers, dysentery, tuberculosis, and skin ailments rose considerably (table 15). No alteration in medical terminology or diagnosis can account for this change.[32] Doctors at both the beginning and the end of the eighteenth century could appreciate the difference between disabilities like blindness and diseases like fever. Their terminology, though often curious by modern standards, still reflected a genuine change in the Hospital population. More inmates were gravely ill at the time of their admission, so more died shortly after their arrival than had in the past when the institution was dominated by healthy or chronically debilitated inmates. Now a patient either died or was cured and left the institution, so the average length of an inmate's stay was drastically reduced. By 1781, 75 percent of the patients stayed less than one year, and 21 percent less than one month.

In short, the Hospital was becoming, if only tentatively and gradually, a hospital in the true sense of the word. Apparently, the directors had come to see the institution's purpose in a new way. Now they hired a

TABLE 15

HEALTH OF INMATES AT THE TIME OF THEIR
ADMISSION TO HOSPITAL

Decade	Healthy (%)	Incurable Diseases (%)	Contagious Diseases (%)	No.
1700–1709	55.7	23.0	21.3	61
1710–1719	66.4	26.4	7.2	110
1720–1729	39.3	44.7	16.0	94
1730–1739	68.5	21.2	10.3	359
1740–1749	82.4	5.4	12.2	279
1750–1759	9.0	65.4	25.6	78
1760–1769	21.9	48.6	29.5	105
1770–1779	22.9	42.0	35.1	205
1780–1789	15.1	39.6	45.3	106
1790–1791	15.0	31.6	53.4	133
N = 1,530				

Source: A.D. Isère, A.H.F. 13, 17, 18, 21, 22.

surgeon to supplement the activities of two doctors and established special wards for the treatment of the epileptic and the pregnant.[33] Not that the Hospital suddenly became an institution of healing, where one was more likely to be cured than killed. The old abuses persisted, and the Hospital remained a depository for the chronically and hopelessly ill. But a new direction had been taken, and old notions and illusions had certainly been shed. The Hospital still employed two *achers* to capture hapless beggars, but they now spent more time preventing thievery within the house than mendicancy without. The directors themselves no longer invoked the old specter of the great confinement of the poor and no longer even mentioned beggars. It is not that they had consciously rejected confinement. Rather, they had just forgotten it and had instead struck out in new directions which would eventually lead to a complete reshaping of the old Hospital.

THE POOR OUTSIDE THE HOSPITAL

New approaches also characterized the directors' handling of another major Hospital activity—the distribution of bread to the needy who lived outside the Hospital walls. These distributions were not themselves new: the Hospital had provided between one and six pounds of bread to each impoverished family on Sundays since the middle of the seventeenth century. In the extremely difficult years between 1712 and 1722, this effort had been, as we have seen, considerably extended; subsequently, distributions were curtailed, but not halted altogether. Then, in 1764 bad harvests and high grain prices returned to Dauphiné, announcing a series of subsistence crises which would plague Grenoble and France during the last decades of the eighteenth century. Twelve hundred pounds of bread were given out each week in 1764, but the directors found this distribution disorderly and wasteful. In 1769 they resolved to draw up lists of the poor and purge those who were not truly needy. These lists survive for the years 1771, 1773, and 1774.[34] They contain the name, address, state of health, marital status, and occupation of the bread recipients, and they provide a basis for comparison with similar lists compiled in the years 1712–1722.[35] Such a comparison permits us to see changes in the incidence of poverty and differences between the priorities of early- and late-eighteenth-century directors.

Unfortunately, the lists drawn up in the 1770s are less informative than their counterparts compiled fifty years earlier. The late-eighteenth-century directors simply did not provide the same richly detailed accounts of the circumstances of the poor. Perhaps they lacked clerical assistance; maybe they were pressed for time. In any event, it was not the number of paupers that caused them to economize on their efforts, for the number of households receiving bread had diminished considerably. In the years between 1712 and 1722, 808 families had depended upon the Hospital for their sustenance. In the 1770s only 680 did so, and 40 percent of these were subsequently thrown off the rolls. If the number of households declined, so too did the number of individuals on the rolls: in the 1770s most of the households which received bread consisted of only one person. In total, fewer people received aid from the Hospital, and as the directors went about their business, the number on relief shrank even more.

The areas of the city where the poor lived had also contracted over the course of the eighteenth century. In the early years of the century, the impoverished had been fairly evenly distributed throughout Grenoble, although there was one pocket of real misery in the Saint Laurent quarter, on the right bank of the Isère (figure 2). In the 1770s Saint Laurent remained the most impoverished neighborhood in the city, and it still provided one-third of the poor on the bread lists. On the other side of the river, the Rue du Boeuf, where the growing leather trades were concentrated, had become both more populous and more miserable. The area to the west of the city around the Rue de Bonne had deteriorated as well, as

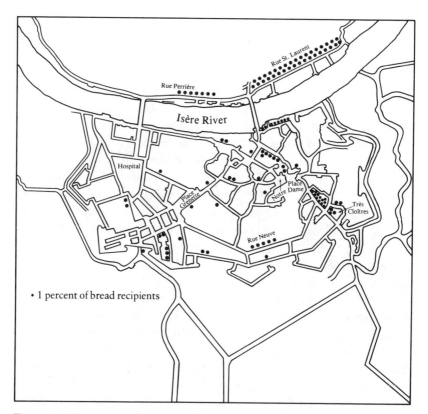

Figure 2.   Homes of the Poor according to the Bread Distribution
            Lists of 1712–1722

had the streets near the Très Cloîtres suburb. At the same time, however,
quarters of affluence had emerged in both the center of the city and along
the Rue Neuve. The poor were evidently being pushed to the margins of
the city, into the populous suburbs south of the town, and a certain
"ghettoization" was clearly under way (figure 3). The process, to be sure,
was far from complete, for a few wealthy souls like the director Bovier
still inhabited the sordid Saint Laurent quarter. But the separation of rich
and poor that would characterize most nineteenth-century cities had obviously begun.

Certain changes also occurred in the kind of individuals who fell into
impoverishment and dependence upon the Hospital. These were not revolutionary changes; the eighteenth century did not create wholly new
forms of poverty in Grenoble, or in France as a whole for that matter.
Widows still remained, as they had for centuries, among the primary vic-

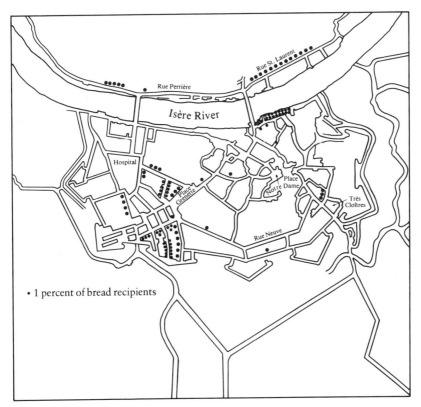

Figure 3.   Homes of the Poor according to the Bread Distribution
             Lists of 1771–1774

tims of impoverishment. The widow Duban, who struggled to support
her two adolescent daughters by selling fruit and old clothes, could have
existed one hundred years before. The widow Olet, a linen-mender with
three children, could have stepped right out of the 1712 register.[36] The
same desperation and hopelessness marked these women's lives as had
marred those of widows fifty years earlier. The widows aside, though, the
poor had changed.

To begin with, the bread recipients had become both older and sicker
in the late eighteenth century. In the early years of the century, almost 50
percent of the recipients had been in good health. By the 1770s, though,
only 16 percent were not afflicted by some sort of debility. If the recipients
were more sickly, it was, to a certain degree, because they were also older.
Heads of household between thirty and forty-five years of age declined
from 35.1 percent in 1712 to less than 1 percent in the 1770s, and those

TABLE 16

BREAD RECIPIENTS IN THE EARLY AND LATE EIGHTEENTH CENTURY

Age	1712–1722 (%)	1771–1774 (%)
1 to 5 years	0.9	1.3
6 to 12 years	2.8	10.0
13 to 20 years	3.1	2.7
21 to 30 years	8.6	1.3[a]
31 to 45 years	35.1	0.7[a]
46 to 60 years	30.1	32.0
61 and older	19.4	52.0[a]
	100.0	100.0
Gender		
Male	42.8	32.5
Female	57.2	67.5[a]
	100.0	100.0
Marital Status		
Married male	38.5	24.6[a]
Married female	5.1	5.0
Widows	34.1	34.3
Unmarried male	4.1	5.6
Unmarried female	18.2	30.5[a]
	100.0	100.0
	N = 680	N = 357

Source: A.D. Isère, A.H.F. 24, 28.

[a]The difference between the two percentages is significant to the fifth percentage level.

over the age of sixty-five grew from 19.4 percent at the beginning of the century to 52 percent at its end (table 16). An even more striking change in the impoverished dependent upon the Hospital came in gender and marital status. In 1712, women outnumbered men on the bread rolls by only 15 percent, but by the 1770s they did so by more than two to one (table 16). These women were neither the widows nor the abandoned wives with children to feed that had populated the 1712 bread list. Many of these women were single and without dependents, which indicates a distinct decline in women's fortunes. Even in the desperate early years of the century, single women, however poorly paid, underemployed or unskilled, could make ends meet provided they had no additional mouths to feed. By the 1770s, however, this was no longer the case. A woman without dependents could not support herself on the meager wages which women's work now apparently brought. Even a woman with no one to feed but herself had to depend upon the Hospital for her daily bread.

The economic position of single women had deteriorated, whereas that of men as a whole had not. This growing impoverishment of unwed females cannot be attributed to greater age or poorer health among unmarried women. The single women were a bit older than their single male counterparts, most of whom were apprentices, but they were younger than the married males on the rolls and healthier than both groups.[37] Apparently, single women were at a new and distinct disadvantage. Poverty seems to have been "feminized," a process that is reflected in the professions of the bread recipients (table 17). None too surprisingly, women's occupations dominate, especially those of laundress and second-hand dealer, or *revendeuse*. More interesting is the fact that few glove seamstresses were among the women who received bread, even though the glove industry employed thousands of Grenobloises. Perhaps the age of the female recipients of bread explains this seeming mystery. Most of these women were over forty, too old for glove sewing, which appears to have been a young woman's occupation. The trade required good eyesight and considerable speed, since the seamstresses were paid by the piece. Years of such work apparently took its toll, for all the individuals who reported to the Hospital in the 1790s with "poor eyes" were glove seamstresses.[38] After sewing gloves for years, a woman lost her eyesight and became slow in her work, so she could no longer make a living stitching gloves. She then fell back upon the more traditional female occupations of laundress and *revendeuse*, for at forty years of age domestic service was no longer a possibility. Therefore, many of the single women who filled the bread lists may have been former glove seamstresses. Evidently, even the growth of glove making, which one would have imagined to be a real boon to Grenoble's single women, did nothing to prevent the general deterioration of women's fortunes.

Although the evidence does suggest that women, especially single women, suffered growing hardship in the course of the eighteenth century, one could object that this conclusion rests upon a spurious comparison of two very differents sets of data. The 1712 bread list made at a time of unprecedented economic crisis, provides, one could argue, a picture of the "conjunctural" poor, of individuals who were abruptly hurled into impoverishment, among them men. By contrast, the 1771 bread list (made after the relatively prosperous years of the mid-eighteenth century)

TABLE 17

SELECTED OCCUPATIONS OF BREAD RECIPIENTS IN THE EARLY
AND LATE EIGHTEENTH CENTURY

Occupation	1712–1724 (%)	1771–1774 (%)
Cobbler	4.4	2.7
Silk-worker	3.0	3.6
Glove seamstress	0.6	6.3[a]
Stocking-maker	2.7	0.9
Wool-carder	0.8	0.9
Ward of Hospital	0.6	6.3[a]
Orphan	3.6	3.6
Chair-carrier	4.0	4.5
Child	3.8	3.6
Flax-comber	2.9	0.9
Tailor	4.2	3.6
Day laborer	7.6	3.6[a]
Weaver	3.8	1.9
Domestic	2.1	3.6
Laundress	2.3	5.4[a]
Spinstress	14.4	7.2
Secondhand dealer	0.8	14.4[a]
Linen-mender	1.3	2.7
Bourgeois	6.4	0.0
Other	30.7	24.3
	100.0	100.0
	N = 512	N = 111

Source: A.D. Isère, A.H.F. 24, 28.

[a]The difference between the two percentages is significant to the fifth percentage level.

supplies a portrait of the "structural" poor, of those who were, whatever the circumstances, always impoverished, and hence principally women.[39] If a bread list existed for a truly disastrous year, say 1789, then a valid comparison could be made, and the assertion that the condition of women had deteriorated would be well founded. Now it is true that the years between 1712 and 1724 were worse than those between 1771 and 1774; however, they were not that much worse. The winters of 1770–1771 and 1773–1774 witnessed soaring grain prices, which attained the same levels they would reach in 1789. Indeed, Pierre Léon has suggested that these years were, for the Dauphinois, just as difficult as 1789.[40] Consequently, there is in fact a valid basis for comparison. Women were more vulnerable than ever before to hard times, and they were probably worse off in good times as well.

Of course, if there were simply more single women in the late eighteenth century, it would come as no surprise that more single women were impoverished. Luckily, two documents can resolve this problem, the *tournées*, or visits of the assessors of the capitation taxes of 1735 and 1789. These are the only two such documents that exist for Grenoble, and both are organized on the basis of household.[41] Consequently, they should provide an indication of the increase or decrease of female-headed households in the eighteenth century. And they show that the number of households headed by single women declined. In 1735, 10.3 percent of the households in Grenoble consisted of single, unmarried women; by 1789 this figure had declined to only 6.3 percent (table 18). If more single women appeared on the distribution rolls of 1771, it was because single women were actually poorer than before, an impression confirmed by the capitation rolls. In 1735, 51 percent of the households headed by unmarried women were exempted because of poverty from taxation; in 1789, 75 percent of the households headed by single females paid a few pennies or nothing at all (table 19).[42]

Widows as a group saw some improvement in their fortunes, because of an influx of middle-class widows from the countryside. But on the whole, unmarried women, especially those who had never been married, suffered a real and distinct erosion of their economic position over the course of the eighteenth century. This deterioration was all the more dramatic in that it was not shared by men. If the capitation rolls are correct, men as a whole experienced a slight improvement, not a decline, in their fortunes during the eighteenth century. In 1735 the tax assessor considered 32 percent of the male-headed households too poor to pay taxes; in 1789 his successor, who was generally much more demanding, deemed only 28 percent desti-

TABLE 18

HEADS OF HOUSEHOLD IN THE CAPITATIONS OF 1735 AND 1789

Households	1735		1789	
	No.	Percent	No.	Percent
Headed by men	1,693	78.2	2,881	81.4
Headed by widows	250	11.5	437	12.3
Headed by other single women	220	10.3	219	6.3
Totals	2,163	100.0	3,537	100.0

Source: A.C. Grenoble, CC 447, CC 463.

TABLE 19

PERCENTAGE OF HOUSEHOLDS IN EACH CATEGORY WHICH WERE
IMPOVERISHED, ACCORDING TO THE CAPITATIONS OF 1735 AND 1789

	1735			1789		
Households	No.	No. Poor	Percent	No.	No. Poor	Percent
Headed by men	1,693	548	32.36	2,881	808	28.0[a]
Headed by widows	250	147	58.8	437	237	54.2[a]
Headed by other single women	220	113	51.36	219	166	75.5[a]

Source: A.C. Grenoble, CC 447, CC 463.

[a]The difference between the two percentages is significant to the fifth percentage level.

tute (table 19).[43] In comparison with women, men fared well during the eighteenth century, no great surprise in an era of economic progress. But the benefits of Dauphiné's commercial renaissance were not shared equally, and only a certain kind of man truly prospered. These were gentlemen, like the doctor Gagnon, who paid 30 livres in taxes, ten times as much as the wealthiest physician in 1735. Or shrewd merchants, like Monsieur Teysseire, a liquor seller, who paid 60 livres, five times as much as his most prosperous predecessors. Sometimes the nouveau riche had no equivalents, rich or poor, on the 1735 rolls. The Dolle brothers, who paid a whopping 77 livres, derived their wealth from a new source, the West Indies trade, and a host of glove merchants, who were assessed 36 livres, owed their prosperity to the growth of the glove trade.

A few men grew rich in the course of the eighteenth century, but even more remained prisoners of poverty. For every prosperous doctor or merchant there were many impoverished laborers; for each wealthy glove manufacturer, a score of destitute glove-workers. In fact, glove-workers constituted the single largest group of individuals exempted because of poverty in 1789. Next to them came the traditional recipients of alms and tax exemptions, the chair-carriers, tailors, flax-combers, and cobblers who had always occupied an important place in the world of poverty.[44] Men as a whole did not see their fortunes deteriorate dramatically as did women, but many men still remained poor. Indeed, males headed, in 1789 as in 1735, the majority of households considered too poor to pay taxes.

And yet, if we return to the bread-distribution rolls, we find that men accounted for only one-quarter of the individuals deemed worthy of a few pounds of bread by the directors of the Hospital General. A curious disjunction exists here between the reality of poverty and the directors' conception of it, a disjunction which brings us closer to understanding their assumptions and tacit requirements. The directors slighted able-bodied males presumably because they considered them capable of supporting themselves and their families, however tiny their wages. In only one instance would this tacit rule be abrogated: when the man in question had a large—extremely large—family. The few men who were assisted by the Hospital had at least five dependents and sometimes more. Pierre Brisard, for example, had six children, three extremely young, and Antoine Cornu had seven offspring, two of whom were ill.[45]

Even such numerous progeny did not necessarily qualify a man for aid in the eyes of the directors. They did not hesitate to exclude even the largest families if the children were more than ten years old. Offspring of this age, the directors reasoned, were old enough to contribute to the family income, and it did not matter much how. If a child begged, that was fine, for begging neither shocked nor troubled the directors, and they did not use the threat of removal from the rolls to frustrate it, as had their predecessors. Nor did they care much about the religious beliefs and practices of the poor. Never did they punish a pauper for his irreligiosity, only for his lack of domestic responsibility. They quickly struck from the lists men like Jean Prat, "a drunk and a weakling," who failed to support his tubercular wife, Suzanne. It is hard to see how depriving the family of bread benefited the unfortunate Suzanne, and the directors sometimes took a more sensible course. They removed Denis Rosset, a carriage-maker who was a "bad subject and beat his wife until he separated from her," from the rolls, but they continued to give bread to his wife. A husband bore responsibility for his family and so too did more distant relations. The directors were quick to remove an individual from the bread lists if they learned that he or she had living relatives, whether rich or poor. They struck the widow Métisseur from the lists when they learned that she had a daughter who exercised the miserable trade of stocking-mender, and they also deprived the widow Duban when it was rumored that she had a laundress daughter. If an individual was utterly alone and sick, then the Hospital owed him assistance. If he had even one impoverished relative, then bread would quickly be withdrawn.[46]

The surest way, however, to be removed from the bread lists was to recover from illness or injury. Almost none of the bread recipients were healthy, particularly the men.[47] As long as a man was unable to work, the directors were happy to provide him and his family with bread. But once he recovered, he and his dependents came off the rolls. Such was the fate of Louis Rambaud, a hod carrier with four children, who overcame an injury sustained at work and therefore saw his family stricken from the rolls. The directors also removed Barnabé Colombet, a "small cobbler" with four children, when both he and his wife recovered, even though the directors themselves said "he could not support his family with his labor."[48] Apparently, the directors granted relief only to those too debilitated or diseased to work. Rarely did they consider unemployment or low wages sufficient misfortune to merit a few pounds of bread. As a result, if an individual, especially a man, was able to work but could not find employment, then he simply did not receive bread, and neither did his children. In this regard, the directors had, in their own quiet way, embraced the ideas of eighteenth-century reformers and even revolutionary legislators. Those who could not work required assistance; those who could work would not get demeaning and undeserved alms. The able-bodied would labor, and the rest would still receive bread, but only under specific conditions.

PETITIONS FROM THE POOR

The new rigor at the Hospital also manifested itself in a new set of procedures and regulations. In the past, intimacy and informality had been the rule: when a pauper needed assistance he either appealed to a patron or presented himself at the Bureau of the Directors. In the eighteenth century, the directors lost their taste for personal contact with the poor. They became squeamish and banished the impoverished from their weekly meetings. Now they required that each pauper submit a written petition to be scrutinized at leisure and a safe distance from the poor. These petitions point to the emergence of a more bureaucratic, less personal stance among the directors, but this is not their principal value. They also provide rare information on the circumstances and demands of the poor, and shed further light on the directors' response to poverty.

Unfortunately, not all of the petitions submitted to the Hospital have survived. Those still in the Hospital archives date, for the most part, from the late eighteenth century, but sheer chance appears to account for their conservation. Not all of the two hundred surviving petitions were requests for the same services, nor did they all meet with either success or failure. To all appearances, this is an utterly random sample, which makes audible the otherwise unintelligible voices of the poor.[49]

It would be naïve, of course, to believe that these petitions express directly and without distortion the thoughts of all the impoverished. First, the petitioners were themselves a rather special group. By their petitions, they displayed an assertiveness and a knowledge of the Hospital's administrative procedures that the lowliest and most marginal of the poor probably lacked.[50] Second, the petitioners were apt to ask only for those services which the Hospital already provided and to phrase their petitions in a way that would please the directors. It is hard to believe, for example, that the petitioners actually "prayed incessantly for the good health and the conservation of the directors," as they claimed in their petitions. Third, like this last phrase, the vocabulary of the petitions was formulaic and stereotypical; every petitioner used the same words and phrases, as if compelled to follow a legal form. Consequently, the language of the petitions sheds no light on the thoughts or attitudes of the impoverished. Finally, the poor did not write these requests themselves, for most were illiterate. They either hired a *maître écrivain* or depended on one of two intermediaries to draw up their petitions.

These were not the traditional intermediaries of the seventeenth century—the magistrates and seigneurs who had provided their clients, dependents, and domestics with a bed in the Hospital. This sort of aristocratic patronage had long disappeared, and more mundane individuals now helped the poor petition the Hospital. Among them were midwives, who ran clinics in their homes where a woman would give birth and then remain for at least a week after her confinement. Frequently, midwives took in penniless, unwed mothers, on whose behalf they petitioned the Hospital to assume responsibility for the unwanted infant and, not coincidentally, the cost of the confinement. Thus Marguerite Resson, a midwife, wrote to the Hospital that a certain Marguerite Biron, native of Saint Laurent parish, had taken refuge in her home for her confinement. "She is," the midwife explained, "impoverished and cannot support this child fathered by a common soldier." Resson assured the directors that the woman was a native Grenobloise and attached a *déclaration de grossesse* to the petition, thereby displaying a knowledge of the Hospital's administrative procedures, for the directors preferred children born of natives and accompanied by a *déclaration de grossesse*.[51] Though far from disinterested—they wanted to receive payment for the birth—the midwives performed a valuable function. They helped young women who were probably ignorant of such matters navigate the complexities of the Hospital's rules and regulations.

There is little doubt as to the selflessness of the other principal intermediary—the parish priest. His importance in securing assistance for his unfortunate parishioners cannot be overstated. Unwed mothers in particular relied upon his assistance. For example, one unwed mother arrived at the Hospital carrying a note from her parish priest which read: "The bearer of this letter is an unfortunate girl ready to give birth, poor, without father or mother, utterly deprived of resources; she is worthy of your charity."[52] The directors, uncharacteristically, admitted her without further ado. Sometimes the priest helped the unwed mother circumvent the Hospital's rules. In 1748 the priest of Froges wrote that a young girl in that village had been raped in a nearby forest. She had no milk to feed her child, and "since I've heard that you will accept no child without some money I have persuaded a charitable person to donate 25 écus for the infant's support."[53] It might be objected that the priests meddled in their parishioners' lives and wielded an excessive power over the poor. Perhaps the priests did both, but that did not prevent their parishioners from coming to them before all others. When an artisan's wife went quite mad and tried to kill him, the artisan called first the priest and only later the local equivalent of the police, the municipal guard.[54]

Those who petitioned the Hospital with or without the help of an intermediary were day laborers, glove or leather workers, cobblers and chaircarriers, domestics and secondhand dealers, in short, the traditional recipients of the Hospital's aid. Widows, none too surprisingly, occupied a large place among the petitioners, and so too did unwed mothers.[55] The single largest group, however, was the group least served by the Hospital: married males with families to feed. Men accounted for almost half of the petitioners, and yet they were virtually absent from the Hospital breadrolls and extremely scarce among the Hospital inmates.[56]

What did these desperate individuals want? They wanted among other things to enter the Hospital General.[57] Old age, debility, and sheer loneliness had forced them to appeal to an institution they were commonly known to loathe and fear. Dependency, that is, the inability to work, caused many, like a domestic too old and too sick to find a position, to resort to the Hospital, for the alternatives were neither numerous nor pleasant. One unusual petition illustrates just how a Grenoblois or in this case a Grenobloise might provide for old age and ill health and yet end up in the Hospital after all. In 1735 a cobbler and his wife appealed to the Hospital to take one Marguerite Mornin, an unmarried woman of seventy-seven years, off their hands. Mornin, who was nearly blind, had promised the cobbler her entire estate, which she claimed amounted to 2,000 livres, in return for sheltering and caring for her until her death. Out of the bargain the cobbler got but 200 livres and more problems than he had ever expected. Mornin turned out to be very ill-tempered and chronically inebriated. She scolded the workers he employed, and they all soon left his service. On one occasion, she drank all his wine and broke everything in his shop. To the horror of the neighbors, she then nearly set fire to the building. Finally, the landlord intervened and insisted she leave. The cobbler was only too willing and literally begged the directors to take the old woman off his hands, which they agreed to do, in return for 5 livres a month until her death.[58]

The cobbler was not the only Grenoblois who asked that the Hospital relieve him of an unwanted guest. Many of the petitioners requested that the directors assume responsibility for an infant or a child who had been abandoned by its parents in the petitioner's home. A schoolmaster, for example, had agreed to take care of a child while the father, a *chamoiseur,* went to Lyon; the father never returned, and the schoolmaster had no intention of sheltering the child permanently. A widow complained that her son and daughter-in-law had fled Grenoble in the middle of the night when they could no longer pay their rent. The grandmother was saddled with the child and could not support it.[59] One did not have to be related to the parents to end up with a child. As one Demoiselle Claudine discovered, a chance encounter could leave an individual with an unwanted infant. In 1758 Claudine was returning from La Tronche when she saw a young girl sitting by the river moaning. She asked her if she was in pain and then offered to accompany her into town. On the way she realized that the girl was pregnant, and no sooner had they entered Claudine's house than the young woman gave birth to a baby girl. Claudine then went out to buy the young woman syrup and meat, and when she returned, the woman was gone but the infant was still there. Neighborliness could bring equally unfortunate consequences, as an artisan's wife, Suzanne Jarron, learned. She had the misfortune to live next door to a midwife who one evening threw out an impoverished girl who had just given birth. Jarron took pity on the girl and brought her into the house. The next day she asked the midwife to take the "creature" off her hands, but the midwife gave her the infant instead. Now Jarron's husband had returned and threatened to beat his charitable wife. After all, as she explained to the directors, she had five children of her own to feed and did not want to give them up.[60]

Not all Grenoblois were as kindly as Jarron or as reluctant to relinquish their own children. Many of the petitioners requested that the Hospital take one of their offspring and send him to a wet nurse in the countryside or house him in the Hospital General. Any number of disasters could precipitate such a request. The death of his wife forced Etienne

Pelin, a glove-worker, to ask the Hospital to take charge of one of his three children. The sudden departure of her husband caused a stocking-er's wife to make similar appeal. One Simon Mathieu experienced a host of such misfortunes. First, he was evicted from his farm when he could no longer pay the rent. Then his wife died, and he was evicted from his apartment in Grenoble. Finally, the country wet nurse who was tending to his two children returned them when he failed to pay her wages, and left them in the street outside his home.[61] Few Grenoblois were as besieged as Mathieu, but many did ask the Hospital to take their children off their hands. Usually, this request came with the birth of an additional child, generally the third.

That the Grenoblois' fortunes were strained at the advent of only the third child is surprising, and it points to one of the grim realities of a workingman's life, a reality consistently overlooked by the Hospital directors. The laborer may well have sought to alleviate his poverty by casting off one of his children, but the root cause of his difficulties was not the number of his offspring but the inadequacy of his wages. Late-eighteenth-century artisans do appear to have had more children than their predecessors; demographic studies have shown that fertility was rising and infant mortality declining very slightly in late-eighteenth-century Grenoble.[62] But the problem for the wage earner was not so much demographic as economic. If a man and a woman both working cannot support three children, then they are not receiving a living wage. Real wages did decline in Grenoble during the eighteenth century, particularly toward the end of the period, and one assumes that those at the very bottom of the scale, the day laborers and chair-carriers who appealed to the Hospital, were those most affected by this decline.[63] Nor was this just a temporary problem precipitated by economic crisis, though soaring grain prices certainly wreaked havoc with the family economy. When artisans asked the Hospital to take charge of a child, they always protested that they would remove the child one day, and some did. But as the directors frequently complained, such temporary arrangements often became permanent. The "artisans' children," as the directors called these legitimate offspring, eventually became adults "raised at the expense of the Hospital."

These children were a heavy burden to the Hospital, but the directors were far more willing to aid them than their fathers. Of those individuals who petitioned to be admitted to the Hospital itself, 74 percent received a flat denial, 13 percent were admitted in return for a cash payment, and 13 percent were placed on the bread lists instead. Sixty percent of those who petitioned the Hospital to take charge of their offspring, in contrast, saw their request granted. The reasons behind the directors' actions are not hard to discern. The administering of the Hospital constituted the single largest item in the directors' budget, and it cost more—approximately 200 livres annually—to house an inmate in the Hospital than it did to send a child to a wet nurse. Cheaper still was the distribution of bread, which became the directors' preferred means of assistance. More than half of those who asked to be placed on the bread lists had their petitions granted, and many individuals who requested other services got bread instead. Only those who asked that their ration of bread be increased received a brusque denial, such a request being, it seems, the height of insolence.

Apparently, the Hospital directors, like eighteenth-century reformers, preferred *secours à domicile*, that is, outdoor relief such as the bread distributions, to incarceration in an old *maison de force*. They too pursued the "deinstitutionalization" of the poor, and though their motives were largely financial, they still made of Enlightenment theory a reality. The directors also displayed another impulse generally identified with the late eighteenth century: a concern for children. They made the young the primary beneficiaries of their largesse, and they assumed responsibility for unwanted children with uncharacteristic equanimity. When it came to children, the directors seemed to cast their financial worries to the wind.

Still, the Hospital directors were not as softhearted as they seemed. They usually capitulated to the request of unwed mothers, who constituted 60 percent of those who asked the Hospital to assume responsibility for a child, but they were much less accommodating when it came to impoverished artisans with legitimate children. This tendency to accept illegitimate infants but to deny admission to legitimate children grew as the eighteenth century progressed and the fortunes of the Hospital diminished. In the 1740s and 1750s, the directors had readily accepted unwanted but legitimate children, sometimes as many as 150 in a year.[64] But as the financial situation of the Hospital deteriorated, so too did the directors' generosity. In 1769 the directors admitted only 100 such children, and by 1789 the number had shrunk to only 34. Demand had not fallen: Grenoble's artisans were no more prosperous and no less eager to relieve themselves of a mouth to feed. The directors' generosity had declined. The drop in the number of legitimate children accepted by the Hospital resulted from a rule adopted by the directors in 1765 which required every legitimate child admitted to have lost one or preferably both parents.[65]

To a certain degree, humanitarian concerns prompted this ruling: the directors believed, probably correctly, that a child would be better off in the bosom of his family, and they even offered to pay artisan women to nurse their own children. Still, finances remained the primary motive, and the directors did not blush to economize at the expense of the child. Throughout most of the eighteenth century, the directors underpaid their wet nurses, which made nurses difficult to obtain and deprived the infants of good care. Economy was necessary because the number of children assisted by the Hospital—in particular bastard children—was always growing. The directors slighted wet nurses and pushed aside legitimate children to make way for the flood of illegitimate and foundling infants which swept over the Hospital in the late eighteenth century. In fact, bastard and abandoned children came to absorb most of the directors' attention and much of the Hospital budget as illegitimacy increased toward the end of the century.

ILLEGITIMACY AND THE HOSPITAL

In the course of the eighteenth century, illegitimate babies came to represent a larger and larger portion of the children assisted by the Hospital. In 1769 such illegitimate and foundling children constituted 60 percent of the children admitted by the Hospital; in 1789 they accounted for over 80 percent. The sheer number of these infants—for they were invariably newborn babies—was also impressive. In 1769 the Hospital admitted 60 foundlings and bastard infants; by 1789 this number had grown to 137.[66] No dramatic change in the director's policies accounted for this increase. Starting in 1784, the Hospital did receive grants from the monarchy for illegitimate infants, but these subsidies covered no more than half of the expenses caused by the children. Moreover, they were paid begrudgingly and only after extremely long delays.[67] Such gifts were, therefore, unlikely to make the directors disregard the Hospital's tremendous financial problems, and in any case, there is no sign that the directors suddenly forgot the deficits and opened the Hospital's doors. On the contrary, they continued to observe a policy of strict economy and the exclusion of all but the most deserving children. They put many obstacles in the path of an unwed mother who wanted the Hospital to assume responsibility for her child, requiring that she provide a *déclaration de grossesse* and baptismal certificates for herself and the infant. In addition, the directors reduced the number of legitimate children the Hospital admitted. Their efforts apparently had some effect, for although the Hospital took charge of more and more illegitimate and foundling infants, the overall number of children admitted each year by the directors grew only slightly.[68]

The Hospital directors were clearly dealing with a phenomenon that was beyond their control—a rise in abandonment and illegitimacy. Since the very end of the seventeenth century Grenoble had boasted an unusually high rate of both, and this problem only increased in the course of the eighteenth century. In the 1700s, 2 percent of the infants baptized in Grenoble's churches had been exposed; by the 1750s this rate had jumped to 5 percent. In sheer numbers this meant that in the year 1720, twelve infants were exposed, and in the year 1760, thirty-three infants were abandoned. Illegitimacy, too, was unusually frequent in Grenoble. In the years between 1696 and 1699, 5 percent of the infants baptized in Grenoble's parishes were described as "natural," or illegitimate. In the 1760s the rate of illegitimacy reached almost 11 percent.[69]

Did the rate of abandonment and illegitimacy continue to rise in the last quarter of the eighteenth century? Here, a lack of demographic studies for the years after 1764 is sorely felt, and any conclusions in this regard are, at best, speculative. Still, there are indications that both abandonment and illegitimacy pursued their upward climb. Certainly, the Hospital directors, who had little choice but to accept any child exposed in the city, admitted more and more foundlings. In 1769 the Hospital received thirty-six exposed babies, and in 1781 it admitted fifty such infants, a number which was quickly surpassed in 1789 when the Hospital accepted almost seventy foundlings. This represents a 28 percent increase in the 1780s alone. Since the number of baptisms increased during this period by only 6 percent, it appears that a rise in the rate of abandonment did occur.[70] The sources of this increase in the number of foundlings must inevitably remain obscure. Were these infants illegitimate? Were they the offspring of rural illicit unions brought to Grenoble to be exposed? Or were they the babies of honest, married artisans who, frustrated by the directors' unwillingness to accept their infants, simply exposed them instead? Unfortunately, the answers to these questions must remain just as mysterious as the pathetic tokens—ribbons, woolen patches, and scrawled notes—which were once attached to the infants and are now conserved in the Hospital archives.[71]

It also seems that illegitimacy rose in the last years of the old regime. To begin with, the Hospital directors accepted growing numbers of illegitimate infants. In 1769 the Hospital admitted thirty-two illegitimate infants; in 1789 it accepted more than twice that number, sixty-eight.[72] This represents a 52 percent increase, and the number of baptisms in Grenoble certainly did not double during the same period. There are, of course, three possible explanations for this increase. The first is that large numbers of rural infants swelled the contingent of children accepted by the directors. The second is that the rate of illegitimacy remained constant but the percentage of infants ending up in the Hospital rose dramatically. The third is, quite simply, that the rate of illegitimacy rose. As for the first possibility, that rural infants swelled the ranks of the children accepted by the Hospital, this is not in fact a possibility. It was not the directors' policy to accept the offspring of rural unions, and documents from the Hospital archives confirm that the directors observed these rules. The second explanation for the growing number of illicit infants at the Hospital is considerably more plausible. If the rate of illegitimacy was constant from 1769 to 1789, then 65 percent of the illicit babies born in Grenoble in 1789 became wards of the Hospital, compared with a mere 28 percent in 1769. This would mean that important and interesting changes had occurred in illegitimacy, specifically in the economic fortunes of the unwed mothers who now had to give up their babies. Finally, it is possible that the rate of illegitimacy simply rose in Grenoble in the late eighteenth century as it did in cities throughout France.[73] My guess is that both of these latter phenomena occurred simultaneously and that they are in fact interrelated. Grenoble began the eighteenth century with an unusually high rate of illegitimacy, and, far from declining, it continued to rise slowly. Then, sometime after 1760, certain changes in the nature of illicit unions occurred which brought more and more infants to the Hospital and set the rate of illegitimacy climbing swiftly, to soar after 1780.

The *déclarations de grossesse* allow us to scrutinize this issue more closely, for they provide information, not obtainable elsewhere, on hundreds of illicit unions. They have distinct advantages, but one should not overestimate their value, for they also pose problems. Among other things, fewer and fewer pregnant women made declarations in the late eighteenth century.[74] Moreover, those who did, did so with greater discretion. The "private" declaration appeared in the late eighteenth century, that is, a declaration received by a notary. Strictly speaking, a notary was unqualified to receive such a document, but his discretion could be counted on, and his honesty was anything but unimpeachable. As an apothecary explained to his pregnant mistress, "one makes a declaration before a friendly notary and he keeps the secret until the baby is born; then he tears up the papers and the woman's honor is preserved."[75] Only upper-class women could afford such a declaration, for it cost at least 4 livres and usually more if it were patently false. A domestic or a working woman could not afford such a sum, but she too could make a "private" declaration, before a parish priest. For the impoverished woman the parish priest had several distinct advantages: he was discreet, he did not charge money, and he could help the unwed mother get her baby accepted by the Hospital General. A large number of women who later confided the care of their infants to the Hospital did in fact take this route, and although it presented benefits to them, it has drawbacks for the historian. The priest never wrote down the details of the woman's seduction, and sometimes he even omitted the seducer's name. Declarations made by priests (and by judges too) tended to be shorter in the late eighteenth century than they were before. They are, consequently, less informative.

They are also deceptive, filled with half-truths and lies. Of the twenty-five declarations made before the Justice in 1789, six amended and corrected earlier fallacious documents.[76] This raises the ugly suspicion that many of the declarations were false, but the documents conserved at the Hospital General are relatively reliable. The directors required that every illegitimate child they accepted be accompanied by a declaration, which seems to have been the main reason women went to the trouble to make them. The directors scrutinized these documents very carefully, for they hoped to make the unwed father support his child. They were usually not successful in this regard, but they still looked closely at each declaration, and when they thought it contained lies, they noted the fact on the back. Then they withheld assistance until the woman in question made a new, truthful declaration, which they appended to the first.[77] Their vigilance therefore insures that the information in some of the declarations is at least plausible if not actually truthful.

The declarations conserved in the G series of the Hospital archives also have the advantage of deriving from a number of pens, those of notaries, priests, and secretaries of Grenoble's municipal court, the Justice. In the Justice archives, declarations are also preserved, and an extensive sample of these documents, particularly those written between 1760 and 1790, was added to the Hospital data. Basically, the declarations from the Justice and the Hospital are similar, and together they form a considerable amount of data, some 1,100 documents.[78] They can provide suggestions, though not firm conclusions, as to why illegitimacy rose in the late eighteenth century and what changes in its nature caused more and more illicit infants to end up at the Hospital General.

What first emerges from the data, however, is not change but permanence. Many of the fundamental features of illegitimacy that we observed at the very beginning of the eighteenth century were still in place at its close. Most of the unwed mothers, for example, were still between the

ages of eighteen and thirty—hardly a surprise, since these years correspond to peak female fertility. More significant is the discovery that the
majority—73 percent—of the unwed mothers were, as always, domestic
servants. There seems to be a strong, structural link between domestic
service and illegitimacy.[79] Certainly the occupation created a proximity
between male and female conducive to intimate relations. But serving as a
domestic may not, in and of itself, have destined a young woman to become an unwed mother. Almost all unwed, fertile women may simply
have been servants, for eighteenth-century society offered few alternatives to single young women.[80] Furthermore, the pregnant servants shared
with other unwed mothers qualities that went beyond mere profession.
Almost all were illiterate, and many were orphaned of father and sometimes of mother as well. Orphan girls seem to have been peculiarly vulnerable to illicit pregnancy; in eighteenth-century Lille the majority of unwed mothers had lost their parents. Just how much the absence of parents
predisposed a woman to an illegitimate pregnancy is hard to determine.
In Grenoble, information on the unwed mothers' parents appears only
haphazardly in the declarations.[81] The place of the mother's seduction
was recorded more consistently, and in 82 percent of all the cases, that
place was Grenoble (table 20).

The town was where young girls went astray. The old notion that peasant girls, fearing for their honor, swarmed into the city and drove up the
illegitimacy rates, simply does not apply to Grenoble.[82] Certainly, unwed
and pregnant peasant girls did occasionally take refuge in town, and their

TABLE 20

PLACE OF SEDUCTION OF UNWED MOTHERS

Decade	Grenoble (%)	Dauphiné (%)	Elsewhere (%)	No.
1720–1729	61.7	33.3	5.0	81
1730–1739	78.2	20.9	0.9	110
1740–1749	84.1	13.6	2.3	88
1750–1759	86.8	13.2	0	91
1760–1769	88.9	9.5	1.6	126
1770–1779	86.0	11.7	2.3	171
1780–1789	88.9	9.2	1.9	303
Totals	82.2	15.8	2.0	970

Source: A.D. Isère, 13 B 652–657; A.H.G. 1–16.

lovers, if they were well off, frequently paid for the voyage. But such purely rural unions accounted for only 16 percent of the illicit births after 1730, and this rate tended to decline toward the end of the century. Not all the unwed mothers, though, were native to Grenoble, born and bred in the city. Forty-six percent of the mothers were migrants, fairly recent arrivals to the town, who had come from villages in Dauphiné to work in Grenoble (table 21). They did not come long distances; most hailed from the villages south of Grenoble, around Vizille and further east, La Mure, and from the Grési-vaudan valley to the north. At the time of their seduction, these women had been living in Grenoble for one to three years, long enough to get pregnant, but apparently not long enough to learn city ways.

Young, ignorant, and a servant by profession—the classic profile of the unwed mother held until the middle of the eighteenth century. Then, its features began to change. In the 1750s women born and bred in Grenoble began to appear in substantial numbers among the unwed mothers, and by 1780 these Grenobloises nearly equaled the migrant women (table 21). At the same time, more and more of the unwed mothers exercised an urban trade other than that of domestic.[83] Secondhand dealers, laun-dresses, day laborers, and, of course, glove seamstresses came to consti-tute about one-third of the unwed mothers in the 1780s (table 22). It is surprising, given their numerical importance in the city, that glove seam-stresses did not predominate among the unwed mothers. Even though the percentage of glove seamstresses did grow over the course of the century, they accounted for only 8.3 percent of the single mothers in the 1780s.

TABLE 21

GEOGRAPHICAL ORIGINS AND RESIDENCES OF UNWED MOTHERS

Decade	Born and Resident in Grenoble (%)	Migrants (%)	Born and Resident in Rural Area (%)	No.
1729–1729	24.0	40.7	35.3	81
1730–1739	31.6	50.5	17.9	95
1740–1749	33.3	53.3	13.4	75
1750–1759	41.6	48.0	10.4	77
1760–1769	47.7	43.0	9.3	107
1770–1779	43.7	41.1	15.2	151
1780–1789	41.7	46.9	11.4	254
Totals	36.2	46.5	17.4	840

Source: A.D. Isère, 13 B 652–657; A.H.G. 1–16.

Less novel but no less independent professions seem to have been more conducive to pregnancy out of wedlock. Laundresses, day laborers, and the practitioners of other lowly but urban professions accounted for a substantially larger proportion—25 percent—of the unwed mothers than before (table 22).

As for the seducers of these unfortunate women, there seems at first to be little change. The army was still responsible for a high percentage of the illegitimate children born in the city, just as it had been in the 1690s and early 1700s when every passage of troops meant a flood of babies nine months later. The soldiers did not leave; in fact, they became a permanent presence in the city with the establishment of a garrison outside the Porte de Bonne in the 1720s. By 1731, 1,000 men inhabited the garrison, a number which grew to 1,900 by 1774.[84] The amorous exploits of these men of arms were well known in the city. "Today," a local gossip reported in 1771, "the artillery regiment departed leaving in its wake, so they say, some 300 children; they also claim that 17 or 18 girls are pregnant at the same time by the same sergeant."[85] Hearsay had probably exaggerated the sergeant's conquests, but the impact of the garrison upon illegitimacy in the first three quarters of the eighteenth century cannot be overstated. As early as the 1730s, Grenoble had attained a rate of illegitimacy twice that of other

TABLE 22

OCCUPATIONS OF UNWED MOTHERS

Decade	Domestics (%)	Urban Professions[a] (%)	Glove-worker (%)	Other[b] (%)	No.
1720–1729	81.3	14.1	1.6	3.0	64
1730–1739	84.2	10.5	2.6	2.7	76
1740–1749	84.4	6.3	6.3	3.0	64
1750–1759	82.8	10.3	1.7	5.2	58
1760–1769	74.1	19.0	5.2	1.7	58
1770–1779	60.8	27.6	7.4	4.2	94
1780–1789	64.1	25.0	8.3	2.6	181
Totals	73.9	17.8	5.0	3.3	595

Source: A.D. Isère, 13 B 652–657; A.H.G. 1–16.

[a]Urban occupations include day laborer, secondhand dealer, laundress, linen-mender, flax-comber, spinner, stockinger, button-maker, and prostitute.

[b]Other includes widows, abandoned wives, and daughters of merchants and members of the legal professions.

French cities, and the army seems to bear responsibility for this precocious rise in bastardy, at least until the last two decades of the century.[86]

Then in the 1780s another group rose to challenge the soldiers' position as the preeminent Don Juans of the city. These were the urban workers who, in the last two decades of the century, came to constitute between 38 and 52 percent of Grenoble's seducers (table 23). The young workers in question came from a variety of trades: day laborers, glove-workers, flax-combers, weavers, and wigmakers predominated on a long list of occupations. One quality did bind all of these laboring men: all were described as *ouvriers*, that is, workers employed by a master artisan or, more often, a merchant-manufacturer. That this new kind of father appeared just when wage-earning urban women also began to dominate among the unwed mothers is no coincidence. A wage-earning man was more likely to seduce a wage-earning woman than a domestic or peasant girl. Sometimes the lovers came from the same profession and met in the same workroom. Bernard Michalet, a glove-worker, encountered and seduced Claudine Coulen, a glove seamstress, in their common place of work. If similar urban occupations created an affinity and an occasion to meet, so too did common, urban origins. Michel Dolivat, an apprentice glove-maker, impregnated his childhood sweetheart, Barbe Mar, who had grown up with him in the Saint Laurent quarter.[87] Because the declarations provide scant information on the putative fathers' origins, it is

TABLE 23

OCCUPATIONS OF UNWED FATHERS

Decade	Soldiers (%)	Peasants[a] (%)	Domestics (%)	Superiors[b] (%)	Workers (%)	No.
1720–1729	16.4	9.0	23.9	29.9	20.9	67
1730–1739	28.1	7.3	25.0	12.5	27.1	96
1740–1749	20.8	6.4	20.8	13.0	39.0	77
1750–1759	34.3	6.5	25.0	18.4	15.8	76
1760–1769	38.1	4.8	18.0	10.5	28.6	105
1770–1779	49.0	2.0	12.8	7.4	28.8	149
1780–1789	34.9	4.8	13.2	8.7	38.4	289
1790	28.0	4.0	4.0	12.0	52.0	50
Totals	26.6	5.9	17.8	13.0	30.9	909

Source: A.D. Isère, 13 B 652–657; A.H.G. 1–16.

[a]Peasants include plowmen (*laboreurs*) and agricultural laborers.
[b]Superiors include members of the legal professions, bourgeois, merchants, and master artisans.

hard to tell just how many illicit unions were based on common, urban roots. Still, it is clear that a new kind of illicit union, a union between city-dwelling, wage-earning men and women, fueled the sudden rise in illegitimacy which occurred in the 1780s.

It is hard—and probably presumptuous—to speculate on the emotional climate within these unions. Still, the declarations do provide a very general indication of the ties that bound unwed father and mother. Some of these unions appear to have been affectionate, honest courtships gone awry. Such relationships were fairly common in the seventeenth century, but in the late eighteenth the circumstance which aborted the marriage was, more frequently than ever before, poverty. In 1789, for example, an apprentice butcher, Pierre Odoz, petitioned the Hospital to assume responsibility for his illegitimate son by a serving girl. The couple, he explained, had planned to get married, but now could not, for both had lost their jobs.[88]

Money played a role in other unions as well, although in quite a different fashion. Prostitution left its traces in the declarations, and it is clear that bawds and harlots still plied their trade in the city streets. Françoise Buisson, for example, an eighteen-year-old Grenobloise, was prostituted regularly by the wife of an ironworker to one Monsieur Bozonnat. This Monsieur Bozonnat, who was either a director of the Hospital or his relative, was quite a consumer of young girls. When Anne Perrin fell prey to the supplications of her landlady, and went to an inn, she met three other prostitutes, all named Charlotte, and the ubiquitous Monsieur Bozonnat. Together the quartet took tea and then had sex, for which Monsieur Bozonnat paid 3 écus.[89]

Such professionals faced growing competition from occasional and part-time prostitutes, for casual prostitution appears to have increased in the late eighteenth century, just as the economic position of single women deteriorated. Poverty forced more and more women to sell their bodies from time to time, as was the case with the flax-comber Benoite Bérard, who surrendered to her employer's demands when, "seeing her in need, he promised to render her services and give her money." Françoise Sauze searched in vain for two months for employment; when she found none she slept with a tobacco seller for a few pennies. Only true desperation could have driven a woman to sell herself for such a small sum, but the road to prostitution was easy enough to take. In 1757 Jeanne Parret had neither worked nor eaten for three days. Famished, she began to beg discreetly in the streets behind the Place Grenette. There she encountered a young man who reprimanded her and claimed that her situation "touched his heart." He gave her an écu and then followed her to her room where he had sexual relations with her. If the border between professional and casual prostitution was increasingly unclear, that between romantic and venal love was all but indistinguishable. More and more seducers offered their lovers vague promises of advancement and phantom hopes of future prosperity. The stocking-mender Benoite Perret, for example, surrendered to her lover when he promised to find her a position as a governess in Lyon. Rose Turc capitulated when a barrister flashed a diamond before her eyes and promised to marry her.[90] Of course, none of these offers materialized, and only the ingenuous woman paid the price.

Late-eighteenth-century seducers may have victimized women, but at least they did not brutalize them. Whereas 25 percent of the unwed fathers in the 1730s raped their prey, only 4 percent in the 1780s assaulted their partners. From rape to seduction: what the putative father had once achieved by violence, he now accomplished with clever promises and subtle manipulation. The sheer cunning of the late-eighteenth-century seducer is impressive, and his skill far exceeded that of his rather coarse and violent seventeenth-century predecessor. A native of Voiron named Jean seduced a glove seamstress with promises of marriage, while carefully hiding both his surname and his wife back in Voiron. A hardware merchant named Mollard offered to marry a young domestic, but when she announced she was pregnant, he refused to help her. He claimed that he was married and therefore exempted from such a burden by law, correct on both points. For sheer finesse, few seducers matched a poultry dealer named Bajat whose modus operandi illustrates just how much life and love had evolved in Grenoble. In 1786 Bajat befriended the family of an extremely young and beautiful girl, and he profited from this acquaintance to spend a great deal of time with her. Eventually, he seduced her by the rather novel means of "having lewd conversations with her" and "loaning her bad books."[91]

A more common means of seduction was the promise of marriage, and women claimed to have received such an offer with greater and greater frequency. By the 1780s virtually all the declarations contained the phrase "under the promise of marriage," and it appeared so often that one is tempted to dismiss it as a convention and nothing more. Perhaps the priests and judges, who were on the whole more discreet than in the past, hoped to preserve a shred of the unfortunate mother's honor. Perhaps the women themselves sought to render a shameful situation a bit less damning. In any event, women claimed to have been offered marriage in circumstances that made such a promise incredible if not impossible. Soldiers frequently told

their credulous lovers that they would marry them—a patent impossibility
since they needed either their officers' permission, rarely given, or their
discharge. In a few cases, the soldiers did claim that they "would have a
discharge very soon," but one still wonders how these young women could
have been so gullible. People do, however, believe what they want to believe, and the Grenobloises' hopes were not utterly without foundation. A
few soldiers from the garrison did settle in Grenoble, marry, have children,
and live to a respectable old age.

Nor did the Grenobloises have reason to disbelieve the other young
men, civilians, who held the phantom of matrimony before their eyes. A
growing proportion of these men were of a social status equal to that of
their lovers, so that marriage was not utterly unthinkable or impossible
(table 24). In the 1720s only 49 percent of the couples occupied a roughly
similar position on the social ladder; by the 1780s, though, almost 74 percent were of equivalent social standing.[92] In contrast to the past, when most
of the seducers hailed from much higher social groups, marriage was now a
distinct possibility.

Consequently, the unwed mothers' hopes, though eventually disap-
pointed, were not unfounded. They were, in any case, certainly intense,
for many women clung to their illusions right to the end. When they made
their declarations, about 10 percent of the hapless mothers refused to

TABLE 24

RELATIONSHIP BETWEEN UNWED MOTHERS AND UNWED FATHERS

Decade	Equals (%)	Employer or Employer's Son (%)	Other Superior (%)	No.
1720–1729	49.2	24.5	26.3	57
1730–1739	56.5	21.7	21.8	69
1740–1749	56.5	18.3	25.2	60
1750–1759	64.0	26.0	10.0	50
1760–1769	65.2	20.5	14.3	44
1770–1779	68.5	15.8	15.7	57
1780–1789	73.8	14.4	11.8	145
Totals	63.4	18.4	18.2	482

Source: A.D. Isère, 13 B 652–657; A.H.G. 1–16.

[a]Equals include couples exercising the same profession and couples when both were wage
laborers. Soldiers were generally excluded unless rank, previous employment, or some indication of family background was included in the declaration.
[b]Superiors include guests in the employer's home and merchants and members of the legal
professions clearly superior in status to the unwed mothers.

identify their lover, in the hope that he would still marry them or at least provide some sort of assistance. Anne Drou, for example, declined to name her lover when she made her first declaration; only three months later, after she had given birth, did she realize that "he probably would not keep his promise" and finally revealed his name. Other women were even more unwilling to relinquish hope. Marguerite Fantoux, who had been impregnated by a fellow day laborer, claimed in her declaration that her suitor might still marry her, even though he had been promising to do so for over three years. Rose Tournon awaited the publishing of the banns for two years. When her lover abandoned her with an unwanted child, she still believed that he would shortly make good his promise. Against all reason, Rose Bourgon believed that an enamel-worker who had already given her two illegitimate children would, this time, lead her to the altar.[93]

Desperately, these women hoped for a salvation that simply did not come. Perhaps other unwed and pregnant girls were more fortunate; perhaps their lovers took them to the altar before their babies arrived. Lacking bridal pregnancy rates, we cannot know how many Grenobloises had their honor rescued in the nick of time.[94] We can speculate on the circumstances that denied a woman a timely reprieve. Many of the unwed mothers were orphans, a condition that probably predisposed a woman to illicit pregnancy. The death of a parent certainly deprived a girl of crucial support and rendered her very vulnerable. Without a father or mother, who could pressure a young man to make good his promises of marriage? One unwed mother, Barbe Mar, attributed her predicament to her father's death. She believed that her lover, a childhood friend, would have neither seduced nor abandoned her if her father had been alive.[95]

The death of a parent thus explains why illegitimacy was not avoided. It may also provide a clue—although not a firm conclusion—to why the illicit unions occurred in the first place. Recently, historians intrigued by the eighteenth-century rise in illegitimacy have come up with two basic explanations for this phenomenon, both of which center primarily upon the unwed mother and her motives. On the one hand, Edward Shorter has argued that working women had more extramarital sex in the late eighteenth century and therefore produced more illicit offspring. These women were motivated by new, individualistic market values, and they sought self-fulfillment in increasingly fulfilling intimate relationships. According to this view, the unwed mothers were the happy vanguard of a sexual revolution.[96] Other historians have vehemently rejected this interpretation and maintained that deteriorating economic conditions caught traditionally-minded, working-class women unawares and prevented illicit unions from being legitimized. In this view, the unwed mothers were the hapless victims of economic circumstances.[97] Both of these interpretations are more suggestive than this short summary indicates, and while I am inclined to agree with the latter view, neither is totally satisfying. Vague notions of impoverishment and victimization and certainly sexual revolutions seem very remote from the lives and motives of the women who concern us here, the unwed mothers of late-eighteenth-century Grenoble.

When these Grenobloises surrendered to their lovers' demands, they decided to take a risk, the risk of becoming pregnant. Against this they weighed the advantage, the advantage of getting married and of enjoying a relatively secure future. Two circumstances probably conspired to make more women more willing to take this risk. First, the outcome if they did not sleep with their lovers was the life of a lonely, impoverished spinner or laundress. The position of older, single women deteriorated, as we have seen, significantly in the course of the eighteenth century, and the only fate that awaited an unmarried girl was a sordid, desperate middle age. Marriage was the only respectable and sensible course for a working woman. Second, these girls had few alternatives to sex; their only assets were their charms, for they lacked the one thing that would allow them to compete otherwise on the marriage market—a dowry. That their fathers were dead is of critical importance here. The young women found themselves in the same position as their mothers, widows, the most chronically impoverished individuals in society. With no dowry and surely no money, these girls had to struggle to find a husband; even though prospective husbands were not of a social class to expect much in the way of a marriage settlement, they still probably wanted the best possible "establishment." Consequently, an orphaned working woman had to take risks to trap a husband and secure a good future, and under the circumstances she made a rational choice.

Therefore, the rise in illegitimacy in the late eighteenth century had less to do with the free market, as Shorter would have us believe, than it had with the marriage market. If, as Moll Flanders remarked, the "market [was] against the fairer sex," as it was in England, then the Grenobloises' decision was all the more comprehensible.[98] Shorter is right, however: young women probably did sleep with their lovers for self-seeking reasons. They did pursue fulfillment, the only fulfillment that eighteenth-century society offered to women, that of marriage. But Shorter's critics are also correct. Impoverishment did play an important role in the rise of illegitimacy in the eighteenth century, for the threat of poverty hung over these women and affected their decisions. As the putative fathers were quick to note, perhaps a bit unfairly, their lovers had been moved as much by "unbound passion" as by the hope of a "good establishment."[99]

This does not mean that these were utterly joyless, mercenary encounters. Self-interest does not exclude passion, and historians of both schools of thought on illegitimacy have been too quick to make assumptions about the emotional climate within these illicit unions. One example will suffice. In 1766 a Grenoble silk merchant brought a complaint to the Justice because he feared that one of his unwed and pregnant workers, Thérèse Cularet, would make a declaration against him. In the course of the trial, his workers painted a vivid picture of the relationship between Thérèse and the true father of her child, another silk-worker, named Coulavel. These two had what could only be described as a tempestuous affair, which they flaunted, much to the chagrin of the other workers. Thérèse was wont to rip off her lover's shirt and bite him on the chest, and she frequently thrust her hands into his trousers exclaiming, "Ah, Coulavel, your cherries are ripe!" In the course of a day's work, the couple would repair for a passionate encounter to various parts of the workshop, and they were once observed frolicking, "in a most immodest posture," in the fields outside the city. The other workers did not approve of these antics, and they complained to both parties. The female workers warned Thérèse not to sleep with Coulavel lest she become pregnant. She responded that Coulavel would take care of her and had an undying love for her, as she did for him. In addition, she announced that he had promised to marry her once his deformed wife was dead; presumably this would be soon, because the wife was about to give birth. When a male silk-worker chided Coulavel, he responded that "he loved Thérèse and always would." Curiously, he added that the child with which she was pregnant was not his anyway.[100]

We cannot know if Thérèse and Coulavel's story had a happy ending; the documents permit no insight on this point. But for most unwed mothers, however joyous the affair, the outcome was bitter indeed: an unwanted child born in shame and, most likely, loneliness. The father's behavior at this point was just as important as that of the mother, and yet the male has been the largely silent partner in the history of illegitimacy, overlooked by historians of both schools of thought.[101] If many things prompted a woman to take risks to get married, other circumstances permitted a man to avoid matrimony easily. Some unwed fathers in the late eighteenth century took the rather drastic step of joining the army. Most, however, simply "lifted their foot," to use the expression of the declarations, and disappeared. In fact, more and more fathers took this route. In the 1740s, only 35 percent of the fathers disappeared into the woods once they learned that their lovers were pregnant. In the 1780s, by contrast, 85 percent took to the road as soon as they heard the news (table 25).

Shame may have caused some of these hasty departures. Upper-class males certainly went to considerable trouble and expense to hide their mistresses' pregnancies. They had the women make false declarations, sent them to nearby cities, paid to have them housed during the last months of their pregnancies, and spirited the children to wet nurses as soon as they were born. A few gentlemen took the preventive step of abortion. One barrister fed his pregnant mistress at least six different remedies, one of which he went all the way to Chambéry to fetch.[102] None had any effect, but perhaps other abortifacients did. For a workingman, however, expensive "remedies" and complicated subterfuges were out of the question. Departure provided the easiest and cheapest means of saving face or, more likely, money.

Fear of the expense that a child would bring may also have prompted many fathers to take to the road. The maintenance of an infant was not inexpensive, and there is evidence that wet nurses' fees were rising in the late eighteenth century. The Hospital, if it could find an unwed father, demanded of him at least 50 livres and sometimes a great deal more.[103] The mere possibility of such a charge may have been enough to send some fathers on the road, but the threat was only as real as the courts chose to make it. Given the rise in illegitimacy, one would expect the judges to have adopted an increasingly rigorous attitude toward unwed fathers or at least

TABLE 25

FATHER'S REACTION TO LOVER'S UNWED PREGNANCY

Decade	Flight (%)	Accepts Child (%)	Pays Confinement (%)	Fights Declaration (%)	Joins Army (%)	No.
1730–1739	60.2	18.8	5.4	5.1	10.5	36
1740–1749	35.7	39.3	17.9		7.1	28
1750–1759	50.4	3.3	23.3	16.4	6.6	30
1760–1769	66.7		15.6	4.4	13.3	45
1770–1779	69.7	4.3	15.2	4.3	6.5	46
1780–1789	85.9	0.9	6.6	3.8	2.8	106
1790	85.7	14.3				27
Totals	68.5	7.0	13.3	5.3	6.0	318

Source: A.D. Isère, 13 B 652–657; A.H.G. 1–16.

to have pursued the same exacting policy espoused at the beginning of the century. Surprisingly, however, the exact opposite appears to have been the case. In the late eighteenth century, a declaration ceased to be a virtual warrant for the errant father's arrest. The judges abandoned the old formula that used to close most declarations, a formula that called for the father to appear before the court. Now, most declarations closed with the curious assertion that the woman in question "had not known others and does not make the present declaration out of vengeance, hate or greed," which indicates that the judges no longer placed unlimited faith in the woman's word. Jurisprudence had taken a new turn, and the virtually unlimited power formerly bestowed upon the mother was curtailed, if not entirely eliminated. No longer could an unwed mother deposit her infant on a father's doorstep by writ alone. The court, eager to avoid the scandals occasioned by the enactment of the edict of 1705, which had authorized such actions, now required a more lengthy and complicated court procedure. It had become very difficult for a woman to force her seducer to accept responsibility for his child.

In fact, one group of putative fathers escaped the grasp of the courts altogether. At some time in the 1740s, the Parlement ruled that married men were not subject to the edict of 1705. The motives behind this ruling are not hard to ascertain. The "scandal" occasioned by living proof of an adulterous union endangered a man's marriage and therefore his family. Such a threat was to be avoided at all costs, and the Hospital often took measures to prevent "scandals." The directors quickly agreed to take the illicit offspring of a domestic and a married gardener once the parish priest explained that the infant "causes a great scandal in the parish and difficulties between the gardener and his wife." On another occasion, the priest of Saint Laurent asked the directors to assume responsibility for a child born to a gravedigger's wife only three months after her marriage. The priest noted that "the husband wants to renounce his wife but will keep her if you rid him of the child."[104] To save the marriage, the directors took the child, and this position represents a retreat from the old paternalism and a new appreciation of the domestic unit. The family now took precedence in the directors' minds, and they were willing to sacrifice the unwed mother to preserve an established marriage.

Now men with families could easily escape responsibility for their illegitimate offspring, and even unmarried men did not have a great deal to fear from the courts. Lawsuits were expensive; few unwed mothers had the funds to initiate and pursue a case. Furthermore, the Hospital tried to avoid such costly litigation, and when persuasion failed, the Hospital had few other means of forcing an unwed father to provide for his child. In short, the unwed fathers of the late eighteenth century had less to fear than their seventeenth-century predecessors. Still, they took to the road at a rate twice as high as in the previous century. They disappeared into the woods when their predecessors would have stood their ground, fought, or simply given in to necessity and opened their purses. What had changed? First of all, the fathers themselves had. Fewer were of an elevated social position, so they were unencumbered by wealth and standing (table 24). The glove- and silk-workers of the eighteenth century were poorer than the gentlemen of the seventeenth, but their poverty alone is not what made them so willing to hit the highway—it was the nature of their poverty. Unlike the unwed fathers of the preceding years who had been peasants, plowmen, and vine owners, the workers had no property, however small, to tie them down. No miserable plot bound them to the land, so when their lovers became pregnant, they could simply pick up and go. Impoverishment alone is too vague and imprecise a concept to explain the rise in illegitimacy; mobility lay behind the flood of unwanted infants.

And this was a particular, new kind of mobility. Of course, the first rise in illegitimacy at the turn of the century had also stemmed from mobility, the mobility created by war and embodied in soldiers. With the establishment of the garrison, soldiers continued to seduce and abandon young Grenobloises, and the city continued to have an unusually high rate of illegitimacy. Then, in the late eighteenth century, the soldiers were joined by a new kind of seducer, a new kind of highly mobile young male, the wage laborer. The silk-workers and glove-workers, the flax-combers and ceramics-workers, who depended upon nothing but a wage for their living, were just as footloose as their military counterparts, if not more so. When they wanted to pick up and leave, they did so without difficulty. Quite a few did decamp and even before they learned of their lovers' pregnancies. A ceramics-worker named Garcin had come to Grenoble from Marseilles to work in the La Tronche ceramics manufactory. He remained in the city for some time, met and seduced a young girl, and then two days later left to work in Lyon.[105] Unencumbered by a peasant's property and paid a regular wage, unlike a domestic, the *ouvrier* glove-worker or tanner could flee the scene without thinking twice and without looking back. The growth of wage labor should therefore be counted among the various factors that precipitated the rise in illegitimacy in the very late eighteenth century. It may also explain why this rise continued, virtually uninterrupted, into the middle of the nineteenth.

The gradual introduction of wage labor also certainly accounted for the flood of infants that washed over the Hospital General. Footloose, wage-earning males tended to father children by impoverished, wage-earning women, who had no choice, once the infant was born, but to offer it to the Hospital General. The directors responded with relative equanimity: they adopted the children and even declined to condemn the sin that had produced them. But the old paternalism, both good and bad, was gone, for if the directors proved generous in regard to bastards, they were much stingier when it came to other paupers. The Hospital General, once reserved for all beggars, now housed the sick; the bread distributions, once meant for all the poor, now went only to women and the old. The impoverished adult male, previously the focus of the Hospital's efforts, suddenly received little attention. No longer did the directors seek to confine him or suppress his "sin and vice." The war against begging and the campaign for souls were so thoroughly obliterated from the Hospital's program that it is hard to believe that they ever served as the institution's foundation. The late-eighteenth-century directors did change the Hospital, but these accomplishments are easy to overlook, for if much was eliminated, nothing much was added. The directors abandoned their predecessors' attempts to assist and repress a large portion of the poor, and quietly, almost by default, left these tasks to the king and the courts, whose efforts we must now examine.

NINE

Vagrants and Criminals in the Eighteenth Century

In 1768 a new institution opened in Grenoble, which the citizens called the Bicêtre after its Parisian equivalent, but which was more properly known as the *dépôt de mendicité,* or beggars' prison. In neither form nor function was the new dépôt very different from older charitable institutions. Like the Hospital General, it occupied a delapidated building, the former Recollets monastery, and like the Hospital, it contained a bewildering assortment of individuals: vagabonds, prostitutes, madmen, thieves, bastard children, and a few honest paupers. Here was yet another house of confinement which mixed the innocent with the criminal, and assistance with repression. Here was yet another *maison de force* where deviance would be cured by that traditional nostrum, confinement. The solution was old, but the problem faced by the dépôt was relatively new: an increase in vagrancy coupled with a shift in criminal patterns. In Grenoble the local criminal court, the Justice, supplemented the work of the dépôt, but both institutions used old tools to deal with a new problem, so neither met with much success. Both, however, tell us a great deal about deviance in the late eighteenth century, and both reveal the fundamental impotence of local elites and even royal authority in the face of new social forces. For the dépôt was not the creation of the Grenoblois; it was the child of a relatively new actor on the charitable scene—the king.

THE KING'S CHARITY: THE DÉPÔT DE MENDICITÉ

Unlike the other charities in Grenoble, the dépôt owed nothing to local initiative. The monarchy had created this institution and scores like it

216

throughout the kingdom to house all those who violated a declaration promulgated in 1764. This edict outlawed begging, and it condemned habitual vagabonds to the galleys and occasional mendicants to the dépôt. If all this sounds familiar, it is because it was. Though the project had been shaped by reform-minded administrators, it resembled the old ordinance of 1724. There were, however, some differences. In 1724 the king had entrusted the enforcement of his laws to the Hospitals General throughout the realm. Royal administrators blamed the failure of the ordinance of 1724 upon these old, inefficient institutions, so this time the monarchy resolved to administer its program itself. Royal intendants, in fact their subdelegates, bore responsibility for the dépôts, and the rural mounted police, the *maréchaussée,* was charged with arresting the beggars and vagabonds. More significantly, this time the king actually intended to bear the cost of the war against mendicancy. The spirit and purpose of the dépôts were old, but their form was new: they were both the creation and the creature of the monarchy alone.[1]

As such, the dépôt must have formed a part of the embryonic national welfare system that, since the pioneering work of Camille Bloch, historians have been so quick to detect in late-eighteenth-century France.[2] Still, historians have looked with considerably more favor on other manifestations of royal beneficence, such as grants to hospitals, or the public works projects, the *ateliers de charité.* Grenoble received both forms of assistance, but from a local perspective neither amounted to a great deal. The royal grants were neither frequent nor generous. Only in 1750, 1752, and 1762 did the Hospital receive gifts from the monarchy, and together they did not come close to reimbursing the Hospital for the debt it had incurred at the monarchy's insistence when enforcing the ordinance of 1724.[3] As for the *ateliers de charité,* they operated only occasionally in Grenoble and employed at most thirty men for periods of no longer than three months at a time.[4] In all fairness, the *ateliers* were intended to succor rural poverty, not urban misery, so Grenoble was naturally slighted in this regard. Still, the monarchy did not lavish vast sums of money on the *ateliers* in rural Dauphiné. To the entire province, it gave only 50,000 livres annually in the years between 1771 and 1789 and sometimes considerably less.[5]

In contrast, the dépôt in Grenoble alone cost the monarchy between 60,000 and 100,000 livres each year from 1768 to 1789.[6] Consequently, it represented the monarchy's most sustained and expensive attempt at public assistance. If some historians have omitted the dépôt from the monarchy's embryonic national welfare system, it is probably because the dépôt sought to repress as much as assist the public. On this point, the royal administrators who created the institution were themselves ambivalent. Some considered the dépôt a temporary prison for vagabonds; others thought of it as a place of rehabilitation, where work would extinguish the beggars' idleness. The latter school of thought tended to prevail in the last years of the old regime, but the ambiguity surrounding the dépôt's purpose was never clarified.[7]

Those who had the misfortune to spend some time in Grenoble's dépôt probably never doubted that it was, indeed, a place of punishment. The Grenoble dépôt qualified as one of the worst in the kingdom, and the intendant Caze de la Bove complained frequently of its maladministration and its physical delapidation. Inmates regularly escaped through its crumbling walls, overcrowding posed a serious problem, and disease was a permanent resident. Sixteen percent of the individuals who entered the institution died, and for some kinds of inmates, internment in the dépôt was tantamount to a death sentence. Infants born in the institution rarely survived more than a week. The insane incarcerated in its cells died on the average within two months of their admission. The care of all these poor souls was entrusted to only two individuals, the concierge and his wife, and consequently discipline and medical care were, to all intents and purposes, nonexistent.[8]

Under these circumstances, it is not surprising that the institution offered little in the way of rehabilitation, which to the royal administrators was nothing but hard work. The inmates did spin cotton and make their own clothes, but there was scant room in the dépôt for any kind of activity. Consequently, what work was offered to the inmates was provided outside the institution. Rural employers took young boys and put them to work in the countryside; anyone in need of a cheap, young laborer could pick him up at the dépôt. A more formal means of rehabilitation was provided to young girls. A certain Monsieur Ducoin had established a lace manufacture in the chateau at Sassenage, and the dépôt regularly supplied him with girls of from six to eight years of age. Ducoin, in return, housed, fed, and employed the girls until they reached fifteen or sixteen. Royal administrators regarded this program as a model of its kind. Whether it actually rid the young girls of their penchant for "idleness," as royal administrators imagined, it did at least give them some skill, and their departure definitely relieved overcrowding.[9]

Usually the concierge dealt with congestion in a more haphazard fashion. The length of an individual's stay in the dépôt was largely determined by the degree of overcrowding in the institution. When there were more than the building could hold, the concierge simply released a few beggars if they promised to occupy themselves. Chronic vagabonds and criminals were not handled so nonchalantly. The *maréchaussée* often dumped them into the dépôt and then quickly transferred them to the local prisons, where escape was not so easy. Escape was certainly no problem at the dépôt: 5 percent of the inmates left the institution in this fashion, specifically through a window in the women's ward. Other inmates left in a convoy escorted by the *maréchaussée*. These convoys were supposed to resettle every beggar in his home and reduce the amount of vagrancy in the kingdom. Of course, they did not have the intended effects. The Grenoble dépôt had to play host to these battalions of beggars as they made their way to Lyon or Savoy, so, given the overcrowding in the institution, the arrival of a convoy usually signaled the sudden departure of other inmates. In addition, though the *maréchaussée* might return a vagrant to his home, it could not make him stay there. The Savoyards dumped at the border by the *maréchaussée* usually waited for the horsemen to depart and then just walked right back into Dauphiné.[10]

Inmates left the dépôt by various means; they also entered it for a variety of reasons, not all of which had been dreamed of by the royal administrators who created the institution. About 5 percent of the dépôt population was simply born there, to mothers of no means or of loose virtue. Camp followers brought in by the military police, and prostitutes incarcerated by the Grenoble chief of police, accounted for about 6 percent of the inmates.[11] Another 5 percent consisted of the raving mad found wandering the roads or offered by their desperate families. Still other individuals came to the dépôt for a "cure," that is, treatment for venereal disease, and a small number were rebellious children from respectable families, locked up by their relatives with the permission of the intendant. Clearly, some of these individuals were not a part of the vagabond population which royal administrators had intended the dépôt to confine. Not even all the inmates incarcerated for "begging" were in fact habitual or professional mendicants. They had been apprehended on the open highway by the *maréchaussée*, but not necessarily in the act of begging. Some simply lacked passports; others were just in search of work. Whatever the royal administrators' intentions, the dépôt punished mobility, not just begging and vagabondage, for anyone who presented a shabby appearance on the open road could find himself at the door of the dépôt.

When an inmate got there, his name, state of health, age, residence, and cause of internment were marked down in a large ledger, presumably by the concierge or a subdelegate's secretary. These ledgers still exist for the years between 1772 and the Revolution, and they contain large amounts of data.[12] Between 1772 and 1790, over 9,000 individuals walked into the dépôt, an unwieldy number, so a sample of one half of the inmates in odd-numbered years was made. Data from 1788 and 1789 were also included because these years hold special interest. Some inconsistency characterized recording procedures, even though the royal government supplied standardized forms for this purpose. But the dépôt registers still provide information on mobility and begging which is unavailable elsewhere.[13]

Moreover, they permit, as does no other source, a comparison with earlier periods, in particular with 1724 and the beggars arrested under the provisions of the ordinance of that year. This is not an easy comparison. In 1724 six Hospital *archers* (or constables) whose competence ranged no further than the city walls, arrested beggars; in 1772 the *maréchaussée*, whose four-man brigades ranged all over rural Dauphiné, apprehended mendicants. The *maréchaussée* had a much broader jurisdiction than the old *archers*, but the two sets of data can be rendered comparable. The beggars arrested by the Voiron brigade and all the inmates brought to the dépôt by convoy from Valence and Lyon have been excluded. Consequently, the beggars who appear in the sample were arrested by the brigade of Grenoble, whose competence included only the area surrounding Grenoble and the Grésivaudan valley. In addition, if the *maréchaussée* horsemen of the late eighteenth century were more efficient than the *archers*, which we have every reason to believe, they were also overworked.[14] Their duties were manifold, and much of their time and energy was expended in the war against contraband, which, in this frontier province, was an unending, costly battle.

Not that the apprehension of individuals took a great deal of effort. To judge by the sheer number of inmates who entered the dépôt, the *maréchaussée* had no trouble reaping a huge harvest. Between 300 and 400 individuals were interned annually in the dépôt during the period 1772–1790, almost twice the number confined in the dépôt at Rennes. In addition, the Grenoble dépôt reported the largest number of entries in the years between 1764 and 1773 of any dépôt in the kingdom, with the exception of Paris.[15] The Dauphinois' reputation for mobility thus seems justified, and this mobility gave all appearances of having increased over the course of the eighteenth century. In 1724 the *archers* of the Hospital General arrested only 119 beggars; in 1775 the *maréchaussée* incarcerated three times that many. The crisis years on the eve of the Revolution exacerbated this tendency and sent a veritable hoard of individuals on the road. In 1789, 540 people were led to the dépôt, but this is just the tip of the iceberg.[16] Many individuals probably escaped the four-man patrols of the *maréchaussée*.

Mobility, and perhaps begging and vagrancy, increased in the course of the eighteenth century, as historians have long suspected. This suspicion is also confirmed by the qualitative changes in mobility that occurred at the same time, for a new kind of transient appeared in the late eighteenth century. He was still usually a male, for men formed the majority of transients by a margin of roughly two to one. But in the crisis years of 1788 and 1789, males literally swamped females (table 26). When women incarcerated for prostitution are removed, females accounted for only 22 percent of the transients arrested in these years. The wanderer was, almost by definition, a man.

Was he healthier or more debilitated than his counterpart from earlier times? At first glance, the late-eighteenth-century transient looks much more pathetic than his predecessors. In 1724, 83 percent of those arrested were sturdy beggars in good health; in the years between 1772 and 1790, only 49 percent were without some form of debility. This apparent deterioration of the vagrant population, though, is deceptive. It reflects a change, not in the transients themselves, but in the variety of functions which the dépôt had to assume. The Hospital, for example, refused to admit the insane who were violent; the dépôt had to take in these "dangerous madmen." Similarly, in the late eighteenth century, the Hospital

TABLE 26
GENDER OF THE INMATES OF THE DÉPÔT

Year	Male (%)	Female (%)	No.
1772	57.9	42.1	126
1773	68.0	32.0	259
1775	65.4	34.6	127
1777	57.1	42.9	91
1779	51.7	48.3	120
1781	59.5	40.5	116
1783	61.7	38.3	201
1785	62.1	37.9	87
1788	62.2	37.8	119
1789	70.1	29.9	274
1790	66.7	33.3	75
Totals	62.9	37.1	1,595

Source: A.D. Isère, II C 1020–1023.

ceased providing treatment for venereal disease; the dépôt had to offer a cure.[17] Fourteen percent of the males who entered the dépôt, and 10 percent of the females, when camp followers are deducted, came to the dépôt for the treatment of syphilis, and it is a measure of the horror which venereal disease inspired that many came willingly, bearing a letter of recommendation from their parish priest. Pregnant women also entered the dépôt voluntarily, with the understanding that their infant, once born, would become a ward of the institution. By 1788 these impoverished and generally unwed mothers constituted almost 10 percent of the inmate population, and they were joined by a substantial number of foundling children. In effect, the flood of illegitimate infants that inundated the Hospital in these years had flowed over into the dépôt. Many of the inmates in the institution were in fact individuals whom the Hospital would not or could not accept.

Whether its creators intended it or not, the dépôt was thus an annex of the Hospital General. It received, in the words of one observer, "all those whom the hospitals cannot contain."[18] Among these individuals were people born outside Grenoble, for the Hospital, once lax on this point, now refused to accept non-Grenoblois.[19] These "strangers" ended up in the dépôt, and most hailed from the villages of rural Dauphiné and, to a lesser degree, southeastern France, in particular Savoy, Comtat Venaissin, and Provence. The beggars of 1724 had had similar origins, so the basic patterns of mobility had not altered dramatically (table 27). But there were changes. Toward the very end of the eighteenth century, the proportion of inmates hailing from very distant regions of France rose slightly, especially in the years 1788 and 1789 (table 28). In 1789 almost a quarter

TABLE 27

ORIGINS OF THE INMATES INCARCERATED IN THE DÉPÔT

Place	1724–1735 (%)		1772–1789 (%)
Grenoble	26.7		25.0
Dauphiné	39.1		46.0
Southeast[a]	10.9		12.7
Faraway[b]	14.4		16.3
Unknown	8.9		0
	$N = 571$ 100.0		$N = 1,613$ 100.0

Source: A.D. Isère, F. 15 and 17; A.D. Isère, II C 1020–1023.
[a]Southeast includes the regions of Provence, Comtat Venaissin, and Savoy.
[b]Faraway includes all other regions.

TABLE 28

ORIGINS OF DÉPÔT INMATES IN THE LATE EIGHTEENTH CENTURY

Year	Dauphiné[a] (%)	Southeast[b] (%)	Faraway[c] (%)	No.
1772	87.4	7.2	5.4	111
1773	69.9	10.9	19.2	239
1775	67.7	14.8	18.0	122
1777	69.7	18.0	12.3	89
1779	70.7	17.2	12.1	116
1781	68.4	15.8	15.8	114
1783	78.6	13.3	8.2	196
1785	80.7	13.3	6.0	83
1788	61.9	13.6	24.5	110
1789	64.0	10.9	25.1	258
1790	69.9	8.2	21.9	73
Totals	71.0	12.7	16.3	1,511

Source: A.D. Isère, II C 1020–1023.

[a]Dauphiné includes Grenoble.

[b]Southeast includes the regions of Provence, Savoy, and Comtat Venaissin.

[c]Faraway includes all other regions.

of the vagrants arrested came from Burgundy, Auvergne, Languedoc, Brittany, Franche-Comté, or other provinces far removed from Grenoble. Not only were there more people on the road in the last years of the old regime, they came from farther and farther away.

Besides these "foreigners" there were a substantial number of natives, that is, Grenoblois. The percentage of Grenoblois apprehended at the end of the eighteenth century is almost equal to the percentage arrested at its beginning (table 27). The similarity is surprising because the horsemen of the *maréchaussée,* unlike their predecessors the sedentary Hospital *archers,* spent much of their time away from Grenoble, patrolling the Grésivaudan and Romanche valleys and the banks of the Drac. Consequently, one would have expected the mounted policemen to have apprehended fewer Grenoblois than the *archers,* who never left the city. But in fact, the policemen of the *maréchaussée* arrested more Grenoblois, in absolute numbers, which suggests that migration to and from the city had increased by the late eighteenth century. This confirms the suspicion of one demographer that Grenoble's population, though constant in size, was continually changing in composition with the comings and goings of temporary migrants.[20]

These mobile, seemingly rootless individuals were not, as contemporaries believed, thieves, vagabonds, and brigands. Only a handful actually fitted into these categories: no more than 3 percent of the individuals registered in the dépôt ledgers had the words "vagabond" or "thief" next to their names. Thieves, vagabonds, and brigands there were in Dauphiné. The prisons bulged with them, and the *prévôtal* court, which had special jurisdiction over wanderers, sent them in increasing numbers to the galleys. But mobility and crime were not perfectly correlated. Grenoble, which had the second largest number of vagrants in its dépôt, also had the second smallest number of rural criminals in its courts.[21] All criminals may have been vagrants, but not all vagrants committed crimes.

Was the average transient a beggar? Here the dépôt registers are ambiguous. The concierge or subdelegate in the years between 1772 and 1788 carelessly noted that almost every individual admitted to the dépôt had been apprehended "begging." In some cases, this is clearly not the case. The camp followers arrested by the military police had probably been caught soliciting, and a number of individuals identified as beggars were also characterized as "lacking a valid passport." Suffice it to say, then, that many of the vagrants who ended up in the dépôt probably did demand alms, but they were not the disabled, adolescent, or aged mendicants who were caught in the years between 1724 and 1735. The late-eighteenth-century beggar was sick; he usually had syphilis. But he was not severely disabled like his predecessors. He did not have the amputations, blindness, or mental retardation that would have made work an impossibility and alms a necessity. More important, few were so old as to be too debilitated to earn a living. On the whole, the dépôt inmates of the late eighteenth century were younger than their predecessors, and many more were in the very prime of life. Twenty-seven percent of the individuals apprehended in the years between 1772 and 1789 were between twenty-one and thirty years of age, in contrast to a mere 13 percent in the period 1724–1735 (table 29).

These young men—for most were men—could work and probably did, but at just what is hard to ascertain. Only in the years between 1788 and 1790 did the concierge record their professions with anything approaching consistency. Even then he noted the occupations of only 40 percent of the adults who entered the dépôt. Perhaps he considered the unskilled workers to have no profession at all and so failed to record their occupation. It is likely that the inmates for whom no profession is noted were in fact day laborers, domestics, and farmhands, for most hailed from rural villages. In addition, many of these men without occupations were apprehended around the time of spring planting and autumn harvest; they may well have been on their way to a new job. As for those

TABLE 29

AGE OF INDIVIDUALS ARRESTED FOR BEGGING

Age		1724–1735 (%)		1772–1790 (%)
1 to 5 years		1.8		9.2
6 to 12 years		9.6		7.3
13 to 20 years		18.2		16.1
21 to 30 years		13.8		27.2
31 to 45 years		16.1		19.7
46 to 60 years		19.3		12.8
61 or older		21.4		7.7
	N = 560	100.0	N = 1583	100.0

Source: A.D. Isère, F. 15 and 17; A.D. Isère, II C 1020–1023.

inmates for whom a profession is given, they too seem to have been between jobs or en route to a location where work might be had. In the case
of 14 percent of these individuals, Grenoble is clearly the destination, for
they were glove-workers. Tailors and apprentice wigmakers, who account
for another 14 percent of the vagrants, may also have been on their way to
a city that catered to the legal profession and its adornment. Another 9
percent of the inmates, flax-combers and wool-carders, may have been
either leaving or heading for Grenoble, for the city did have a small textile
industry. And 6 percent of the inmates who claimed they were silk-
workers were clearly going to or coming from Lyon.[22]

What all of these workers had in common was an urban trade that had
to be exercised in a city. Such was not the case with the vagrants of the
years between 1724 and 1735. Most of them were professional beggars
too old or too young to work; those few who did have occupations exercised trades like cobbler, gardener, or weaver, which were as much at
home in the countryside or rural *bourg* as they were in the city. Indeed,
only 24 percent of the beggars incarcerated in the years between 1724 and
1735 claimed a city as their place of residence. In the late eighteenth century, however, 36 percent of the transients came from towns and cities,
places like Valence, Vienne, Romans, Marseille, and Lyon. These urban
folk certainly contributed to the rise in mobility at the very end of the
eighteenth century, and they were themselves more mobile because they
were wage earners. They worked in particular kinds of manufactures,
those in which, with the exception of tailoring and wigmaking, some
slight accumulation of capital had occurred and some concentration of
labor was under way. This suggests that while economic hardship still

sent many on the road, particularly during crisis years, economic prosperity and development also fueled mobility.

Finally, were these transients truly marginal to society? As far as contemporaries were concerned, any traveler was, by definition, threatening, dangerous, and definitely déclassé. The speed with which the Dauphinois peasants identified the traveler as a brigand is amply illustrated by the alacrity with which the Great Fear spread throughout lower Dauphiné in 1789.[23] Certainly, there were a few thieves, vagabonds, and deserters in the midst of the mobile population. Former wards of the Hospital—bastard girls become camp followers, and abandoned boys turned thief—stand out in this group, as if the Hospital were creating its own underclass. But the majority of transients were neither criminal nor marginal. They were simply mobile workers. The marginal classes did, as Nicole Castan has persuasively argued, grow in the late eighteenth century, but so too did the mobility of the "normal" population.[24] We would find it hard to consider a glove-worker or a worker in ceramics manufacture "marginal" to the business of eighteenth-century society. He may have been young, footloose, and probably unmarried, but that does not make him a tenant of the underworld. A rise in mobility as much as an increase in vagrancy occurred in the late eighteenth century, but the distinction was a fine one and impossible for contemporaries to make. Wedded to old notions of delinquency, they tried to master a new situation with an old-fashioned, inefficient institution, the dépôt. They responded to a rise in mobility almost hysterically by locking up everyone in the hope of incarcerating a few criminals.

If rogues and thieves were far from numerous at the dépôt, where were they? To find these inhabitants of the underworld we must abandon the dépôt and turn to the courts, to Grenoble's criminal bench, the Justice.

CRIMINALITY IN THE LATE EIGHTEENTH CENTURY

Like the dépôt, the Justice had to contend with new social forces in the late eighteenth century. New forms of deliquency emerged, and a new type of criminal appeared, both of whom strained the resources of the archaic court. Now the judge saw before him, not a crude, violent delinquent, but a subtle, greedy criminal who could easily elude arrest. Now he dealt, not with violent assault, but with secret theft, which was difficult to punish. For good or ill, Grenoble acquired in the last years of the old regime a modern type of criminality whose causes were numerous and complex but whose consequences were obvious. Now, when the Grenoblois stepped outside of his home, he had to fear for his pocketbook.

He did not, however, have to fear for his life. Grenoble in the late eighteenth century was much more tranquil than it had been in the past. The streets rarely witnessed violence, and fisticuffs and assaults were much less frequent than they had been a century before.[25] The bands of soldiers that preyed upon young girls had vanished; the gangs of youths who had fought pitched battles in the darkened streets had moved their escapades elsewhere. On the whole, public space was less often sullied by bloodshed, and the fact is all the more amazing in that public space itself had increased in the course of the eighteenth century. Grenoble now possessed a theater, a concert hall, a public garden, and a troop of tightrope walkers. Surprisingly enough, the theater was never the scene of conflict. Though tickets were cheap, it catered to a fairly well-heeled audience, and provided the stage, not for brawls, but for discreet tension between the bourgeoisie and nobility, such as the famous snubbing of Barnave's mother by a noblewoman. Even the public garden, where all social classes mixed freely, saw only isolated incidents of conflict.[26]

One of these rare events occurred in 1789, but it involved verbal, not physical, violence. A widow called La Guichard came upon the wife of one Courbassière, a lawyer at the Justice. She greeted her with the words "there is the whore Courbassière who has stolen my lover; I think I'll give her a few blows and tear out her hair." True to her promise, La Guichard ripped off Courbassière's wig and then paraded around the garden, shouting "here is the fake chignon of the whore Courbassière." She next proceeded to the Courbassières' home on the rue Montorge where she cursed Monsieur Courbassière, calling him a cuckold and announcing to a crowd of one hundred amused witnesses that she had nursed his wife through the pox. The merriment occasioned by this conflict between the two women was not unusual. Women, in particular market women, provided a kind of comic counterpoint to the otherwise straitlaced life of the city, and the local gossip, Letourneau, generally so stuffy, recorded their bon mots with delight. The usual social constraints did not apply to these women, and they enjoyed a sort of license which allowed them to cross class lines. Their privilege, however, was limited to words alone; rarely were women involved in violent incidents, and only occasionally did they give or receive blows, at least in public.[27]

Women certainly never set foot in the one area of the city where violence remained endemic—the cabaret.[28] Here, blood continued to be spilled, and if Grenoble seemed less violent than in the past, it was because violence was circumscribed, limited to this one, traditionally volatile area. Wine and liquor certainly rendered the cabaret a dangerous place: a few drinks sufficed to make enemies of friends and combatants of acquaintances. But it was not so much what was served as who was served that made the cabaret the premier locus of crime. The tavern was a purely male domain, frequented by young, working-class men between the ages of twenty and thirty. These individuals accounted for most of the crime in the city, and age was more important than profession. Flax-combers, glove-workers, soldiers, and peasants battled it out, and they had little in common save their age and their love of drink. One trade, however, did stand out for its sheer rowdiness—the wigmakers. One evening in 1766, for example, a group of apprentice wigmakers were returning from a tavern where they had been performing a professional ritual, the toasting of a new journeyman. A woman on the third floor of a house inadvertently dumped a chamberpot on one of the wigmakers, which prompted his co-workers to pelt the house with small stones, crying "whore," "bitch," and so forth. The woman urged the wigmakers to go, "for somebody will call the guard." Her warning came too late, for an ill-tempered barrister whose window had been broken had already summoned the forces of order.[29]

That professional rituals brought young men like the wigmakers together and then led them into trouble was not unusual. A new solidarity among workers emerges from the criminal records, along with a new pride in profession. In 1773 a turner, a cabinetmaker, and a carpenter went to a cabaret to relax. There they quickly fell to discussing the relative merits of the city's professions, and the carpenter remarked that the turners "were not regulated, because they had no banner and their rules were not approved by the Court." The turner replied that his profession was as ordered as the carpenter's and then observed that one should not malign any profession. The carpenter disagreed and a fight ensued. Professional disputes apparently caused conflict, but rarely did this tension erupt into violence in the work place. The *atelier* was seldom the scene of disputes, but an incident did occur in 1774. The glove-workers in the workshop of sieur Aymé wanted a new apprentice to pay his "bec jaune," or traditional admission fee. They joked with him about it, but he did not take the hazing lightly and in a sudden rage thrust a tanner's knife into the stomach of one of the other workers.[30]

Bloodshed may have occurred between workers, but it rarely marked the relationship between masters and journeymen. Indeed, violent conflicts between members of different social strata were exceedingly rare in

eighteenth-century Grenoble, mainly because the elite had left the ring.
The merchants, shopkeepers, lawyers, and manufacturers who in the seventeenth century had occasionally indulged in fisticuffs, now resolved
their tensions another way, through litigation. The distrust of the courts
so often evidenced by earlier Grenoblois appears to have disappeared,
and litigation, instead of being avoided, became something of a municipal
sport. No affront was too trivial or too intimate to be aired in court. In
1783, for instance, one Pierre Vert, a merchant, was left standing at the
church by his fiancée. Jilted but not ashamed, Vert lodged a criminal complaint against an innkeeper whom he accused of spreading malicious gossip and undoing his engagement.[31]

Vert's disgrace might have led to fisticuffs in the past, but now it led to
the court. Thanks in part to the Grenoblois' litigiousness, violence tended
to diminish in the city. Nor was this just a false impression created by the
records or by an inert prosecuting attorney. Such violent crime as there
was in eighteenth-century Grenoble was pursued vigorously by the *procureur du roy,* the functional equivalent of a district attorney. When three
young workers exchanged blows in a cabaret and one was wounded seriously, the victim refused to press charges, claiming that he, as much as the
others, had precipitated the conflict. The *procureur* would hear none of it.
He seized the case, pushed it through the courts, and saw that the perpe-
trator paid 30 livres in damages to the victim and 6 livres "for an affront
to public order" to the poor of Saint Laurent parish.[32]

Along with the prosecuting attorney, another member of the forces of
order, the *garde bourgeoise,* appears to have taken its duties more seriously
in the late eighteenth century. This ancient corps was responsible for patrolling the city, and it constituted the only real police force in Grenoble.
Though few in number, the guards appear to have discharged their responsibilities more efficiently in the late eighteenth century and to have provided
a modicum of security unavailable in the past. One measure of the guard's
greater efficacy was the speed with which it now appeared at the scene of a
crime. In the past, it took hours for the guard to arrive, and sometimes it
never appeared at all. In the late eighteenth century, it did arrive and sometimes even before the neighbors, who never hesitated to barge into a conflict. Another measure of the guard's new efficiency was the fact that the
Grenoblois actually called upon it for assistance. In the past, a person who
feared a beating had recourse only to his neighbors. Now, the victim alerted
the guards and allowed them to deal with the malefactor.

By our standards, Grenoble was still a rude, unpoliced society where
persons and property enjoyed little protection. Still, a certain progress

had been made in one hundred years. The forces of order were marginally more efficient, and bloodshed was less common in public places. Violence was circumscribed, contained in certain well-defined areas, like the cabaret, and assault was usually limited to verbal abuse and lengthy court proceedings. Violence had been chased from the public arena, but now, as in our own time, it erupted in private, in the home. Domestic tensions, previously so well contained that not a single case opposing family members came before the Justice during the seventeenth century, now spilled into the courts.[33] Apparently, families could no longer resolve their internal differences, and parents now looked to the court to discipline their children. Dominique Cuchet, for example, brought a criminal complaint against her own daughter and accused her of stealing and selling all her furniture. Claude David, in a similar vein, had the *huissiers* arrest his son for robbery and claimed that bitterness over a marriage contract had prompted the theft.[34] Rebellious and embittered children were not the only family members to lash out at their closest relatives. Parents, too, occasionally vented their wrath on their offspring. A man named Dupont, for example, long complained that his son kept bad company and stayed out too late. One night the son returned home after his parents had retired, and knocked on the door. Dupont's wife begged him to let the son in, but he refused. Finally, the wife got up to open the door, which only sent Dupont into a rage and he began beating her. The son now entered and struck his father, who in turn stabbed his son in the stomach with a cobbler's knife. The son, his intestines pouring out, stumbled into the street to be met by the guard. Curiously, under questioning, Dupont only regretted that he had not killed his son instead of merely wounding him.[35]

Like differences between parents and children, disputes between spouses now came before the court. The crime of passion and jealousy, previously absent from judicial archives, suddenly appeared in the court records. In 1789, for example, one Pierre Jacob, an innkeeper, lodged a criminal complaint against another innkeeper named Gand, who had ambushed him, beaten him, and left him for dead. This was not the first time that Gand had struck. Several weeks earlier, according to a witness, Gand had spied Jacob kissing his wife and had beaten him bloody. A more intriguing case of jealousy came before the Justice in 1764. A merchant named Chalvet suspected Louis Blanc, a goldsmith, of courting his wife. He tried to catch Blanc in the act, but finally devised another way of confirming his worst suspicions. Chalvet had a friend go to his wife and tell her that Blanc was waiting for her in the municipal garden. The wife coolly responded that she did not care and ignored the invitation. The friend reported all this to Chalvet who nonetheless continued to suspect the worst. Finally, by sheer chance, he discovered Blanc and his wife in a most compromising position, flew into a jealous rage, and knifed the man.[36]

A crime of passion but also of stealth: the sieur Chalvet stalked his prey coolly and shrewdly, and his modus operandi was not unusual. Most of Grenoble's criminals replaced brute force with cunning, and they, like their brothers the seducers of unwed mothers, used tricks and not fists to achieve their ends. These were more refined criminals, and they generally indulged in that most refined and modern of crimes—stealing. Thievery came to account for a substantial portion of the cases brought before the Justice at the end of the eighteenth century even when the growth of litigation is taken into account, and the most profitable and cunning form of theft was breaking and entering. In 1779, thieves burned out the lock on the door of the shop of the famous cabinetmaker Hache and made off with 40 livres. In 1783, burglars entered the home of a former magistrate while he was in the country and took an even larger sum of money. Priests were a favorite target, for the thieves knew when a curé would be out of the house, during mass. Inns too saw a considerable amount of theft. In 1774 a band of robbers stopped at an inn, and while two of them kept the innkeeper's wife occupied below, three others entered the first story and took everything they could lay their hands on.[37]

Not all thieves were this clever. Much thievery was perpetrated by isolated individuals who almost on impulse filched a few coins or some linen. In 1764, for example, Jean-François Teyssier, twenty-three and a cook, stole three handkerchiefs from an inn where he was having supper. Later he claimed to have drunk too much and to have wandered into a room where he saw the handkerchiefs and pocketed them, without thinking. A similar sudden, inexplicable surrendering to temptation characterized the crime of Jacques Robert, a domestic. For two years he had served the noblewoman Dame Herculais, when one night, while she was dining at the home of the first president of the Parlement, Robert suddenly pocketed some of the silverware. Horrified at what he had done, Robert held on to the silver for more than a year and then quietly tried to sell it, only to be apprehended.[38]

Whether by impulse or with considerable premeditation, the Grenoblois were stealing more—and more frequently—from one another. In this regard, Grenoble was no different from other cities in France.[39] Though stealing was still relatively rare by modern standards, it was distinctly on the rise, yet another sign, albeit an unpleasant one, of Grenoble's growing modernity. But were there indeed more thieves in the city or were the inhabitants just more willing to report the crime? The evidence points in both directions. The Grenoblois do seem to have abandoned their penchant for settling accounts themselves. When a flax-comber was robbed while sleeping in a cart parked on the Place Grenette, he did not take out after the thief himself, even though he knew who he was. Instead of risking his own neck, he fetched the guard and had them arrest the malefactor. The greater efficiency of the guard probably encouraged other Grenoblois to seek its help, and the renewed energy of another official— the *procureur* of the Justice—also prompted them to report theft. In the late eighteenth century, the *procureur,* unlike his predecessors, was quite eager to prosecute cases of thievery. He seized every instance of the crime, so that a victim was not, as in the past, forced to pursue a thief through the courts himself. In addition, he prosecuted these cases "a l'extraordinaire," which meant, among other things, that the court, not the plaintiff, bore the cost of the trial. Small wonder then that the Grenoblois left the apprehension and punishment of thieves up to the court and avoided the scenes, endless law suits, and sheer bodily harm that had occurred in the past when they took the law into their own hands. Significantly, in the late eighteenth century, every complaint concerning a false accusation of theft, once a staple of the judicial records, was lodged, not against a private individual, but against the *procureur,* that is, the court.[40]

If the Grenoblois could abandon vigilantism, their country cousins could not. Rural Dauphinois did not enjoy the same advantages as city dwellers, and they continued to pursue thieves themselves. When a farmer in Vizille was robbed at midnight of two horses, he did not call upon the *maréchaussée,* for it would have taken them days to arrive. Instead, he had his domestics saddle up and ride to every major crossroads in the area. As he expected, they soon apprehended the thief and retrieved the horses. Of course, not every country dweller had eight domestics to secure his property; most were, quite literally, at the mercy of criminals. If conditions in this regard had improved in the city, they certainly had not in the country. The only police force, the mounted horsemen of the *maréchaussée,* were too few in number and too far away to provide any protection. The local seigneurial courts were more interested in hearing lucrative civil cases than in prosecuting penniless criminals. Thieves appear to have been aware of the country dwellers' vulnerability, for at least two bands of Grenoble thieves went to surrounding villages when they wanted to steal. Significantly, when they were apprehended, it was inside the city walls.[41] An archaic situation thus persisted in the countryside, but in the city, reported thievery increased because the thief was more likely to be caught.

Thieves might also have been caught, in a figurative sense, in a new set of assumptions about private property.[42] The apparent increase in thievery could reflect nothing more than a new definition of what constituted theft. In a society in which payment in kind often accompanied wages, this posed a serious problem. A worker usually enjoyed certain privileges, whether in regard to food, cast-off materials, or whatever, along with his wages; if an employer suddenly decided to retract these customary privileges, the worker could find himself, to his surprise, a thief. Such seems to have been the problem of one stevedore who was accused of filching wood while loading a boat on the banks of the Isère. At his trial, he explained that the stevedores were traditionally allowed to keep one or two pieces of wood when they loaded a boat as a supplement to their wages. The wood merchant denied this, and the stevedore was banished.[43]

The transition to wholly wage labor created problems, but they were neither particularly numerous nor frequent, perhaps because this transition was, as yet, far from complete. It is surprising that domestics were not embroiled in difficulties more frequently, for their remuneration consisted almost solely of payment in kind—that is, food, shelter, and clothing. What jurists called "domestic theft," that is, theft by a servant of a master's goods, did become a bit more common, but this increase did not stem from a redefinition of the domestic's privileges.[44] Rather, it reflected a new view of the master's duties and obligations toward his servants. In the past, masters had been loath to drag their servants through the public courts. They were, after all, members of the master's household, and he bore sole responsibility for their behavior. If they stole, he would discipline them himself or just look the other way. By the late eighteenth century, this view had begun to change, as one particular incident illustrates. In 1766 the servant of Monsieur Teysseire, the inventor of ratafia, was apprehended at night carrying a case of the liquor, which it was assumed he had stolen. Monsieur Teysseire allowed the case to go to court and eventually much further. When he testified at the trial, he contradicted the servant's claim that he (Teysseire) had ordered the servant to deliver the liquor to an inn—a claim which would have explained why the servant was abroad at night with the ratafia. Twice the servant begged Teysseire to remember the order, that is, to save him; twice Teysseire refused. The servant was sentenced to death by strangulation on the Place de Breuil. In this case, Teysseire had sent his own servant to the scaffold.[45]

Teysseire may have condemned his domestic to death, but he did not bear complete responsibility for this sad incident. His servant had clearly stolen the ratafia, for he had confessed as much when first apprehended. Different attitudes toward domestics and property cannot account for the plague of thievery that struck Grenoble in the late eighteenth century, nor can more consistent reporting of the crime. What did cause the increase in theft? Teysseire's invention, the ratafia, may hold the clue. If more people stole in the eighteenth century, it may well be because there was, quite simply, more to steal. More cash, first of all: the seventeenth-century thief had to content himself with altar cloths, handkerchiefs, and chickens, but his successor had money before his eyes. In inns and cabarets, money tempted him, all the more because it could be spent without recourse to a fence, still a dangerous business. At the same time, these were substantial sums even when inflation is taken into account. The pockets of the flax-comber robbed on the Place Grenette contained 40 livres, and the sack of a common farmhand 30 livres. Seventeenth-century laborers had probably never seen, much less possessed, so much cash, and they certainly never imagined the even vaster sums possessed by newly enriched Grenoblois. Now there were men like Monsieur Teysseire among the wealthy, a whole new group of nouveau riche who provided new temptations and opportunities.[46]

Under these circumstances, did theft constitute, as Arlette Farge has suggested, "a kind of resistance, an implicit condemnation of the social order"?[47] Perhaps in Paris it did, but in provincial Grenoble most likely not. To all appearances, theft remained, as in the past, a heinous act, condemned by official and popular opinion alike. "Thief" and "banished"—the latter being the most common punishment for thievery—remained, as before, the epithets that the common Grenoblois hurled at one another in rage, just as the traditional lexicon for women—"whore" and "trollop"—still held. And some variations were added. One woman accused a man of "trying to ruin the whole city," and another, an innkeeper's drunken mother-in-law, claimed that her son-in-law robbed all his clients and then buried them in the garden. But the cry of "thief" still raised the Grenoblois' ire and was intended to do so.[48]

If the average Grenoblois despised the robber, it was because he was frequently his prey. The list of victims in the eighteenth century contains such humble individuals as washerwomen, flax-combers, glove-workers, blacksmiths, farmhands, and domestics of all sorts. A large number of thefts did occur in inns, but it would be hard to consider these humble establishments, barely distinguishable from simple cabarets, bastions of the ruling class. And the seasoned robber's chosen prey was, of course, other thieves. In 1784 a sixty-year-old locksmith called Frappe ran afoul of the law. He stole some money from a shop where he was repairing the locks and then fled the city. For a while he wandered and then decided to head for Savoy. Along the way he stopped in a cabaret, where 20 écus were picked from his pocket. There he also encountered two men who volunteered to lead him to the border, telling him that they rendered this service to deserters all the time. When the trio arrived at a remote spot, the two men informed Frappe that he must share his ill-gotten gains or "pass through their hands." Only the timely arrival of an innocent peasant saved Frappe's skin, but his booty was gone.[49]

Preferring to prey upon their own kind, Grenoble's thieves were not rebels. Some social tensions were revealed in the criminal records, but they did not involve theft. The seizure of an indebted individual's goods by the *huissiers* of the court could raise the neighborhood, as it had in the seventeenth century. When a glove-maker was arrested for defaulting on a 100 livres loan, dozens of men and women from the Rue du Boeuf ran to his assistance when they heard the cry "the huissiers are here!"[50] But this kind of incident was anything but new, and the tensions it revealed had always been a part of Grenoble society and had always been easily contained. On the whole, the rich had little to fear from the criminals, least of all a challenge to their political dominance. After the work of Georges Rudé and others, it is probably not necessary to stress that criminals rarely formed a part of rebellious crowds.[51] Their mobility and their destitution made them unlikely to stand and fight the dominant elements in society. One example will suffice. In May 1788 a certain Josserand, deserter and convicted thief, came to Grenoble in search of work. "The troubles" (that is, the riot known as the Day of the Tiles) and the subsequent disorder made work hard to come by. So Josserand quickly left the city and its turmoil for the countryside, where he filched several items from some inns.[52] Thieves like Josserand posed little threat to the rich, not even to their property. A battalion of domestics stood between their silverplate and the thief, and the new patterns of habitation in the city removed the rich even further from the impoverished. It is significant that only two magistrates—still the wealthiest individuals in Grenoble—fell victim to theft; in one of these cases, the malefactor was one of the magistrate's own servants. The truly rich were only vulnerable to "domestic theft," which may explain why this crime carried such horrific penalties.

In fact, few domestics were among Grenoble's thieves, as best we can tell. The truly successful robber, after all, does not get caught and leaves no records. Most cases of breaking and entering, the only really lucrative form of theft in eighteenth-century Grenoble, remained unsolved, so these most professional of thieves elude us as they did the authorities. Did Grenoble in fact possess a small underworld? It is exceedingly hard to tell, for the literary sources which shed so much light on the lower depths of Parisian society do not exist in provincial Grenoble. No Mercier or Rétif lovingly painted the city's thieves and whores. Grenoble's only chronicler, Letourneau, did not share these Parisians' *nostalgie de la boue*—a measure of a provincial's proximity or distance from the poor, depending on how one looks at it. Indeed, Letourneau rarely mentioned the impoverished and then only to condemn them as "rascals" and rejoice in their confinement in the *dépôt de mendicité*.[53]

Only the judges of the Justice showed much interest in the underworld, and their curiosity was very limited. The crime in question was all that really concerned them, and they paint only the most cursory portrait of the criminal. The defendant was almost invariably a male; women stole infrequently and then only very small, insignificant amounts. He was also generally young, between the ages of eighteen and twenty-five, although there were older thieves and a few teen-agers as well. Typically, a criminal had gotten off to a bad start very early. Claude Nicoud had no profession, for "his father refused to do anything for him," and Nizier Genevois had been thrown out of the paternal home in Allemond at seventeen years of age. And if apprenticeship in crime began anywhere, it was in the army, for an extraordinary number of Grenoble's thieves had spent some time in some capacity in the troops. Our thief Nizier Genevois had been a soldier in both the French and Savoyard armies and had deserted from both. Jean-Baptiste Magnin had been the servant of an officer in the Scotch regiment before he took up a life of crime. Among those who had not been in the army, no particular profession predominates. Farmhands, wigmakers, carpenters, masons, and those "with no fixed profession" fell into thievery, though many did so after having dropped out of their chosen calling. Bardin, formerly a weaver, had "quit" his profession to take up the lowly occupation of *portefaix,* and Frappe the locksmith had become a farmhand after impoverishment forced him to pawn his tools. Once a man was on the decline, the descent into thievery was easy. However, the one quality that all of Grenoble's thieves shared was mobility. They were an extremely well-traveled group, whose itineraries had covered all of France. Joseph Morel, twenty, had been born in nearby Crolles, but had spent five years with the army in Brittany. Gaspard Rougier, a wigmaker, had lived for two years in Paris, and Jean Josserand, born in Lans, had spent three years in the galleys.[54]

Given what we know about the links between crime and mobility in the old regime, the thieves' travels come as no surprise—nor does their impoverishment. Marie Mansion, a destitute, sixty-year-old secondhand dealer, told the judge that "misery" caused her to filch some bread from an inn. Louis Marguiaud, an eighteen-year-old apprentice mason, explained that it was winter when he had stolen some iron from a blacksmith and he could find no work. "Hunger," he told the judge, had forced him to steal, an act which he now bitterly regretted. Eighteenth-century criminals frequently invoked their destitution, much more frequently than did their seventeenth-century predecessors. But this does not mean that the average criminal at the end of the old regime was more impoverished than his predecessor. What these protestations of poverty do indicate is that a new dialogue had developed between the judge and the accused.[55] Now, the judge took into account mitigating circumstances, and the thieves were all too happy to provide them. Drunkenness was often invoked as a cause of diminished responsibility. Josserand, the former galley prisoner, told the judge he had been drunk when he filched some handkerchiefs, and he begged the magistrate to take into account "the modicity of his means and his extreme youth." Anne Grosset, a recent widow, asked the judge to bear in mind that she was "troubled by the death of her husband" at the time of her crime and "did not know what she was doing." Sometimes the court was moved: Anne Grosset received no punishment for her crime, and in 1790 a member of a band of thieves was exonerated "because of his youth."[56]

The court could be merciful. Banishment was the most severe punishment prescribed to most criminals, even the most hardened. But the court could also be extremely cruel. The judge did not take into account the extreme youth of the servant who robbed Teysseire. This teen-ager went to the gallows despite his age. Leniency was balanced by arbitrary cruelty, and the judge, if warmed by stories of impoverishment, did not hesitate to throw many poor individuals into jail on the flimsiest of pretexts. A twenty-five-year-old carter complained that he had languished for seven months in prison after an enemy accused him of theft. A sculptor was held for nearly a year on a vague suspicion that he had stolen. The judge did not even require a suspicion to lock up an individual. When a merchant was robbed in 1782, the judge's first action was to imprison all of the man's domestics. When a former magistrate had his house robbed a year later, the judge followed the same procedure: he confined all the domestics before the investigation even began.[57] Such instances of preventive detention tended to multiply toward the end of the old regime, and they may reflect the court's growing impotence in the face of rising theft.

After all, though the forces of order were somewhat more efficient than in the past, their effectiveness by no means equaled that of modern police forces and courts. Before the mobile, clever criminal, the court was pretty helpless. Those who committed the crime of breaking and entering always slipped through the judge's fingers, and given the proximity of the Savoy border and the paucity of policemen, it is surprising that any thieves at all were brought to justice. Even the amateurish, ill-fated Frappe the locksmith roamed for a full year over Dauphiné before being apprehended. The courts could do little to stem the flood of thefts, and their impotence was even greater in rural areas. The fact that the judges, as members of the elite, were rarely touched themselves by theft made them no less uneasy in the presence of this new, growing phenomenon. Like the royal administrators who established the *dépôt de mendicité*, the judges faced a new situation and tried unsuccessfully to make old institutions master it. The court's contradictory response to thievery, swinging as it did between leniency and rigor, may have constituted a feeble attempt to control a novel situation with archaic, administrative tools.[58]

It may also have stemmed from new attitudes toward the poor. We have seen signs of innovation at the Hospital General: the directors quietly discarded some old notions and moved discreetly toward new concepts. At the charity schools too, the late eighteenth century witnessed the demise of certain concerns and the birth of new approaches to poverty. Enlightenment attitudes toward the poor are not yet entirely clear. We must abandon the dépôt, the Hospital, and the court and enter the notary's study. We must capture the Grenoblois in that act which revealed the most about their social vision, the making of their last wills and testaments.

TEN

Patterns of Charity: 1730–1789

Having arrived at an advanced age, Claude Drevon decided to prepare for death. Thus, on May 30, 1780, the former barrister called his notary to his home on the Rue Brocherie and there dictated his final will and testament. He hurried through the initial formalities, recommending his soul to God and electing as his burial place the cemetery of Saint Hugues. When the notary asked, as the law required, if he wished to make any pious bequests, he answered simply and curtly, "no." Drevon then addressed himself to the problem which preoccupied him most that day—the division of his estate. To his eldest married daughter he left 400 livres, the unpaid balance of her dowry; to his four younger daughters he left 4,000 livres to be divided equally among them; to his younger son he gave 14,000 livres, and to his wife an annual pension of 400 livres. The bulk of his estate he bequeathed to his universal heir, his elder son. When the notary had taken all this down, M. Drevon signed his will, and the notary went back to his office.[1]

Five years later another Grenoblois also prepared himself for death and made out his final will and testament. This time it was M. Jean Baptiste Claude Planelly de la Valette, *chevalier d'honneur* at the Chambre des Comptes of Dauphiné and descendant of one of the oldest and most prestigious families in the province. Unlike the barrister Drevon, M. de la Valette did not call his notary; instead he closeted himself in the library of his *hôtel particulier* on the fashionable Rue Neuve and wrote out his will personally. But he too was eager to tackle the problem which concerned him most that day, in his case the salvation of his immortal soul. He began his testament by commending his soul to God, begging His forgiveness

239

for his numerous sins, and requesting the intercession of his advocate, the Virgin Mary, and his Savior, Jesus Christ. He then asked to be buried in the cemetery of the parish of Saint Hugues and set aside several hundred livres so that an "annual" of masses could be said in the church immediately after his death. He also commanded that eighty masses be said by the Recollets and Augustinians and sixty more by the Capucins and the Carmelites and left to the Poor Claires 100 livres without specifying the purpose of the gift. Then M. de la Valette provided for his dependents: to the poor on his estates at Viviers and la Buisserate in the Grésivaudan valley, he left 400 livres, and to his immediate household, his domestics, he bequeathed small amounts of money. Having fulfilled his spiritual and social duties, M. de la Valette quickly took care of his family obligations. To his unmarried daughter, he left 40,000 livres to serve as her dowry, and to his son, an officer in the cavalry regiment of Orléans, he bequeathed the bulk of his estate. M. de la Valette then signed and sealed his will. Only years later, after a series of events which he could not possibly have imagined, would the contents of M. de la Valette's will be revealed on the 24 Frimaire Year III.[2]

How different were these two experiences and how varied the documents they produced. In the seventeenth century, men with less in common than Drevon and de la Valette had nonetheless produced wills of greater similarity. The Grenoblois who sat down to write their testaments in the years between 1680 and 1729 had brought to the event the same feelings about death, the same spiritual preoccupations, and the same vision of the poor. A kind of consensus reigned within Grenoble society at the very height of the Counter Reformation. But by the end of the eighteenth century, this unanimity had dissolved into discord. When Drevon and de la Valette wrote their wills, no one type of spirituality and no one social vision prevailed in Grenoble. Instead, there were at least two positions on the Church, two forms of religiosity, two visions of the poor—in short, two opposing views of society. The thousands of wills in the notarial archives, once sampled, allow us to trace the emergence of these two conflicting streams of thought and examine the cultural and social rifts that riddled Grenoble society on the eve of the Revolution.[3]

WILLS AND TESTAMENTS

These divisions manifested themselves clearly in the realm of poor relief. Some individuals continued to support the institutions that Grenoble had inherited from the Counter Reformation; some, like their ancestors, still left money to the Hospital General in their wills. None too surprisingly, those who remained most faithful to the Hospital were those who had created it: the magistrates. In the 1780s, 57 percent of the magistrates remembered the Hospital in their testaments, and though this rate was slightly lower than in the past, it was still the highest in the city (table 30). Surprisingly, those least loyal to the institution were those charged in the late eighteenth century with its administration: the merchants, and the lawyers, *huissiers,* and notaries who made up what Grenoblois called the *basoche.* Barely 27 percent of the practitioners of the law remembered the Hospital in their wills in the 1780s, and only 17 percent of the merchants bothered to leave a penny to the old *maison de force* (table 30).

The lawyers' and merchants' indifference to the Hospital General extended to all forms of poor relief, formal or informal. Fewer and fewer members of the legal and mercantile communities bequeathed money to the poor, either the paupers of the Hospital General or the indigent who flocked to funerals and roamed the streets. Only a third of the lawyers and a quarter of the merchants left money to any form of charity in the 1780s, and their negligence constituted a virtual rejection of all existing means of relief (table 31). It also stood in direct opposition to the practices of the magistrates, who remained true to their traditions. Like their ancestors, the magistrates still remembered the poor in their wills, and in

TABLE 30

PERCENTAGE OF URBAN TESTAMENTS CONTAINING BEQUESTS
TO THE HOSPITAL GENERAL

Decade	Magistrates	Basoche	Bourgeois	Merchants
1720–1729	67	31	33	11
	(39)	(51)	(3)	(36)
1730–1739	37	24	17	22
	(27)	(49)	(18)	(32)
1740–1749	48	31	45	26
	(27)	(49)	(11)	(27)
1750–1759	38	32	24	4
	(26)	(40)	(17)	(26)
1760–1769	37	15	9	21
	(30)	(40)	(11)	(19)
1770–1779	47	15	44	7
	(15)	(27)	(9)	(14)
1780–1789	57	27	14	17
	(23)	(30)	(7)	(24)

Note: The figures in parentheses are the absolute numbers of testators in each category.

TABLE 31

PERCENTAGE OF TESTAMENTS CONTAINING CHARITABLE BEQUESTS

Decade	Nobles	Magistrates	Basoche	Bourgeois	Merchants
1720–1729	66	80	45	33	33
	(41)	(40)	(66)	(3)	(58)
1730–1739	68	70	39	34	29
	(28)	(27)	(61)	(35)	(41)
1740–1749	52	66	45	54	24
	(23)	(29)	(56)	(13)	(31)
1750–1759	55	73	52	53	24
	(22)	(26)	(48)	(30)	(33)
1760–1769	75	77	35	31	32
	(36)	(31)	(48)	(16)	(25)
1770–1779	51	78	35	56	25
	(43)	(18)	(34)	(16)	(20)
1780–1789	50	70	33	38	25
	(36)	(23)	(36)	(21)	(32)

	Total Percent	Average Donation (in livres)
1720–1729	40	648.89
	(323)	(126)
1730–1739	28	293.42
	(397)	(105)
1740–1749	30	401.57
	(304)	(89)
1750–1759	33	314.69
	(307)	(99)
1760–1769	29	332.31
	(333)	(95)
1770–1779	30	179.88
	(276)	(80)
1780–1789	27	261.50
	(326)	(89)

Note: The figures in parentheses are the absolute numbers of testators in each category.

the 1780s, 70 percent still bequeathed money to the Hospital or the paupers outside its walls (table 31). Despite the defection of the lawyers and
merchants, traditional charity still enjoyed the staunch support of the
aristocratic magistrates.

But aristocrats by their very nature are few in number, and they alone
could not sustain Grenoble's poor. As fewer and fewer individuals beneath the tiny judicial elite made bequests to the poor, so the overall rate
of charitable giving declined. In the 1720s about 40 percent of the

Grenoblois left some money to the poor in their wills; but in the 1780s this rate had dropped to only 27 percent (table 31). Of course, these figures are based on a sample, and a shift in the composition of the sample could account for the apparent decline. But regression analysis (which eliminates such distortions) confirms that a real and significant decline in charitable giving occurred in the course of the eighteenth century (table 32). And this decline was accompanied by a drop in the size of those few bequests which still made their way to the poor. In the 1780s the average bequest for the relief of the poor was only a third the size of the average bequest for the same purpose made in the 1720s (table 31). Fewer people were giving to the poor, and those who still made bequests were giving less. The upshot was a general and significant decline in the amount of

TABLE 32

PERCENTAGE OF TESTATORS MAKING CHARITABLE BEQUESTS:
SELECTED REGRESSION AND TOBIT RESULTS

Variables	Regression Coefficient	Tobit
Date	−0.005	−3.99
	(2.11)	(4.41)
Nobles	0.451	1,141.09
	(14.14)	(13.42)
Magistrates	0.584	1,141.09
	(16.45)	(16.00)
Basoche	0.265	716.44
	(9.48)	(8.96)
Bourgeois	0.290	809.93
	(7.45)	(8.03)
Merchants	0.175	571.04
	(5.71)	(6.57)
Plowmen	0.059	163.33
	(1.459)	(1.23)
Domestics	−0.043	−220.61
	(1.12)	(1.29)
Female	−0.003	−60.74
	(0.20)	(1.20)
Literacy	0.048	251.19
	(2.31)	(4.32)
Urban	−0.039	−37.46
	(1.74)	(0.57)

Note: In the regression equation, the dependent variable was whether or not the testator made charitable bequests. In the tobit equation, the dependent variable was the amount of money spent on charitable bequests, which was zero for testators who left nothing for charity. Both the regression and the tobit equation included a constant term. The numbers in parentheses are t-statistics or measures of significance. For an explanation of their meaning, see table 2.

charity—a development which goes a long way toward explaining the agonies of the Hospital General and other charitable institutions in the late eighteenth century.[4]

Of course, it is possible that the Grenoblois suffered, not declining altruism, but diminishing fortunes, and that their niggardliness stemmed, not from the will, but from the pocketbook. And if magistrates saw their incomes grow, while merchants and lawyers saw theirs decline, then the differing charitable styles of these groups would reflect differing economic circumstances, not contrasting impulses. As always, economic climate could shape charitable giving, and we must determine the degree to which it did so before concluding that a genuine decline in altruism occurred. The testaments themselves provide material for such an analysis in the form of dowries and bequests to family members. These legacies suggest that the Grenoblois held their own financially in the eighteenth century and that some groups, such as merchants and lawyers, enjoyed a real improvement in their fortunes. The average dowries given by members of the legal and mercantile communities to their daughters increased, even when inflation is taken into account, and so too did the money they left to their second sons and other dependents. The magistrates did not suffer either, even if their economic ascension was not quite so dramatic.[5] On the whole, Grenoblois above the level of the laboring poor saw their economic position consolidated or improved in the course of the eighteenth century. But growing wealth did not lead to larger charitable bequests. When the charitable gifts are expressed as a ratio of all family bequests, a distinct decline emerges. In the 1720s charitable gifts amounted to 6 percent of all family bequests; by the 1780s they accounted for barely 1 percent. Economic misfortune did not account for this drop; diminishing generosity did.

What accounted for this decline in altruism? One hundred years earlier a growth in religious giving had accompanied an increase in charitable donations. Counter Reformation Catholicism had stimulated charity and produced an unprecedented outpouring of testamentary alms. Was the reverse now true? Were religious and charitable bequests still tied? Certainly, the links between the two sorts of beneficence remained strong, indeed the correlation between gifts for religious and charitable purposes was greater than ever before.[6] And the rate of religious giving followed the same course as that of charitable giving: precipitous decline. In the 1720s, 75 percent of the Grenoblois remembered the church in their wills, but by the 1780s only 53 percent did so (table 33). In addition, the size in real terms of the average bequest for spiritual purposes fell from 222 livres at the beginning of the

TABLE 33

PERCENTAGE OF TESTAMENTS CONTAINING PIOUS BEQUESTS

Decade	Percent	Average Bequest (livres)
1720–1729	75	222.35
	(323)	(242)
1730–1739	72	167.06
	(397)	(284)
1740–1749	74	95.37
	(304)	(224)
1750–1759	66	82.05
	(307)	(204)
1760–1769	61	114.17
	(333)	(204)
1770–1779	51	62.07
	(276)	(140)
1780–1789	53	67.78
	(326)	(173)

Note: The figures in parentheses are the absolute numbers of testators in each category.

century to only 67 livres at its close (table 33). Regression analysis removes the possibility that this drop is just an artifact of the sample and confirms what we have already suspected: a decline in religious giving brought in its wake a drop in charitable bequests (table 34).

The regression coefficients also reveal that this drop in pious bequests was largely the work of one particular group: the *basoche*. The *huissiers,* notaries, and lawyers were the least likely of all prosperous Grenoblois to remember the Church in their wills (table 34). Their neglect is all the more surprising considering their former fidelity. In the 1720s, 85 percent of the lawyers and notaries had included pious legacies in their wills, making the *basoche* one of the most seemingly devout groups in Grenoble (table 35). But defections began shortly thereafter, and by the 1760s only 35 percent of the *basoche* left money to the Church. Thereafter, the rate dropped to a mere 21 percent, and those few lawyers and notaries who still left money to the Church gave it a mere 37 livres, a paltry sum for a group that included the sons of the opulent Périer and the wealthy Teysseire.[7]

To all appearances, the lawyers and notaries abandoned post-Tridentine Catholicism, but before concluding that they were disbelievers we must be sure that the data are not distorted, that the decline in pious bequests does not reflect the emergence of new sentiments unrelated to religion. New attitudes toward death, for instance, could produce new

TABLE 34

PERCENTAGE OF TESTAMENTS CONTAINING PIOUS BEQUESTS,
AND SIZE OF PIOUS BEQUESTS: SELECTED REGRESSION
AND TOBIT RESULTS

Variables	Regression Coefficient for Likelihood	Coefficient for Amount
Date	−0.004	−1.72
	(8.39)	(5.65)
Nobles	0.158	192.05
	(4.46)	(8.93)
Magistrates	0.319	343.05
	(8.11)	(14.81)
Basoche	0.046	44.82
	(1.47)	(2.43)
Bourgeois	0.235	55.23
	(5.47)	(2.03)
Merchants	0.162	33.01
	(4.77)	(1.55)
Plowmen	0.103	9.75
	(2.31)	(0.34)
Domestics	0.084	12.59
	(4.80)	(0.46)
Female	0.079	17.66
	(3.96)	(1.43)
Literacy	0.054	42.34
	(2.36)	(4.65)
Urban	0.013	35.36
	(0.17)	(2.26)

Note: In the first regression equation, the dependent variable was whether or not testators made pious bequests. In the second regression equation, the dependent variable was the amount of money spent on pious bequests, which was zero for testators who left nothing to the Church. Both regressions included a constant term. The figures in parentheses are t-statistics or measures of significance. For an explanation of their meaning, see table 2.

patterns of religious giving which would create the illusion of declining piety.[8] It is true that the lawyers assumed a new stance before their own demise. They refused to perform the gestures so dear to their ancestors: the election of burial in a monastery or church and the orchestration of a solemn funeral complete with hundreds of requiem masses.[9] The lawyers "denied" death, to use Michel Vovelle's phrase, but at the same time they also repudiated post-Tridentine Catholicism.[10] They ignored the injunctions of the Church and placed their souls in danger. They gave proof, not just of a new indifference to death, but of a new indifference to the fate of their immortal souls which came perilously close to outright disbelief.

Of course, the lawyer who declined to choose a burial site or organize his funeral left these matters, by default, to his heirs. His omission may have stemmed, not from declining faith in the Church, but from growing confidence in his heirs, and a new family sentiment could have emptied eighteenth-century wills of their religious content. Michel Vovelle, the undisputed expert in these matters, was himself troubled by this possibility, but it seems unlikely that Grenoble's lawyers were moved by domestic sentiment alone.[11] The true believer, however devoted to his heirs, simply would not leave in their hands a matter as important as his Eternal Salvation. The fervent post-Tridentine Catholic would not ignore his soul or omit the religious bequests that would secure his salvation. Only the skeptic who doubted the efficacy of redemptive masses or questioned the intercessory powers of the Church would fail to leave money for prayers. Religious doubt, not just family devotion, lay behind the lawyers' reluctance to make pious bequests, and their falling rate of religious giving derived primarily from growing indifference if not apostasy.

Here was a new sensibility, but should we call it "dechristianization"? Even Michel Vovelle, who has been most closely associated with the term, expressed some doubts about its appropriateness, and other historians have rejected it as too sweeping.[12] Basically, opinion has settled into two camps: those who believe that the French were stripped of their Catholicism and Christianity in the eighteenth century, and those who contend that a new spirituality, more "inward" and pure but no less Catholic, triumphed in the age of the Enlightenment.[13] The latter interpretation probably comes closest to the truth, for the lawyers who ignored the Church in their wills did not reject all Christianity, or even all Catholicism. They simply refused to purchase postmortem masses and by so doing, repudiated only a specific institution, the regular clergy, and a specific doctrine, the salvation of souls by prayer. This was, nevertheless, both a sweeping gesture: the friars and the masses alike were central to post-Tridentine Catholicism—and an unequivocal one: the great majority of lawyers refused to leave even a penny to the regular orders for masses. But the *basoche* was neither heathen nor atheistic. Most lawyers probably accepted Christian doctrine while rejecting Catholic ritual; some even continued to patronize Catholic institutions while ignoring the regular clergy. A few lawyers still supported the Christian schools and the Brothers of Charity, though less zealously than in the past, and a handful still left money to the parish clergy, though less generously and never for masses. The lawyers certainly were not fervent post-Tridentine Catholics like their ancestors, but they were not pagans either. Most likely they remained Catholics, but Catholics with a new kind of religious sensibility.

In this endeavor they were joined by the workingmen of Grenoble. They too rejected certain elements in Counter Reformation Catholicism, but they did so more reluctantly and less hastily than the *basoche*. The workingmen had, after all, come late to resurgent Catholicism. Only in the early eighteenth century did they begin to make religious bequests in substantial numbers, and not until the 1730s did the majority remember the Church in their wills. Subsequent events should not obscure the importance of this conversion. It was among the working people that the Counter Reformation Church won its most difficult and impressive victory. Against all odds, the Church had succeeded in converting the working people, but it was not a very durable conversion.

In the late eighteenth century, some workingmen ceased to make religious bequests: their rate of giving dropped to 35 percent (table 35). Flaxcombers and glove-workers, laborers in Grenoble's most "advanced" industries, led the way in this defection, but even those who lagged behind did not necessarily cling to traditional spirituality or even the Church. When workingmen embraced Counter Reformation Catholicism, they reshaped it to fit their own needs. They absorbed the discipline and self-restraint inherent in this doctrine, and they certainly accepted the fundamental religious tenets of resurgent Catholicism. But they also recast this spirituality into a form congenial to workingmen. When laboring Grenoblois made religious bequests, after all, their gifts went, not to the monastery, but to a confraternity, an organization which stressed solidarity within profession, mutual aid, and common devotion. The late-

TABLE 35

PERCENTAGE OF PIOUS BEQUESTS IN TESTAMENTS BY MALES ONLY

Decade	Basoche	Workers	Merchants
1720–1729	85	59	61
	(36)	(41)	(33)
1730–1739	76	56	82
	(38)	(66)	(28)
1740–1749	66	67	81
	(35)	(67)	(16)
1750–1759	61	58	71
	(33)	(54)	(21)
1760–1769	35	50	77
	(26)	(54)	(13)
1770–1779	41	35	36
	(17)	(45)	(14)
1780–1789	21	35	52
	(19)	(49)	(21)

Note: The figures in parentheses are the absolute numbers of testators in each category.

eighteenth-century laborer favored these confraternities, whether they were brotherhoods established in chapels devoted to the patron saint of his profession, the Jesuit associations of the Young and Old Artisans, the Penitents, or the Rosary sodalities. The laborer did ask these institutions to pray for the redemption of his soul; but he did not entrust such prayers to clergymen. He asked his equals, fellow workingmen and members of the confraternity, to assure his salvation—a choice which reveals a certain distrust, if not disapproval, of the clergy. Consequently, his gifts constituted a reaffirmation of solidarity with other workingmen, not an endorsement of the Church and its doctrine. Like the glove-worker who refused to make a religious bequest, the tanner who bestowed a few pennies on a confraternity performed an unconventional, even unorthodox gesture.

The laborers joined the *basoche* in apostasy, and behind them came the merchants, who ventured upon this path with no small amount of trepidation. Their pattern of benefaction seems uneven, incoherent, plagued by sudden reversals and inexplicable hesitations. The problem here lies, not with the merchants themselves, but with the category "merchant." Like the rubric "master artisan," which in the late eighteenth century ceased to apply to more than a dozen individuals, the label "merchant" no longer reflected the economic realities of Grenoble society. On the eve of the Revolution, individuals as diverse as small shopkeepers and grand *négociants,* simple peddlers and merchant-manufacturers called themselves "merchants," but they had nothing in common save the label. The wills themselves do not provide sufficient information to allow us to introduce more precise distinctions into this category, but they do permit us to glimpse two distinct forms of testamentary behavior. On the one hand, the *négociants,* the great wholesale merchants, adhered to a pattern of religious giving similar to that of the lawyers, their social and economic equals. Monsieur Périer, for example, made a token gift of 25 livres to each "convent" and then, in the next breath, bestowed the fabulous sum of 70,000 livres on each of his dependents.[14] Merchant-manufacturers were even stingier: be they glove merchants or flax producers, they gave not a penny to the Church. The highest levels of the world of commerce manifested the same rejection of Counter Reformation Catholicism as did the lawyers. But the small shopkeepers and retail dealers tended to espouse the same values and institutions as the workers, who, by income and inclination, were closer to them. Like the laborers, the shopkeepers had a seemingly high rate of giving to the Church, but in fact their bequests went to confraternities, especially the Penitents. Divided by economic and social circumstance, the merchants were torn between two different forms of religiosity, but for all their indecision, they still belonged with the skeptics.

If conflicting impulses rent the merchants, a veritable chasm split one group of domestics from another. As in the past, servants were divorced from their social equals, the laborers, and they continued to move in the world of their social superiors, their employers. They absorbed their cultural values from their masters—magistrates, lawyers, or merchants—and when religious differences appeared among the employers, they also cropped up among the employees. The domestics who served magistrates, for example, displayed a consistently high rate of religious giving throughout the eighteenth century.[15] At the end of the period, as at its beginning, 80 percent of the magistrates' servants remembered the Church in their wills, and their gifts went to the aristocratic nuns of Saint Claire or the traditional "four convents." In contrast, domestics who served in the homes of humbler folk, lawyers and merchants, were much less faithful to traditional spirituality. These servants, like their employers, began to desert the Church in the mid-eighteenth century, and by the 1780s only half of the domestics remembered to make pious bequests in their wills. Bound to different masters and therefore to different spiritual values, the domestics were poised between two conflicting types of religiosity. This precarious position gave them an ambiguous cultural role in Grenoble society as a whole. Daniel Roche has quite rightly stressed the domestics' function as cultural intermediaries, dispensing to their social equals the values they acquired in the homes of their social superiors, their masters.[16] But the effect of this cultural mediation became more and more unclear as the eighteenth century wore on. Certainly, the domestics continued to function as a link between the prosperous and the common folk, but now they dispensed, not one set of values, but two, each diametrically opposed to the other.

In addition, changes in the composition of the domestic labor force precipitated changes in the domestics' religious impulses. In the eighteenth century, women came to predominate among servants, and women, whatever their occupation, background, or social standing, had their own, particular pattern of religious giving.[17] As the regression coefficients reveal, gender suddenly became a determining factor in pious bequests (see table 34). Women had previously lagged slightly behind men in pious giving, but then in the early eighteenth century they abruptly overtook men and maintained a position of clear superiority throughout the rest of the century. In the 1760s, for example, only 57 percent of the men made religious bequests, whereas over 65 percent of the women remembered the Church in their wills (table 36). Women, whether rich or poor, noble or commoner, remained steadfastly faithful to Counter Reformation Catholicism, whereas their husbands abandoned the Church. A certain pattern had emerged, a pattern that would characterize French religious life throughout the nineteenth century: the husband and father drifted away from Catholicism, but the wife and mother remained the Church's staunch ally within the home.[18]

What bound women so tightly to the Church? Had they developed their own specifically feminine forms of spirituality which sustained their devotion? Wills can provide only partial answers to these questions, but they do reveal that women had distinct tastes and predilections when it came to religious bequests. The convents, in the true sense of the word, continued to attract women's generosity. Whatever their social group, women supported the prestigious Saint Claire convent, not so much because it was aristocratic but because it was the only female order in Grenoble that accepted bequests for masses. Similarly, women continued to support other monasteries, in particular those which housed confraternities, like the Rosary sodalities at the Carmelites and the Dominicans, and the Third Order in the Recollets, or the Penitents of Saint Joseph parish. What all these groups had in common was a "mixed" composition, that is, a membership made up of both men and women. These groups pro-

TABLE 36

PERCENTAGE OF TESTAMENTS MADE BY MEN AND WOMEN
CONTAINING PIOUS BEQUESTS

Decade	Men	Women
1720–1729	71	81
	(200)	(123)
1730–1739	73	70
	(219)	(178)
1740–1749	67	82
	(168)	(136)
1750–1759	65	69
	(182)	(125)
1760–1769	57	65
	(169)	(164)
1770–1779	51	51
	(142)	(134)
1780–1789	50	56
	(161)	(165)

Note: The figures in parentheses are the absolute numbers of testators in each category.

vided women with an active spiritual life which females apparently could
not acquire elsewhere, not even in their parish church. If women remained faithful to the Church, it was probably because of these feminine
groups, for while secular society increasingly confined women to the
home, Catholicism offered them an independent spiritual life outside the
domestic sphere.

The rift between men's and women's religious practices ran the length
of Grenoble society, from the bottom of the social scale up to the lawyers
and merchants near its summit. But here it stopped. Those at the very
peak of Grenoble society—the magistrates and nobles—were not troubled by such divisions. Both men and women in this aristocracy were exceptionally faithful to the spirituality—Counter Reformation Catholicism—which they had embraced before all others.[19] In the late eighteenth
century, they still clung to the religiosity which they had largely shaped;
on the very eve of the Revolution, 91 percent remembered the Church in
their wills, just as they had one hundred years before (table 37). At first
glance, the judges' cousins, the nobles, seem considerably less devout, but
the nobility was a varied and irregular group which contained prestigious
dukes and country *hobereaux*. When the rural gentlemen are removed,
the nobles come close to equaling the magistrates in piety, for over 65

TABLE 37

PERCENTAGE OF RELIGIOUS BEQUESTS AMONG NOBLES,
MAGISTRATES, AND BOURGEOIS

Decade	Nobles		Magistrates	Bourgeois
	Rural	*Urban*		
1720–1729	75	66	90	100
	(6)	(35)	(40)	(3)
1730–1739	89	91	85	83
	(4)	(24)	(27)	(35)
1740–1749	91	94	86	92
	(6)	(17)	(29)	(13)
1750–1759	59	62	92	83
	(4)	(18)	(26)	(30)
1760–1769	83	82	97	63
	(8)	(28)	(31)	(16)
1770–1779	65	66	83	75
	(11)	(32)	(18)	(16)
1780–1789	56	65	91	67
	(7)	(29)	(23)	(21)

Note: The figures in parentheses are the absolute numbers of testators in each category.

percent made religious bequests on the eve of the Revolution, just as they had in the 1720s. Together, the nobles and magistrates formed the most pious group in Grenoble, and the regression coefficients confirm this impression (table 34). They also reveal that the aristocracy was followed in short order by a group with whom they had (to all appearances) little in common—the rentiers, or bourgeoisie, as they were called at the time. These men and women who lived on income from their rural estates possessed neither fabulous wealth nor ancient pedigrees, but that did not stop them from mimicking the spiritual proclivities of their social superiors. Although some decline occurred over the course of the eighteenth century, the bourgeois were still among the most devout individuals in the city: 67 percent remembered the Church in their testaments on the very eve of the Revolution (see table 37).

If the nobility, the magistracy, and the bourgeoisie were traditional in the frequency of their bequests, they were equally traditional in the objects of their gifts. Like their ancestors, the magistrates and nobles lavished huge sums of money on the regular clergy, always for the salvation of their immortal souls. Sebastien Flodard Bally de Montcarra, seigneur and honorary master at the Chambre des Comptes, left annual pensions totaling 650 livres to a host of religious houses. Equally generous were the bequests of François de Galien de Chabons, a nobleman who was seigneur of Plassages and president à mortier of the Parlement. He left the huge sum of 1,200 livres to the ladies of Saint Claire in return for an infinity of masses, and he also gave considerable sums of money to the local monasteries, with which he had a "long" and "personal" affiliation.[20]

The magistrates and nobles appear to have remained utterly faithful to post-Tridentine Catholicism, and their devotion comes as no small surprise. Eighteenth-century aristocrats in general and those of Grenoble in particular were reputed to have been freethinkers at best, debauched libertines at worst. After all, rumor has it that Grenoble's aristocrats served as models for the cynical characters in Choderlos de Laclos' novel Les Liaisons dangereuses. Laclos did indeed spend some time in the garrison at Grenoble, and he may well have drawn upon his experiences there when shaping his characters, but the best example of a provincial noble which his novel provides is not the debauched Madame de Merteuil, but the excruciatingly devout La Presidente de Tournevel, who had many equivalents in eighteenth-century Grenoble.[21]

There is of course another picture of the eighteenth-century aristocracy, one that in recent years has gained considerable popularity. Historians have replaced the debauched libertine with the enlightened free-

thinker, and the liberal aristocrat now dominates the literature.[22]
Certainly, a reform-minded aristocracy existed in late eighteenth-century
Dauphiné. The Parlement embraced a number of progressive causes, including physiocracy, the abolition of torture, and the toleration of Protestants, and many magistrates were known to be involved in Freemasonry,
albeit Masonry of the mystical, Lyon sort.[23] Still, when the noble or magistrate made his last will and testament he manifested the most conservative, traditional impulses. His attachment to liberal causes did not prevent
him from performing the same gestures as his ancestors and endorsing the
Church and post-Tridentine Catholicism. A curious inconsistency seems
to characterize the aristocrats' behavior, and their relationship to the Enlightenment bears further investigation.

One point, however, seems clear: the aristocrats remained true to the
Church, and their fidelity set them at odds with their immediate social
inferiors, the *basoche*.[24] Upon this critical issue, noble and commoner
could not agree, and a serious breach opened up within the Grenoble elite
for the first time. On occasion, this division could be bridged and temporary unanimity achieved, as the events of 1788 and 1789 would demonstrate. But the rift was, nevertheless, wide and deep, for it went beyond
mere spiritual issues.[25] Social and political problems were too entangled
with the Church to make this just a religious dispute. Differing views of
society, and opposing notions about the poor, divided aristocrat from
lawyer and noble from commoner, as the Grenoblois' testaments clearly
demonstrate.

Take, for example, the wills of two seemingly like-minded, progressive
Grenoblois: the lawyer Barnave, father of the famous delegate to the Constituent Assembly, and the marquis de Barral, magistrate and industrial-
ist, father of the infamous sans-culotte mayor. When these gentlemen
made their wills in the 1780s, both included bequests to the Hospital
General. The lawyer Barnave left to the institution the modest sum of 100
livres, whereas the marquis bestowed upon the Hospital the substantial,
even lavish gift of 3,000 livres.[26] Size was not, however, what distinguished the two legacies. The lawyer Barnave asked that his gift go for the
support and feeding of the poor. The marquis, on the other hand, requested that his legacy purchase masses to which the poor would add
their special prayers for his redemption. For the lawyer Barnave, the poor
had lost their particular religious aura; for the marquis, however, they
retained their mystical intercessory powers. One bequest was secular, almost progressive; the other was religious, even archaic. Here we have two
sets of social assumptions, assumptions apparently shared by Barnave's

and Barral's respective social groups. On the very eve of the French Revolution, not one member of the *basoche* asked that the poor pray for his soul; more than 15 percent of the magistrates, however, purchased the special, intercessory prayers of God's paupers.

For the aristocrats, the poor were still Christ's poor, but they were also the seigneur's. The old seigneural ethic was not dead—far from it. The marquis de Barral certainly did not fail to remember "his" poor—the tenants of his estates—along with God's. To the poor of Allevard and Saint Pierre d'Allevard, he left 100 livres, and to the impoverished of Chapelle du Bard and Pinot, where his holdings were less extensive, he left 60 livres. Other great lords followed suit. The count of Saint Vallier, Nicolas Amédée de la Croix de Chevrières, asked that 100 livres be distributed in each parish within his estates on the day of his death. Similarly, Bally de Montcarra requested that 100 livres be dispensed to the occupants of Saint Jean d'Octavon, Gilon, Parans, and other places, all communities where he was seigneur. Sometimes these bequests took the form of grain, just as they had for centuries: the Count of Herculais instructed his heirs to open the granary in his chateau the day of his funeral and allow the inhabitants of Saint Gervais to take what they needed. Other times, the seigneur requested that his bequest be converted into medicine to be dispensed to the sick. Always, however, the testator asked that his heirs preside over the distribution, whether it was grain, medicine, or just money, thereby reasserting the family's personal ties with the tenants.[27]

The fundamental form of these seigneurial bequests had not changed, nor had their purpose. These bequests were still designed to display the seigneur's beneficence and to assert his paternal solicitude for his dependents, that is, his peasants. Nor had the seigneurs' propensity to make such gifts declined. While other types of bequests to the "free" poor— shoes for paupers in the funeral cortege and cloth for widowed women— disappeared, those to peasants persisted right up to the Revolution. About the same percentage of magistrates and nobles remembered "their" peasants in their wills as had done so one hundred years before (table 38). Apparently, the old feeling of seigneurial obligation, the traditional need to display lordly paternalism, remained strong among the Dauphinois aristocracy. They at least still observed the old forms and the old rituals. To all appearances, they were still attached to their traditional obligations and probably to their traditional privileges and prerogatives as well.

No such sentiments gripped the lawyers, notaries, and great merchants of Grenoble, many of whom possessed land in the countryside.

TABLE 38

PERCENTAGE OF BEQUESTS TO PEASANTS IN TESTAMENTS

Decade	Nobles and Magistrates	All Others	Average Bequest by Nobles and Magistrates (in livres)
1720–1729	31	4	445.94
	(81)	(242)	(25)
1730–1739	45	3	262.32
	(55)	(342)	(25)
1740–1749	27	6	219.70
	(52)	(252)	(14)
1750–1759	42	5	187.81
	(48)	(259)	(20)
1760–1769	46	5	216.25
	(67)	(266)	(31)
1770–1779	43	6	117.04
	(61)	(215)	(26)
1780–1789	39	4	138.10
	(59)	(267)	(23)

Note: The figures in parentheses are the absolute numbers of testators in each category.

Their holdings were sometimes as large as those of the magistrates, and nothing prevented them from possessing a seigneury or exercising a lord's high justice. Still, they felt absolutely no need to reenact these feudal rituals: not one lawyer or merchant left bequests to "his" peasants in the years between 1760 and 1789. Only a few rentiers imitated the manners of the aristocrats (table 38). In general, the seigneurial theater produced by these bequests belonged to the aristocrats alone, and their attachment to these archaic rites points once again to the chasm that had come to separate them from their immediate social inferiors. If religion divided the magistrates and the lawyers, then a certain social view also divorced the aristocracy from the *basoche*.

The late-eighteenth-century aristocrat still performed the traditional gestures, but this does not mean that he did so graciously or with generosity. Bequests to the peasants had never provided real, sustained relief to the poor; that was not their purpose. But in the late eighteenth century, they provided even less comfort to the impoverished, for their size declined radically. In the years between 1720 and 1729, the average seigneur had given his peasants 444 livres; on the eve of the Revolution, the lord deigned to provide them with no more than 138 livres (table 38). Typically, the grandfather of the marquis de Barral left to his tenants 800 livres

plus huge bequests in grain; the marquis himself, however, left "his" peasants only 190 livres. The contrast was probably not lost upon the peasantry, nor was it unrelated to the rising tension in rural Dauphiné on the
eve of the Revolution. The retraction of communal rights and the increase
in seigneurial demands about which the peasants complained in the late
eighteenth century were not new.[28] Many times in the past seigneurs had
pressed their peasants to the breaking point. But in the summer of 1789
the rupture came. Perhaps the lords' hollow paternalism was among the
factors contributing to this break. Perhaps the patent emptiness of seigneurial beneficence, now exposed for all to see, led to a demystification
of seigneurial rule and in the end its downfall.

We know too little about the situation in rural Dauphiné on the eve of
the Revolution to determine the effect of the aristocrats' abdication of
responsibility. We do know that they also failed to meet their responsibilities in the city. In Grenoble the magistrates abandoned the Hospital General, an institution which they had created. They no longer sat on its
board of administration, and they no longer tended to the tedious problems of its daily administration. In the city as in the country, the old manifestations of seigneurial paternalism tended to disappear, to be replaced,
albeit tentatively, by the good works inspired by another, new social ethic.

This new social ethic manifested itself only partially and belatedly in
the Grenoblois' wills. In the 1780s the ties between religion and charity
broke down, and a new kind of altruism emerged of which the *basoche,*
as always, was the harbinger. On the eve of the Revolution, only 21 percent of the lawyers made religious bequests, but over 32 percent gave
money to the poor. Something other than post-Tridentine Catholicism
inspired these bequests, but just what, is hard to say. Testamentary charity was old-fashioned, and wills cannot reveal much about new attitudes.
More informative are the pamphlets and essays written by enlightened
progressive-minded Grenoblois, which provide a more complete picture
of the new secular, social ethic.

PAMPHLETS AND ESSAYS

Surprisingly enough, there are not a large number of such essays. Historians generally believe that the Enlightenment witnessed an outpouring
of concern for the poor which took the form of numerous pamphlets,
treatises, and proposals. The sheer quantity of this writing has impressed
historians and convinced them that the "humanité" and "bienfaisance"
so often invoked in the late eighteenth century was in fact real.[29] Grenoble

certainly had an Enlightenment and a group of individuals, among them lawyers, doctors, and *négociants,* who embraced the new ideas and put their thoughts down on paper. But the Grenoble "community" of the Enlightenment, to use Daniel Roche's phrase again, gave little thought to poverty, at least in writing. The local Académie Delphinale heard papers on botany or technical subjects and did not encourage writings on social or political topics. No flood of pamphlets on the poor and no outpouring of essays on poor relief marked the Enlightenment in Grenoble. To determine what constituted the "new ideas" about poverty, we must rely, unfortunately, upon only two authors: Achard de Germane and the abbé Reymond.

That a cleric should deal with the right succoring of the poor is no surprise. Poor relief had always been the special preserve of the clergy, in Grenoble as in the rest of France. But Reymond was no traditional clergyman. In 1776 he published *Le Droit des curés,* a tract which laid out the bitter grievances of the lower clergy against their superiors. Reymond had led the Dauphinois "revolt of the curés," which pitted the lower clergy against the ecclesiastical hierarchy, and when that movement met with success on the local level, he shifted his attention to France as a whole. In 1771 he wrote another pamphlet, *Le Droit des pauvres,* which again focused on the conflicts between the upper and lower clergy, but which also addressed the question of the poor. And in 1789 he published yet another tract, *Le Cahier des curés du Dauphiné,* in which he called for a sweeping national reform of the Church. When the Revolution did come, Reymond found himself, ironically, a member of the upper clergy: he became a constitutional bishop of Grenoble.[30]

Considering Reymond's extraordinary career, it comes as a surprise that when he attacked the question of poverty, he did so from the most traditional angle, that of begging. "Of all the ills of society," he wrote in 1789, "the greatest is a host of beggars." This "moral and political plague," he added, "has the most pernicious consequences," for it was always an "apprenticeship of crime." "Everyone knows that beggars do not have much religion and less honesty," remarked Reymond, "and they do not long resist the temptation to steal." The equation between begging and crime was not new, nor were Reymond's notions about the origins of begging. "A pernicious penchant for idleness which enervates and corrupts" lay at the root of poverty, and begging was just one manifestation of the pauper's laziness.[31]

Thus far nothing could have been more traditional than Reymond's analysis of poverty. His fellow clergyman, the Père Guévarre, could have written these same lines seventy years before. But Reymond broke with tradition when he considered the means employed in his day to eliminate mendicancy. For these he had nothing but scorn. The dépôts were cruel and self-defeating. His parishioners, he remarked, returned from this "violent" institution "with all the vices that had sent them there in the first place." The hospitals too were "useless." "It is well known," Reymond asserted, "that the administration of the hospitals is very expensive and that salaries and the maintenance of buildings take up one-third of the revenues, revenues which are lost to the poor." In addition, the air in these old *maisons de force* was unhealthy and the personnel "hard and pitiless." Even the laws prohibiting begging were ineffective and, worse yet, unjust, for what was needed was "not a prohibition but a remedy."[32]

To Reymond's mind, the correct "remedy" varied with the pauper. For the impoverished sick, he would first abolish the hospital and return the ill to their homes where the air was superior, and their families more attentive than the callous hospital staff. As for the sturdy poor, Reymond had an old solution but with a new purpose. *Bureaux de charité*, he explained, should be established in every parish in France; some 80,000 would do. The Père Guévarre too had great faith in the *bureaux de charité*, but he considered their primary function the distribution of alms. Not Reymond; for him, alms only encouraged idleness. The *bureaux* would distribute only one item, work. "It is essential," he asserted, "for good morals and for society as a whole that every sturdy beggar be given the habit of work; the *bureaux* will make this their sole objective." They would provide labor by bringing rural employers into contact with the poor; in other words, they would function as employment bureaus. They might also administer *ateliers de charité*. But their primary task would be the extinguishing of the vice of idleness through work.[33]

The question of funding naturally arose, and Reymond was all too happy to address it. Who was responsible for the poor? he asked. Very quickly he responded—the Church. Its wealth, he maintained, was the patrimony of the poor, given over in stewardship to its ministers, principally the parish clergy. At this point, Reymond entered into the very heart of his argument, for he proposed a radical redistribution of the wealth of the French Church. First, he suggested that one-twenty-fourth of the *dîme* be turned over immediately to the *bureaux de charité*. Second, he called for one-quarter of the Church's real property to be distributed for charitable purposes—in other words, to the *bureaux*. Finally, he demanded that the superfluous wealth of the Church, which lay in the hands of the idle upper clergy, be restored to the poor through the *bureaux de charité*. As the Revolution approached, Reymond made even more sweeping demands. In 1789 he suggested that all the collegiate churches in France be abolished and their property redistributed to the *bureaux de charité*. At the head of these little institutions would be, of course, the parish clergy. They were the natural benefactors of the poor, for their proximity to the impoverished gave them insight into the needs of the destitute.[34]

As for the unfortunate beggars, they would, if this system were enacted, simply disappear. "The habit of work would spare morals," Reymond claimed, "and the children of the next generation would not be tempted to beg." On the contrary, they would "applaud the laws that punish mendicancy." Now the prohibitions against begging could be enforced with the necessary ferocity, for only those still sunk in criminal idleness would demand alms. As for the rest, the great majority, they would once again be "useful" to society, and society itself would enjoy a host of benefits. "Other than the destruction of begging," Reymond proclaimed, "the security of the roads would be insured and the nation would enjoy the fruits of the indigents' labors; religion too would benefit because its ministers would no longer live in opulence, which is contrary to the designs of the Great Institutor."[35]

Reymond's project was a curious mixture of the old and the new. He approached poverty in a traditional fashion, from the vantage point of begging, and proposed traditional remedies, *bureaux de charité* and *ateliers de charité*. His condemnation of casual almsgiving had antecedents in the views of the Company of the Holy Sacrament, and one of his more radical proposals, the promotion of the lower clergy, had its roots in the Counter Reformation. Nevertheless, Reymond's project was novel in several respects. These innovations are easy to overlook, for it is not so much what was included as what was omitted that lent novelty to Reymond's views. To begin with, the hospitals-general received scant attention. Indeed, they cropped up only when Reymond condemned them. Furthermore, the urban poor were virtually overlooked in favor of the rural poor. Christian charity and its obligations were never mentioned, and moral imperatives were strangely absent from a pamphlet written by a cleric. For Reymond, poor relief was an utterly secular affair, a "political problem" in which the Church was incidental, and "utility," not God's word, was the measure of success. The assumptions upon which seventeenth-century poor relief was built were quietly and discreetly discarded. In fact, the poor themselves were shoved aside, for Reymond's primary concern was the reform of the church, not the succoring of the poor. The impoverished were incidental, an ornament and nothing more, in a discourse whose subject was as much ecclesiastical privilege as impoverishment.

Somewhat more to the point was the work of Achard de Germane. A lawyer and a director of the Hospital General of Grenoble, Achard was also an essayist of some local repute. Economics was his speciality, and in 1788 he read a paper on the branches of industry most appropriate to Dauphiné before the Académie Delphinale.[36] In 1789 he won first prize in a contest sponsored by the Academy of Valence with a second paper, this one on the suppression of begging. Both of these essays were the work of a well-read, provincial gentleman who had somehow absorbed, if not digested, all the major currents of Enlightenment thought. Montesquieu, the physiocrats, Rousseau, and Adam Smith all left their mark on Achard and on his two essays. Therefore, it is surprising that many of Achard's views on poverty were so traditional. He shared with Reymond a horror of begging: "the leprosy of society," he called it, and referred to its practitioners as the "tribe" of beggars. Achard even clung to the old notion of false beggars who "covered themselves in rags to inspire pity, whose excuse is usually a sick husband or wife and children dying of hunger." Such tribulations, Achard explained, "are only ruses to deceive the sensitive man, and alms are nothing but the reward of laziness." Who then was responsible for the beggar's poverty? The beggar himself, for he was "willingly useless," in other words, wantonly idle. In this state "everything escapes him, even the horror of his own fate, and misery deprives him of reason." In fact, Achard concluded, "degradation gives him the sentiment of nonexistence, . . . and he does not, so to speak, exist."[37]

The pauper may not exist, but he must still be punished. "I know," Achard remarked, "that one should be indulgent toward men and that one should pardon them; but to render them happy one must sometimes be severe." "Punishment and reward," he asserted, "are the tools which the administrator must use to force people to bend to his will." Punishment in particular should be used upon the poor, for they did enormous harm both to themselves and to society as a whole. They were no longer a religious scourge, threatening the righteous with their sin. Now they were an economic affliction bringing hardship to all. To the proprietor of rural estates they brought high costs, for the "exploitation of the land becomes more expensive for lack of workers." To the manufacturer they brought high wages, "for the scarcity of workers renders labor more expensive." And to everyone they brought high prices, for costly labor meant costly, less competitive goods. It was not that work was unavailable. The beggar refused to work and abandoned the countryside, where work was plentiful, for the city and a life of wanton poverty. Achard shared his contemporaries' delusion that the population of France was declining and draining toward the cities. "The cultivator," he explained, "sees with envy and longing the advantages of the artisan which are a luxury to him; this is what causes there to be so many workers in cities who cannot make a living and are reduced to begging." Under these circumstances, Achard maintained, "mendicity acquires men while agriculture loses them."[38]

These wantonly idle, voluntarily unemployed individuals should not receive alms, and Christian charity should not be, as in the past, the foundation of public assistance. Like his seventeenth-century predecessors, Achard could not condemn casual almsgiving too vehemently. "These disorderly alms," he explained, "do great harm, for they flatter the idleness of the beggars and exempt them from work." The consequences of such charity were, Achard believed, "pernicious, for these alms are of no utility and confer only temporary benefits on the beggar." The old *maisons de force,* however, were more useful. Unlike Reymond and many of his other contemporaries, Achard believed that the hospitals-general had an important role to play. They were to be the asylum of "those who have worked all their lives and whom age and sickness have rendered unable to make a living." These paupers were, Achard explained, "the respectable poor," and they deserved all the care they received. Beggars were another question, and the institution that dealt with them, the *dépôt de mendicité,* was as evil as the mendicants themselves. "These are," Achard asserted, "very bad establishments," where the inmates were apt to become "even lazier." The beggars needed assistance, but only in the form of work: "the legislator should provide work and nothing else."[39]

Indeed, work constituted the only truly effective means of abolishing begging. "The method," Achard stated confidently, "of preventing mendicancy is to occupy sturdy beggars in the cultivation of the earth." Achard, like many of his contemporaries, had an almost mystical faith in the value of work. Its effects were ennobling. Not only did it preserve the pauper from begging, it restored his "courage" and "reason," in short, his humanity. His children, too, would benefit, for "education," that is, work, would extinguish the idleness they often acquired from their parents. In fifteen or twenty years, Achard assured his readers, begging would disappear altogether, and the economy would enjoy a true renaissance.[40]

But who would provide this work? Who would force the innately lazy pauper to apply himself? Achard had two responses. First, he cited Montesquieu's assertion that the State owed all its citizens subsistence, and he understood this to mean work. However, Achard was not interested in *ate-*

liers de charité or other public works projects. These projects obstructed the free flow of labor and drove up wages. Moreover, they were unnecessary, for work already existed in abundant quantities in the countryside. The State need only set the pauper on to it. This could be achieved, Achard suggested, if the hospitals-general functioned as employment bureaus, sending the beggars to rural employers. There, the pauper would receive only the tiniest wage, but he would not be tempted to return to begging. Free market forces would take care of that. Once the hoards of paupers had been returned to the countryside, the price of labor would fall and with it the price of all goods. The pauper would be able to support his family; if he could not, his "courage" and "self-interest" (now revived by labor) would prompt him to seek other, more remunerative employment.[41]

In this fashion, the State would secure the prosperity of the poor and would fulfill its "sacred duty." But the rich too had a duty; they too bore responsibility for the poor. "The patrimony of the poor," Achard solemnly stated, "can only be found among the wealthy." Achard then launched into a Rousseauist panegyric of suffering humanity and its tender *sensibilité*. But should the humane rich provide alms to their miserable brothers? Absolutely not; the duties of the rich lay elsewhere. The Academicians of Valence neatly summarized Achard's position in a poem appended to his essay. "Divine providence," the poem began, "has caused the rich to appear along with the indigent, for one needs hands, the other needs a wage, and everything is thus well arranged in life, for one half of the world is served by the other." In Achard's view, therefore, mutual needs and duties still bound the rich and poor, as they did in the seventeenth century; however, these links were no longer expressed with alms. "How blind men are," exclaimed Achard; "they prefer to give alms and diminish their fortune . . . when they could enrich themselves by offering a salary instead!"[42]

Consequently, the duty of the rich was to heed their own self-interest. If the pauper needed encouragement on this point, so too did the rich man. "It is necessary," Achard proclaimed, "to stimulate the wealthy citizens . . . and to tempt their self-interest, which is the motor of all men." The self-interest of the rich could be stimulated in a number of ways. First, the grain trade should be freed. Here, Ashard raised the old battle cry of the physiocrats and pursued it through a number of pages. Second, the roads should be improved, a favorite subject of Achard, so that commerce would flourish. Finally, as far as Valence itself was concerned, the court and the university had to be abolished. This may seem a peculiar proposition, but it went right to the heart of Achard's argument. The rich were distracted by the university and the courts from their own self-interest. They pursued careers which were rewarded with esteem, but which failed to enrich them and provided no solace—work—for the poor. Achard's fellow competitor, Reynaud de Lagardette, stated the problem more forthrightly. In his essay, which is appended to Achard's, he lambasted "the vile prejudice" against men of commerce. Only when the *négociant* was held in proper esteem would industry and commerce flourish and poverty disappear. On this point, Achard was filled with optimism. "Man," he assured the reader, "has need only of the enlightenment of personal self-interest; if my system is followed, I dare to conclude that in fifteen or twenty years a regeneration of society will occur!"[43]

Achard's optimism certainly set him apart from his seventeenth-century predecessors, who thought that they could relieve poverty, but never imagined that they could abolish it. A number of other assumptions fundamental to Achard's argument also put him at odds with his ancestors. First, though he had considerable faith in human self-interest, he had less confidence in human institutions. The Hospital he suffered only because it would care for the sick; the *dépôt de mendicité* and public works projects he roundly condemned. Achard wanted, like the other directors of the Hospital General, to deinstitutionalize the poor and leave their relief to "that universal motor of all human actions, self-interest," in other words, to market forces. In this scheme of things, the Church had absolutely no role, and Achard showed not the slightest interest in morality or religion. Here was, perhaps, the single most important difference between Achard and his ancestors. For Achard, the poor were purely economic beings, and they concerned him only to the degree that they hampered the economy. Economics had replaced religion as the basis of discourse on the poor, and this change alone rendered Achard's work innovative.

But the secular, economic tone of Achard's discussion did not have the revolutionary consequences that one might expect. For all his novelty, Achard shared many assumptions with his predecessors. Like seventeenth-century Grenoblois, Achard believed that the pauper bore sole responsibility for his own misery. The pauper's refusal to work, his stubborn idleness, was now his vice, but it was no less his problem. Like his forerunners, Achard also had a nearly magical solution to this problem: work. Work had replaced confinement as the panacea that would transform the pauper and society as well. Nor was Achard any more capable than his forerunners of developing a radical critique of economic arrangements. His delusion, shared by most of his contemporaries, that work was readily available in the countryside, allowed him to reduce an economic problem to a personal quirk.[44] It was not that the poor could not find work or that they were insufficiently remunerated for their labor; it was that they chose not to work. Again, poverty was a moral as much as an economic problem, and this conviction permitted Achard to ignore the real sources of poverty in the late eighteenth century: unemployment, underemployment, and low wages. The genuine complaints of the poor—their inability to feed their families—Achard dismissed as ruses and clever feints. Like his fellow directors at the Hospital, he refused to recognize that the poor were poor because they were not paid enough money to support their families. For Achard, the pauper was impoverished because he wanted to be, because he suffered from a moral flaw—habitual laziness.

Historians are wont to talk about progress when discussing eighteenth-century attitudes toward the poor, but it is by no means clear that Achard's system would have led to more or better relief for the destitute. His secular, economic perspective did not prevent him from repeating the errors of his ancestors, nor did it prompt him to call for an extension of relief. Achard did denounce old, inhumane, and inefficient institutions (a step forward), but he did not propose new institutions to take their place.[45] Work, Achard argued, was the best means of relief, but neither society nor the State were obliged to provide it. Achard absolutely rejected the *ateliers de charité* or public works projects and never contemplated the State-financed, national welfare system discussed by some of his contemporaries. For him, the State had only the most limited role in public assistance: the providing of information on jobs, not jobs themselves. In fact, the State served the poor best by serving the rich most, by encouraging commerce and industry, which would lead to the creation of jobs. No direct relief would be provided to the poor; the market, working unencumbered, would tend to their needs. No alms, public works projects, or bread distributions would be necessary. That "universal motor of all human actions, self-interest," would make the poor, and poor relief with them, obsolete.

Inevitably, Achard's system would have led to the diminution, if not outright demise, of poor relief, and this was precisely what was happening in late-eighteenth-century Grenoble. The new "altruism" elicited only a handful of testamentary bequests from the Grenoblois and even fewer donations to the Hospital General. The directors of the Hospital restricted relief. They generally excluded the able-bodied from their institution and struck sturdy paupers from the bread-distribution rolls. Perhaps the most progressive Grenoblois believed, like Achard, that work acquired in the marketplace was the only suitable means of relief. Perhaps the directors shared Achard's faith in the market. In any event, a number of exterior circumstances encouraged them to limit poor relief and ignore the poor. The Hospital was broke, and its finances showed no signs of improving. Certainly, there were plenty of paupers, but most were harmless women and children. The poor hardly forced themselves into the consciousness of the rich. They posed little threat to the elite's property and less to its political dominance. The occasional grain riot did cause alarm, but such incidents were always contained and never truly threatened authority. For the time being, the Grenoblois could afford to overlook the poor and ignore their needs.

But the time was quickly arriving when this would no longer be possible. Even as Achard and Reymond wrote, events were occurring which would change the political equation and force the poor upon the consciousness of the rich. The Revolution would create new circumstances, and the Grenoble elite would respond by creating new types of poor relief. The years between 1789 and 1794 witnessed a renewed energy on the part of the rich and a feverish (if not always fruitful) activity in the domain of poor relief.

ELEVEN

The Revolution: 1789–1814

In October 1794 the municipal council of Grenoble received the famous Ventôse decrees from Paris. These were, according to historians, the Jacobin dictatorship's most radical piece of social legislation, for the decrees required that common lands be sold to support the indigent. The Grenoble municipality received these decrees with great enthusiasm, but there was one problem: Grenoble had no commons to speak of. No matter, proclaimed the city government, "nothing will stand in the way of this manifestation of beneficence." Having disposed, after a fashion, of the Ventôse decrees, the municipal council next turned to a petition from the Hospital General, which it greeted with far less enthusiasm. The Hospital directors complained—and not for the first time—that the Revolution had deprived the institution of income and foisted upon it unprecedented numbers of paupers. The municipal council claimed to be distressed by the Hospital's predicament, but denied that it was responsible. The Convention had placed the Hospital, and all institutions like it, under the protection of the nation, not the city of Grenoble. On this score, no "manifestation of beneficence" was forthcoming.[1]

The meeting of October 1794 was in some ways typical of the fate of public assistance in revolutionary Grenoble. It raises two important questions. Did the Revolution lead to "great manifestations of beneficence"? Or did it leave the poor equally, if not more, desperate? In general, historians have provided two sets of answers to these questions. The first praises the principles enunciated by the revolutionaries, but concedes that circumstances prevented their implementation.[2] The second, in contrast, deplores these same principles and contends that they led to the wanton destruction of existing means of relief and therefore to greater suffering among the poor.[3] The first implies that the Revolution had little real impact upon public assistance; its only legacy was some noble, but intangible, principles. The second insists that the Revolution wreaked havoc with poor relief; it left in its wake only destruction and misery for the poor. According to the first school of thought, the revolutionaries did not go far enough; according to the second, they went all too far.

As the events of the municipal meeting of 1794 illustrate, both interpretations can easily be applied to the history of poor relief in Grenoble. After all, the Ventôse decrees were never enacted in Grenoble or anywhere else for that matter. At the same time, the Hospital of Grenoble, like so many other charitable institutions in France, was seriously undermined by the Revolution, and its very existence was threatened. Both historical interpretations fit; consequently, neither is entirely satisfactory. Both interpretations are too simplistic, for they fail to take into account the different stages of the Revolution and the changes in policy and circumstance that accompanied shifts in regime. Furthermore, both share a common, Parisian perspective. As local studies appear, it becomes increasingly obvious that the history of public assistance in provincial France was more complex and more complicated than was previously imagined.[4] The laws issued in Paris were shaped, often deformed, by local conditions and regional peculiarities, so that national decrees frequently had unintended and unforeseen consequences. The legacy of the Revolution to local communities was neither completely disastrous nor entirely beneficial. It was at once something more than noble principles and something less than wholesale destruction. In provincial France the Revolution changed poor relief, but in ways that historians have often failed to appreciate.

In order to evaluate accurately the Revolution's legacy, we must follow the intricate, often uneven, development of poor relief in Grenoble in the years between 1789 and 1814. This development falls into three basic periods which coincide with changes in the city's political climate. The first period runs from 1790 to the fall of 1793, a time when old-regime projects and reforms were pursued with new energy. The second period concerns the months between February 1793 and the fall of 1794, when famine and a radical sans-culotte movement forced the municipal authorities to extend relief to unprecedented numbers of paupers. The last and final period runs from the beginning of 1795 through the Empire, when the Jacobin experiment in public welfare was abandoned, and authority in matters of poor relief, as in everything else, eventually passed from the municipality to the prefect.

In the years between 1790 and 1793, however, local governments enjoyed almost complete autonomy in matters of poor relief, more autonomy than they had known since the sixteenth century. The events of 1789 had strengthened municipal institutions and greatly extended their prerogatives in all domains, including that of poor relief. Moreover, the central government rarely interfered in these years. The Constituent Assembly, through its famous Committee on Mendicity, was busy collecting data, not issuing legislation, so the actual provision of relief was left up to municipal, district, and departmental authorities. Significantly, all of these officials chose to continue—even to enlarge—efforts that were under way before the Revolution. The *ateliers de charité*, or public works projects, so favored by Enlightenment reformers did not cease to operate. On the contrary, more money was poured into them, and Grenoble saw more paupers assisted in this manner than under the old regime. Attempts to improve the *dépôt de mendicité* were also continued. In 1790 the new departmental directory ordered a review of the old institution. The official charged with this task began by making the first, frank admission of the dépôt's real function: "This dépôt," he wrote, "which began as an asylum for beggars has become with time a hospital for those afflicted with venereal disease." Such was indeed the actual function of the dépôt, and the official concluded that it was "infinitely useful" in this form. He also suggested that the plan (originated by the intendant Caze de la Bove) to move the dépôt to a more salubrious location be adopted. The departmental authorities agreed, but when an audit of the concierge's books uncovered serious irregularities, the proposal was postponed.[5]

The Grenoblois continued the programs of the eighteenth century, but they also drew upon an older tradition. The first years of the Revolution witnessed a rebirth of personal charity, but in a new guise and with a new purpose. In late December 1789, just as municipal elections got under way, an announcement appeared in one of the local newspapers, *Les Affiches du Dauphiné*, which proclaimed that a Société Philanthropique was to be established in the city. It explained that the Revolution had caused considerable hardship for the indigent and urged the Grenoblois to alleviate this suffering by joining the new organization. A gift of 72 livres, a rather substantial sum, would secure membership, and it could be delivered to the publisher of the paper, Giroud. Though seemingly benign in purpose, the Société Philanthropique aroused suspicion in some quarters. *Les Affiches du Dauphiné* was the mouthpiece of the more conservative elements in Grenoble society, those committed to a strong monarchy and a very limited suffrage. The paper's publisher, Giroud, was commonly known to sympathize with the rightist faction in the city and to maintain ties with Grenoble's conservative delegate to the Constituent Assembly, Mounier.[6]

A few months later another charitable endeavor appeared. This time the sponsoring body was the local, radical club, which supported wide suffrage and limited monarchy, the Société Populaire.[7] Its president, the abbé Fairin, announced its creation at a municipal council meeting. The abbé told the city officers that the Société Populaire had been touched by the sufferings of the poor and had taken up a collection among its members. He explained that "the time when a nation passes from servitude to liberty is a terrible crisis for the indigent class," and that "unjust and powerful men try to enrich themselves at the expense of the unfortunate." These nefarious individuals, he remarked, "cut their domestics' salaries, fire their workers and send their wealth abroad to the enemies of the Nation." The Société Populaire wanted to help the victims of these evil persons, and its members, among them the marquis de Barral, the citizen Barnave, and the company of Périer, Berlioz, and Rey, had already donated between 12 and 300 livres apiece to do so. Later the Société sent its members into the streets of the Saint Hugues and Saint Joseph parishes to collect alms, so that by August of 1790 the Société had collected over 6,000 livres, and another 3,500 livres would be added by the end of the year. All of this money went to a fund, the Caisse des Pauvres, which was administered by the municipality.[8]

One might well wonder what prompted this sudden burst of charitable zeal. Clearly, despite some similarities, this was not the old Catholic charity come to life after a half-century of quiescence. A certain political viewpoint lay behind both the Société Philanthropique and the Société Populaire, and both represented a certain stance vis-à-vis the Revolution. The Société Philanthropique was closely tied to Mounier and the local "monarchists," and the Société Populaire grouped together more progressive individuals like Barnave. In the spring and summer of 1790, these two factions were at war with each other, and the correct course of the Revolution was a hotly contested issue in Grenoble. Both factions needed the support of the population as a whole, and the Société Philanthropique was the more candid in this regard. "Charity," it explained in the newspaper announcement, "is the most noble and generous means of preserving the multitude from the seduction of those who wish to lead them into all sorts of excess."[9] Presumably, the author was speaking of the Société Populaire, which was probably just as eager to "preserve the multitude from

the seduction" of its opponents. Eventually, victory would go to the Société Populaire, which triumphed in the municipal elections and had the
pleasure of forcing the publisher Giroud to pay "damages" to the Caisse
des Pauvres. But the outcome of this struggle was by no means clear in the
winter or even the spring of 1790.[10]

Political struggles and political motives thus lay behind the sudden rebirth of charity in the first years of the Revolution. Yet these alms, though
hardly disinterested, were no less effective and no less welcome to the
poor. Unfortunately, the Société Philanthropique has left no record of its
activities; we cannot know how many—if any—paupers received assistance from it. On the other hand, the Caisse des Pauvres, which was sponsored by the Société Populaire and the municipality, did keep accounts,
and they reveal that the Caisse supplied bread either free or at a reduced
price to an unspecified number of individuals at a time of very high grain
prices. Whatever their motives, the philanthropists of 1790 provided genuine and much-needed assistance. The conflicts of the Revolution, far
from frustrating charity, produced an outpouring of alms not seen in Grenoble for many years.[11]

The effect of the Revolution on the institution which remained Grenoble's primary purveyor of relief, the Hospital General, was not quite so
clear-cut. The consequences of the legislation issued from Paris in the years
between 1789 and 1791 were ambiguous. The abolition of feudalism and
the Civil Constitution of the Clergy, both sometimes considered the death
knell of France's hospitals, had little effect on the Hospital General of Grenoble. Feudal dues had never provided the institution with any significant
income; they were not missed. The transformation of the church lands into
biens nationaux also failed to disturb the Hospital. Like most charitable
institutions in France, it was temporarily exempted and continued to enjoy
possession of all its estates. But the abolition of market taxes in 1789 dealt a
terrible blow to the Hospital's fragile finances, for the institution's principal
and most regular source of income were just such taxes, the octrois. The
municipality did promise to reimburse the Hospital for money lost because
of the suppression of these taxes, but these funds were not immediately—
or indeed ever—forthcoming. Burdened with the debts it had inherited
from the old regime and deprived of its most reliable source of income, the
Hospital was nearly broke by 1790. In September of that year, the directors
all but proclaimed bankruptcy: they resigned en masse and handed the
institution over to the municipal government.[12]

The municipality reacted violently to this unwanted gift. It trotted out
the old edict of 1699, which had virtually excluded municipal officers

from the administration of the Hospital, and accused the former directors of trafficking in *assignats*. This charge was probably unjustified, but it does reveal the deep rift which had come to separate the Hospital from the municipal government. In 1790 most of the late-eighteenth-century directors had abandoned the *maison de force* for more powerful and prestigious offices in the new municipality and the new department of the Isère. At the Bureau of the Hospital, there remained only a few aristocratic canons, two magistrates, the increasingly reactionary Achard de Germane, and the abbé Brochier, who would shortly take up his position as self-appointed refractory bishop in exile in Savoy. The progressive municipal officers thus had some reason to distrust the directors, and they had even more reason to refuse any responsibility for the Hospital itself. The municipal government, like the Hospital, had inherited substantial debts from the old regime, whereas the Revolution had only increased its expenses. The municipal council did not want to add the Hospital to its seemingly insurmountable financial problems, and it therefore appealed to the departmental authorities.[13]

On December 13, 1790, the departmental authorities resolved the issue: they forced the municipal council to assume responsibility for the Hospital and ordered it to appoint new directors from within its own ranks. Thus, two hundred years of semi-independence came to an abrupt end, and the Hospital was returned to the municipality. For the next decade, the Bureau of the Hospital General would be an extension of the municipal government and would reflect that body's composition. Henceforth, the aristocratic magistrates and canons would disappear, to be replaced by municipal officials and appointees. In 1791 the city named to the Bureau men from the legal professions, like the lawyers Dumas and Blanc and the notary Martinais, and wealthy merchants, like the glove trader Laville, the *négociants* Dolle and Ferouillet. A new group of Grenoblois now dominated the Bureau, but the invasion of the lawyers and merchants was not so much an innovation as a confirmation of trends already evident before the Revolution. In the late eighteenth century, men whose eminence was based on trade and talent, not land and privilege, had begun to infiltrate the Bureau. Among them were men like the elder Teysseire and Périer, and both returned to the Bureau to occupy their old places. So too did the adroit marquis de Barral, now mayor of the city and, curiously enough, a prominent radical. As far as the composition of the Bureau was concerned, the first years of the Revolution simply accelerated changes already under way.[14]

The Hospital's financial agonies, which had also originated in the old regime, persisted too. The departmental directory bestowed upon the institution, at the time it returned it to the municipality, a grant of 15,000 livres. This sum did not come close to solving the Hospital's problems nor compensating for the loss of the octrois. Scarcely a month later, the municipality asked the Department for permission to levy a surcharge on the city's capitation tax. The Department refused, citing the numerous complaints it had already received from the overtaxed citizens of Grenoble. In October the municipal government had recourse to the oldest of expedients: one of its members, the wealthy flax merchant and future sansculotte, Navizet, loaned the Hospital 30,000 livres. Even a sum this huge was insufficient, and within weeks the Hospital needed more money. At first the municipality offered to loan the Hospital funds, but it retracted the offer, noting that "all available money from taxes has already been earmarked for other uses." The city council did resolve to assist the Hospital in acquiring reimbursement for the rentes it had owned on the Hôtel de Ville of Paris. The municipality wrote to the departmental and national authorities, but in neither case did it receive any response. A year after the city government took charge, the Hospital was in no better shape financially.[15]

The Hospital's agonies were certainly nothing new, and they would not warrant close scrutiny were it not for one fact: they reveal that financial problems on both the local and the national level plagued institutions of poor relief even before the event most often cited as their downfall— the war. Months before the declaration of hostilities, Grenoble's Hospital was already on the brink of bankruptcy for reasons succinctly stated by the city attorney, Delhors. In a published report, Delhors began by invoking the many setbacks suffered by the Hospital since 1789: the suppression of the octrois, the loss of the rentes on the Hôtel de Ville, and the end of alms and charitable gifts. He then described the problems which had beset the institution since the municipality had assumed its administration. The most important of these was the persistent and well-founded rumor that the Hospital's estates would soon be proclaimed *biens nationaux*. This rumor had produced two serious difficulties for the institution. First, the farmers who rented the Hospital's estates had simply ceased paying rent. As a result, the institution no longer received any income from its property, although it still paid taxes on these estates. Second, the Hospital's creditors, suspecting that their collateral was about to vanish, had besieged the institution, demanding their money. The new directors did not feel that they could refuse, and at a time of near bankruptcy they handed over 10,343 livres to the Hospital's creditors. As always, the legacy of the old regime—debts—lay heavily upon the Hospital General, but the Constituent Assembly's hesitations had aggravated the problem. The Assembly would have done better to nationalize the Hospital's estates outright, thereby sparing the institution taxes and irate creditors while depriving it of no income. In this instance, it was not the speed but the lumbering pace of the Assembly's actions which created difficulties for the Hospital.[16]

The new directors, Delhors claimed, had dealt with this dreadful situation as best they could. They had ceased accepting loans and they had reduced the Hospital's expenses by cutting the inmate population. On neither score was Delhors entirely accurate. The Hospital did continue to take loans, at least from members of the city council and the Hospital Bureau. And the directors really did not show much inclination to reduce the number of individuals dependent upon the Hospital. On the contrary, the policy of exclusion practiced by the eighteenth-century directors had been reversed. Now most individuals who asked to be admitted to the Hospital were accepted, and anyone who requested bread received it. Moreover, the new directors had installed a device which forced them to assume responsibility for just about any unwanted infant in the city. "Touched by humanity," the directors had erected a kind of lazy susan equipped with a bell at the Hospital door. When someone placed an infant in this contraption and rang the bell, the concierge wheeled the child inside to warmth and safety. Many lives were probably saved by this machine, but the Hospital's fortunes were certainly hampered. Now the Hospital had to admit any infant, and it had lost the ability to scrutinize each case closely. The result was a clear increase in the Hospital's expenses, for the directors felt that those "innocent by virtue of their recent birth" could not be turned away. Despite the Hospital's serious financial difficulties, the directors' altruism was seemingly unbounded.[17]

Still, the Hospital had pressing needs, and its finances, as Delhors put it, had to be "revolutionized" if the institution were to survive. He had two proposals. First, he suggested that the authorities in Paris and at the Department of the Isère make good on their promise to reimburse the Hospital for funds, such as the income from the old octrois taxes, that had been lost because of the Revolution. The Department agreed and referred the Hospital to Paris; Paris in turn ordered the Hospital to appeal to the Department. Two years later, no reimbursement had materialized. Delhors' second proposal bore a quicker fruit, albeit a bitter one. He suggested that the Hospital General annex the hospice run by the Brothers of Charity, which included a small military hospital. Delhors and the municipal council reasoned that a military hospital would provide dependable income from the Ministry of War and would ease crowding within the Hospital as well. What they had not counted on was the coming war, its duration, and the sheer size of the armies it would call into being. In the winter of 1792, after lengthy negotiations, the Hospital agreed with the Ministry of War to take on between 300 and 400 ailing soldiers and then won full possession of the newly christened Military Hospital. But by September there were over 950 soldiers housed in the new hospital, and the fees paid by the ministry did not compensate for their expense. By January of 1793 a problem had appeared which was soon to become chronic. The Ministry of War was at least three months behind in its payments to the Hospital, and there was little hope that the funds would arrive in the near future.[18]

At this time, the municipal authorities asked for a report on the progress of the Hospital General. Its finances had been "revolutionized," but not with the expected results. The institution's fiscal health was, at best, precarious, and old problems persisted, in particular the debts inherited from the old regime. Still, the Revolution certainly had not destroyed the old *maison de force*. By various expedients, the municipal government and the directors had kept the Hospital alive, and had even extended its services to a larger number of individuals. Now, however, the institution would face a new set of challenges, for circumstances changed radically in the winter of 1793. Among other things, the long-awaited "definitive reorganization of poor relief"—that is, the enacting of national legislation—finally got under way.

The first really significant national decree promulgated in Grenoble was the law of June 1793, which promised monetary assistance to the fathers of large families, pregnant women, the old, the sick, and orphaned or abandoned children.[19] The Department of the Isère promised that funds would be made available, and the municipal council appointed officials in each section of the city to help the poor meet the requirements of the law. These requirements were quite complex, for the law insisted that every pauper prove his eligibility with a sheaf of documents. A disabled individual, for example, had to provide a copy of his baptismal certificate, a paper stating that he paid no taxes, and two medical certificates, signed by different physicians, describing the nature of his illness or disability. The intent of these rules was benign: only the truly needy would receive assistance. But in a society where the poor were largely illiterate, their effect was nefarious: many worthy individuals were excluded because they could not assemble the necessary documentation. Two months after the publication of the law of June 1793, only 143

Grenoblois had appealed for aid, and most of these individuals had not amassed all of the required papers.[20]

Clearly, there were more than 143 destitute individuals in Grenoble; the Hospital General alone distributed bread to over 700 families every Sunday. The municipal authorities therefore resolved to abandon the cumbersome, new bureaucratic procedures and start afresh, using the records of the Hospital General as a basis. This time 720 individuals, or 420 households, were deemed worthy of aid, and the fruit of the authorities' labors—a list of indigents—allows us to compare their intentions with the assumptions of their predecessors, the Hospital directors of the late eighteenth century.[21] When the lists established in 1793 are brought together with the lists compiled in 1771 through 1774, remarkably few differences emerge (table 39). In both sets of data, the very old predominate, and the sick and disabled form the majority of recipients. Contrasts are minimal because the revolutionary authorities and the directors of the late eighteenth century shared the same notions about who was worthy of public assistance. Both groups believed that only individuals incapable of work should receive assistance; both made only one exception to this rule, fathers of large families. During the Revolution, the unspoken assumptions of the directors of the eighteenth century simply became written law. In this regard, the Revolution worked no revolution in poor relief; it simply affirmed and confirmed trends already begun at the end of the old regime.

Still, there were slight differences between the lists of 1793 and 1771. In 1793, occupations exercised by men tended to predominate for the simple reason that there were more male recipients in that year (table 39). The law of June 1793 made special provisions for men burdened with large families, and sometimes these families could be very large indeed. Jean Buissière, for example, had five children between the ages of two and ten, and he also supported his seventy-four-year-old mother, all on the small wages of a mason. Of course, the directors of the Hospital General in the late eighteenth century had also looked kindly upon workingmen weighed down by numerous progeny. But they had never been this beneficent. The revolutionary authorities proved more willing than their predecessors to assist those who could work, and they admitted more readily that a man's wages did not always suffice to feed a family. The result was that more individuals were supposed to receive aid under the new regime than under the old. In 1771 only 357 Grenoblois had been aided by the Hospital General; in 1793 over 720 citizens were promised the assistance of the state.[22]

But not all were to profit equally from the government's generosity. One group in particular was slighted by the new legislation: single

TABLE 39

COMPARISON OF THE RECIPIENTS OF AID IN 1793 WITH RECIPIENTS
OF AID IN THE PERIOD 1771–1774

	1771–1774 (%)	1793 (%)
Gender		
Men	32.5	40.4
Women	67.5	59.6
	100.0	100.0
Age		
1 to 5 years	1.3	0.5
6 to 12 years	10.0	1.2
13 to 20 years	2.7	1.2
21 to 30 years	1.3	1.4
31 to 45 years	0.7	17.9
46 to 60 years	32.0	25.1
61 and older	52.0	52.6
	100.0	100.0
Health		
Well	16.0	21.3
Sick	84.0	78.7
	100.0	100.0
Marital Status		
Married male	24.6	39.7
Married female	5.0	9.9
Widow	34.3	31.8
Unmarried male	5.6	0.5
Unmarried female	30.5	18.2
	100.0	100.0
	N = 357	N = 720

Source: A.D. Isère, A.H.F. 28; A.C. Grenoble, LL 250–251.

women. In 1793 there were many fewer old, unmarried women on the list of recipients than there had been in the late eighteenth century, and it is hard to believe that the numbers or sufferings of these women had been reduced by the Revolution. Perhaps these women still received bread from the Hospital, as they had in the past, and were therefore not entirely without aid. But the revolutionary legislation still took absolutely no notice of this chronically impoverished group and made no provision for them. The Revolution was very hard on women, particularly single women: it held out for them not even the hollowest promise of relief.

Unfortunately, hollow promises were all that the indigents included on the lists ever received: despite all the list making and document collecting, the law of June 1793 was never actually implemented in Grenoble. The district had provided too little money, a mere 2,600 livres, a sum which the municipality did not hesitate to call "ridiculous." The city appealed for an increase, but the Department pointed to the Grenoblois' casual attitude toward the law's stipulations and refused to grant any money whatsoever.[23] Moreover, the events of the next two years rendered the edict of 1793, for all its good intentions, inadequate and obsolete. In the years between 1793 and 1795, so many Grenoblois found themselves dependent upon the municipal authorities and the Hospital General for their daily bread that the edict with its complicated procedures and detailed regulations seemed ridiculous. At this time, the city entered a period of such intense and prolonged suffering that the municipality and the Hospital General had to invent new forms of relief. They had to adopt a much more generous stance in the face of unprecedented misery, and they had to respond to pressure from a newly powerful political left.

Problems began as early as the summer of 1792. In August of that year Grenoble experienced difficulties in provisioning its markets, for the first time since 1790, and the city boasted the highest grain price in all of France. Relief did not come with the harvest, for it was deficient, and scarcity was exacerbated by the presence of an ever-growing army, which deprived civilians of their daily bread. Violence frequently erupted at the market, and by the spring of 1793 the specter of famine hung over the city. Added to these tensions was a grave political crisis. In May and June of 1793, the Department of the Isère flirted with federalism while its neighbor Lyon broke decisively with the Convention. Grenoble remained loyal to the Republic, but conservative elements in the city were seriously compromised, and even moderates saw their fortunes decline as a radical, sans-culotte movement appeared in the city. Already in February, local sans-culottes who called themselves the Bonnets Rouges seized control of the market and forced merchants to sell grain at low prices. In April, citizens of the first (Saint Laurent) and seventh (Très Cloîtres) sections had accused seven members of the municipal council of collusion with aristocrats, priests, and other traitors to the Republic. In comparison with its Parisian equivalent, this local sans-culottes movement was pretty conservative. Prosperous artisans like the flax dealer Chanrion and the glove merchant Laville headed the movement and maintained control of it throughout 1793 and 1794. But the Bonnets Rouges still terrified the local authorities, who had little choice but to bow to their wishes, especially during the Year II and the reign of the Committee of Public Safety. The Parisian government sent a series of envoys to Grenoble who supported and encouraged local radicals. A list of thirty-three suspects was drawn up, all of whom were arrested immediately; refractory clergy were pursued, and the loyalty of established figures like Claude Périer and the former marquis de Barral was called into doubt.[24]

Twice the envoys of the Committee of Public Safety purged the municipal government, and the Hospital Bureau of Directors quickly reflected the swing to the political left. Men of the law disappeared, and radicals like the mayor Dumas and the sans-culotte Joseph Chanrion replaced them, together with a number of artisans and small shopkeepers. Some of the former directors came to grief. Delhors was denounced by the Société Populaire, now called the Jacobin Club. Stendhal's grandfather, the doctor Gagnon, was proscribed though never imprisoned. Other former directors, far from suffering under the new political regime, simply adjusted and adopted (at least in public) suitably Jacobin sympathies. Navizet, Rey, and Dolle, all wealthy *négociants,* continued to occupy seats on the Hospital Bureau, and Périer saved himself by several timely "patriotic" gifts of grain. Even the marquis de Barral, now an "honorary sans-culottes" was eventually reappointed to the Bureau.[25]

The Terror disturbed the Hospital Bureau, but it did not destroy it. Nor did the legislation passed in Paris during late 1793 and 1794 bring the institution to its knees, as some historians have argued. The Convention's policies had only slight if any impact on the Hospital. The enforcing of punitive measures against the refractory clergy, for example, hardly exercised the directors of the Hospital General, even though most were vehement Jacobins. In January 1794 the directors politely asked the Sisters of Saint Martha, the Providence hospital's nursing order, if they wanted to swear allegiance to the new Constitutional Church. When the ladies refused, the directors just as politely asked them if they would remain in the Hospital until new nurses could be found. The directors then reimbursed the order for the 1,800 livres it would lose at the time of its departure.[26] Similarly, the notorious decree of 23 Messidor Year II, which nationalized the hospital's estates and which has often been described as the death knell of France's charitable institutions, had virtually no impact on the Hospital General of Grenoble. The directors had long since ceased receiving income from the Hospital's estates, and they were overjoyed to be relieved of the taxes which the estates entailed. They did resolve to carry out the clerical work that nationalization required, but they never actually completed this task. All their energies had to be directed toward providing the Hospital and its poor with bread.[27]

Provisioning became difficult as early as the spring of 1793. In May of that year, the Hospital directors appealed to the district, and received 96,000 livres from the national treasury. This sum, however, hardly sufficed to meet a crisis that was only growing with each day. In 1794 and 1795 the directors frequently found themselves with only enough grain to last a week or even a few days. Again and again, they appealed to the district, but their entreaties fell upon deaf ears. Meanwhile, the Hospital inmates and the Grenoblois who depended on the institution were on the verge of starvation, so the directors took matters into their own hands. At first, the problem lay in getting enough money to meet soaring grain prices. The directors could expect no help from the municipality, which was equally besieged. So they advanced the Hospital money out of their own pockets. Then it became increasingly difficult to find any grain at any price, so severe was the scarcity. At this point, the director Rey took to the roads in search of grain. He traveled to Geneva, scoured Burgundy, visited villages throughout the Bugey, and descended to Marseille in the hope of importing grain from Italy. On the way, he often arrived at markets only to discover that the agents of the army had preceded him: everything had been requisitioned. Desperate, Monsieur Rey negotiated a huge purchase of rice in Marseille, which was substituted for the usual bread. By such expedients the Hospital somehow survived, and so too did the extraordinary number of paupers which it had come to assist.[28]

For the directors did indeed assist a growing number of paupers. They did not respond to the crisis as had their eighteenth-century predecessors by reducing the number of individuals dependent upon the Hospital. On the contrary, they increased the Hospital's burdens and boasted that they "employed every means to relieve all suffering humanity." To a certain degree, this extension of the Hospital's services was unintentional and perhaps unwanted. In August 1794 the Providence hospital, which had provided medical care, went broke. The alms upon which it had once survived had now vanished. The municipality gave the Providence and all its possessions to the Hospital General, thereby increasing the Hospital's physical size and the number of mouths it had to feed. The army also thrust hoards of sick soldiers and deserters upon the beleaguered directors. In March

1794 over 900 soldiers were cared for in the Hospital, three times as many as the original contract with the Ministry of War had specified. But this burden did not prevent the directors from admitting more and more impoverished Grenoblois to the Hospital. In the spring of 1794 the Hospital housed 630 paupers, almost twice as many as it had sheltered in the late eighteenth century, and that number soon grew to over 700.[29]

Impressive as the growth in the inmate population was, it was small compared with the increase in the number of individuals who received assistance in the form of bread outside the Hospital walls. For decades the directors had dispensed bread each Sunday, but in the winter of 1794 they added a distribution on Tuesdays and then increased the length of these distributions from a few hours a day to twelve. Finally, in the fall of 1794 they resolved to give out bread continually, "en permanence," so that all who needed it would be accommodated. Obviously, the number of families who depended on the Hospital had increased. In April 1794, 700 households received bread, twice as many as had received it in the late eighteenth century. A year later, this number had swelled to an extraordinary 2,000 families (roughly 6,000 individuals), nearly a third of Grenoble's population.[30]

At first glance, the directors of 1793 and 1794 appear to have surpassed their predecessors; never before had so many individuals received assistance from the Hospital. But then never before had so many individuals needed assistance. Two phenomena combined in 1793 and 1794 to create unprecedented misery: bad harvests and the war. The first was not new. In the late eighteenth century, deficient harvests had produced scarcity and high grain prices. But grain prices had never reached such heights before. In January 1794 wheat sold for 37 livres the *quartal;* in October it sold for 700 livres the *quartal.* Runaway inflation contributed to this rise and to the miseries of the average Grenoblois. Wages did not keep pace with the price increase, and a worker in one of the national workshops made only 20 francs a day, but had to pay 18 francs for a one-pound loaf of bread.[31]

The municipal authorities knew the cause of this rise in prices: the war. War was not, of course, new to Grenoble, but the sheer size of the republican armies were. The army of the Alps placed an enormous strain on already deficient supplies and drove up the price of everything from tobacco and lodging to firewood and grain. The motherland's crusade brought little comfort to the Grenoblois. Admittedly, the Parisian government did set up national workshops in the city, which provided considerable employment. But these workers saw their wages consumed by high prices, and they too found it difficult to feed themselves. The army did indeed, as the municipal authorities frequently complained, make a difficult situation almost unbearable.[32]

The war created hardship for many, if not all, the Grenoblois, and the Hospital may well have met only part of this need. But its efforts were amply supplemented by the work of the Jacobin municipal council, which undertook, in 1793 and 1794, a small experiment in controlled economics. This improvisation was uncharacteristic and repellent to many municipal officers, whose professed Jacobinism did not diminish their deep attachment to free market practices. The crisis was such that they had to bury their convictions and improvise new means of relief and new solutions. First, however, they exhausted the old expedients. In the spring of 1793 when scarcity first appeared, the municipality imposed a surcharge on city taxes to provide funds for grain purchases. Then, it very reluctantly returned to the archaic, paternalistic regulations that had governed the marketplace in the old regime. When scarcity persisted, the municipality banned the sale of white bread and authorized only "equality bread"—coarse dark loaves. Finally, it rationed bread, allowing each citizen a mere pound a day.[33]

By harvest time 1794, scarcity was so severe that none of these measures proved effective. The municipality consequently improvised a massive program of controlled prices combined with public assistance. A four-tiered system emerged from the experiment: those who were absolutely destitute received bread gratis at the Hospital; those somewhat better off received both free bread and bread at 25 sous a pound; those who could only afford bread at 25 sous received it at that price and those able to pay 50 sous but no more got bread at that price. The cost of this program was considerable: the municipality paid 3 livres 5 sous for each pound of bread. And the dimensions of the experiment were enormous: according to the lists compiled by section commissioners, 67 percent of the Grenoblois received bread at a reduced price, and the rate went as high as 98 percent in the impoverished Très Cloîtres and Saint Laurent quarters. In the winter of 1794–1795, the program was extended even further; at that time, 16,000 Grenoblois, about 80 percent of the whole population, received assistance in the form of bread from the municipal government.[34]

With a program that involved 80 percent of the community, the Grenoble municipality of the years 1793 through 1795 came as close as anyone to realizing the principles established by the Committee on Mendicity.[35] At that time, subsistence was the right of every individual, and the municipality, that is, the State, took it upon itself to insure this right. "It is not a favor that one does these people," a municipal officer explained, "it is the discharging of a debt incumbent upon society."[36] The Jacobin municipality, though relatively conservative, extended aid to so many individuals that this ceased to be charity and became real public assistance. It would be wrong, however, to conclude that the municipal officers had an utterly benign view of the poor and dispossessed. On the contrary, the municipality found time, in the midst of the crisis, to denounce in the most vehement terms the habitually idle and deviant.

In December 1793 an officer remarked that "if ever men should be at work it is now in the current, difficult circumstances." The nation needed the labor of every citizen, and those who chose not to work—the idle—should be incarcerated in the *dépôt de mendicité*. In a similar vein, another officer observed that Grenoble was "filled with beggars, and the only way to destroy this plague is to lock them up." Jacobinism had not extinguished the fear of beggars; nor had it banished contempt for the more raucous manifestations of popular culture. Under pressure from the radical Société Populaire, or Jacobin Club, the municipality closed all the cabarets in the city, "for these places only encourage the corruption of morals." It also launched a veritable campaign against prostitutes and loose women. In February 1794, commissioners from each section burst into homes and dragged out women they suspected of prostitution or "corrupt morals." Sixty women were subsequently incarcerated in the *dépôt de mendicité* to the eventual embarrassment of the municipality: not all were in fact prostitutes.[37]

This new interest in the morals of the people did have a benign side. If the people were to be good republicans, they had to be taught to be good republicans, and this pedagogic task began, logically, at the primary level. Despite the economic crisis, the municipality, at the urging of the Société Populaire, undertook an ambitious effort to provide every child in Grenoble, rich or poor, with a republican education. To a certain degree, this pedagogic effort was a response to legislation from Paris. But it also sprang from the deepest concerns of the city's radicals. In October 1793 two representatives of the Société Populaire broke into a municipal meeting and proclaimed that the Société had seen "the utility of some sort of public instruction in the Rights of Man and the Constitution." The Société proposed to establish schools for this purpose and to open them to young Grenoblois of both sexes. Of course not just anyone could teach in these schools. Former religious were suspect, and so too were the old Propagation and Orphans pensions, which were summarily closed. By April 1794, however, twelve primary schools were operating in the city, and the teachers were receiving a salary, albeit a miserable one, from the municipality. In the fall of 1794, more than 800 students—sons and daughters of day laborers, glove-workers, carpenters, and other modest folk—attended these schools and received some sort of instruction, absolutely free of charge. The municipality continued to worry about the teachers' political sentiments, but a certain point had been made: charity schools had become public schools, and what had once been a part of poor relief now became one of the rights enjoyed by every citizen.[38]

The municipality's accomplishments in the realm of primary education, as in that of public assistance, were impressive, but they did not long survive Thermidor Year II and the purge several months later of Jacobin elements within the city government. The new conservative municipality showed little interest in education; only a brief revival occurred in 1797 when the coup d'état of Fructidor Year V swept some Jacobins back into city hall. The massive bread-distribution programs were also gradually dismantled. Since the harvest of 1795 was relatively plentiful and the municipality strapped for funds, the new city government first raised the price of bread, then reduced the number of recipients, and finally halted the distributions altogether. Other forms of relief also fell by the wayside. The edict of June 1793 had never received any real application; it was not revived. The families of soldiers who had previously received money from the national government saw no aid after 1794. There was only one, rather ephemeral initiative in poor relief. In November 1795 a Bureau de Bienfaisance was established in accordance with national legislation. A tax on theater tickets was supposed to provide poor-relief funds, which would be distributed by the municipal officers in charge of the Bureau. But on the first day of the Bureau's operation, paupers besieged the institution, demanding assistance "with great insolence." The municipal officers were frightened, and they closed the Bureau; it did not reopen. In 1802 the prefect observed that the Bureau had for all intents and purposes never existed.[39]

The Hospital General too set about dismantling the achievements of 1793 and 1794. First, the Jacobins were driven from the Bureau: moderate professional men like the engineer Renauldon and the lawyer Martinais replaced the radicals like Chanrion, Navizet, and Dumas.[40] Second, the directors, no longer subject to sans-culotte pressure, vowed to follow a policy of economy, that is, retrenchment. They began by denying admission to the Hospital to all but the most desperate. In February 1796 they toured the Hospital's wards and ejected all the inmates who could receive treatment at home. They also gradually reduced the bread distributions.

First, they converted these distributions into money, which represented a substantial savings for the institution but a real hardship for the poor. Then they considered ending them altogether. On this point, the directors hesitated. Public assistance, they observed, had already been considerably reduced, and "public assistance insures public tranquility."[41] They worried that violence would occur, but the social calm that reigned throughout 1795 proved their fears groundless. In March 1796 the directors suspended bread distributions until the financial situation of the Hospital improved. Then, the appearance of the Bureau de Bienfaisance in 1796 provided the directors with the pretext they had been waiting for. In principle, if not in fact, the Bureau was supposed to dispense relief to domiciled paupers, so the Hospital could abandon all forms of bread distribution. Never again would it provide bread or any other form of relief to the poor outside its walls.[42]

Meanwhile, the Hospital directors redoubled their efforts to extract some monetary assistance or compensation from the authorities at the district, department, and national levels. As always, their entreaties met with failure, and in 1796 even this avenue of assistance was closed. The national decree of Vendémaire Year V returned to France's hospitals the property made *biens nationaux,* or nationalized, in 1794. The decree was at least partially benign in intent, for it meant to restore the hospitals to fiscal health. But in Grenoble its consequences were utterly disastrous. The Hospital received no benefit from its restored estates, because the farmers were either unwilling or unable to pay rent. In addition, the return of the properties meant the return of the tax collector. As in 1792, the Hospital again found itself in the position of paying taxes on land that brought it no income. Furthermore, now in possession of its estates, the Hospital was expected to discharge all of its old debts. In August 1797 the directors agreed with surprising equanimity to "meet this obligation to humanity" and to pay the 25,844 livres owed to some 6,000 creditors. In this task the directors would receive no help from the national authorities. When Paris had returned the estates to the hospital, it had effectively washed its hands of the institution and its poor.[43]

In all fairness, the local authorities were not much more generous in their treatment of the poor. In 1795 the Grenoble municipality, previously so munificent, suddenly turned its back on the poor, and the directors of the Hospital General shortly followed suit. What accounted for this sudden about-face? Was it precipitated by a decline in poverty? A number of factors contributed to the new stance in the face of impoverishment, but a decrease in hunger and want was not among them.

If anything, misery increased after 1795, for at that time the Grenoblois began to feel the effects of the war full force. The national workshops which had once provided some compensation for the miseries endured by the Grenoblois were summarily closed by the Paris government. Now the unemployed joined the ranks of the impoverished. So too did more and more widows, women who had lost their husbands and consequently their livelihoods to the endless war. By 1796 fifteen new widows had appeared on the Rue Saint Laurent alone, and the fate of these women was almost certain destitution.[44]

The war also brought with it an increase in the most dreaded form of poverty—vagabondage. The roads of rural Dauphiné seemed alive, but not with the relatively harmless, traveling workers of the eighteenth century. Reports of cutthroats and thieves poured into the Department of the Isère and the municipal government, particularly in 1796 and 1797, and the *dépôt de mendicité* suddenly sheltered, not just persons afflicted with venereal disease, but real, dangerous criminals.[45] Some of these vagabonds were prisoners of war who had been ejected from the dépôt in Valence when it became overcrowded. Most, however, were deserters, whether from the French or Austrian armies. Joseph Kaliche, for example, had deserted from the armies of the Empire and then taken to a life of crime along with four other Austrians. More common was the case of Pierre Bernard, a native of the Ain, who with five other deserters roamed the Rhone valley, burning and stealing. A man who deserted his unit apparently had little choice but to turn to a life of crime, and there were plenty of deserters. In 1797 and 1798, 75 percent of the criminals incarcerated in Grenoble's prisons were deserters or soldiers, accused of vagabondage, riot, extortion, theft, and arson.[46] In other parts of France, the recrudescence of vagabondage in 1795 and 1796 may have constituted a return to criminal patterns of the old regime.[47] But in Dauphiné, this wave of vagabonds was new and the distinct creation of the Revolution, more specifically the revolutionary war.

If war created new forms of poverty, it also exacerbated the old. Illegitimacy gave all indications of rising during the Revolution, particularly in the years following the declaration of war. Unfortunately, no precise statistics and no *déclarations de grossesse* permit us to measure this increase accurately. Demographic studies of Grenoble during the Revolution have yet to appear, and unwed mothers ceased making declarations, much to the chagrin of the directors of the Hospital General, around 1790.[48] Still, the directors frequently pointed to the growing numbers of illegitimate and abandoned infants, and the Hospital's records, though incomplete and sketchy, suggest that their complaints were justified. In 1792 the Hospital had some 500 children at nurse in the countryside. In 1798 it had over 800. Given the ferocious infant mortality which swept away at least three-quarters of these children before they reached their first birthdays, it is possible that the Hospital admitted over 1,200 infants in the years between 1792 and 1798, and probably more. In any event, the Hospital's burdens nearly doubled in the course of the Revolution, and the directors knew the culprit: the army. "The defenders of the homeland," they complained, "have littered this country with their offspring." Many young unwed mothers seduced by soldiers only discovered that they were pregnant after their lovers were well on their way to the front. The result was a flood of illegitimate children for whom, the directors stated emphatically, "the homeland is responsible."[49]

During the first years of the Revolution, Paris had discharged its obligations toward the infants and provided the Hospital General with subsidies for their support.[50] Then, in 1795, these grants began to arrive with greater and greater delays until, in 1797, they ceased to arrive at all. A new sort of crisis gripped the Hospital. The nurses' husbands besieged the institution on several occasions and threatened to return the Hospital children if they were not paid on the spot. Many times they came perilously close to giving the infants back, but somehow the directors always placated them. They paid the nurses in tobacco instead of the nearly worthless *assignats,* they borrowed money, they loaned the Hospital money out of their own pockets, and always they redoubled their appeals to the authorities. The latter solution rarely worked, and in 1799 it had been over two years since the nurses had received a penny from the Hospital.[51]

In that year, the Hospital sent an employee to the Grésivaudan valley to check on the infants in nurse there. What he saw appalled him. Some of the nurses, having barely enough food for their own families, had neglected the infants and fed them no more than four ounces of black bread "which they threw to them as to dogs." Others had simply abandoned the children, who were now to be seen wandering aimlessly in the forests and on the highways. An unknown number of these infants had been devoured by wild animals. Those who survived "hardly resembled humans." They were so malnourished that they could not or had never learned to walk. "Like animals they crawl on all fours," remarked the employee, "and they no longer have the faces of humans." The employee suggested that carts be sent throughout the valley to rescue these hapless children, and he himself had retrieved thirty or forty. Worse yet, he feared that the situation was no better in the Oisans mountains, where some four hundred additional children were in peril.[52]

Who was to blame? At first the Hospital representative harangued the municipal authorities in the villages of the Grésivaudan: they should have seen to it that the children were properly cared for. But the village officers explained that they had frequently begged the nurses to be patient and wait for the government to keep its promises. The nurses were not swayed. They pointed out that their taxes had been raised threefold in the past years. Why, they asked, could the government not pay them what it owed? The Hospital official had no answer to this question, and when he returned to Grenoble he put it to the individual in charge of all such matters, the prefect. The prefect promised the directors of the Hospital that he would obtain, if not the sums owed the nurses, at least a token payment from the national government. Two months later, the directors had yet to see a penny, and, ironically, the tax collector was pressing them for the Hospital's back taxes.[53]

At this point, the Hospital records break off; we lose track of the foundling children. The correspondence of the Hospital's manager, however, reveals that under the Empire, the nurses were still waiting for their payment.[54] Nothing seems to have changed as far as the foundlings were concerned, or in the whole realm of poor relief, for that matter. The Napoleonic regime continued the policies of the Directory, which might best be described as benign neglect. The Hospital General was left to its own devices and its own dwindling finances. Voluntary charity was encouraged as a means of alleviating the government's burden, but the Grenoblois' altruism could not be reawakened. A return to the status quo ante of the late eighteenth century occurred. At least Grenoble was fortunate enough to have an unusually talented prefect, the mathematician Fourier, who took some interest in the poor. He established a soup kitchen, attempted to enforce the laws against begging, and tried without success to set up a "maternal bureau" to collect alms for mothers who nursed their own children. On the whole, though, no major innovations in poor relief occurred in this period. The Jacobin experiment in public assistance was definitely over.[55]

What brought the improvisation to an end? The foundling children may well provide the answer. If they were so grievously neglected, it was because children are easy to ignore. They cannot voice their demands, and they pose no serious threat to the prevailing regime. The same might be said of the poor in the years after 1794. When the popular movement died, so too did any serious attempt to provide public assistance. When the sans-culottes flexed their muscles, the authorities threw themselves into poor relief. The connection seems obvious enough, but historians have been reluctant to underscore it. Contemporaries were not so shortsighted. The Grenoble municipal council freely admitted that its grain distribution program "served to prevent public disorder" and "assure public tranquility." It is not sheer coincidence that the municipality extended assistance to unprecedented numbers of individuals just when a radical sans-culotte movement, in the form of the Bonnets Rouges, appeared in Grenoble. Like all of Grenoble's revolutionaries, these sans-culottes were rather moderate, but this made them no less alarming to the elite. For its part, the elite responded by compromising, temporizing, and finally mounting a huge public assistance program. Its hegemony remained secure, but this does not vitiate the relationship between the popular movement and public assistance. One image sums it up: the sans-culottes of the Bonnets Rouges collecting (or extorting) "patriotic gifts" for the poor from the frightened, but obliging, négociants of the Grande Rue.[56]

But when the Bonnets Rouges disappeared, so too did the bread distributions, the aid to foundling children, the casual admissions to the Hospital General—in short, all the elements of the Jacobin improvisation in public assistance. The Revolution thus appears to have left only the most fleeting imprint on Grenoble's institutions of poor relief. As for the poor themselves, there is no question that the event created enormous hardship for those traditionally disadvantaged elements in French society, women and children. Circumstances increased their suffering, and the government did nothing to alleviate their misery.[57] And the Revolution created new forms of poverty. It produced a form of vagabondage new to Dauphiné and promoted lawlessness and crime. It is hard to see what benefit the poor actually derived from the Revolution. To them, the legacy of the Revolution might well have been, as historians have frequently remarked, nothing but hollow promises and several "beaux principes."

But principles are important, and there is no question that in the years 1790 through 1795 the revolutionaries had the best of intentions and the most ambitious of plans. The question remains: why did they fail? The war has often been cited as the culprit. Certainly, it exhausted the State's finances and created innumerable difficulties. But the Grenoblois experienced difficulties in obtaining money from the departmental and national authorities as early as 1790, long before the war. The war alone cannot account for the revolutionaries' failure.[58] Their curious mixture of restraint and boldness, of conservatism and radicalism, may do so. The experience of the Hospital General is, in this regard, instructive. Like the revolutionaries in Paris, the Grenoble directors carried with them throughout the Revolution the legacy of the old regime—that is, its debts. Just when the Hospital appeared on the verge of recovery, its debts came back to haunt it and exhaust its income. One wonders what would have happened had the directors simply wiped the slate clean, repudiated the profligacy of their predecessors, and made a fresh start. One also wonders what achievements in public assistance could have been wrought had the Parisian revolutionaries followed suit and placed the new regime on a sounder financial footing. The debts incurred by the monarchy were something concrete, something the revolutionaries could affect, unlike the economic climate and bad harvest. Had they chosen to repudiate them, the whole Revolution might have looked quite different. But such a repudiation flew in the face of the Parisian revolutionaries' most cherished convictions, just as it clashed with the Grenoble directors' deepest impulses. Both had an almost religious faith in the rituals of credit, and both tried valiantly to discharge what the directors once called their "duty to humanity." That their other duties to humanity suffered is, under the circumstances, not surprising.

In some ways, the revolutionaries did not go far enough: they were too conservative, too punctilious. But in others, they were much too visionary, too far ahead of their own times and capabilities. From Paris, they issued uniform decrees which they assumed would produce uniform results. When these decrees were applied to local institutions, like the Hospital General of Grenoble, they often had unintended consequences, with the result that essentially benign legislation was often either ineffective or downright destructive. From the decree of June 1793 to the edict of Vendémaire Year V, the revolutionary legislation foundered on the rocks of local conditions and peculiarities. What was good for some hospitals was not necessarily beneficial for the Hospital of Grenoble or other charitable institutions.[59] The revolutionaries failed to take into account the multitude of local circumstances and original institutions which made up eighteenth-century France. They legislated as if they lived in a centralized, homogenous state, whereas what they actually had to contend with was a decentralized patchwork of varied institutions and peculiar customs.

At times the revolutionaries simply failed to realize just how much of the old regime persisted into the new. They had such high expectations and such great aspirations that they were doomed, in a sense, to at least partial failure. In 1791, when the city attorney of Grenoble tried to persuade the departmental authorities to levy a tax for support of the poor, he proclaimed that this measure was but a temporary expedient. Soon the definitive reorganization of poor relief would be completed, and the poor would vanish altogether. Soon no one would pay any taxes at all![60] Small wonder then that the revolutionaries' achievements fell short of their aspirations and that historians have tended to emphasize their failure in the domain of public assistance. Measured against their lofty ambitions, the revolutionaries' achievements could only seem minimal.

Still, the revolutionaries did work some beneficial and lasting changes in public assistance. These were not the sweeping changes they had wished, but they were changes nonetheless. In Grenoble at least, the legacy of the Revolution consisted of more than a few noble principles, and the events of the years 1789 through 1814 had a real, concrete impact upon institutions and attitudes. The Hospital General is a case in point. The Revolution neither destroyed nor "revolutionized" the old institution. The Hospital survived well into the nineteenth century. It was a different institution, but not a radically different one. The Revolution simply accelerated and confirmed trends already under way in the late eighteenth century. In the last years of the old regime the directors had begun to transform the Hospital into a purely medical institution, exclusively concerned with the care of the sick. The Revolution completed their work.

Ironically, it was the very hardship suffered by the institution which produced this change. The financial difficulties experienced by the Hospital after 1795 forced the institution's directors to reorder their priorities. When bankruptcy threatened the Hospital, the directors had to abandon the bread distributions and with them the Hospital's most important attempt at poor relief. When the Hospital could no longer feed all its inmates, the directors had to eject all but the most gravely ill and remove those who were chronically, but not mortally, sick. When the Providence hospital dissolved, the directors had to assume that institution's burdens and provide medical care for more individuals. By 1799 the Hospital General was the only institution in Grenoble providing medical treatment, and, perforce, medical treatment was all it provided. To be sure, its wards still sheltered some children and some elderly inmates, but this was the legacy of the old regime, not the creation of the new. The directors generally refused to assume responsibility for the illegitimate children presented to them, and they tried to exclude the chronically ill and permanently disabled, who had once been the primary occupants of the institution. To a certain degree, the Hospital ceased to be a repository for the detritus of society. It became instead an institution for the treatment of the sick, a task which absorbed all of its energies and all of its diminished finances.

The shift in the Hospital's purpose is made clear by the admission book for the Year VIII (1799–1800). Admittedly, not all of the Hospital's inmates appear in this document, for the soldiers of the military sections of the institution and approximately one-third of the other inmates were not included. Still, this register reveals important changes in the kind of person admitted to the Hospital and, by extension, the kind of services offered there.[61] For example, the inmates of the Year VIII (1799–1800) were more likely than their predecessors to be adults. They were individuals in the prime of life between the ages of twenty-one and sixty, not helpless children or debilitated old folk (table 40). In addition, a greater number than in the past had families. Married men and women account for 35 percent of the inmates in 1799–1800, whereas they constituted only 6 percent of the inmates in the eighteenth century. These were not the lonely, utterly desperate individuals who had once hoped to make the Hospital their permanent home. Most stayed in the institution for only a month and none for more than five months. They resided for a much shorter period of time in the Hospital than did their forerunners, because they did not suffer from permanently debilitating diseases. Only a handful of the inmates of the Year VIII suffered from mental illness, retardation, loss of a limb, or that vague but chronic condition "infirmness." Now the inmates of the Hospital had contagious and sometimes curable diseases like dysentery, tuberculosis, colic, skin ailments, and a host of fevers.[62] To all appearances, these individuals came to the Hospital for medical treatment; once they had received it, they were discharged. They were really no longer inmates at all. Now they were patients, and the Hospital was a medical institution.

There were other signs of the Hospital's new vocation as well. A course in midwifery, first established by the intendant Caze de la Bove, continued and was even enlarged during the Revolution. The departmental authorities showed considerable interest in the course and supplied funds for a larger number of countrywomen to receive free instruction and a small stipend. The surgery school previously run by the Brothers of Charity also survived the Revolution, transferred to the military section of the Hospital General and administered by lay doctors. More students were admitted to the course, which resulted in a decided benefit for the Hospital inmates. During their course of study, the students assisted the demoiselles, or lay nurses, and they probably provided what little conscientious and competent care was available in the institution.[63]

Ironically, the greatest changes—and maybe improvements—in medical care within the Hospital came about as a result of its greatest curse—

TABLE 40

HOSPITAL INMATES IN 1790 AND THE YEAR VIII

	1790 (%)	Year VIII (%)
Age		
1 to 5 years	1.5	1.3
6 to 12 years	17.3	4.6
13 to 20 years	15.0	17.1
21 to 30 years	6.3	22.5
31 to 45 years	5.5	20.0
46 to 60 years	14.2	22.1
61 and older	40.2	12.5
	100.0	100.0
Marital Status		
Married male	0.0	21.7
Married female	9.3	12.9
Widow	17.5	12.9
Unmarried male	38.1	17.1
Unmarried female	35.1	35.4
	100.0	100.0
Health		
Healthy	15.0	0.0
Chronically diseased/disabled	31.6	2.8
Suffering from contagious/curable disease	53.4	97.2
	100.0	100.0
	N = 133	N = 240

Source: A.D. Isère, A.H.F. 22, 1 and 2.

the war. In 1808 an army doctor sent by the Ministry of War to practice in the military section of the Hospital complained to his superiors about conditions there. He described the neglect to which the soldiers were subjected, and he characterized the Hospital buildings as drafty and insalubrious. He charged that the Hospital personnel were unconscientious, ignorant, and amateurish, and he complained that they obeyed the directors, not the physicians. The directors lodged some weak countercharges, but the Ministry of War sided with the doctor. Changes were ordered, among them an increase in the chief medical officer's authority.

The Restoration did return the bishop and several notables to the Hospital Bureau, but henceforth, ultimate authority in all matters concerning the internal administration of the Hospital lay with the doctors. Whether this change in authority benefited the patients is not clear. A distinct improvement probably did result from a change in the nursing personnel: by 1814 the incompetent demoiselles had been replaced by a professional corps of nurses, the nuns of a religious order. Now the Hospital's journey from *maison de force* to a house of healing was complete.[64]

The Revolution thus changed Grenoble's oldest charitable institution; it also created its newest. In 1803 a novel kind of organization for the alleviation of hunger and want appeared in the city. For once, it was not staffed by lawyers and merchants; its members were those who in the past had more often been the recipients than the distributors of aid—the laboring poor. For this group in particular, the Revolution had been a bitter but most instructive experience. Some practical knowledge of politics had been acquired, and considerable hardship endured. As far as poor relief was concerned, the workingmen had learned a valuable if bitter lesson. If they were to receive comfort in sickness or hunger, it would not come from the local elite or the national authorities. The workingmen had only themselves to depend on, and so in 1803 the glove-workers created the first mutual aid society in Grenoble or, for that matter, in France as a whole. They were soon joined by other workingmen, by cobblers, masons, flax-spinners, and carpenters. In 1809, 712 Grenoblois belonged to mutual aid societies, and there were seven such organizations providing assistance in times of unemployment and sickness. The imperial authorities discouraged the movement, but in 1818 it resurfaced stronger than ever. By 1830 there were sixteen mutual aid societies, and by 1848, thirty-five, with over 6,000 members altogether.[65] Here was the Revolution's most enduring legacy, and the beginning of a new era in the relationship between the rich and the poor.

Conclusion

With the emergence of the mutual aid society, we come to a convenient stopping point. The story of the rich and the poor in Grenoble does not, of course, come to such an abrupt end. As for the rich, they got richer. Of the former directors of the Hospital General, the Périer clan profited from the Revolution to purchase vast estates and to establish themselves as the premier bankers of France. Achard de Germane, the local social philosopher, fled Grenoble in 1792, became a favorite in emigré circles, and then returned at the Restoration with valuable and lucrative contacts. Doctor Gagnon, Stendhal's grandfather, was proscribed during the Terror, but survived to resume his position as a director of the Hospital General in 1816. Only the marquis de Barral suffered: after having been an "honorary sans-culottes" and a Baron of the Empire, he was ostracized politically because of his motley collection of honors. As for the poor, they probably got poorer. To be sure, the glove industry flourished in the nineteenth century, but prosperity brought with it industrialization and the destruction of the trade's craft traditions. The laboring poor became the working class, and their transformation made the history of relations between the rich and the poor a different story.

This is a good point, therefore, at which to survey the terrain covered and to establish what we have learned in the course of the journey. As for poverty and the economic circumstances which created it, established notions need some refinement. Contemporaries remarked that periodic subsistence crises hurled those without reserves into poverty; Olwen Hufton has amended this notion and argued that the disruption of the family economy brought on destitution. Both theories contend that sudden misfortune created poverty, and both theories are supported by the Grenoble data. However, each could benefit from some reformulation. The Grenoblois who lived a hand-to-mouth existence was vulnerable to subsistence crises, but he was particularly vulnerable at particular periods of his life. Youth and old age placed an individual at severe risk, and even the relatively secure could succumb to disease or destitution at these times. Misery, therefore, depended as much on age as on grain prices. As for the family economy, it had less and less to do with poverty as the eighteenth century progressed. Those who had never formed a domestic unit and therefore failed to suffer from its disruption—older single women— found themselves chronically impoverished. Functioning family economies—families with only two children and both spouses at work—also had trouble surviving. Gradually, a new kind of poverty emerged which was not the product of subsistence crises and not the result of domestic misfortune. Insufficient wages lay behind the new misery and created a chronic form of poverty which persisted in both good times and bad.

As there were changes in the causes of poverty, so too were there changes—more radical changes—in the culture of the poor. This study allows us to glimpse only the general outlines of this alteration; future work will undoubtedly add many important nuances to the picture. But we can see that between the early seventeenth and the late eighteenth century, the Grenoble poor underwent, for lack of a better phrase, a process of acculturation. The adherence of the laboring poor to Counter Reformation Catholicism, as evidenced in their wills and testaments, is one manifestation of this process. The general decline of violence demonstrated in judicial records is another. The old raucous habits decried so often by the Brothers of the Holy Sacrament disappeared, and the Church triumphed, at least partially, over the cabaret. The laboring poor thus embraced the values of discipline and restraint preached by Catholicism, but not without altering these values to suit their own purposes. Within the confines of resurgent Catholicism, the laboring poor constructed their own spirituality, which stressed the dignity of labor and pride in profession. For them the triumph of Lent over Carnival was not an unmitigated tragedy: the discipline and self-respect acquired in the seventeenth and eighteenth centuries would stand the working class in good stead during the struggles of the nineteenth.

The poor changed; so too did the rich who ministered to them. In the seventeenth century, aristocrats dominated charity. Judges from the sovereign courts and nobles from the highest ranks of the army and the Church created Grenoble's charitable institutions and funded them. They also administered them: the "brothers" who staffed the confraternities and the directors who ran the Hospital General all shared ancient lineage, powerful office, and vast, seigneurial estates. Noblesse oblige inspired charity, but not for long. In the eighteenth century, the aristocrats decamped, and another kind of Grenoblois took charge of poor relief. The directors of the Hospital General were now men of humble origins: lawyers, businessmen, bankers, and doctors, gentlemen who sprang from the world of commerce and industry and boasted neither distinguished pedigrees nor powerful office. These were men whom one might label "bourgeois" or "middle class" if these terms were not so loaded or ambiguous. Whatever one calls them, they were different from their aristocratic predecessors, and inclined, as one would expect, to maintain different relations with the poor.

One hundred years before, during the seventeenth century, the aristocrats had conceived of their ties to the impoverished as personal, total, and reciprocal. An "artificial family," that is, a confraternity, dispensed their aid and made of public charity an extension of private altruism. Intimacy reigned between benefactor and pauper. To obtain admission to the Hospital General, a pauper had to appear personally before the Bureau, and when the directors preferred their domestics or dependents, no one was scandalized. In fact, this sort of personal favoritism was institutionalized: the most popular endowments—those for hospital beds or apprenticeships—specified that the donor's heirs choose the recipients among their clients or domestics. In general, the aristocrats made no distinction between public and private; they treated the impoverished just like their personal retainers or dependents. They gave them material aid, but they also supplied them with spiritual guidance, moral support, and when called for, harsh discipline. Mere alms were not enough; the benefactor, like a father, had more complex responsibilities. He had to bestow upon the pauper spiritual and moral benefit as well as monetary aid. He had to see to the good of the soul as well as of the body. As for the poor, they were expected to return undying loyalty, respect, and absolute obedience. Charitable relations were paternalistic, multistranded, and moral as well as economic.

In the eighteenth century, these ties became simpler, less personal, and more bureaucratic. The benefactor still provided aid, but he no longer supplied spiritual supervision or moral guidance. He did not feel obliged to save the pauper's soul or assure his good behavior. Relations between rich and poor were shorn of their moral content, and simple, distant relationships supplanted the old, multistranded ties. Now a public institution instead of a private confraternity dispensed aid, and there a new bureaucratic spirit reigned. The Hospital directors now interposed between themselves and the poor a set of clear, written rules, which replaced the casual admittance procedures of the past. Now, written petitions rather than personal appeals opened the doors of the Hospital, and the directors' clients (if they had any) enjoyed no advantage or privilege. Consistency and a certain impartiality were achieved, but at the expense of intimacy and flexibility. A sheaf of petitions and papers now kept the poor at a safe distance from the directors, and with the Revolution these bureaucratic procedures became so involved that they hindered rather than facilitated the administration of relief. Still, they achieved their primary purpose: personal contact with the poor was eliminated, and a more distant relationship, regulated by rules, stripped of moral content, and embodied in cash alone, took its place.

This change in the quality of charitable relations derived from sweeping changes in French society. If poor relief functions as a mirror, as I have argued at the beginning of this book, then here it reflects France's journey toward modernity. In the seventeenth century, charitable relations were paternal, personal, and multistranded just like all other social relations. The seigneur, like the benefactor, provided his tenants with more than just land; he also gave them protection, moral guidance, and aid. The lowly artisan like the pious donor provided his workers with more than just money; he also supplied them with food, shelter, spiritual instruction, and when necessary, punishment. Social ties possessed strong moral and religious as well as economic qualities; the bonds between master and servant or lord and peasant involved more than the exchange of money or goods. In the eighteenth century, all this changed with the gradual triumph of wage labor over domestic labor. By the last years of the century, the merchant-manufacturer no longer provided his laborers with moral guidance or spiritual support; he just gave them a wage. By the same token, the benefactor no longer bore responsibility for the pauper's soul; he just provided him with monetary assistance—if that. Social relations lost their moral content and became embodied in cash alone. For Marx, this change in social relations formed a part of the transition from feudalism to capitalism. For Weber, the switch from personal to bureaucratic power belonged to the growth of modern society. However one describes it, there is little dispute as to the basic agenda; much more controversial is its interpretation.

For some historians, mainly conservatives and royalists, the demise of traditional social ties was tragic. This minority glorifies seigneurial paternalism and assumes that it provided genuine shelter from hunger and want. Nothing could be further from the truth. The clearest manifestation of seigneurial beneficence—the deathbed bequest of any of Grenoble's great seigneurs—obviously did nothing to ease the pain of the peasantry, nor was relief its principal intention. On the contrary, the lords sought by such legacies to display their dominance and assert their undisputed superiority. Certainly, as the admirers of seigneurialism argue, the lord was obliged (at least in principle) to help his dependents. But, as they fail to notice, he was also licensed to abuse them. The seigneur could determine their religion, dictate their behavior, and deprive them of their liberty. At the limit, he could actually do them violence, as the history of the Congregation for the Propagation of the Faith amply demonstrates. Alms were plentiful in the seventeenth century, but for the poor this constituted, at best, a mixed blessing.

Under these circumstances, the demise of traditional ties and the advent of modern social relations in the eighteenth century brought with it positive benefits. On this point, the majority of historians of poor relief agree. They cannot deplore too strongly seventeenth-century charity or praise too loudly Enlightenment philanthropy. In some respects, they are correct. The eighteenth century did see the rich adopt, if not "humanity" and "philanthropy," then at least a less punitive stance. The moral police of the past disappeared and with it the notion that poverty could be extinguished by locking up the poor. The Enlightenment did lead to a more humane treatment of the poor, and historians who emphasize the point do not err. But they do exaggerate. In Grenoble the late eighteenth century saw no sweeping innovations in poor relief and certainly no increase in the number of individuals receiving assistance. The directors of the Hospital General did undertake a few reforms, all in accordance with enlightened thinking on poverty. They "deinstitutionalized" the poor, that is, they preferred bread distributions outside the Hospital walls to confinement within the institution. They began transforming the old *maison de force* into a genuine hospital, admitting sick individuals and improving medical care. They provided aid only to the "deserving poor," that is, the sick and the very young. In short, they met the demands of humanity. But they also served the financial interests of the Hospital General. "Deinstitutionalization" meant relieving the Hospital of paupers; transforming it into a medical facility entailed excluding desperate individuals; and serving only the "deserving poor" meant serving only a few of the poor. Some might get better care, but many got only benign neglect. The "able-bodied" poor—that is, men with large families and older single women—received little aid. The number of people on the bread lists dwindled; the percentage of petitions accepted by the Hospital declined. Overall, the number of individuals supplied with assistance, far from rising, actually fell. The Hospital served humanity more by serving it less. Nor did other institutions suddenly arise to fill the gap. The Grenoblois created no new formal sources of relief in the late eighteenth century; they also failed to continue informal means. Testamentary bequests declined, as did donations by the living. Apparently, the new philanthropy made fewer demands on the individual than did the old charity. Eighteenth-century Grenoblois did not do the poor as much harm as had their ancestors, but they did not do them as much good either.

Enlightened Grenoblois were not, therefore, much better than their forerunners; but they were not much worse either. To judge them inferior or superior to their ancestors is short-sighted, for in both the seventeenth and the eighteenth century poor relief was inadequate, insufficient, and unsuccessful. In both centuries, benefactors failed in certain respects: they neither eliminated poverty nor succeeded in alleviating misery. And they suffered from certain crucial intellectual limitations: all believed that the pauper himself bore sole responsibility for his plight, that he alone, not anonymous forces, created poverty. Benefactors in both centuries failed, therefore, to develop a radical critique of prevailing economic arrangements. The aristocrats of the seventeenth century never imagined that the distribution of wealth was anything but just; the lawyers of the Enlightenment, like Achard de Germane, never seriously questioned the existence of economic inequities. Certainly, neither ever tried to redistribute wealth or minimize social and economic differences. Even the Committee on Mendicity at its most radical assumed that poverty was, for the able-bodied, a temporary condition necessitating only occasional relief. Short-term assistance was, therefore, all that was needed, and temporary relief from misfortune, insurance rather than genuine welfare, was all that was ever provided.

This leaves us with an intriguing problem: why did the Grenoblois provide more charity at certain times and much less at others? What accounts for their relative parsimony or generosity? In the years between 1680 and 1730, for example, the Grenoblois were exceptionally generous; in the latter half of the eighteenth century, by contrast, they were unusually stingy. Given that poverty was much more severe in the earlier period, we could conclude, as some historians have done, that the rich were "responding to poverty." This, however, is just a restatement of fact, not an explanation. We come closer to a solution if we bear in mind that charity constituted insurance. In this case, aid was most likely to be forthcoming when a sizable proportion of the community needed insurance, when they or their kin were vulnerable to misfortune. In the years between 1680 and 1730, economic crisis was so prolonged and intense that almost everyone beneath the aristocracy was at risk. A lawyer, for example, might not have to fear poverty personally. But in the event of his death, his widow and children might well find themselves dependent upon charity for their daily bread. The bread-distribution rolls of the Hospital General contained enough examples of such formerly "respectable" women and children to make this a real possibility. Conversely, in the late eighteenth century, poverty ceased to menace many Grenoblois, and the flood of alms dried to a trickle. Economic difficulties had not disappeared: in the last years of the century subsistence crises reappeared. But the growth of industry and trade had greatly enriched the middle segments of society and provided them with a shelter against disaster. The lawyer with a hand in the glove trade and one small estate did not have to fear, as had his less well endowed greatgrandfather, that his widow would be dependent upon public assistance. In fact, the widows of lawyers and merchants were not among the poor on the capitation rolls of 1789. Prosperity had provided a cushion and removed some old incentives for almsgiving.

But not all: economic circumstances alone cannot account for the Grenoblois' generosity or lack thereof. Cultural factors encouraged or discouraged generosity, and the impact of resurgent Catholicism cannot be ignored. As the Grenoblois' wills and testaments demonstrate, Catholicism encouraged charitable giving, and it did so in a rather simple, straightforward way. It successfully attached personal benefit to the common good by promising benefactors distinct rewards—Eternal Salvation—and misers distinct penalties—Eternal Damnation. In short, Catholicism overcame what political scientists call the "free rider problem."[1] A good Catholic could not ignore the poor and allow his neighbor to bear the whole burden of almsgiving; he could not take a "free ride." If he did, he faced a rather awesome and sure punishment: Hell. If he contributed to the relief of the poor, though, he could look forward to a substantial reward: Heaven.

Catholicism therefore stimulated the social conscience, but it did not necessarily supply effective relief to the poor. Seventeenth-century charity, however plentiful, never equaled or even mitigated the sufferings of the poor. In fact, such questions of efficacy and sufficiency were largely irrelevant to the Catholic benefactor. He was concerned, not with the pauper's material well-being, but with his spiritual welfare, with his soul.

If Catholicism joined self-interest to the common interest, it also linked individual salvation to the righteousness of the community as a whole. A good Catholic could not afford to ignore his sinful neighbor; his personal salvation depended on the redemption of the whole community. Therefore, he not only left alms to the poor, he also sent them to school, dragged them to church, punished them for immorality, and incarcerated them in a *maison de force*.

When Counter Reformation Catholicism died, so too did this successful, but rather sinister, social ethic. In the late eighteenth century, many Grenoblois—like many other men throughout the kingdom—abandoned post-Tridentine Catholicism. Why they or their fellow Frenchmen did so is by no means clear. Historians have been too preoccupied establishing the meaning, chronology, and social composition of this phenomenon to speculate on its deeper social causes. The forces that lay beneath Frenchmen's defection from the Church will undoubtedly be unearthed some day, but that is not the task of the present study. Suffice it to say that, as the anthropologists tell us, religions symbolize and explain the world to their adherents; therefore, post-Tridentine Catholicism ceased to symbolize and explain the world to some Grenoblois, males of the middle and working classes.

While we cannot fully explain the Grenoblois' defection from Catholicism, we can at least account for their seeming indifference to the poor. When Catholicism faded, the old links between self-interest and the common good dissolved, and the flood of alms dried up. Achard de Germane put his finger on the problem when he observed that men were driven by self-interest, and only when their self-interest was stimulated would they give to the poor. Achard suggested that, under the circumstances, employing the poor and growing rich from their labor was the only feasible form of charity. Other eighteenth-century thinkers had less cynical responses to the problem. Some extolled sensibility and claimed there was an innate altruism conferred upon all men by their humanity. Men, so the argument went, tended to their brothers because they were men. Another school of thought took a more jaundiced view of human nature and added an element of coercion. The State, these thinkers claimed, should dispense aid and force all citizens to contribute, that is, pay taxes. While some authors could maintain both sentiments, this did nothing to alter the essential problem: French men and women, for a variety of reasons, no longer had any incentive to assist the poor.

And in the course of the eighteenth century, they showed less and less inclination to relieve hunger and want—until the Revolution. Cultural and economic factors alone cannot account for the Jacobin experiment in social welfare, nor for the developments in poor relief that preceded it. Politics must be considered, but historians of poor relief have not generally done so. They have ignored political considerations and assumed that French benefactors did so as well. The reasons for this neglect are obvious: the poor were utterly disenfranchised under the old regime and generally denied the vote during the Revolution. Still, to ignore politics, even in this setting, is to take an excessively narrow view of political activity. Many acts qualify as political gestures, even charitable "gifts." In the seventeenth century, for example, a benefactor reaped positive, even concrete political benefits from his "altruism." He could place his clients in the Hospital General, act as an intermediary with the directors on their behalf, and generally strengthen his ties with his dependents. The new institutions, like the Hospital General and the charitable confraternities, only rendered his political investment less costly. They placed at his disposal greater resources and provided him with more effective ways of demonstrating his patronage and securing loyalty. Moreover, as the political scientists remind us, patronage does not just reaffirm dependency; it also creates it.[2] By his charitable gifts the benefactor did not only, to quote Bossuet, "build up heavenly treasure"; he also accumulated earthly, political capital.

Eighteenth-century benefactors found it neither so easy nor so profitable to reap political benefits from charity. First, they had fewer resources than their predecessors. The Hospital General was nearly broke, and the middle classes had neither the income nor the inclination to compensate for this loss. Furthermore, other patrons had entered the market and offered stiff competition. Now midwives and especially priests acted as intermediaries and helped the poor receive assistance without asking for eternal loyalty in return. At the same time, the greater mobility of the poor rendered a "charitable" investment highly risky; after all, there was little likelihood that a client would be around to return the favor. And those most likely to need aid in the eighteenth century—the very young, the very old, and the female—were also those least likely to make valuable clients. Finally, the eighteenth-century Grenoblois had little to fear from the poor, for they posed no real threat. The seventeenth-century benefactors had done their job well: the impoverished were superficially orderly and obedient. Aside from a few minor disturbances at the grain market, which were easily mastered if each party played its traditional role, the poor posed no real threat and manifested little discontent. At least, they did not express their grievances effectively.

The Revolution changed all this, not because it changed the poor, but because it altered the political environment in which the poor acted. Now, national events lent to even the most cursory protest considerable reasonance, while all the fragility of the new municipal government rendered the support of all segments of the population vital. Small wonder then that the years between 1790 and 1792 witnessed a sudden resurgence of charity as competing factions from within the elite bid for the support of all Grenoblois. In 1793 and 1794 the laboring class emerged as a positive, active political force which had to be reckoned with, not just wooed. The conjunction of popular protest and social welfare underscores the link between popular political action and poor relief. In a world in which the old religious incentives had lost their force, only pressure from "below" would stimulate the elite to provide assistance on a large scale. Only when the putative recipients of relief played an active political role would social welfare be forthcoming. The remark is as true for seventeenth- and eighteenth-century France as it is today.

Appendix A

COMPOSITION OF THE SAMPLE OF WILLS: 1620–1729

Social Group	Number	Percent
Nobles	353	11.5
Magistrates	319	10.4
Basoche	528	17.2
Bourgeois	210	6.9
Merchants	388	12.6
Master artisans	341	11.1
Plowmen	140	4.6
Workers (artisans and day laborers)	426	13.8
Domestics	67	2.1
Soldiers	118	3.8
Peasants	14	0.4
Unknown	164	5.6
Totals	3,068	100.00
Residence of Testator		
Urban	2,521	82.1
Rural	535	17.4
Unknown	12	0.5
Totals	3,068	100.0
Gender of Testator		
Male	1,873	61.0
Female	1,195	39.0
Totals	3,068	100.0

Appendix B

PERCENTAGE OF TESTATORS MAKING BEQUESTS TO THE HOSPITAL:
SELECTED REGRESSION RESULTS

Variables	Coefficients	t-Statistics
Date	0.005	2.40
Nobles	0.126	4.28
Magistrates	0.509	13.85
Basoche	0.234	7.85
Bourgeois	0.196	4.92
Merchants	0.147	4.48
Plowmen	−0.058	1.31
Domestics	−0.065	1.09
Female	0.017	1.02
Urban	0.130	5.47
Literacy	0.077	3.65

Note: Regression coefficients for the variables immigrant, family status, and sick have been omitted from this table. For an explanation of the variables, see table 1.

Appendix C

COMPOSITION OF THE EIGHTEENTH-CENTURY SAMPLE
OF TESTAMENTS: 1730–1789

Social Group	Number	Percent
Nobles	188	9.71
Magistrates	154	7.93
Basoche	283	14.57
Bourgeois	131	6.74
Merchants	182	9.37
Master artisans	120	6.18
Laborers	98	5.04
Workers	543	27.96
Domestics	124	6.38
Soldiers	16	0.82
Unknown	103	5.30
Totals	1,942	100.00
Residence		
Grenoble	1,517	78.32
Rural	423	21.68
Unknown	2	0.10
Totals	1,942	100.00
Gender		
Male	1,041	53.60
Female	901	46.39
Totals	1,942	100.00

Notes

CHAPTER ONE

1. Henri Beyle (Stendhal), *La Vie d'Henri Brulard,* p. 101.
2. François de Bonne, Duc de Lesdiguières, *Actes et correspondance de Lesdiguières,* ed. Charles Douglas and Pierre Roman. 3 vols. (Grenoble, 1884). Vol. 3, pp. 462–467.
3. Charles Dufayard, *Le Connétable de Lesdiguières,* p. 578.
4. Lesdiguières, *Actes et correspondance* 3:462–467.
5. On the Wars of Religion, see Nicolas Chorier, *Histoire générale du Dauphiné* 2:600–743.
6. Dufayard, p. 3.
7. This process was accomplished by the royal intendants who were gradually introduced into Dauphiné and Grenoble. (Edmond Esmonin, "Les Intendants du Dauphiné, des origines à la Révolution," in *Etudes sur la France du XVIIe et XVIIIe siècles,* ed. Edmond Esmonin, pp. 71–113.)
8. On the *procès des tailles,* see Antoine La Croix, "Claude Brosse et le procès des tailles"; Scott Van Doren, "War, Taxes and Social Protest: The Challenge to Authority in Sixteenth Century Dauphiné."
9. On the uprising in Dauphiné in 1580, see Emmanuel Le Roy Ladurie, *The Carnival of Romans;* Scott Van Doren, "Revolt and Reaction in the City of Romans: 1580."
10. Raoul Blanchard, *Grenoble: Étude de géographie urbaine,* p. 43.
11. Blanchard, pp. 77–78.
12. Vauban, cited in Blanchard, p. 77.
13. Edmond Esmonin, "Le Recensement de Grenoble en 1725," in *Etudes sur la France du XVIIe et XVIIIe siècles,* p. 460.
14. Pierre Léon, *La Naissance de la grande industrie en Dauphiné* 1:90.
15. Léon, *La Naissance de la grande industrie* 1:175–311.
16. Like all Parlements in the old regime, the Parlement of Dauphiné heard both civil and criminal cases, and it acted as a legislative body as well (Jean Egret, *Le Parlement du Dauphiné et les affaires publiques dans la deuxième moitié du XVIIIe siècle* 1:1–16). The Parlement employed in 1697 four presidents, two *chevaliers d'honneur,* forty-six counselors, and six *gens du roy* (Guy Allard, *Dictionnaire historique du Dauphiné,* p. 283).
17. The Chambre de l'Edit consisted of one president, six Catholics, and six Protestant counselors (Allard, *Dictionnaire historique,* p. 234).
18. In 1697 the Chambre des Comptes consisted of six presidents, eighteen *maîtres,* two *correcteurs,* four secretaries, and an *avocat-général* and a *procureur du roy* (Allard, *Dictionnaire historique,* p. 227).

19. Allard, p. 305.

20. Almost all the communities in Dauphiné had seigneurs, and though not all were magistrates, the largest, most lucrative, and ancient lay in the hands of judges (Bernard Bligny, ed., *Histoire du Dauphiné*, pp. 249–254).

21. Egret, *Le Parlement du Dauphiné* 1:32.

22. Esmonin, "Le Recensement de Grenoble en 1725," in *Etudes sur la France du XVIIe et XVIIIe siècles*, p. 460.

23. Allard, p. 253.

24. Esmonin, "Le Recensement de Grenoble en 1725," pp. 90–110.

25. Archives Communales de Grenoble, BB 80.

26. Pierre-Henri Bordier, "Le diocèse à l'arrivée de Le Camus," pp. 163–171.

27. In 1515, when the consuls began to reform Grenoble's public welfare system, the city possessed four hospices: the Aumône Saint Hugues, intended to dispense bread to the poor; the Hôpital Saint Antoine, meant for the victims of Saint Anthony's fire but used as a hospital for victims of all ailments; the Hôpital Saint Jacques, which was a hospice for pilgrims; and the Hôpital de l'Isle, which served as an asylum for plague victims. There were also four leprosariums located on the outskirts of the city. None of these institutions performed any charitable functions at the beginning of the sixteenth century (Auguste Prudhomme, *Catalogue des archives hospitalières de Grenoble*, Grenoble, 1898, pp. i–x).

28. A. C. Grenoble, BB 4; BB 10; BB 7; BB 6; BB 12; BB 18.

29. During this period the functions and prerogatives of the Bureau des Pauvres were assumed by the Conseil de la Santé. A good study of this process appears in Auguste Prudhomme, "Etudes historiques sur l'assistance publique à Grenoble," *Bulletin de l'académie delphinale* 9(1985): 122–350.

30. A. C. Grenoble, GG 245–252.

31. A. D. Isère, Archives Hospitalières, E. 4 April 10, 1627.

32. A. D. Isère, A.H.E. 4 March 21, 1627; E. 29.

33. A. C. Grenoble, BB 100; BB 95; A. D. Isère, A.H.E. 4 June 2, 1627.

34. A facsimile of the plaque appears in Auguste Prudhomme, *Catalogue des archives hospitalières*, p. 63.

CHAPTER TWO

1. A. D. Isère, 26 H. 221.

2. A. D. Isère, 26 H. 201.

3. The body of literature on religious confraternities is considerable and is growing every day. For France, see Philip Benedict, *Rouen during the Wars of Religion;* Louis Pérouas, *Le Diocèse de La Rochelle de 1648 à 1724;* Philip T. Hoffman, *Church and Community in the Diocese of Lyon, 1500–1789.* Charitable confraternities have received considerable attention from historians of Renaissance Italy. See Brian Pullan, *Rich and Poor in Venice;* Richard Trexler, *Public Life in Florence;* Ronald Weissman, *Ritual Brotherhood in Renaissance Florence.*

4. Gabriel Le Bras, *Etudes de sociologie réligieuse*, pp. 423–462.

5. Women's charitable confraternities existed in Toulouse, Aix-en-Provence, Valence, and Romans, and of course in Paris where the most famous example of this sort of sodality, the Ladies of Charity, established by Saint Vincent de Paul, spearheaded all sorts of good works (Pierre Coste, *Les Dames de charité*, Paris, 1933). Women, both lay and religious, were also involved in charity schools (see Judith C. Taylor, "From Proselytizing to Social Reform").

6. A. D. Isère, 26 H. 201.

7. Pierre Dutour, *Mémoires curieux sur l'histoire des moeurs et la prostitution en France au XVIIe et XVIIIe siècles* (Paris, 1854), pp. 87–88.

8. The Madeline hospice was different from the medieval asylums set up for retired prostitutes. Its intent was not to shelter aging whores, but to reform young prostitutes. On medieval prostitutes' asylums, see Jacques Rossiaud, "Prostitution, Youth and Society in the Towns of Southeastern France in the Fifteenth Century."

9. A. D. Isère, 26 H. 221.

10. The membership of the Orphans confraternity in the years between 1636 and 1702 comprised the following:

Noblewomen	18.5%
Magistrates' wives	56.0%
Lawyers' wives	16.5%
Bourgeois (rentiers)	9.0%
Total	100.0% $(N = 66)$

11. For the most recent statement of this notion, see Nancy Roelker, "French Noblewomen and the Reformation," *Archiv fur Reformationsgeschichte* 63 (1972): 170.

12. For a more detailed discussion of the spirituality promoted by women's confraternities, see Kathryn Norberg, "Women, the Family and the Counter Reformation: Women's Confraternities in the Seventeenth Century," *Proceedings of the Western Society for French Historical Studies* 6 (1979): 55–63.

13. A. D. Isère, 26 H. 221; on the medieval view of poverty, see Michel Mollat, *Etudes sur la pauvreté au Moyen Age* (Paris, 1974); "Conclusion," in *Assistance et charité,* Cahiers de Fanjeaux, no. 13 (Toulouse, 1978), pp. 389–408.

14. A. D. Isère, 26 H. 201; 221.

15. A. D. Isère, 26 H. 201.

16. Ibid.

17. A. D. Isère, 26 H. 221; 201.

CHAPTER THREE

1. René de Voyer d'Argenson, *Les Annales de la Compagnie du Saint-Sacrement,* p. 193.

2. Voyer d'Argenson, p. 195.

3. Raoul Allier, *La Cabale des dévots.* Since Allier, the Parisian Company has been the subject of only one major study, Emmanel Chill's "The Company of the Holy Sacrament, 1660–1666: Social Aspects of the French Counter-Reformation." A useful summary of Mr. Chill's findings appears in "Religion and Mendicity in Seventeenth-Century France," *International Review of Social History* 7 (1962): 400–425

4. The Company register is now in the Bibliothèque Municipale of Grenoble in the Fonds dauphinois under the number R. 5765. How the register came to reside with the family papers of the Gigou de Chapolay at the Chateau of Meffray is not clear, but there is one possible explanation. The last member of the Company to die was Louis Grimaud, seigneur de Becsque, owner of the chateau. He died without heirs, and the chateau subsequently changed hands a number of times before the Gigou family purchased it. When the family bought the chateau it apparently got the papers of Louis Grimaud—and of the Company—in the bargain.

5. There are several studies of provincial companies, among them A. Auguste, *La Compagnie du Saint-Sacrement de Toulouse: Notes et documents;* A. Leroux, "Extraits du registre de la Compagnie du Saint-Sacrement de Limoges," *Bulletin de la société archéologique et historique du Limousin* 23 (1885): 58–76; 45 (1896): 388–416; Georges Guigues, *Les Papiers des dévots de Lyon, 1630–1731;* M. Sauriau, *La Compagnie de Saint-Sacrement de l'Autel de Caen* (Paris, 1913).

6. The Grenoble register has been the subject of only two other studies. Abbe Lagier published extracts from it in "La Compagnie du Saint-Sacrement de Grenoble," *Bulletin de la société d'archéologie et de statistique de la Drôme,* 50–51 (1916): 17–49; 141–179. More recently, Paul Bordier, a student at the University of Grenoble, wrote an excellent study of the Company (Paul Bordier, "La Compagnie du Saint-Sacrement de Grenoble 1652–1666"). Mr. Bordier's thesis goes beyond the Company to consider religious life in Grenoble on the eve of the Counter Reformation. A precis of his work can be found in P. Bordier, "Le Diocèse de Grenoble à l'arrivée de Le Camus."

7. Letter from Monsieur de Foresta, dated February 9, 1640, cited in Raoul Allier, *La Compagnie du Saint-Sacrement de Marseille: Documents,* pp. 141–142.

8. Letter from the Parisian Company to the Marseille Company, cited in Allier, *La Compagnie du Saint-Sacrement de Marseille,* pp. 23–24.

9. Letter from the Parisian Company to the Marseille Company, dated March 1, 1654, cited in Allier, *La Compagnie du Saint-Sacrement de Marseille,* pp. 192–193.

10. Bordier, "La Compagnie du Saint-Sacrement de Grenoble," pp. 21–24; 40–41.

11. Ibid., pp. 25–27.

12. For the lineage of the Brothers, see the articles under each surname in Guy Allard, *Dictionnaire historique du Dauphiné.*

13. Bordier, "La Compagnie du Saint-Sacrement de Grenoble," p. 28.

14. B.M. Grenoble, Fonds dauphinois, R. 5765, "Rôle des communions et des visites des pauvres," pp. 39v, 40, 58, 74.

15. The Brothers did not actually bury the poor; they said masses for the redemption of the paupers' souls (B.M. Grenoble, Fonds dauphinois, R. 5765, p. 77). As for reconciling enemies, the Brothers preferred to reconcile enemies within families (B.M. Grenoble, Fonds dauphinois, R. 5767, pp. 138, 203, 220v).

16. On the Le Puy scheme for the distribution of used clothing, see B.M. Grenoble, Fonds dauphinois, R. 5765, p. 40.

17. On the desperate financial situation of the Hospital and its haphazard administration, see A. D. Isère, A.H.E. 5–6.

18. A. D. Isère, A.H.E. 6.

19. B.M. Grenoble, Fonds dauphinois, R. 5765, pp. 67v, 71, 141v.

20. Ibid., pp. 199, 200v, 201.

21. Ibid., pp. 60, 67.

22. *Project charitable,* B.M. Grenoble, Fonds dauphinois, O. 7736, pp. 1–4.

23. B.M. Grenoble, Fonds dauphinois, O. 7736, pp. 1–6.

24. Brothers of the Holy Sacrament, cited in A. Auguste, *La Compagnie du Saint-Sacrement de Toulouse,* p. 47. This passage is taken from a pamphlet published a few years before the *Projet charitable* and which bears a striking resemblance to it. It is likely that the Grenoble Brothers used the Toulousain pamphlet as a model.

25. B.M. Grenoble, Fonds dauphinois, R. 5765, pp. 129v, 153.

26. Ibid., p. 107v.

27. Ibid., p. 237.

28. Ibid., pp. 114, 123v, 125, 126, 238, 263, 267.

29. Ibid., pp. 149, 167v. On magical beliefs surrounding the Host, see Keith Thomas, *Religion and the Decline of Magic.*

30. B.M. Grenoble, Fonds dauphinois, R. 5765, pp. 73, 74, 75v, 86, 129v, 189v.

31. Ibid., pp. 17, 33, 36, 76, 92, 99v.

32. Ibid., pp. 40v, 65v, 79, 133, 165, 232, 252.

33. Ibid., pp. 81v, 191v, 217, 250.

34. Ibid., pp. 91v, 158v, 195, 217.

35. Ibid., pp. 63v, 75, 76, 147.

36. Ibid., pp. 101v, 103, 125, 267v.

37. Ibid., pp. 35, 85, 86, 113v, 114, 114v, 127, 192.

38. Ibid., pp. 57, 139, 161v, 165, 178, 195, 201, 217, 223, 237.

39. Ibid., pp. 39v, 102v, 124, 128v, 158v.

40. Ibid., pp. 28, 38, 54, 82, 101, 134, 211, 246, 280v.

41. Ibid., pp. 74v, 89v, 117, 196.

42. Ibid., pp. 89, 126v, 127v, 128, 223, 238, 246.

43. Ibid., p. 223.

44. Ibid., p. 249.

45. Ibid., pp. 127v, 156, 200.

46. Ibid., pp. 76, 124, 128v, 194, 244, 258, 265.

47. The Justice was a seigneurial court and had the same powers as such courts throughout France. It heard all sorts of petty civil and criminal cases, received *déclarations de grossesse,* made death inventories and acted as a probate court, levied fines, and even had the power to impose the death penalty. In this case, convicted criminals were granted auto-

matic appeal before the Parlement. The Justice, which was staffed by a magistrate, a prosecuting attorney, and several *huissiers,* also had jurisdiction in some villages near Grenoble. The Justice itself has never been the subject of a sustained study, but helpful information can be found in Guy Allard, *Dictionnaire historique du Dauphiné,* p. 33.

48. Most of the Justice's records before 1670 have disappeared, but this poses no serious problem. It is highly unlikely that basic patterns of criminality changed dramatically in the ten years that separate the Company's activities from the beginning of the Justice archives.

49. The justice dispensed by the Grenoble court was very expensive indeed. A dead man found drowned in the Isère or lifeless on a public highway had to pay, literally out of his pockets, a considerable sum of money, 40 livres, for the honor of having the cause of his death determined and his body removed. These court costs had important implications for the reporting of crime. Some plaintiffs may have sought informal means of redress rather than risk being saddled with legal fees. Still others may have undertaken cases in the hope of dishonoring their enemy publicly and ruining him financially to boot. Consequently, the plaintiff's ability to pay court costs and his inability to use informal means of redress, not the crime itself, determined which crimes appear in the records and which do not. For an insightful discussion of these problems, see Nicole Castan, *Justice et répression en Languedoc à l'époque des lumières.*

50. Here my approach will be similar to that used with such success in Yves Castan, *Honnêteté et relations sociales en Languedoc, 1715–1780.*

51. The Justice criminal records for the years 1674 through 1688 are currently classed 13B 364 to 370 of the Archives Départementales of the Isère. Since this series is currently being reclassed, these numbers may well change in the near future.

52. A. D. Isère, 13 B 366.

53. A thorough explication of the deficiencies of old-regime justice appears in Nicole Castan, *Justice et répression,* pp. 85–130.

54. A. D. Isère, 13 B 370.

55. A. D. Isère, 13 B 365 and 374.

56. A. D. Isère, 13 B 374.

57. B.M. Grenoble, Fonds dauphinois, R. 5765, p. 127v.

58. A. D. Isère, 13 B 370.

59. A. D. Isère, 13 B 369.

60. A. D. Isère, 13 B 368.

61. Ibid.

62. A. D. Isère, 13 B 369.

63. A. D. Isère, 13 B 366.

64. A. D. Isère, 13 B 370.

65. A. D. Isère, 13 B 366–370.

66. Two weak links appear in the family system of seventeenth-century Grenoble: the troubled relationships between brothers, on the one hand, and the tension-filled relations between stepparents and stepchildren, on the other. Both occasionally caused violence (A. D. Isère, 13 B 365 and 366).

67. A. D. Isère, 13 B 370.

68. A century later in Languedoc, young males would still predominate among those tried for criminal offenses (Nicole Castan, *Les Criminels de Languedoc: Les Exigences d'ordre et les voies du ressentiment dans une société pré-révolutionnaire (1750–1790),* p. 38).

69. A. D. Isère, 13 B 370.

70. See in particular Yves-Marie Bercé, "Aspects de la criminalité au XVIIe siècle."

71. A. D. Isère, 13 B 370. For the notion of honor in the eighteenth century, see Yves Castan, *Honnêteté et relations sociales.*

72. A. D. Isère, 13 B 651. On honor in mediterranean society, see J. G. Peristiany, ed., *Honor and Shame: The Values of Mediterranean Society.*

73. A. D. Isère, 13 B 367 through 380.

74. A. D. Isère, 13 B 380.

75. A. D. Isère, 13 B 365 and 380.

76. Some of this material was used by Jacques Solé in "Passion charnelle et société urbaine d'ancien regime: Amour vénal, amour libre et amour fou à Grenoble au milieu du règne Louis XIV."

77. A.D. Isère, 13 B 370.

78. Ibid.

79. A.D. Isère, 13 B 369–370.

80. Ibid.

81. Of these men, one was the husband of a procuress, who had become smitten with one of his wife's girls, and the other two were men who had seduced servant girls and then prostituted them to friends and relatives (A.D. Isère, 13 B 370; 13 B 648–649).

82. A.D. Isère, 13 B 370.

83. Ibid.

84. B.M. Grenoble, Fonds dauphinois, R. 5765, p. 218; A.D. Isère, 13 B 370.

85. A.D. Isère, 13 B 370.

86. Because the prosecuting attorney seized a prostitution case as soon as it came before the court, it is hard to tell just who reported the prostitutes. The neighbors seem the logical choice. In one instance, it is clear that they had also informed their landlady of the whore's activities and tried to have her evicted before going to the Justice (A.D. Isère, 13 B 370).

87. A.D. Isère, 13 B 364–370. Youths had long played a similar role in France, as Jacques Rossiaud has shown in "Prostitution, Youth and Society in the Towns of Southeastern France in the Fifteenth Century."

88. A.D. Isère, 13 B 370.

89. Monique Bornarnel, "La Population de Grenoble 1680–1764: Etude socio-démographique," p. 68.

90. See chapter 5.

91. A good description of the content, purpose, and legal history of the *déclaration de grossesse* appears in Marie-Claude Phan, "Les Déclarations de grossesse en France (XVIe-XVIIIe siècles): Essai institutionnel," p. 88.

92. B.M. Grenoble, Fonds dauphinois R. 5765, p. 249. Unwed mothers throughout France seem to have been unwilling to make *déclarations*. While historians of the eighteenth century have lavished a considerable amount of attention on this document, those of the seventeenth century have generally ignored it, probably because there are so few declarations before 1700.

93. A.D. Isère, 13 B 648.

94. A.D. Isère, 13 B 648–649.

95. A.D. Isère, A.H. G. 2

96. A.D. Isère, 13 B 648–649.

97. A.D. Isère, 13 B 648.

98. Ibid.

99. Ibid.

100. On the traditional functions of the *déclaration de grossesse,* see Marie-Claude Phan, "Les Déclarations de grossesse en France," pp. 86–87.

101. A.D. Isère, 13 B 648–649.

102. A.D. Isère, 13 B 648.

103. A.D. Isère, 13 B 369.

104. A.D. Isère, 13 B 365–367.

105. B.M. Grenoble, Fonds dauphinois R. 5765, p. 246.

106. On Grenoble's libertines, see Jacques Solé, "Passion charnelle et société urbaine," pp. 211–213.

107. B.M. Grenoble, Fonds dauphinois R. 5765, p. 124.

108. Ibid., pp. 73v, 75v, 108, 112, 135, 141, 164v.

109. This particular "progressive view" of English poor relief is best expressed by T.K. Jordan, *Philanthropy in England 1480–1660.*

110. On Puritan poor relief, see the work of Christopher Hill, *Society and Puritanism in Pre-revolutionary England.*

111. Perhaps the best example of this tendency to focus on the Church at the expense of the laity is Pierre Broutin's *La Réforme pastorale en France.* This is not to deny the importance of historians like Broutin; their work has been some of the most illuminating on the Catholic Reformation.

112. Peter Burke, *Popular Culture in Early Modern Europe.*

113. Boris Porchnev, *Les Soulèvements populaires en France de 1623 à 1648.*
114. Michel Foucault, *Madness and Civilization,* trans. Richard Howard.
115. B.M. Grenoble, Fonds dauphinois R. 5765, p. 261v.
116. Ibid., pp. 73, 73v, 156, 163, 223v, 251.
117. Ibid., p. 220v.
118. Perhaps the most succinct statement of Mousnier's position has appeared in Mousnier, "Recherches sur les soulèvements populaires en France avant la Fronde."
119. Voyer d'Argenson, *Les Annales de la Compagnie du Saint-Sacrement,* p. 249.
120. A.D. Isère, A.H.E.6.

CHAPTER FOUR

1. Pierre Barbéry, *L'Oeuvre de la Propagation de la Foi de Grenoble et de Lyon,* pp. 86–87.
2. Barbéry, p. 43. Neither the Parisian nor the Grenoble Propagandists bothered to write down their statutes; therefore, the citations in the text come from the Lyon congregation's statutes. Presumably, they are similar to the rules observed by both the Parisians and the Grenoblois.
3. Congregations were also established in Metz, Puy, Rennes, Alençon, Saint Lô, Toulouse, Chambéry, Avignon, Tours, and Loudun. Only a handful of these congregations have left any record of their activities, so secondary works on the Propagation are few indeed. The Montpellier group has been the subject of a series of published documents entitled "Procès-verbaux de la Propagation de la Foi de Montpellier," *Bulletin de la société de l'histoire du protestantisme français* 26–27 (1878): 113–115; 159–161; 213–220. On the history of the Grenoble congregation in the eighteenth century, see Henri Terrebasse, *Notes et documents pour servir à l'histoire des protestants du Dauphiné: Les Maisons de la Propagation de la Foi.* An overview of the Propagation's activities appears in Olivier Douen, *La Révocation de l'édit de Nantes à Paris* 2:229–262.
4. All of the records of the Propagation can be found in the Departmental Archives of the Isère in the series 26 H or regular clergy. The documents are of two sorts: the minutes of the Congregation's meetings and miscellaneous correspondence. Both are unbound.
5. An unflattering but amusing portrait of this Grenoblois appears in Elie Benoist, *Histoire de l'édit de Nantes* 3:173.
6. Barbéry, pp. 86–87.
7. Jules Michelet, "Précis de l'histoire de France," in *Oeuvres complètes,* ed. Paul Villareix. 5 vols. (Paris, 1973). See vol. 3, p. 173.
8. Douen 2:262.
9. Bourdaloue, cited in A. Cans, "La Caisse du clergé de France et les protestants convertis," *Bulletin de la société de l'histoire du protestantisme français* 60 (1902): 236.
10. Bossuet, cited in Douen 2:238–239, n. 3.
11. A.D. Isère, 26 H. 101–105.
12. A.D. Isère, 26 H. 101–104.
13. The Propagation was unusual in that it admitted both men and women; but the women, the "Sisters," always played a subordinate role. Apparently, the women met separately from the men, and the "Sisters" were supervised by a male, usually an almoner. In addition, the officers elected by the ladies were subject to approval by the men's group. The Maison de la Propagation, however, was the women's special domain, and they administered it almost single-handedly. Despite the limitations imposed upon them, the ladies were the most assiduous of Propagandists. Bishop Le Camus considered them more devoted to the confraternity than the male members were (Barbéry, p. 51).
14. A.D. Isère, 26 H. 104. Rumors frequently circulated that the "principal ladies of the R.P.R." were planning to storm the Orphans and liberate all the Protestant children. Of course, the Protestant ladies meant the Propagation, but their confusion was understandable. In 1675 one Protestant woman did succeed in "stealing" her own child from the Propagation (A.D. Isère, 26 H. 104).

15. On the social composition of **Grenoble** Protestantism, see P-G Geisendorf, "Les Conséquences démographiques de la révocation de l'édit de Nantes en Dauphiné," and Madeline Sauvan-Richou, "La révocation de l'édit de Nantes à Grenoble." On rural Protestantism in Dauphiné, see Pierre Bolle, "Une Paroisse reformée du Dauphiné à la veille de la révocation de l'édit de Nantes: Mens-en-Trièves."

16. In 1676 the ladies of the Propagation in conjunction with Bishop Etienne Le Camus launched a major campaign for the protection of Grenoble's domestics. They divided the city into several quarters and assigned each lady the task of watching over all Catholic domestics employed by Protestants in that area. The ladies also tried to convert Protestant domestics (A.D. Isère, 26 H. 104–105).

17. Author not cited, "Procès-verbaux de la Propagation de la Foi de Montpellier," *Bulletin de la société de l'histoire du protestantisme français* 26 (1878): 116–117.

18. Pierre Jurieu, *La Politique du clergé de France, avec les derniers efforts de l'innocence affligée* (Amsterdam, 1682), pp. 112–113.

19. On the geographical distribution of Protestants in Dauphiné, see Pierre Bolle and Jean Godel, *Les Protestants en Dauphiné au XVIIe siècle,* Information régionale, C.R.D.P. de Grenoble, no. 12 (Grenoble, 1972).

20. Etienne Le Camus, in "Correspondance inédite de l'evêque de Grenoble, Le Camus avec Monsieur de Barillion, evêque de Luçon, au sujet de leurs campagnes contre l'hérésie, 1682–1696," *Bulletin de la société de l'histoire du protestantisme français* 3 (1855): 569–580.

21. Alexis Muston, *Histoire populaire des Vaudois,* pp. 203–255.

22. Père Meynier, "Etat sommaire de la religion dans la vallée du Pragelas," cited in Alexis Muston, *History of the Waldensians* (London, 1869), pp. 205–206.

23. "Procès-verbaux des conversions faites dans la vallée du Pragelas," cited in Muston, *History of the Waldensians,* p. 210.

24. A.D. Isère, 26 H. 118, 102, 104, 105.

25. Arnaud, *Histoire des Protestants du Dauphiné* 2:151.

26. A.D. Isère, 26 H. 118.

27. On the "traffic in souls," see Jean Orcibal, *Louis XIV et les protestants,* pp. 39–56.

28. Benoist 3:351.

29. A.D. Isère, 26 H. 118.

30. Orcibal, p. 54.

31. A.D. Isère, 26 H. 105; Etienne Le Camus, "Mémoire concernant les nouveaux-convertis du diocèse de Grenoble, 1689," in *Mémoires des évêques de France sur la conduite à tenir à l'égard des reformés,* ed. Jean Lemoine (Paris, 1902), p. 275; Paul Pellisson, cited in Jurieu, p. 152.

32. On the Protestant reaction to the "commerce in souls" see Orcibal, p. 47.

33. Antoine Arnaud, cited in Douen 1:521.

34. Louvois, cited in Douen 1:521–522.

35. A.D. Isère, 26 H. 118; 104. In 1677 the king established five parish churches in the Pragelas and provided them with priests. The Propagation contributed to the project both financially and with gifts of ornaments. In an attempt to rally the Vaudois to the Church, the priests organized celebrations for feast days, in particular those of the village patron saint. The ladies of the Propagation provided the banners used in these celebrations (A.D. Isère, 26 H. 104).

36. Muston, *History of the Waldensians,* p. 220.

37. Jesuit missionary, cited in Muston, *History of the Waldensians,* p. 208–209; Le Camus, cited in Pierre Bolle, "Le Camus et les protestants," in *Le Cardinal des montagnes: Etienne Le Camus,* ed. Jean Godel, p. 153; Abbé de Musi, cited in Arnaud 2:156–157.

38. A.D. Isère, 26 H. 101–107.

39. One of these schools was established by the ladies of the Propagation and had the express purpose of providing primary education to young women. The Progagandist efforts, however, were not entirely positive; frequently they only supplied schoolteachers after having driven the Protestant schoolmaster out of the village. The distribution of catechisms was a relatively common practice among devout Frenchmen, but the Propagandists added a new element: they also distributed secular books, mainly Latin classics (A.D. Isère, 26 H. 104–107).

40. A.D. Isère, 26 H. 104; Congregation of Montpellier, cited in "Procès-verbaux de la Propagation de la Foi de Montepellier," p. 115.

41. A.D. Isère, 26 H. 101, 102, 104, 107.

42. Louis XIV, *Memoirs for the Instruction of the Dauphin,* trans. Paul Sonnino (New York, 1970), p. 155.

43. Abbé de Musi, cited in Arnaud 2:155–156.

44. A.D. Isère, 26 H. 102.

45. A.D. Isère, 26 H. 113.

46. A.D. Isère, 26 H. 111.

47. A most illuminating discussion of this belief in the wholeness of the Christian community among German city dwellers appears in Bendt Moeller, *Reichstadt und Reformation.*

48. Léon Lallemand, *Histoire de la charité* 2:156.

49. A.D. Isère, 26 H. 117.

50. A.D. Isère, A.H.E.7 November 27, 1689; Arnaud 3:25–32.

51. A.D. Isère, 26 H. 104 and 105.

CHAPTER FIVE

1. A.D. Isère, A.H.E.8.

2. Léon, *La Naissance de la grande industrie en Dauphiné* 2:92; Bernard Bligny, ed., *Histoire du Dauphiné,* pp. 289–337.

3. A.D. Isère, 26 H. 207.

4. A.D. Isère, 26 H. 272–273.

5. B.M. Grenoble, Fonds dauphinois, R. 1414.

6. B.M. Grenoble, Fonds dauphinois, O. 7733.

7. A.D. Isère, A.H., Supplément IV.

8. A.D. Isère, A.H.E. 7–9.

9. A.D. Isère, A.H. IV. E. 4.

10. A.C. Grenoble, CC. 1173; CC 1183.

11. A.D. Isère, A.H.B. 4–5.

12. All remarks concerning the Hospital directors are based on the minutes of the meetings of the Bureau de la Direction, A.D. Isère, A.H.E. 6–10.

13. Monsieur Canel was one of the most important figures in the history of Grenoble's charitable institutions. He was involved in just about every charitable endeavor in the city and was so respected by the intendant that he was named one of the commissioners of the *révision des feux.* Son of a reputedly wealthy but not very prestigious Dauphinois family, he had been educated in Paris at Saint Sulpice and then returned to Grenoble. His piety was as celebrated as his charity. (Anonymous document cited in Maurice Virieux, "Jansénisme et molinisme dans le clergé du diocèse de Grenoble au début du XVIIIe siècle," *Revue d'histoire de l'église de France,* 60 [1974]: 314–315.)

14. A.D. Isère, 26 A.H. IV. E. 2.

15. Intendant Bouchu in *Correspondance des controlleurs-generaux,* ed. Boislisle (Paris, 1883), vol. 1, p. 333; A.D. Isère, A.H.E.9 April 23, 1724; A.H.E.7 December 1, 1706; A.H.E.10 June 27, 1735.

16. A.D. Isère, A.H.F. 1.

17. See Marcel Giraud, "Crise de conscience et d'autoritié à la fin du règne de Louis XIV."

18. On the administration of the edict of 1724 in Grenoble, see A.D. Isère, A.H.F. 1.

19. A.D. Isère, A.H.E.7 August 15, 1691.

20. On the history of the ordinance of 1724, see Jean-Pierre Gutton, *L'État et la mendicité dans la première moitié du XVIIIe siècle: Auvergne, Beaujolais, Forez, Lyonnais.*

21. A.D. Isère, A.H.E.7 May 6, 1703; March 22, 1707.

22. A.D. Isère, A.H.E. 7–9; A.H.B. 5.

23. A.D. Isère, A.H.E.6 February 25, 1680.

24. Guévarre was active throughout the southeast of France and had organized confinements in a number of cities (P. Joret, "Le Pére Guèvarre et les bureaux de charité," *Annales du Midi* 1 [1889]: 340–393).

25. A.D. Isère, A.H.E.9 July 6, 1712.

26. Guévarre, cited in P. Joret, "Le Père Guévarre et les bureaux de charité," p. 390.

27. A.D. Isère, A.H.E. 203. Between July and October 1712 the Hospital received over two hundred gifts from individuals as diverse as the first president of the Parlement, a card-maker, a group of tavern keepers, and several domestics.

28. A.D. Isère, A.H.E.8 September 1, 1712.

29. Guévarre wrote the pamphlet while staying in Rome at the request of the pope. Later he used it in all of his missions, changing the title according to the location. (P. Joret, "Le Père Guévarre et les bureaux de charité," p. 365.)

30. A.D. Isère, A.H.E. 203.

31. A copy of *Mendicité abolie* can be found in the Bibliothèque Municipale de Grenoble, Fonds dauphinois, O. 7735.

32. A.D. Isère, H. 207.

33. Ibid.

34. A.D. Isère, A.H. IV. E. 2.

35. A.D. Isère, A.H.E.11 October 11, 1712.

36. B.M. Grenoble, Fonds dauphinois, O. 7735, pp. 8–9.

37. Ibid., pp. 32–33.

38. Ibid., p. 1.

39. A.D. Isère, 26 H. 272.

40. B.M. Grenoble, Fonds dauphinois, R. 1414.

41. A.D. Isère, A.H.F.1.

42. Louis Pérouas, *Le Diocèse de La Rochelle, 1648–1724,* pp. 347, 385. On Jansenism in Grenoble, see Bruno Neuveux, "Le Camus et les jansénistes français," in *Le Cardinal des montagnes,* ed. Jean Godel, pp. 91–121; Jean Egray, "Le Renouveau et ses limites (1621–1715)," in *Histoire du diocése de Grenoble,* ed. Bernard Bligny, pp. 119–149.

43. For the reasons explained in chapter 3, the figures given concerning the increase in theft are, at best, only approximate. They are meant as a general indication of trends, not as a precise measurement.

44. A.D. Isère, 13 B 370–380.

45. A.D. Isère, 13 B 648.

46. A.D. Isère, 13 B 370 and 374.

47. A.D. Isère, 13 B 370 and 380.

48. A.D. Isère, 13 B 380.

49. Monique Bornarel, "La Population de Grenoble 1680–1764," p. 68.

50. A.D. Isère, A.H.F.1.

51. It is not clear why declarations are more numerous in this period. Obviously, the rise in illegitimacy played a role. So too did the improved quality of the Dauphinois clergy thanks to the reforms of Bishop Etienne Le Camus. Episcopal statutes required that every priest enjoin an unwed mother to make a declaration, and at the end of the seventeenth century many single mothers remarked that they made a declaration after seeing their parish priest. Also, the court adopted an increasingly rigorous policy in regard to unwed fathers, so many women may have seen the advantage of making a declaration.

52. A.D. Isère, 13 B 648–651.

53. A.D. Isère, 13 B 648–649; A.H.G. 2–4.

54. A.D. Isère, A.H.E.7 August 6, 1693.

55. A.D. Isère, A.H.G. 2–4.

56. Unwed parents also provided false information when baptizing their illicit offspring. In 1715 Françoise Savoy and her lover François Arbor, a soldier, pretended at their infant's baptism to be married, and the child was listed in the parish register as legitimate. Only when they exposed the baby later did the truth come out (A.D. Isère, 13 B 380).

57. A.D. Isère, 13 B 649.

58. These written agreements lie buried, unfortunately, in the notarial registers. It is significant that Nicole Castan has found such out-of-court settlements to have been very common in eighteenth-century Languedoc (Nicole Castan, *Justice et répression,* pp. 20–21).

59. A.D. Isère, 13 B 648; A.H.G. 4.

60. Unwed mothers continued to suffer from the disapproval of the community. Indeed, more and more of the women who made declarations came from villages outside Grenoble. Apparently, they had come to the city to have their child and escape the disapproval of their neighbors. City women also fled their homes once their pregnancy became evident. Louise Telman, a resident in Die, came to Grenoble to "hide her weakness," and many pregnant Grenobloise may have gone to nearby towns to conceal their condition (A.D. Isère, A.H. G. 4).

61. A.D. Isère, 13 B 648–651.

62. A rise in illegitimacy may derive from any number of sources that have nothing to do with values or religious beliefs. For instance, economic conditions may, in and of themselves, produce a higher rate of illegitimacy, as Richard Easterlin has demonstrated in an extremely convincing theoretical article, "The Economics and Sociology of Fertility: A Synthesis," in *Historical Studies in Changing Fertility,* ed. Charles Tilly, pp. 191–194. Moreover, the increase in bastardy occurred just when religious belief peaked in Grenoble, as we shall see in chapter 6.

63. A copy of the ordinance of 1724 can be found in A.D. Isère, A.H.E. 1.

64. The Grenoble registers of the beggars confined in the years between 1724 and 1730 appear in A.D. Isère, A.H., F. 15 and F. 17.

65. A.D. Isère, A.H.F. 1.

66. In St. Etienne, 333 beggars were incarcerated (Jean-Pierre Gutton, *L'Etat et la mendicité,* p. 202). At Aix-en-Provence, 470 individuals were confined specifically for begging (Cissie Fairchilds, *Poverty and Charity in Aix-en-Provence,* p. 102).

67. A.D. Isère, A.H.F. 15.

68. A.D. Isère, A.H.F. 15 and 17.

69. Jean-Pierre Gutton found adolescent and even child beggars to be extremely common in 1724 (*L'Etat et la mendicité,* pp. 204–208).

70. A.D. Isère, A.H.F. 15. In all these cases there was no significant variation in age, health, or residence during the years that the royal ordinance was in force.

71. In principle, seasonal migrants were not to be arrested by the *archers.* Such were, at least, the provisions of the ordinance of 1724, but it is possible that the *archers* did indeed confine some migrating peasants. Still, it seems that the crises of 1724 through 1726 sent otherwise sedentary Dauphinois on the road.

72. In the Forez too the true vagabonds formed only an infinitesimal proportion of the beggars. The beggar who faked disease and disability was not, however, a fantasy. In both Aix-en-Provence and the region around St. Etienne, such "false" beggars were confined during the enforcing of the ordinance of 1724 (Fairchilds, *Poverty and Charity in Aix-en-Provence,* p,. 114; Jean-Pierre Gutton, *L'Etat et la mendicité,* pp. 218–219).

73. Such criminal vagabonds were more likely to find their way into the hands of the rural police, the *maréchaussée,* whose area of competence was limited to the area outside the city walls.

74. A.D. Isère, A.H.F. 15 and 17.

75. See chapter 8.

76. A.D. Isère, A.H.F. 1.

77. A.D. Isère, A.H.F. 24, p. 101.

78. See Fairchilds, *Poverty and Charity in Aix-en-Provence;* Gutton, *La Société et les pauvres: L'Exemple de la generalité de Lyon* (Lyon, Société d'Edit les Belles Lettres, 1971).

79. A.D. Isère, A.H.E.7 April 30, 1712.

80. A.D. Isère, A.H.F. 24.

81. Ibid., p. 291.

82. Ibid., p. 291.

83. Ibid., p. 18.

84. Ibid., p. 102.

85. Ibid., p. 679.

86. Ibid., p. 365.

87. Ibid., pp. 217, 255, 683.

88. Léon, *La Naissance de la grande industrie* 1:99–123.

89. A.D. Isère, A.H.F.24, p. 224.
90. Ibid., p. 310.
91. Gutton, *La Société et les pauvres,* p. 53.
92. A.D. Isère, A.H.F. 24, p. 304.
93. Ibid., p. 398.
94. Ibid., pp. 162, 422, 436, 473.
95. Ibid., p. 139.
96. Ibid., p. 637.
97. Ibid., p. 9.
98. Ibid., p. 62.
99. Ibid., p. 149.
100. Ibid., pp. 455, 576.
101. See chapter 6.

CHAPTER SIX

1. A. D. Isère, Froment III E. 1.470 (20) pp. 70–71v.

2. In *La Mort à Paris aux XVIe, XVIIe et XVIIIe siècles,* Pierre Chaunu and his team of fifty-one students read and analyzed the "discourse of death" contained in some 10,000 Parisian wills made between 1550 and 1789. The first half of the book contains a general survey of the literature on death by Chaunu himself. In a similar vein is Philippe Ariès' masterful study of attitudes toward death, *L'Homme devant la mort,* which covers the whole of western Europe from antiquity to the present.

3. This study owes a considerable debt to Michel Vovelle's *Piété baroque et déchristianisation en Provence aux XVIIIe siècle.*

4. Brian Pullan, *Rich and Poor in Venice,* p. 14.

5. I have used testaments proved before the court of the *bailliage* of Grésivaudan, which can be found in the B series of the Archives Départmentales de l'Isère. A number of these documents were lost during the Revolution, so I supplemented this source with testaments proved before a lesser court, the Justice or seigneurial court, of Grenoble, cataloged under 13 B. These records are in the process of reclassification, so the catalog numbers may change.

6. I calculated the number of documents in the Grenoble archives by first counting the number of documents in each notarial register I read and by then establishing the average number of documents per register for each five-year period. I then determined the number of registers filled by Grenoble's notaries in this period by consulting the archival inventory and then multiplied the number of registers times the average number of documents for each period. To determine the percentage of wills in this output, I divided the number of wills in each notarial register I read by the number of documents in that register. My estimate of 2 percent seems reasonable, for Jean-Paul Poisson in a study of notarial archives throughout France has come up with the same figure (Jean-Paul Poisson, "La Pratique notariale aux XVIIIe siècle").

7. Of all multivariate statistical techniques, multiple regression analysis, or ordinary least squares, is the most familiar to historians and requires no explanation. However, those who would like an example of regression analysis in historical work will find J. Morgan Kousser, "Ecological Regression and the Analysis of Post Politics," a model study with a clear explanation of regression. Tobit is a related technique developed for the analysis of what are called limited dependent variables—variables such as votes, occupations, or testamentary bequests. Like regression, tobit produces coefficients that measure the positive or negative effects of various independent variables upon a dependent variable, and as in the case of regressions, we can check for the significance of these effects by examining t-statistics for the appropriate coefficients. Strictly speaking, tobit is more appropriate than regression for analyzing bequests in wills, which are either absent or positive, but never negative. Tobit also takes into account more information than regression does, for it includes both the chances that a testator makes a bequest and the size of any bequest made. The tobit estimate will therefore be the final arbiter for the effects of any independent variable. For more information on tobit analysis, see G. S. Maddala, *Econometrics* (New York, 1977), pp. 162–182,

and James Tobin, "Estimates of Relationships for Limited Dependent Variables." Particularly relevant is Philip T. Hoffman, "Wills and Statistics: Tobit Analysis and the Counter Reformation in Lyon," *Journal of Interdisciplinary History* 14 (1984): 813–834. For the use of related techniques dealing with limited dependent variables, see J. Morgan Kousser, "Making Separate Equal: Integration of Black and White School Funds in Kentucky," *Journal of Interdisciplinary History* 10 (1980): 399–428. I am indebted to J. Morgan Kousser for introducing me to tobit analysis.

8. For the economic history of Dauphiné in this period, see Léon, *La Naissance de la grande industrie* 1:93–132.

9. Here as everywhere else in this study, all figures in money amounts cited in the text and tables have been converted to constant value livres using a decennial index of grain prices in the Grenoble market established by Henri Hauser *Recherches et documents sur l'histoire des prix en France de 1500 à 1800*, pp. 370–371. Consequently, neither inflation nor deflation distorts the data. (See the note on monetary amounts at the end of the Introduction.)

10. Average Bequests to Charity: 1620–1729 (livres)

1620–1629	192
1630–1639	68
1640–1649	185
1650–1659	237
1660–1669	299
1670–1679	421
1680–1689	433
1690–1699	137
1700–1709	224
1710–1719	499
1720–1729	649
N = 2,772	

11. See Léon, *La Naissance de la grande industrie*, vol. 1.

12. When date is included as an independent variable in a regression equation for dowries, the t-statistic is only 0.589, or insignificant, indicating that there was little change in the size of dowries. In addition, there is a slight negative coefficient.

13. When the number of heirs listed in the will was put into the regression equation, the resulting t-statistic was a mere 0.17, indicating that the number of heirs had no influence on a testator's decision to make or not make charitable bequests.

14. A. D. Isère, B. 1031 (1672).

15. When family status is included in the regression equation, the resulting t-statistic is 0.40, which indicates that family status did not influence charitable giving.

16. Establishing social categories for the old regime always poses difficulties. This is especially true in the case of wills and testaments where information on wealth and income is partial or absent altogether. Consequently, I have adopted the professional categories used by the Grenoblois themselves. If a testator called himself a counselor at the Parlement, he has been coded as such and then placed in the larger category "magistrate." It should be noted that magistrates (who certainly were noble) were coded separately from the nobles who did not possess offices at the sovereign courts. Generally, the former were wealthier than the latter and of more ancient lineage. Obviously, I am held hostage by the data, for an individual might bestow upon himself a title that was much too lofty and undeserved. In a city like Grenoble where legal professions predominated, this problem is not as acute as it might be elsewhere: a man either was or was not a lawyer, a counselor, or a notary. Once one descends the social scale, however, serious problems emerge. The Grenoblois called themselves "merchants," but this vague title covered a host of different social situations. Where feasible, I have introduced as many nuances as possible, but the paucity of wills here at the bottom of the social scale makes large, aggregate categories a necessity. For example, day

laborers and simple artisans have been included in the same category because there were too few of either who made wills to constitute separate groups. In addition, very little differentiated the flax-comber and the day laborer who worked in a master flax-comber's shop. Neither owned the means of production, and each received both wages and payment in kind. Membership in a guild was not significant in Grenoble, for the guilds were notoriously weak—and nonexistent in some trades. As for women, I have used the husband's occupation as an indication of social group. Since their status was derivative in the old regime, this seems appropriate. Where a testator gives no indication of his occupation (frequently the case with women), I have simply excluded that will from the data.

17. The correlation coefficient for literacy and nobility is only 0.07; the correlation coefficient for literacy and magistrates is much higher, 0.39. The nobles were much less likely than their judicial cousins to be literate.

18. When religious giving is included as an independent variable in the regression equation for the percentage of Grenoblois making charitable gifts, the resulting coefficient is 0.173 with a t-statistic of 8.08. In other words, a Grenoblois who made a pious bequest was, all other things being equal, 17 percent more likely than his impious neighbors to remember the poor in his wills.

19. Vovelle, *Piété baroque*, pp. 55–56.

20. When all forty-odd notaries were thrown into the regression equation, only one was even marginally significant. That notary was Toscan, who served the magistrates of Grenoble. Consequently, the effects of the notary and social group are confused in this case, and the significance of the Toscan variable reflects the significance of the magistracy in religious giving.

21. When a testator's ill health is included as an independent variable in the regression equation, the resulting t-statistic is only 0.747. In other words, a testator's state of health had no effect on his decision to include or omit religious bequests in his will.

22. Despite their generic title, the *artes moriendi* were more concerned with life than death. They advised the pious to live in the fear of death and prescribed a host of spiritual exercises and devotions. In addition, Daniel Roche has estimated that 80 percent of the literate public knew of such books (Daniel Roche, "La Mémoire de la mort: Recherche sur la place des arts de mourir dans la librairie et lecture en France aux XVIIe et XVIIIe siècles"; Roger Chartier, "Les Arts de mourir [1450–1600]").

23. Natalie Zemon Davis, "Some Tasks and Themes in the Study of Popular Religion"; Robert Muchembled, *Culture populaire et culture des élites.*

24. Ariès, *L'Homme devant la mort*, p. 231.

25. A.D. Isère, B. 1011 (1661); Bonnier III E. 1.009 (5) p. 183; B. 1014 (1679); B. 1008 (1680); B. 1011 (1663).

26. A.D. Isère, B. 1008 (1639); B. 1014 (1673); B. 1012 (1667); B. 1015 (1689).

27. A.D. Isère, B. 1008 (1642).

28. A.D. Isère, B. 1016 (1697); B. 1014 (1678); B. 1015 (1684); B. 1014 (1671); Lavorel III E. 1.094 (18) p. 130v.

29. Chaunu, *La Mort à Paris*, pp. 356–359; Vovelle, *Piété baroque*, pp. 94–100.

30. Percentage of Bequests for Masses Alone

	Magistrates	Others
1620–1629	57	20
1630–1639	92	16
1640–1649	88	23
1650–1659	86	27
1660–1669	91	40
1670–1679	85	41
1680–1689	79	43
1690–1699	78	50
1700–1709	78	56

	Magistrates	Others
1710–1719	75	55
1720–1729	88	62
N = 2,772		

31. "New converts" were deducted by using the list of magistrates and nobles found in Arnaud, *Histoire des Protestants du Dauphiné* 2:436–446.

32. A. D. Isère, B. 1019 (1725).

33. Percentage of Magistrates Making Bequests for Spiritual Purposes

	For Masses	For Other Spiritual Purposes
1620–1629	57	86
1630–1639	92	92
1640–1649	88	88
1650–1659	86	86
1660–1669	91	97
1670–1679	85	85
1680–1689	79	85
1690–1699	78	81
1700–1709	78	81
1710–1719	75	81
1720–1729	88	90
N = 319		

34. In 1680, the rate of charitable giving among the magistrates was 82 percent, whereas only 79 percent of the magistrates made bequests for masses. In the following years, the rate of charitable giving was only slightly lower than the rate of giving for masses.

35. A. D. Isère, B. 1015 (1684); Dou III E. 1.182 (36), p. 33.

36. A. D. Isère, B. 1015 (1714); Aubert III E. 1.185 (36), p. 15v.

37. Michel Vovelle found that this refusal to make religious bequests and command lavish funerals constituted proof of Jansenism. He found such traces of heresy in wills from all over Provence, but prudently chose to analyze the progress of Jansenism through testaments only in the diocese of Senez where the Jansenist movement is well known and well documented (Michel Vovelle, *Piété baroque*, pp. 459–497).

38. The best source on Jansenism in Grenoble is a secret document analyzed by Maurice Virieux in "Jansénisme et molinisme dans le clergé du diocèse de Grenoble au début du XVIIIe siècle," pp. 279–319; see also Bernard Bligny, ed., *Histoire du diocèse de Grenoble*, pp. 150–153.

39. A. D. Isère, 13 B. VI 450 (1676).

40. Percentage of Rural Nobles Making Religious Bequests

1620–1629	0	1690–1699	64
1630–1639	33	1700–1709	60
1640–1649	31	1710–1719	67
1650–1659	33	1720–1729	67
1660–1669	66	1730–1739	73
1670–1679	67	1740–1749	31
1680–1689	55	N = 108	

41. A.D. Isère, Revol III E. 1.179 (16) p. 165v; Patras III E. 1.438 (4) p. 331; Blain III E. 1.001 (27) p. 229; Duclot III E. 1.229 (17) p. 3.

42. An equally impressive conversion occurred among noble officers. None of these nobles made religious bequests in the years between 1620 and 1639; by 1700 the rate had risen to 85 percent. Here Vauban's reforms and the construction of a permanent garrison at Grenoble may have helped to render these formerly young and rustic men urbane, settled, and pious Catholics.

43. In the sample of Protestant wills which will be discussed later in this chapter, 21.3 percent of the wills came from master artisans. Consequently, master artisans represent a substantial proportion of the Protestant sample and perhaps of the Protestant population as well.

44. After 1670, 26 percent of all the artisans made bequests to confraternities as opposed to only 4 percent of higher social groups. This former figure may seem small, but it represents only the beginning of a trend. The workingmen's attachment to confraternities really manifested itself in the mid-eighteenth century when between 59 and 65 percent of the male workers included legacies to confraternities in their wills (see chapter 10).

45. Bequests to parish churches represent only 9 percent of the pious bequests made after 1700.

46. Only 52 percent of the domestics serving common folk made religious bequests in the years between 1620 and 1729; over 89 percent of the domestics employed by nobles and magistrates made religious bequests.

47. For the domestics' social background, see chapter 8, which analyzes the *déclarations de grossesse* made by young servant girls.

48. Percentage of Religious Bequests Not for Masses

1620–1629	32	1690–1699	17
1630–1639	22	1700–1709	22
1640–1649	36	1710–1719	17
1650–1659	17	1720–1729	19
1660–1669	13	1730–1739	25
1670–1679	14	1740 1749	24
1680–1689	12		

49. A.D. Isère, B. 1017 (1714); Toscan III E. 1.433 (8) p. 231; Patras III E. 1.438 (28) p. 168.

50. A.D. Isère, B. 1012 (1657); B. 1018 (1721); B. 1013 (1672).

51. A.D. Isère, Chancey III E. 1.077 (8) p. 88.

52. For examples of bequests for the establishing of missions, see A.D. Isère, B. 1013 (1672); 13 B 6 473 (1685); B. 1018 (1721); B. 1014 (1676).

53. Examples of bequests for the schooling of rural youth are A.D. Isère, B. 1013 (1672); Froment III E. 1.420 (20) p. 70v; Toscan III E. 1.433 (8) p. 35.

54. A.D. Isère, Froment III E. 1.420 (20) p. 70v; A.D.B. 1016 (1682).

55. A list of such benefactors can be found in the Archives Hospitalières F. 31.

56. Pierre Chaunu, *L'Europe des deux réformes;* Jean Delumeau, *Le Catholicisme entre Luther et Voltaire;* Philip Benedict, *Rouen during the Wars of Religion;* Natalie Davis, "The Sacred and the Body Social in Sixteenth-Century Lyon."

57. Conflict between Protestant and Catholic at the Hospital General revolved around problems of financing and free access of the clergy of both faiths to the hospital wards. Bickering continued into the 1640s but ceased thereafter when Protestants no longer sought admittance to the Hospital. (See A.D. Isère, A.H.E. 6 December 19, 1639; February 14, 1653; E.5 January 23, 1639; April 10, 1639; E.6 February 14, 1653.)

58. See A.D. Isère, A.H.D. 11.

59. Pierre Bolle, "Le Camus et les Protestants," in *Le Cardinal des montagnes,* ed. Jean Godel, pp. 143–159.

60. Practitioners of all kinds of skilled trades from sculptor to stockinger appear in the Protestant sample. Rather than enumerate each profession, suffice it to say that no single trade dominates in the sample.

61. While 14 percent of the artisans in the Protestant sample were involved in glove making, only 3 percent of the Catholic artisans were a part of that trade.

62. Natalie Davis has found that many Protestants in sixteenth-century Lyon were

members of relatively new, unestablished trades. Because they were poorly integrated into the community, these artisans drifted toward Protestantism (Natalie Z. Davis, "Strikes and Salvation," in *Society and Culture in Early Modern France*).

63. Geographical Origins of Testators

	Protestant	Catholic	t-statistic
Born in Grenoble	43.7%	69.1%	−4.68
Born outside Grenoble	56.3%	30.9%	−4.68
$N = 3,402$			

64. Residence of Protestant and Catholic Testators

	Protestant	Catholic	t-statistic
Grenoble	71%	83%	−4.64
Outside Grenoble	29%	17%	−4.64
$N = 3,402$			

65. Protestants were just as anxious as their Catholic neighbors to prevent conflict within their families. Also, they frequently admonished in the most strident of tones their principal heirs to keep the faith and force others within the family to do so. All of this suggests that the pressures exerted upon Protestants could lead to conflict as easily as intimacy. A. D. Isère, Patras III E. 1.438 (19) p. 154; B. 1009 (1651); Duclot III E. 1.214 (52) p. 184; Patras III E. 1.438 (39) p. 317v.

66. A good summary of Protestant theology on death appears in Chaunu, *La Mort à Paris*, pp. 252–292.

67. Obviously, the propensity of any Protestant to make such an affirmation of faith varied with circumstances. In a study of Protestant and Catholic wills in Lyon and Nimes, Wilma Pugh has found that persecution could affect rates of charitable giving in the Protestant community. Although Professor Pugh's argument is convincing, she considers only the quantity—not the quality—of charitable giving and therefore tends to overlook the qualities which characterized Protestant beneficence whatever the pitch of persecution (Wilma Pugh, "Catholics, Protestants and Testamentary Charity in Seventeenth-Century Lyon and Nimes," *French Historical Studies* 11 (1980): 479–504). Protestant wills and testaments can certainly be used as a test of the vitality of the Protestant community, as Michel Vovelle has shown in a regrettably brief article, "Jalons pour une histoire du silence: Les Testaments dans le sud-est de la France du XVIIIe siècle," *De la cave au grenier*, pp. 387–403.

68. Natalie Zemon Davis, "The Sacred and the Body Social in Sixteenth-Century Lyon."

69. A. D. Isère, B. 1011 (1661); Blanc III E. 1.364 (29) p. 602; Patras III E. 1.439 (29) p. 602.

70. A. D. Isère, 13 B VI 610 (1728).

71. A. D. Isère, B. 1008 (1642); Aubert III E. 1.185 (48) p. 103v.

72. Arnold Van Gennep, *Le Folklore du Dauphiné* 1:179–191.

73. For examples of such bequests, see A. D. Isère, B. 1015 (1685); Duclot III E. 1.214 (48) p. 514v; Hebrail III E. 1.401 (4) p. 162v; Mailhet III E. 1.186 (16) p. 312; Marchand III E. 1.107 (11) p. 60v; Dou III E. 1.182 (25) p. 184v.

74. A. D. Isère, B. 1016 (1677).

75. A. D. Isère, Duclot III E. 1.129 (21) p. 96.

76. A. D. Isère, Rosset III E. 1.092 (21) p. 32v.

77. Percentage of Decline in Bequests for Clothing Paupers

	Urban Testators	Rural Testators
1620–1629	8	9
1630–1639	2	4
1640–1649	3	2
1650–1659	2	5

	Urban Testators	*Rural Testators*
1660–1669	3	6
1670–1679	2	9
1680–1689	0	6
1690–1699	1	2
1700–1709	1	3
1710–1719	0	2
1720–1729	0	2
1730–1739	1	2
$N = 2,772$		

78. A. D. Isère, 13 B VI 522 (1715); 13 B VI 533 (1730).
79. A. D. Isère, 13 B VI 488 (1675); B. 1020 (1723).
80. A. D. Isère, B. 1021 (1758).
81. A. D. Isère, B. 1015 (1681).
82. A. D. Isère, B. 1021 (1758).
83. A. D. Isère, B. 1014 (1678).
84. A. D. Isère, B. 1013 (1670).
85. A. D. Isère, B. 1017 (1714); B. 1015 (1656); B. 1015 (1656).
86. Recent research on the so-called feudal reaction of the late eighteenth century has established that such a reaction was hardly unique to the prerevolutionary period. A small feudal reaction occurred each time a new generation of seigneurs took power (William Doyle, "Was There an Aristocratic Reaction in Pre-Revolutionary France?" in *French Society and the Revolution,* ed. Douglas Johnson (Cambridge, 1976), pp. 3–20).
87. A. D. Isère, B. 1012 (1670).
88. Le Roy Ladurie, *Carnival of Romans,* pp. 1–59. See also Bernard Bonin, "La Vie rural en Dauphiné: 1550–1720."
89. A. D. Isère, B. 1018 (1723); B. 1012 (1670); Aubert III E. 1.185 (31) p. 169; B. 1014 (1676).
90. Evolution of Seigneurial Bequests

	Percent of Testators	*Average Size of Bequests* (livres)
1620–1629	15	73
1630–1639	15	289
1640–1649	16	187
1650–1659	17	234
1660–1669	23	388
1670–1679	28	379
1680–1689	42	168
1690–1699	28	115
1700–1709	28	333
1710–1719	31	445
1720–1729	45	262
$N = 2,772$		

91. A. D. Isère, B. 1015 (1656).
92. A. D. Isère, B. 1016 (1682).
93. A. D. Isère, A.H.F. 30–32.

CHAPTER SEVEN

1. "Avis au sujet des écoles chrétiennes," B. M. Grenoble, Fonds dauphinois, C. X. 183.

2. The little schools of Grenoble have been the subject of two articles: Yves Poutet, "Les Ecoles de la rue Saint Laurent à Grenoble, 1707–1963"; Gerard Chinéa, "L'Enseignement primaire à Grenoble sous la Révolution."

3. Traditionally, historians of the Enlightenment have believed that the philosophes wanted to enlighten the people and extend education to the masses with only slight reservations. This view is expressed in James Leith, "Modernization, Mass Education and Social Mobility in French Educational Thought, 1750–1789," in *Studies in Eighteenth Century,* ed. R. F. Brissenden (Toronto, 1973), vol. 2; Peter Gay, *The Enlightenment: An Interpretation* 2:489–499; Harry C. Payne, *The Philosophes and the People.* Recently, at least one historian has taken a quite different view of the prevailing attitude in the eighteenth century and argued that Enlightenment thinkers did not, for a variety of reasons, want to see the "people" enlightened. This interpretation appears in Harvey Chisick, *The Limits of Reform in the Enlightenment: Attitudes toward the Education of the Lower Classes in Eighteenth-Century France.*

4. B. M. Grenoble, Fonds dauphinois, D. X. 183. The pamphlets published by the Bureau des Ecoles Charitables can be found in the Fonds dauphinois of the Bibliothèque Municipale of Grenoble. The institution's account books are in the Archives Départmentales, series D. 58.

5. B. M. Grenoble, Fonds dauphinois, R. 4521.

6. B. M. Grenoble, Fonds dauphinois, X. 183.

7. The best sources on the Christian Brothers remains Georges Rigault, *Histoire de l'Institute des Frères des Ecoles Chrétiennes.* Also of interest is Yves Poutet, "L'Enseignement des pauvres dans la France du XVIIe," and *Le XVIIe siècle et les origines lasalliens* (Rennes, 1970).

8. B. M. Grenoble, Fonds dauphinois, R. 4521.

9. Rigault, *Histoire de l'Institut* 2:199.

10. B. M. Grenoble, Fonds dauphinois, R. 4521.

11. Poutet, "Les Ecoles de la rue Saint Laurent," pp. 112–113.

12. Rigault, *Histoire de l'Institut* 1:549.

13. For information on the Jesuit colleges and other secondary educational institutions, see W. Frijhoff and D. Julia, *L'Ecole et société dans la France de l'ancien régime;* François Dainville, "Effectifs des collèges et scolarité aux XVIIe et XVIIIe siècles"; and Roger Charier, M. Compère, Dominique Julia, *L'Education en France du XVIe au XVIIIe siècles.* Jean de Viguerie, *L'Institution des enfants, pp. 225–253.*

14. Rigault, *Histoire de l'Institut* 1:580–581.

15. Rigault, *Histoire de l'Institut* 2:200–207.

16. B. M. Grenoble, Fonds dauphinois, U. 3248.

17. According to the Bureau account books to be found in the Archives Départmentales de l'Isère, D. 58, the income (in livres) of the Bureau was, by decade, as follows:

1710–1719	6,218
1720–1729	5,693
1730–1739	9,012
1740–1749	9,250
1750–1759	7,786
1760–1769	6,645
1770–1779	4,537

18. A. D. Isère, D. 56 and 58.

19. Léon, *La Naissance de la grande industrie* 1:156; Pierre Barral, *Les Périers dans l'Isère au XIXe siècle d'après leur correspondance familiale.*

20. B. M. Grenoble, Fonds dauphinois, R. 9053.

21. B. M. Grenoble, Fonds dauphinois, D. X. 183.

22. A. D. Isère, 26 H. 272.

23. B. M. Grenoble, Fonds dauphinois, D.X. 183.

24. B. M. Grenoble, Fonds dauphinois, U. 3248.

25. B. M. Grenoble, Fonds dauphinois, D.X. 183.

26. A. D. Isère, 26 H. 272.

27. A. D. Isère, L. 286.

28. A. D. Isère, II. C 91; Léon, *La Naissance de la grande industrie* 1:305.

29. Lèon, *La Naissance de la grande industrie* 1:195; Léon Cote, *L'Industrie gantière et l'ouvrier gantier à Grenoble.*

30. A. D. Isère, A.H.F. 24.

31. François Furet and Jacques Ozouf have also stressed the role of the urban and rural masses in the instruction of the French and have credited these humble individuals, as much as seventeenth-century benefactors, with the growth of literacy in the old regime (François Furet and Jacques Ozouf, *Lire et écrire: L'alphabétisation des français de Calvin à Jules Ferry*).

CHAPTER EIGHT

1. A.D. Isère, A.H.E. 27 April 7, 1786.

2. A. Cugnetti, *L'Hôpital-Général de Grenoble* 2:397.

3. A. D. Isère, A.H.E. 54–135.

4. A. D. Isère, A.H.E. 203.

5. The Hospital acquired money by borrowing from a variety of individuals—for example, from the marquise d'Agoult, a noblewoman, and from Dominique Guédy, a glove-worker (A. D. Isère, A.H.E. 26). In return, the Hospital paid interest in the form of *rentes viagères*. Sometimes the Hospital also borrowed money from institutions, in particular religious institutions like the Ursulines of Briançon who provided the Hospital with 4,500 livres at 4 percent interest in 1754 (A. D. Isère, A.H.E. 26).

6. For information on most of these directors, see Pierre Léon, *La Naissance de la grande industrie* 1:156,259,279. On the business associates of the Dolle and the Raby, see Léon, *Les Dolles et les Rabys: Marchands et spéculateurs dauphinois dans le monde antillais du XVIIIe*. On the Périers, see Pierre Barral, *Les Périer dans l'Isère au XIXe siècle d'après leur correspondance familiale* (Paris: 1964).

7. On Hélie and his role in the revolt of the curés, see Michel Bernard, "Revendications et aspirations du bas-clergé dauphinois à la veille de la Révolution," p. 337.

8. Léon, *La Naissance de la grande industrie* 1:243–250; Jean-François Belhoste, *Histoire des forges d'Allevard.*

9. Pierre Vaillant, "Intellectualité d'une société provinciale à la fin de l'ancien regime: La Fondation de la bibliothèque municipale de Grenoble." A list of the members of the Académie Delphinale can be found in the Bibliothèque Municipale de Grenoble, Fonds dauphinois, R. 8706.

10. Gaspard Bovier, *Journal du séjour à Grenoble de J-J Rousseau sous le nom de Renou*, p. 19; Henri Rochas, *Bibliographie du Dauphiné* 2:172–174.

11. Stendhal, *La Vie d'Henri Brulard*, in *Oeuvres complètes*, ed. Pierre Larrive (Paris: Editions de la Pléiade, 1956).

12. The directors who accompanied Mounier and Barnave to the Assembly at Vizille were Barthélemy, Flauvan, de Legalière, Hélie, Lemaître, Barral, Pascal, Gagnon, Barthelon, Dupy, Botut, and Périer. See *Chroniques dauphinoises*, ed. François Champollion-Figeac. 2 vols. (Vienne, 1885). Vol. 1, pp. 438–441.

13. Charles Perrosier, "Correspondance d'Achard de Germane avec Monsieur de la Coste," *Bulletin de la société d'archéologie et statistique de la Drôme* 19–24 (1885–1891): 24; Rochas, *Bibliographie du Dauphiné* 1:33; Stendhal, *La Vie d'Henri Brulard*, pp. 73–137; Barral, *Les Périers de l'Isère*, pp. 33–34; François Vermale, "Le Père de Casimir Périer pendant la Révolution," *Annales de l'Université de Grenoble* 9 (1934): 22–52; Rochas, *Bibliographie du Dauphiné* 1:82–83.

14. See Daniel Roche, *Le Siècle des lumières en province: Académies et académiciens provinciaux, 1670–1789.*

15. Jean-Joseph Mounier, cited in Louis de Lanzac de Laborie, *Jean-Joseph Mounier: Un Royaliste en 1789*, p. 195.

16. Joseph Barnave, *Introduction à la révolution française*, p. 10.

17. A. D. Isère, A.H.E.28 September 6, 1787; A.H.E.23 February 21, 1763; A.H.E.3.

18. A. .D. Isère, A.H.E.20 December 21, 1761; A.H.E.26 January 29, 1781.

19. A. D. Isère, A.H.E.19 March 24, 1761; A.H.E.24 May 3, 1779; A.H.E.26 June 23, 1783; A.H.E.20 September 26, 1763.

20. A. D. Isère, A.H.E.20 September 26, 1763; A.H.E.24 February 17, 1776; A.H.E.26 January 29, 1781; A.H.E.28 November 27, 1786; A.H.E.24 January 13, 1777.

21. A. D. Isère, A.H.E.22 February 25, 1771; A.H.E.24 August 4, 1776; A.H.E.25 May 1, 1779; A.H.E.26 March 10, 1783; A.H.E.28 April 16, 1787.

22. The following analysis is based on a sample of one-half of the names inscribed in the registers F. 13 (1724), F. 17 (1731), F. 18 (1741), F. 21 (1771), F. 22 (1781 and 1791). This makes for a sample of 1,745 cases. In 1724 and 1763, the syndic just made a general survey of the inmates residing in the Hospital at the end of the year, a document different from the registers of entries, kept on a daily basis in other years. In order to simulate a series of admissions registers, the date of each case is the date of entry of that individual. Consequently, a person appearing in the general survey of 1763 but admitted in 1759 is placed under the rubric 1750–1759.

23. A. D. Isère, A.H.F. 17, p. 127; F. 13, p. 15; F. 21, p. 15; F. 13, p. 30.

24. On old age in traditional societies, see Peter Stearns, *Old Age in Pre-Industrial England and France;* also, edited by Stearns, *Old Age in Pre-Industrial Europe* (New York, 1981); Peter Laslett, "The History of Aging and the Aged," in *Family Life and Illicit Love in Earlier Generations,* ed. Peter Laslett, pp. 174–214.

25. The difficulties posed by translating old diseases into modern terminology have been explored by Jean-Pierre Peter in "Disease and the Diseased"; Peter, "Les Mots et les objets de la maladie"; Jean-Pierre Goubert, *Malades et medecins en Bretagne.*

26. There is no pattern to the individuals whom certain diseases struck. However, men tended to have had limbs amputated more frequently than women, for men account for 88 percent of the amputees. Women were more likely to have problems with their eyes, for almost 60 percent of the individuals with "bad eyes" were women. Also, almost all of the women suffering from this affliction were glove seamstresses.

27. A. D. Isère, A.H.F. 20, pp. 7, 28v, 36v, 37.

28. A. D. Isère, F. 13, p. 32; p. 38v.

29. For an insightful discussion of the reformers' hospital program, see Michel Foucault, *The Birth of the Clinic: An Archaeology of Medical Perception.*

30. The mortality rates quoted here do not generally include foundlings and other infants brought to the Hospital. These were usually registered in a separate ledger. The years between 1740 and 1749 have been excluded because the infants were included in the Hospital register in these years and therefore skew the data.

Years	Mortality Rate (%)
1700–1709	21
1710–1719	26
1720–1729	31
1730–1739	19
1750–1759	23
1760–1769	26
1770–1779	26
1780–1789	26
1790–1791	40
N = 1,745	

31. Once again infants are not included in these mortality figures, and data from 1741 have been omitted because the infants recorded in that year alone skew the data.

Years	Mortality Rate among Healthy Inmates (%)
1700–1709	24
1710–1719	18
1720–1729	14
1730–1739	15
1750–1759	17
1760–1769	4
1770–1779	6
1780–1789	6
N = 733 *	

32. A.D. Isère, A.H.F. 22. It could be argued that this change in the nature of the inmates' diseases reflects a change in diagnosis of disease. Greater precision does character- ize the nomenclature of the years after 1760, but because I have grouped diseases into ex- tremely broad categories, I do not think diagnosis determined the disease.

33. A.D. Isère, A.H.E. 21 January 5, 1767; A.H.E. 25 March 23, 1778.

34. A.D. Isère, A.H.F. 28. These bread lists are organized according to street and neighborhood. Apparently, they were made as the directors toured each quarter.

35. See chapter 5.

36. A.D. Isère, F. 28.

37. Only 38 percent of the single women were sixty-one years of age or older; 75 percent of the males were older than sixty-one years. Consequently, single women were, on the average, about forty-six years of age. They were healthier than their male counterparts too. Fifty-five percent of the single women were in good health, whereas only 45 percent of the men were sound in body.

38. All of the glove seamstresses who entered the Hospital in the late eighteenth cen- tury had impaired eyesight (A.D. Isère, A.H.F. 22).

39. The distinction between "structural" and "conjunctural" poor is that of Jean- Pierre Gutton, which has proved so useful that it has been widely adopted by historians.

40. Léon, La Naissance de la grande industrie 1:224–225.

41. Unfortunately, several sheets are missing from the 1735 capitation rolls, and 1,336 households of a total 2,163 escape scrutiny. These missing pages, however, did not concern the most impoverished areas of the city, nor have we any reason to believe that single women were not evenly distributed throughout the city at this time. In addition, no censuses exist for the latter part of the eighteenth century, so the capitation rolls, the only such tax documents ex- tant, provide the only means of determining whether the number of single women grew or diminished over the course of the century (A.C. Grenoble, CC 447 [1735] and CC 463 [1789]).

42. Of course, privileged individuals were always exempted from the capitation tax. They paid some money, but only for their domestics, and this roll is separate from the rolls dealt with here. In these documents, poverty was the only reason for exemption.

43. It is immediately obvious that the tax assessor of 1789 was much more exacting than his predecessor. He was happy to demand several pennies from individuals who fifty years earlier would have been utterly exempt. He, unlike his more charitable predecessor, granted absolute exemptions only to the most destitute. These differences in assessment tend to skew the data. In 1735, 37 percent of the Grenoblois received such exemptions; in 1789, only 18 percent received them, making a 17-point decline in poverty. This is highly unlikely given what we know about the disastrous year of 1789. When those assessed less than one livre are included among the exempted in 1789, a more reasonable and plausible picture emerges. In that year, 35 percent of the Grenoblois were assessed less than one livre

or nothing at all. Such a slight decline in impoverishment is conceivable, so those assessed a few pennies were included among the 1789 exemptees in order to compensate for the differences between the two tax collectors.

44. In 1789 the glove seamstresses were the single largest group on the list of impoverished, constituting 12 percent of those who could not pay taxes. Male glove-workers, however, were not far behind, for they constituted 9.3 percent of the impoverished. These figures reflect the importance of the glove industry in Grenoble. The rest of the occupations on the list of exempted households run the gamut from chocolate seller to flax-comber, with no particular occupation predominating.

45. A. D. Isère, A.H.F. 28.

46. Ibid.

47. Of the handful of bread recipients who were in good health, 55 percent were female and 45 percent were male.

48. A. D. Isère, A.H.F. 28.

49. These petitions are scattered throughout the G series of the Archives Hospitalières in the Archives Départementales de l'Isère. Chronologically, they stretch from 1740 to 1790, but the largest number, some sixty, come from the year 1777.

50. The petitioners were not very elevated either. Cobblers account for 7.5 percent, glove-workers for 6.8 percent, domestics 5.3 percent, chair-carriers 5.3 percent, and day laborers 16.5 percent. The occupations of the rest of the petitioners run the gamut, with a heavy concentration of midwives, for reasons that will emerge during the discussion (A. D. Isère, A.H.G. 4–16).

51. A. D. Isère, A.H.F. 11.

52. A. D. Isère, A.H.F. 16.

53. A. D. Isère, A.H.F. 9.

54. A. D. Isère, A.H.F. 15 and 10.

55. The marital status of the petitioners was as follows (%):

married male	45.1
married female	7.7
widows	23.9
unmarried males	6.8
unmarried females	12.6
children	3.9
$N = 227$	

56. Indeed, married males tended to be more numerous among the petitioners as time went by: in the years between 1780 and 1789, 60 percent of the petitioners were married men.

57. Twenty-four percent of the petitions sent to the Hospital requested that the petitioner be admitted to the institution as an inmate.

58. A. D. Isère, A.H.F. 10. The directors frequently asked that an individual wanting to end his days in the Hospital provide some money by way of compensation. Usually the directors asked for more than 5 livres a month, and the individuals who provided money were referred to as *pensionnaires*.

59. A. D. Isère, A.H.F. 14 and 16.

60. A. D. Isère, A.H.F. 8 and 10.

61. A. D. Isère, A.H.F. 11 and 16.

62. Monique Bornarel, "La Population de Grenoble 1680–1764," p. 152.

63. On the decline in real wages, see Léon, *La Naissance de la grande industrie* 1: 303–310.

64. Data on the legitimate and the illegitimate children accepted by the Hospital can be found in the G series of the Archives Hospitalières. The Hospital kept separate sets of registers, one for legitimate, another for illegitimate, and yet another for foundling children,

giving the names of the infants and the location and wages paid to their wet nurses in the countryside. Both legitimate and illegitimate children under fifteen years of age were sent to wet nurses, either to nurse or to work (A. D. Isère, A.H.G. 18–38).

65. A. D. Isère, A.H.E.23 February 13, 1774.

66. A. D. Isère, A.H.G. 32–39.

67. In 1784 the Hospital received 4,626 livres from the king; in 1785, 7,060 livres; in 1786, 8,733 livres; and in 1787, 10,267 livres. In 1785, the expenditure for children came to 14,886 livres. The king provided only 7,060 livres (A. D. Isère, A.H.E. 25).

68. Between 1769 and 1780, the Hospital admitted between 100 and 140 infants each year; in 1786 this number jumped suddenly to 170. However, the number of legitimate children admitted to the Hospital declined dramatically. In 1769, 100 infants were handed over to the Hospital by their parents. In 1789 the directors accepted only 34 such children (A. D. Isère, A.H.G. 32–39).

69. Bornarel, pp. 67–68.

70. The figure on the number of baptisms in Grenoble comes from documents from the Fonds Chaper of the Archives Départementales de l'Isère, cited in Bornarel, p. 74.

71. These peculiar tokens are interspersed in the G series of the Archives Hospitalières of the Archives Départementales de l'Isère.

72. The number of illicit children admitted by the Hospital had increased slowly since the 1760s. At that time approximately thirty infants were admitted each year. In the 1770s this figure gradually rose to thirty-seven infants, and then, in the 1780s, climbed to over fifty in 1786, only to soar to sixty-eight in 1789 (A. D. Isère, A.H.G. 32–39).

73. For illegitimacy rates in several French cities, see Jean-Louis Flandrin, *Familles: Parenté, maison, sexualité dans l'ancien société*, pp. 176–184; Edward Shorter, "Illegitimacy, Sexual Revolution and Social Change in Modern Europe," pp. 272–273; on abandonment, see Claude Delaselle, "Abandoned Children in Eighteenth-Century Paris," in *Deviants and Abandoned*, ed. Robert Forster (Baltimore, 1978), pp. 47–81.

74. Just why this was the case is not clear. The main reason a woman made a declaration was to protect herself from prosecution for infanticide in the event that her unwanted child died, a real possibility in this era of high infant mortality. Perhaps the courts prosecuted infanticide less vigorously than in the past, so that many women took the risk and saved their honor by not making a declaration. Only a thorough investigation of the judicial records, now only partly classified, would resolve this problem. In any event, a similar diminution in the number of pregnant women who made declarations appears to have occurred throughout France (Marie-Claude Phan, "Les Déclarations de grossesse en France").

75. A. D. Isère, 13 B 653.

76. A. D. Isère, 13 B 657.

77. When a certain Marie Espard claimed she did not know the name of her seducer, the directors gave her only bread until she revealed the truth (A. D. Isère, A.H.G. 9).

78. There are small differences between the declarations in the Justice and those in the Hospital. The unwed mothers who went to the Justice were older, more literate, and certainly more assertive than their hapless sisters whose infants ended up at the Hospital. Thirteen percent claimed they wanted to pursue their seducers through the court. Prostitutes also made their declarations before the Justice. So that these differences do not skew the data, I have sampled very extensively in the Justice records for the years between 1750 and 1789 to be sure that the changes I detected in these years were real and characteristic of illegitimacy as a whole in the eighteenth century.

79. Jean-Pierre Gutton has investigated this link in his insightful study of domestics, *Domestiques et serviteurs dans la France de l'ancien régime*, pp. 206–213. Sexual relations between husband and servant also constituted a frequent grounds for separation among eighteenth-century married couples (Allain Lottin, "Vie et mort du couple: Difficultés conjugales et divorces dans le nord de la France au XVIIe et XVIIIe siècles," pp. 71–72).

80. We have no way of estimating what proportion of women were domestics in eighteenth-century Grenoble. There are no censuses for the period. Capitation records lump together male and female servants, and servants themselves did not pay the capitation tax. Their masters paid for them, but these records are unhelpful. These documents contain only

the name of the master and the amount he was assessed for his servants. There is no indication of just how the assessment was arrived at and no mention of the gender of the domestics.

81. The illiteracy of the mothers reflects the general illiteracy of all women of their particular class. More interesting is the fact that they were orphaned. They shared this quality with other unwed mothers in France. In Lille, 70 percent of the single mothers had lost their parents (Allain Lottin, "Naissances illégitimes et filles mères à Lille au XVIIIe siècle," p. 20). In Aix, 50.8 percent of the unwed mothers were orphans (Cissie Fairchilds, "Female Sexual Attitudes and the Rise of Illegitimacy: A Case Study," pp. 636–637).

82. A rise in rural illegitimacy did occur in Provence (Fairchilds, "Female Sexual Attitudes," pp. 652–653). A similar increase may well have occurred in rural Dauphiné, but it is obscured by the increase in illicit unions in Grenoble.

83. The increase between the 1720s and 1780s in the percentage of women exercising urban, independent professions, including that of glove-worker, is significant: it has a t-statistic of 3.17. The decrease in the proportion of domestics is also significant (the t-statistic is 2.84). As for the percentage of women born and bred in Grenoble, here too there is a significant increase, with a t-statistic of 2.91.

84. Bornarel, pp. 103–107.

85. Pierre-François Letourneau, cited in Edouard Esmonin, "La Société grenobloise au temps de Louis XV d'après les Miscellanea de Letourneau," in *Etudes sur la France du XVIIe et XVIIIe siècles,* p. 492.

86. Lille, for example, had an illegitimacy rate of only 4.5 percent in 1740, whereas Grenoble had a rate of 8 percent as early as 1730 (Lottin, "Naissances illégitimes et filles mères," p. 290; Bornarel, p. 68).

87. A. D. Isère, G. 11; 13 B 653.

88. A. D. Isère, G. 16.

89. A. D. Isère, 13 B 657 and 654.

90. A. D. Isère, 13 B 653; 656; A.H.G. 16.

91. A. D. Isère, G. 12; 14; 13 B 657.

92. The increase in couples of equivalent social standing between 1720 and 1780 is significant (t-statistic of 2.47).

93. A. D. Isère, A.H.G. 15; 13 B 657.

94. Bridal pregnancy did rise in other parts of France. On this question, see Jean-Louis Flandrin, *Le Sexe et l'occident,* pp. 272–275.

95. A. D. Isère, 13 B 653.

96. Shorter has expressed his views in "Illegitimacy, Sexual Revolution and Social Change in Modern Europe"; "Female Emancipation, Birth Control and Fertility in Early Modern Europe," *American Historial Review* 68 (1973): 605–640; *The Making of the Modern Family.*

97. This second view has arisen largely in reaction to Shorter's interpretation. Among its proponents are Louise Tilly, Joan W. Scott, and Miriam Cohen, "Women's Work and European Fertility Patterns"; Louise Tilly and Joan W. Scott, "Women's Work in Nineteenth Century Europe," *Comparative Studies in Society and History* 7 (1975): 55–58; Fairchilds, "Female Sexual Attitudes," pp. 627–667. Though not necessarily of this school, the work of Jean-Louis Flandrin is of considerable interest, particularly his *Le Sexe et l'occident.*

98. For the English marriage market, see Lawrence Stone, *The Family, Sex and Marriage in England,* pp. 192–216.

99. The complaint that the unwed mothers had given their favors in the mercenary desire to find a "good establishment" was also voiced by the parents of unwed fathers when they found themselves saddled with an illegitimate grandchild (A. D. Isère, A.H.G. 15).

100. A. D. Isère, 13 B 420.

101. If the father's reaction is frequently overlooked, it is because it is extremely hard to know just how he dealt with his lover's pregnancy. The declarations in the Hospital archives are extremely useful in this regard, for the directors frequently noted just what had become of the father.

102. A. D. Isère, 13 B 653.

103. In 1785 the Hospital demanded that a glove-worker pay 200 livres all at once if the

institution was to assume responsibility for his illegitimate grandson (A. D. Isère, G. 15). In this instance, the Hospital seems to have adjusted its demands to the means of the man in question. Younger, less established men were asked for considerably less.

104. A. D. Isère, A.H.G. 14 and 16.

105. A. D. Isère, A.H.G. 6.

CHAPTER NINE

1. An excellent discussion of the origins of the dépôts appears in Thomas M. Adams, "An Approach to the Problem of Beggary in Eighteenth-Century France: The *Dépôts de Mendicité.*"

2. See Camille Bloch, *L'Assistance et l'état en France pendant la Révolution.*

3. The Hospital received 10,000, livres in 1750, 6,000 livres in 1752, and 6,000 livres from the revenues of the *vingtième* tax in 1767 (A.D. Isère, A.H.E. 15, 17, and 18).

4. For information on the *ateliers* and their functioning, see A.D. Isère, II C. 1010–1015.

5. M. Gueymard, M. Charvet, M. Pilot, and Albin Gras, *Statistique générale du département de l'Isère,* 3 vols. (Grenoble, 1846). Vol. 3, p. 520. An excellent discussion of the *ateliers* and their insufficiency appears in Olwen Hufton, *The Poor of Eighteenth-Century France 1750–1789,* pp. 182–193.

6. M. Gueymard, et al., *Statistique générale du départment de l'Isère* 3:520–521.

7. The confusion and ambivalence of royal administrators, even the most progressive, is discussed in Adams, "An Approach to the Problem of Beggary," pp. 122–245, 382–498.

8. A.D. Isère, II C. 1013–1015.

9. On Ducoin's lace manufacture, see A.D. Isère, L. 286.

10. A.D. Isère, II C. 1020–1023.

11. The monarchy had a special arrangement with the military police to incarcerate prostitutes found "with the troops." Grenoble was not the only dépôt to hold camp followers (see Adams, "An Approach to the Problems of Beggary," p. 117). In principle, the lieutenant of police had no authority in regard to the dépôt, but in fact he brought prostitutes to the institution with the tacit approval of the intendant and his subdelegate.

12. A.D. Isère, II C. 1020–1023.

13. An excellent source for the study of mobility would be the passports delivered by the authorities to individuals undertaking voyages outside Grenoble. Unfortunately, such passports are preserved only for the years between 1740 and 1743 (Maurice Virieux, "Les Migrations en Dauphiné").

14. The *maréchaussée* and its functions have been the subject of several local studies of which the most recent and complete is Ian A. Cameron, *Crime and Repression in the Auvergne and the Guyenne, 1720–1790.*

15. A.D. Isère, II C., 1022; Adams, "An Approach to the Problem of Beggary," pp. 74–121; "Etat des mendiants et vagabonds qui ont été renfermés dans les dépôts ... pendant l'année 1773 et les précedentes," in Hufton, *The Poor of Eighteenth-Century France 1750–1789.* Appendix 4, pp. 389–390.

16. A.D. Isère, II C. 1022.

17. The Grenoble dépôt was not the only dépôt to provide some treatment for venereal disease (Adams, "An Approach to the Problem of Beggary," p. 117). The treatment of venereal disease preoccupied the Grenoble intendant, and he solicited studies of the etiology and cure of syphilis (A.D. Isère, II C. 32). It is doubtful that the remedies provided at the dépôt actually effected a cure, but the concierge nevertheless proclaimed diseased inmates "cured" after two months (A.D. Isère, II C. 1020).

18. The abbé Montlinot, cited in Adams, "An Approach to Beggary," p. 111.

19. A.D. Isère, A.H.E. 17 April 12, 1751.

20. Monique Bornarel, "La Population de Grenoble 1680–1764," p. 77.

21. Nicole Castan, "Summary Justice," in *Deviants and the Abandoned in French Society,* p. 124.

22. No other professions predominate among the transients, but stockingers, ceramics-workers, tanners, and glove seamstresses were present in substantial numbers (A.D. Isère, II C. 1020–1023).

23. Pierre Conard, *La Grande peur en Dauphiné*.

24. Nicole Castan, "Summary Justice," p. 112. A similar argument for a slightly later period appears in Michel Vovelle, "From Beggary to Brigandage: The Wanderers in the Beauce during the French Revolution."

25. Violence was less common, but conflict was still endemic. In the late eighteenth century, disputes continued to break out, and insults continued to be hurled. Because the Grenoblois retained their prickly sense of honor, many of these cases ended up in the court, and the criminal complaint filed by a private person remained the most common sort of case. Now, however, verbal violence did not always lead to physical violence, and the Grenoblois were more likely to vent their rage in relatively private places, like their homes or stairways, than on public thoroughfares. The marketplace did remain the backdrop for some fisticuffs, but on the whole blows were less frequently exchanged than in the past.

26. Vital Chomel, ed., *Histoire de Grenoble*, pp. 205–212; Jean-Jacques Chevallier, *Barnave ou les deux faces de la Révolution*.

27. A.D. Isère, 13 B 348; Edmond Esmonin, "La Société grenobloise au temps de Louis XV d'après les Miscellanea de Letourneau," in *Etudes sur la France du XVIIe et XVIIIe siècles*, pp. 490–491.

28. On this point Grenoble was less advanced than larger cities like Toulouse where women did frequent cabarets. See Nicole Castan, *Les Criminels en Languedoc: Les Exigences d'ordre et les voies du ressentiment dans une société pré-révolutionnaire (1750–1790)*, pp. 198–199.

29. A.D. Isère, 13 B 420.

30. A.D. Isère, 13 B 424.

31. A.D. Isère, 13 B 433.

32. A.D. Isère, 13 B 430.

33. A change in the attitude of the court cannot account for the greater incidence of domestic violence in eighteenth-century criminal records. The Justice magistrates were even less inclined than their predecessors to meddle in domestic affairs. As we have seen, they would not press the demands of an unwed mother if her seducer was a married man (see chapter 8). The judges did not toy gladly with the family.

34. A.D. Isère, 13 B 415, 420.

35. A.D. Isère, 13 B 420.

36. A.D. Isère, 13 B 418, 438.

37. A.D. Isère, 13 B 424, 425, 430, 433, 438.

38. A.D. Isère, 13 B 418.

39. André Abbiateci et al., *Crimes et criminalité en France aux XVIIe et XVIIIe siècles;* Arlette Farge, *Vivre dans la rue à Paris au XVIIIe siècle;* Pierre Deyon, *Le Temps des prisons;* Yves Castan, *Honnêteté et relations sociales en Languedoc, 1715–1780.*

40. A.D. Isère, 13 B 433, 438.

41. A.D. Isère, 13 B 420, 425. On the inadequacy of rural justice, see Nicole Castan, *Justice et répression*, pp. 85–129; Olwen Hufton, "Le Paysan et la loi en France au XVIIIe siècle."

42. A redefinition of private property did lead to a seeming increase in theft in late-eighteenth-century England (Douglas Hay et al., *Albion's Fatal Tree*, pp. 1–34).

43. A.D. Isère, 13 B 425.

44. On domestics and criminality, see Jean-Pierre Gutton, *Domestiques et serviteurs*, pp. 203–206.

45. A.D. Isère, 13 B 420.

46. It is impossible to demonstrate conclusively that the Grenoblois of the eighteenth century were wealthier than their predecessors. However, an economic renaissance, amply documented by Pierre Léon in *La Naissance de la grande industrie*, had occurred in the region, and the capitation tax analyzed in chapter 8 does suggest a small, but significant increase in wealth. The reader should bear in mind that this prosperity was not shared equally by all. Some Grenoblois saw their fortunes deteriorate in the face of economic growth. Prosperity did create new forms of poverty (see chapter 8).

47. Arlette Farge, *Le Vol des aliments à Paris*, p. 233.

48. A.D. Isère, 13 B 418, 424, 430.

49. A.D. Isère, 13 B 418, 424, 435, 438.

50. A.D. Isère, 13 B 430.

51. Georges Rudé, *The Crowd and the French Revolution.*

52. A.D. Isère, 13 B 435.

53. Pierre-François Letourneau, "Miscellanea," 4 vols., Bibliothèque Municipale de Grenoble, Bd 658.

54. A.D. Isère, 13 B 418, 420, 425, 438.

55. Yves Castan has also found that judges in the late eighteenth century in Languedoc began to take into account mitigating circumstances (*L'Honnêteté et les relations sociales,* pp. 493–529).

56. A.D. Isère, 13 B 425, 435.

57. A.D. Isère, 13 B 433.

58. The general breakdown of the courts in the face of rising criminality has been described by Nicole Castan in "Summary Justice," pp. 129–138.

CHAPTER TEN

1. Archives Départmentales de l'Isère, Girard III E. 1. 432 (38).

2. A.D. Isère, Toscan III F. 1. 433 (23).

3. For an explanation of the sampling technique employed, see chapter 6. The sample consists of 1,942 wills made between the years 1730 and 1789. Wills represent about 3 percent of the documents in the notarial archives, and there are approximately 143,535 documents in the 365 registers filled between 1730 and 1789. Therefore, my sample represents about 43 percent of the total available wills. The social composition of the sample is explained in Appendix A.

4. It could also be argued that an edict promulgated in 1749, which strictly limited the size of bequests to institutions enjoying the right of *mainmorte,* produced this decline in charitable giving. Royal administrators certainly aimed at institutions like the Hospital General when they wrote the edict. But the Hospital General of Grenoble was never actually subject to the law: the Parlement of Dauphiné refused to register the edict and in 1755 obtained an outright exemption for the Hospital (A. Cugnetti, *L'Hôpital-Général de Grenoble* 2: 386–391).

5. In the 1720s the average lawyer gave his daughter a dowry of about 2,000 livres; in the 1780s he could afford to bestow upon her between 4,000 and 6,000 livres. The magistrates were able to give their daughters much larger dowries, dowries on the average of about 19,000 livres. The size of the magisterial dowries remained constant throughout the century, and some judges bestowed unprecedented sums on their daughters when they married them in Paris. The disparity between the judges' and the lawyers' dowries reflects different family policies as much as differences in income. The lawyers usually married their daughters in Grenoble to other lawyers and some merchants, which was much less ambitious and more economical than the magistrates' family policy. The reader should recall that all monetary amounts in this text and the tables have been treated to correct for inflation (see note on monetary amounts at the end of the Introduction).

6. The correlation coefficient between charitable giving and pious giving is .285.

7. In the 1720s the average religious bequest by a member of the *basoche* amounted to over 166 livres. By the 1760s the average bequest came to no more than 47 livres, and it only diminished thereafter.

8. A more detailed discussion of eighteenth-century attitudes toward death appears in John McManners, *Death and the Enlightenment: Changing Attitudes to Death among Christians and Unbelievers in Eighteenth Century France;* René Favre, *La Mort dans la littérature et la pensée française au siècle des lumières.*

9. The lawyers were somewhat more advanced than the other Grenoblois when it came to attitudes toward death, but the rest of the population was not far behind. In the 1770s only 6 percent of the Grenoblois chose a particular site for their grave, whether in a church or a cemetery, and none made any special provision for their funeral.

10. Michel Vovelle, *Mourir autrefois: Attitudes collectives devant la mort aux XVIIe et XVIIIe siècles,* pp. 139–166. Not all Grenoblois were indifferent to death or dying. A veritable obsession with premature burial gripped women and nobles and several requested that

their bodies be waked for at least forty-eight hours and observed for signs of decomposition. Rumors of a premature burial had led to a near panic in 1771 and the opening of several graves in Saint Hughes cemetery (Pierre-François Letourneau, "Miscellanea," B.M. Grenoble, Bd. 658, 4 vols.; vol. 4, pp. 1497–1501). Vovelle has found a similar phenomenon in Provence (Vovelle, *Piété baroque*, pp. 79–81).

11. Vovelle, *Piété baroque*, pp. 611–612.

12. Ibid., pp. 610–614.

13. A good summary of the debate on dechristianization appears in McManners, *Death and the Enlightenment*, pp. 440–444.

14. A.D. Isère, Toscan III E. 1.433 (13).

15. Percentage of Pious Bequests in Testaments Made by Domestics

	Domestics Serving Magistrates	Domestics Serving Commoners
1720–1729	80	50
	(2)	(5)
1730–1739	71	67
	(6)	(14)
1740–1749	85	67
	(3)	(13)
1750–1759	100	24
	(17)	(4)
1760–1769	63	55
	(11)	(8)
1770–1779	80	25
	(12)	(5)
1780–1789	87	56
	(16)	(15)

$N = 131$

16. Daniel Roche, "Les domestiques comme intermédiaires culturels," and *Le Peuple de Paris: Essai sur la culture populaire au XVIIIe*.

17. On the feminization of domestic service, see Cissie Fairchilds, "Masters and Servants in Eighteenth-Century Toulouse."

18. A similar disparity between male and female testamentary behavior occurred in both Paris and Provence (Pierre Chaunu, *La Mort à Paris*, pp. 333–336; Vovelle, *Piété baroque*, pp. 322). On women's attachment to religion in the nineteenth century, see Bonnie Smith, *Ladies of Leisure: The Bourgeoises of the Nord* (Princeton, 1982).

19. Percentage of Religious Bequests in Testaments Made by the Men and Women of the Magistracy

	Men	Women
1720–1729	87	100
	(31)	(9)
1730–1739	79	92
	(14)	(13)
1740–1749	81	92
	(16)	(13)
1750–1759	92	92
	(13)	(13)

	Men	Women
1760–1769	95	100
	(20)	(11)
1770–1779	77	100
	(13)	(5)
1780–1789	87	100
	(15)	(8)

$N = 194$

20. A.D. Isère, B. 1021; Toscan III E. 1.433 (23).

21. Edmond Esmonin has suggested that a few Grenoblois served as models for Choderlos de Laclos' novel (Esmonin, "La Société grenobloise au temps de Louis XV d'après les Miscellanea de Letourneau," in *Etudes sur la France du XVIIe et XVIIIe siècles*, pp. 491–493).

22. This new position on the aristocracy has been best stated by Guy Chaussinand-Nogaret in *La Noblesse au XVIIIe siècle. De la féodalité aux lumières*.

23. Jean Egret, *Le Parlement du Dauphiné* 1:122–204; Pierre Barral, "Un siècle de franc-maçonnerie grenobloise"; Louis Trénard, *Lyon de l'Encyclopédie au préromantisme*.

24. Michel Vovelle has also found that nobles and middle-class testators had different patterns of religious giving in Marseille, and he too stresses the differences between these two groups (Vovelle, "L'Elite ou le mensonge des mots," p. 55).

25. Recently, François Furet has stressed the unity, not the diversity, of the prerevolutionary and revolutionary elite. See François Furet, "Le Catéchisme révolutionnaire"; also *Penser la révolution française* (Paris, 1980), pp. 1–45. Furet's interpretation has acted as a necessary and welcome corrective to an older, outdated Marxist view, and it has greatly enhanced our understanding of the Revolution. Certainly, the Dauphinois elite could achieve unanimity; it did so in 1788 at the Assembly of Vizille. But the compromise proved short-lived and broke down only a few months later at the Estates of Romans (Egret, *Les Derniers Etats du Dauphiné: Les Etats de Romans*). As Furet himself has remarked, the revolutionaries spent the rest of the Revolution trying to re-create the compromise of 1789. The Dauphinois appear to be no exception, but their efforts underscore not the unity but the division between aristocrat and commoner.

26. A.D. Isère, Toscan III E. 1.433 (16), p. 37; B. 1022.

27. A.D. Isère, Toscan III E. 1.433 (23); Toscan III E., 1.433 (8), p. 19; Toscan III E. 1.433 (23), p.44.

28. Dauphiné awaits a historian of rural life on the very eve of the Revolution, but helpful indications can be found in Bernard Bligny, ed., *Histoire du Dauphiné*, pp. 248–288; Léon, *La Naissance de la grande industrie* 1:305–308; Egret, *Le Parlement du Dauphiné* 2:60; 100–103; Pierre Conard, *La Grande peur en Dauphiné*, pp. 5–37.

29. The best statement of this view and the most complete treatment of late-eighteenth-century views on poverty is Harry C. Payne, *The Philosophes and the People*.

30. On Reymond and the revolt of the curés, see Michel Bernard, "Revendications et aspirations du bas-clergé dauphinois à la veille de la Révolution," p. 337; Jean Godel, *La Réconstruction concordataire dans le diocèse de Grenoble après la Révolution;* Bernard Bligny, ed., *Histoire du diocèse de Grenoble*, pp. 165–196.

31. Abbé Reymond, *Le Cahier des curés du Dauphiné* (Lyon, 1789), p. 147; Reymond, *Le Droit des pauvres* (Geneva, 1781), p. 8.

32. Reymond, *Le Droit des pauvres*, pp. 15, 124–125.

33. Reymond, *Le Cahier des curés*, pp. 192–193; *Le Droit des pauvres*, pp. 117, 135–136.

34. Reymond, *Le Cahier des curés*, pp. 130, 149, 156; *Le Droit des pauvres*, pp. 83–84.

35. Reymond, *Le Droit des pauvres*, pp. 190–192, 196–197.

36. Antoine Achard de Germane, "Essai sur les branches de l'industrie qui convient le mieux aux cantons de la province de Dauphiné; et sur les moyens d'exciter le progrès dans l'agriculture dans ceux qui ne seroit susceptibles d'aucun genre d'industrie sans nuire au

rétablissement des bois. Mémoire couronné par la société littéraire de Grenoble dans sa séance publique de 12 mars 1789." B.M. Grenoble, V. 4731.

37. Achard de Germane, *Essai sur les moyens locaux les plus assurés et les moins dispendieux de faire cesser le fléau de la mendicité à Valence sans que les pauvres tant citoyens qu'étrangers soit moins secourus* (Valence, 1789), pp. 13, 87, 96.

38. Ibid., pp. 56, 79, 88.

39. Ibid., pp. 56, 77, 79, 81.

40. Ibid., pp. 61, 78–79.

41. Ibid., pp. 79, 83, 103–104.

42. Ibid., pp. 1, 41, 75, 80.

43. Ibid., pp. 44–50, 85, 116.

44. An insightful discussion of the philosophe's mistaken belief that French population was declining and that the countryside had insufficient labor appears in Harvey Chisick, *The Limits of Reform in the Enlightenment*, pp. 33–45; see also Payne, pp. 33–45.

45. I do not mean to challenge the notion that the Enlightenment produced real and significant improvements in the care of the poor. I do think that these changes have been exaggerated by historians and that the continuity between seventeenth- and eighteenth-century poor relief has been overlooked.

CHAPTER ELEVEN

1. Archives Communales de Grenoble, LL 7, p. 410.

2. The most important proponent of this view was Camille Bloch, whose pioneering work in this field remains the foundation for any study of poor relief during the Revolution. A good summary of Bloch's position appears in the introduction to *Assistance publique (1789–An VIII): Recueil de textes*, eds. Camille Bloch and Alfred Tuetey.

3. The proponents of this particular thesis are principally Léon Lallemand and Paturier, both rather conservative historians whose works were written at the end of the last century (Léon Lallemand, *La Révolution et les pauvres;* Louis Paturier, *L'Assistance publique à Paris sous l'ancien régime et pendant la Révolution*).

4. Two excellent studies that focus on local conditions are Colin Jones, *Charity and Bienfaisance: The Treatment of the Poor in the Montpellier Region 1740–1805;* and Alan Forrest, *The French Revolution and the Poor.* These books make considerable use of provincial archives and constitute the most sustained and insightful analyses of poor relief during the Revolution to date. They are essential to any understanding of the problem.

5. On the *ateliers de charité,* see A. D. Isère, L. 661; for the *dépôt de mendicité,* see A. D. Isère supplément, L. 51.

6. B.M. Grenoble, Fonds dauphinois, O. 850. On the election of January 1790, see Vital Chomel, ed., *Histoire de Grenoble*, pp. 226–228.

7. The Société Populaire was actually called the Société des Amis de la Constitution at this time, but its name changed as often as did the political winds during the Revolution. For the sake of clarity, I shall call it the Société Populaire, the name by which it is best known, throughout the following discussion.

8. A. C. Grenoble, LL 1, p. 28; LL 248; Roger Tissot, *La Société populaire de Grenoble sous la Révolution*, pp. 39–44.

9. B. M. Grenoble, Fonds dauphinois, O. 850.

10. A. C. Grenoble, LL 248; Egret, *La Révolution des notables: Mounier et les monarchistes*, pp. 214–215; Vital Chomel, ed., *Histoire de Grenoble*, pp. 226–230.

11. A. C. Grenoble, LL 248.

12. A. C. Grenoble, LL 2, p. 23v.

13. A. D. Isère, L 54, p. 403.

14. A. D. Isère, 1 L 1, pp. 1–2v; 1 L 2, p. 23v.

15. A. C. Grenoble, LL 2, pp. 60, 85v, 94.

16. A. C. Grenoble, LL 1, p. 136; Jean Baptiste Delhors, *Rapport sur la situation de l'Hôpital de Grenoble* (Grenoble, 1791); A. D. Isère, L 662.

17. A. C. Grenoble, LL 662; A. D. Isère, A.H., 1 L 1.

18. A. C. Grenoble, LL 2, pp. 141, 152; A. D. Isère, L 57, p. 334v; A. C. Grenoble, LL 3, p. 3.

19. Bloch, *Assistance publique (1789–An VIII),* pp. 100–111.

20. A. C. Grenoble, LL 250; LL 6, p. 107.

21. A. C. Grenoble, LL 251.

22. Ibid.

23. A. C. Grenoble, LL 250.

24. A. C. Grenoble, LL 2, p. 182; LL 3, p. 74; Auguste Prudhomme, *Le Féderalisme dans l'Isère et Francis de Nantes;* François Vermale, *Le Pain à Grenoble (1793–1796);* R. Delanchenal, *Un Agent politique à l'armée des Alpes: correspondance de Pierre Chépy (1793–1794)* (Grenoble, 1894); Chomel, ed., *Histoire,* pp. 234–240.

25. A. D. Isère, A. H. 1 L 2, p. 189v.; A. C. Grenoble LL 3, p. 198.

26. A. D. Isère, A. H. 1 L 2, p. 163v.; p. 170.

27. Ibid., p. 213.

28. A. D. Isère, A. H. 1 L 2, pp. 86, 148; 1 L 3, pp. 14, 14v, 39, 78v, 123.

29. A. D. Isère, A. H. 1 L 3, p. 124v.; 1 L 2, pp. 81v, 213v.

30. A. D. Isère, A. H. 1 L 2, p. 184v.; 1 L 3, pp. 73v, 81v.

31. A. C. Grenoble, LL 7, p. 148; LL 9, pp. 11, 70.

32. A. C. Grenoble, LL 6, pp. 78, 91, 134.

33. A. C. Grenoble, LL 3, pp. 103, 161; LL 7, p. 4; LL 8, pp. 67–72.

34. A. C. Grenoble, LL 8, pp. 67–72; LL 7, p. 148; LL 9, p. 11.

35. On the work of the Committee on Mendicity, see Camille Bloch and A. Tuetey, *Procès-verbaux et rapports du Comité de Mendicité de la Constituante.*

36. A. C. Grenoble, LL 8, p. 67.

37. A. C. Grenoble, LL 3, pp. 308, 313; LL 5, pp. 61, 222.

38. A. C. Grenoble, LL 3, pp. 198, 300, 314; LL 5, p. 220; LL 6, p. 94; LL 226; for a more detailed discussion of primary education in Grenoble during the Revolution, see Gerard Chinéa, "L'Enseignement primaire à Grenoble sous la Révolution," pp. 121–160.

39. A. C. Grenoble, LL 9, p. 62; LL 10, pp. 1, 85, LL 251.

40. A. D. Isère, A. H. 1 L 3.

41. A. D. Isère, A. H. 1 L 3, p. 191v.

42. A. D. Isère, A. H. 1 L 3, p. 192v; 1 L 4, p. 24; 1 L 3, p. 134v.

43. A. D. Isère, A. H. 1 L 3, p. 181; 1 L 4, pp. 8, 11v, 61, 106, 134.

44. A. C. Grenoble, LL 251.

45. A. C. Grenoble, LL 9, p. 149.

46. A. C. Grenoble, LL 107.

47. See Vovelle, "From Beggary to Brigandage: The Wanderers in the Beauce during the French Revolution."

48. The Hospital directors maintained that unwed mothers ceased making declarations because no one "has any faith in them anymore." But the directors' relative willingness to accept any child also discouraged the making of declarations (A. D. Isère, A. H. 1 L 2, p. 171).

49. A. D. Isère, A. H. 1 L 2, p. 171; 1 L 5, pp. 18, 99.

50. A. D. Isère, A. H. 1 L 3, pp. 59v.; 112v.

51. A. D. Isère, A. H. 1 L 4, pp. 14v, 22; 1 L 3, p. 172; 1 L 4, p. 30; 1 L 5, pp. 19v; 30v.

52. A. D. Isère, A. H. 1 L 5, pp. 98v–100.

53. A. D. Isère, A. H. 1 L 5, p. 109v; 3 L 1.

54. A. D. Isère, A. H. 3 L 2.

55. Prudhomme, *Histoire de Grenoble,* pp. 662–663.

56. Chomel, ed., *Histoire,* p. 231; on the sans-culotte movement in Grenoble, see Tissot, *La Société populaire;* Prudhomme, *Histoire de Grenoble,* pp. 628–629.

57. On the trials of women during the Revolution, see Olwen Hufton, "Women in Revolution 1789–1796," pp. 44–56. The works of Richard Cobb also provide poignant insight into the hardships endured by the poor in the Revolution; among Professor Cobb's numerous books, *The Police and the People: French Popular Protest, 1789–1820: Reactions to the French Revolution* (Oxford, 1972), and *Death in Paris, 1795–1801* (Oxford, 1978) are, perhaps, the most evocative.

58. In his study of poor relief during the French Revolution, Alan Forrest, surveying the whole of France, came to the same conclusion that the war alone cannot account for the inability of the revolutionaries to finance their relief programs; he too found that financial problems began long before the war (*The French Revolution and the Poor*, pp. 172–173).

59. Many hospitals in France had means of financing their services which were quite different from those of the Hospital of Grenoble. Many did in fact rely upon their estates for most of their income, and Revolutionary legislation consequently affected these institutions differently. For a good discussion of the differing financial practices of the hospitals in the old regime, see Forrest, *The French Revolution and the Poor*, pp. 34–51. A study of a particular institution whose fate during the Revolution was not precisely identical to that of the Hospital of Grenoble is Forrest, "La Révolution et les hopitaux dans le départment de la Gironde."

60. A. D. Isère, L 150.

61. A. D. Isère, A. H. 1 Q 2. This study is based on a random sample of one-half of the individuals whose names appear in the admission register for the Year VIII.

62. A. D. Isère, A. H. 1 Q 2.

63. A. D. Isère, L 532; L 91; L 58, p. 212.

64. A. D. Isère, A. H. 1 3 2; 1 L 14, p. 3.

65. A. D. Isère, 1 X 2; Chomel, ed., *Histoire*, pp. 260–262. On the significance of the mutual aid societies for the working-class movement, see William Sewell, *Work and Revolution*, p. 260.

CONCLUSION

1. See Mancur Olson, *The Logic of Collective Action*.

2. Samuel L. Popkin, *The Rational Peasant: The Political Economy of Rural Society in Vietnam*, pp. 13–15.

Archival Sources

ARCHIVES DÉPARTMENTALES DE L'ISÈRE (A. D. ISÈRE)

Most of the sources used in this study can be found in this archive. The series B 1004–1020 provides wills and testaments opened before the Bailliage of Grésivaudan. Series 13 B 364–438 contains the criminal records of the Justice of Grenoble, the city's primary civil and criminal court. The records of the Justice are now in the process of classification; the numbers could change. The series II C concerns the Intendancy of Dauphiné and therefore contains numerous documents of interest, in particular the records of the *dépôt de mendicité* in Grenoble. In the series III E all the registers of notaries active in Grenoble before the Revolution can be found. Series 12 H includes the records of many of Grenoble's confraternities; the documents of the Propagation, Madelines, and Orphans groups are to be found in this series, as well as the records of a number of small hospices. For the Revolution, the L series, which contains the records of the departmental and district authorities, is invaluable.

The Archives Hospitalières, a supplement to the H series, provides information on Grenoble's hospitals, in particular the Hospital General. Here one finds the deliberations of the directors, the accounts of the institution, and lists of inmates. The G series of this archive also contains many *déclarations de grossesse,* and the H series includes important information on the benefactors of the institution. The Hospital's records for the years 1790–1815 are catalogued in the supplement 1 L 1–15. The deliberations of the Revolutionary directors as well as patient-entry books can be found in this supplement.

ARCHIVES COMMUNALES DE GRENOBLE (A. C. GRENOBLE)

The municipal records for the old regime, now housed in the city hall, are indispensable for any study of Grenoble. They are catalogued under the series A.C. AA–GG and concern city council deliberations, municipal finances, education, public health, and disease. The municipal records of the Revolutionary period are in the supplement LL, and they contain the municipal government's deliberations, lists of bread recipients, and records of the *dépôt de mendicité.*

BIBLIOTHÈQUE MUNICIPALE DE GRENOBLE (B. M. GRENOBLE)

The manuscript collection of the Bibliothèque Municipale de Grenoble includes the Fonds dauphinois, a large collection of pamphlets, documents, and books concerning Grenoble and Dauphiné. Here can be found the register of the Company of the Holy Sacrament and information on Grenoble's charity schools, as well as other manuscripts relating to the history of public assistance in the city.

Selected Bibliography

Abbiateci, André; Billacois, François, et al. *Crimes et Criminalité en France aux XVIIe et XVIIIe siècles.* Cahiers des Annales 3, Paris, 1971.

Adams, Thomas M. "An Approach to the Problem of Beggary in Eighteenth-Century France: The *Dépôts de Mendicité*." Ph.D. dissertation, University of Wisconsin, 1972.

Allard, Guy. *Dictionnaire historique du Dauphiné.* Grenoble, 1697. Reprinted, Geneva, 1970.

Allier, Raoul. *La Cabale des dévots.* Paris, 1902.

———. *La Compagnie du Saint-Sacrement de Marseille: Documents.* Paris, 1909.

Ariès, Philippe. *L'Homme devant la mort.* Paris, 1977.

d'Argenson, René de Voyer. *Les Annales de la Compagnie du Saint-Sacrement.* Edited by Beauchet-Filleau. Marseille, 1900.

Arnaud, E. *Histoire des Protestants du Dauphiné.* 3 vols. Paris, 1875.

Auguste, A. *La Compagnie du Saint-Sacrement de Toulouse: Notes et documents.* Paris, 1913.

Babéry, Pierre, *L'Oeuvre de la Propagation de la Foi de Grenoble et de Lyon.* Montauban, 1913.

Barnave, Joseph. *Introduction à la révolution française.* Edited by Fernand Rudé. Paris, 1960.

Barral, Pierre. *Les Périers dans l'Isère aux XIXe siècle d'après leur correspondance familiale.* Paris, 1964.

———. "Un siècle de franc-maçonnerie grenobloise (1750–1850)." *Cahiers d'histoire* 2 (1957): 373–394.

Belhoste, Jean-François. *Histoire des forges d'Allevard.* Grenoble, 1982.

Benedict, Philip. *Rouen during the Wars of Religion.* Cambridge, 1981.

Benoist, Elie. *Histoire de l'édit de Nantes.* 3 vols. Delft, 1695.

Bercé, Yves-Marie. "Aspects de la criminalité au XVIIe siècle." *Revue historique* (1969): 33–42.

Bernard, Michel. "Revendications et aspirations du bas-clergé dauphinois à la veille de la Révolution." *Cahiers d'histoire* 2 (1956): 330–350.

Beyle, Henri (Stendahl). *La vie d'Henri Brulard*. Paris: Editions de la Pléiade, 1968.

Blanchard, Raoul. *Grenoble: Étude de géographie urbaine*. Paris, 1912.

Bligny, Bernard, ed. *Histoire du Dauphiné*. Toulouse, 1973.

———. *Histoire du diocèse de Grenoble*. Paris, 1979.

Bloch, Camille. *L'Assistance et l'état en France pendant la Révolution*. Paris, 1908.

Bloch, Camille, and Tuetey, Alfred. *Procès-verbaux et rapports du Comité de Mendicité de la Constituante*. Paris, 1911.

Bloch, Camille, and Tuetey, Alfred, eds. *Assistance publique (1789–An VIII): Recueil de textes*. Paris, 1908.

Bolle, Pierre. "Une Paroisse reformée du Dauphiné à la veille de la révocation de l'edit de Nantes: Mens-en-Trièves." *Bulletin de la société de l'histoire du protestantisme français* 112 (1965): 109–135; 231–239; 322–346.

Bonin, Bernard. "La Terre et les paysans en Dauphiné au XVIIe siècle." Ph.D. dissertation, University of Grenoble, 1980.

Bordier, Pierre-Henri. "La Compagnie du Saint-Sacrement à Grenoble, 1652–1666." Ph.D. dissertation, University of Grenoble, 1970.

———. "Le diocèse à l'arrivée de Le Camus." In *Le Cardinal des montagnes: Etienne Le Camus, évêque de Grenoble (1671–1707)*, edited by Jean Godel. Grenoble, 1974. Pp. 163–171.

Bornarel, Monique. "La Population de Grenoble 1680–1764: Étude socio-démographique." Ph.D. dissertation, University of Grenoble, 1976.

Bovier, Gaspard. *Journal du séjour à Grenoble de J-J Rousseau sous le nom de Renou*. Grenoble, 1964.

Broutin, Pierre. *La Réforme pastorale en France*. Paris, 1965.

Burke, Peter. *Popular Culture in Early Modern Europe*. New York, 1979.

Cameron, Ian A. *Crime and Repression in the Auvergne and the Guyenne, 1720–1790*. Cambridge, 1981.

Castan, Nicole. "Summary Justice." In *Deviants and the Abandoned in French Society*, edited by Robert Foster. Baltimore, 1978. Pp. 111–157.

———. *Les Criminels de Languedoc: Les Exigences d'ordre et les voies du ressentiment dans une société pré-révolutionnaire (1750–1790)*. Toulouse, 1980.

———. *Justice et répression en Languedoc à l'époque des lumières*. Paris, 1980.

Castan, Yves. *Honnêteté et relations sociales en Languedoc, 1715–1780*. Paris, 1974.

Chartier, Roger. "Les Arts de mourir (1450–1600)." *Annales* 31 (1976): 51–75.

Chartier, R.; Compère, M.; and Julia, Dominique. *L'Education en France du XVIe au XVIIIe siècles*. Paris, 1976.

Chaunu, Pierre. *L'Europe des deux réformes*. Paris, 1981.

———. *La Mort à Paris aux XVIe, XVIIe et XVIIIe siècles*. Paris, 1978.

Chaussinand-Nogaret, Guy. *La Noblesse au XVIIIe siècle. De la féodalité aux lumières*. Paris, 1976.

Chevallier, Jean-Jacques. *Barnave ou les deux faces de la Révolution*. Paris, 1936.

Chill, Emmanel. "The Company of the Holy Sacrament, 1660–1666: Social Aspects of the French Counter-Reformation." Ph.D. dissertation, Columbia University, 1960.

Chinéa, Gerard. "L'Enseignement primaire à Grenoble sous la Révolution." *Cahiers d'histoire* 17 (1972): 121–160.

Chisick, Harvey. *The Limits of Reform in the Enlightenment: Attitudes toward the Education of the Lower Classes in Eighteenth-Century France.* Princeton, 1981.

Chomel, Vital, ed. *Histoire de Grenoble.* Toulouse, 1976.

Chorier, Nicolas. *Histoire générale du Dauphiné.* 2 vols. Lyon, 1672. Reprinted, Grenoble, 1971.

Cobb, Richard. *The Police and the People: French Popular Protest, 1789–1820.* Oxford, 1970.

Conard, Pierre. *La Grande peur en Dauphiné.* Paris, 1904.

Cote, Léon. *L'Industrie gantière et l'ouvrier gantier à Grenoble.* Paris, 1903.

Cugnetti, A. *L'Hôpital-Général de Grenoble.* 2 vols. Grenoble: Presses Universitaires de Grenoble, 1980.

Dainville, François. "Effectifs des colleges et scolarité aux XVIIe et XVIIIe siècles." *Population* 10 (1955): 455–488.

Davis, Natalie Zemon. "The Sacred and the Body Social in Sixteenth-Century Lyon." *Past and Present* 90 (1981): 40–70.

———. *Society and Culture in Early Modern France.* Stanford, 1980.

———. "Some Tasks and Themes in the Study of Popular Religion." In *The Pursuit of Holiness in Late Medieval and Renaissance Religion,* edited by Charles Trinkhaus and Heiko Oberman. Leiden, 1974. Pp. 307–336.

De Certeau, Michel. "Politique et Mystique, René d'Argenson." *Revue d'ascetique et de mystique* 39 (1963): 45–82.

Delumeau, Jean. *Le Catholicisme entre Luther et Voltaire.* Paris, 1971.

Deyon, Pierre. *Le Temps des prisons.* Paris, 1979.

Douen, Olivier. *La Révocation de l'édit de Nantes à Paris.* 2 vols. Paris, 1894.

Duby, Georges, ed. *Histoire de la France urbaine.* 3 vols. Paris, 1981.

Dufayard, Charles. *Le Connétable de Lesdiguières.* Paris, 1898.

Egret, Jean. *Les Derniers Etats du Dauphiné: Les Etats de Romans.* Grenoble, 1942.

———. *Le Parlement du Dauphiné et les affaires publiques dans la deuxième moitié du XVIIIe siècle.* 2 vols. Grenoble, 1942.

———. *La Révolution des notables: Mounier et les monarchistes.* Paris, 1950.

Esmonin, Edmond. *Etudes sur la France du XVIIe et XVIIIe siècles.* Paris, 1964.

Fairchilds, Cissie. "Female Sexual Attitudes and the Rise of Illegitimacy: A Case Study." *Journal of Interdisciplinary History* 8 (1974): 627–667.

———. "Masters and Servants in Eighteenth-Century Toulouse." *Journal of Social History* 12 (1979): 368–393.

———. *Poverty and Charity in Aix-en-Provence.* Baltimore, 1976.

Farge, Arlette. *Le Vol des aliments à Paris.* Paris, 1978.

———. *Vivre dans la rue à Paris au XVIIIe siècle.* Paris, 1979.

Favre, René. *La Mort dans la littérature et la pensée française au siècle des lumières.* Paris, 1979.

Flandrin, Jean-Louis. *Familles: Parenté, maison, sexualité dans l'ancien société.* Paris, 1976.

———. *Le Sexe et l'occident.* Paris, 1981.

Forrest, Alan. "La Révolution et les hôpitaux dans le département de la Gironde." *Annales du Midi* 86 (1974): 381–402.

————. *The French Revolution and the Poor.* New York, 1981.

Forster, Robert. *The Nobility of Toulouse in Eighteenth-Century France.* Baltimore, 1960.

Foucault, Michel. *The Birth of the Clinic: An Archaeology of Medical Perception.* Translated by John Hurley. New York, 1977.

————. *Madness and Civilization.* Translated by Richard Howard. New York, 1965.

Frijhoff, W., and Julia, D. *L'Ecole et société dans la France de l'ancien régime.* Paris, 1975.

Furet, François. "Le catéchisme révolutionnaire." *Annales* 27 (1971): 255–289.

————. *Penser la Révolution française.* Paris, 1978.

Furet, François, and Ozouf, Jacques. *Lire et écrire: L'alphabétisation des français de Calvin à Jules Ferry.* 2 vols. Paris, 1977.

Garden, Maurice. *Lyon et les lyonnais au XVIIIe siècle.* Paris, 1970.

Gay, Peter. *The Enlightenment: An Interpretation.* 2 vols. New York, 1966, 1969.

Geisendorf, P-G. "Les Conséquences démographiques de la révocation de l'édit de Nantes en Dauphiné." *Cahiers d'histoire* 6 (1961): 245–264.

Giraud, Marcel. "Crise de conscience et d'autorité à la fin du règne de Louis XIV." *Annales* 7 (1952): 172–203.

Godel, Jean. *La Réconstruction concordataire dans le diocèse de Grenoble après la Révolution.* Grenoble, 1968.

————, ed. *Le Cardinal des montagnes: Etienne Le Camus, évêque de Grenoble (1671–1707).* Grenoble, 1974.

Goubert, Jean-Pierre. *Malades et médecins en Bretagne.* Paris, 1974.

Guigues, Georges. *Les Papiers des dévots de Lyon, 1630–1731.* Lyon, 1922.

Gutton, Jean-Pierre. *Domestiques et serviteurs dans la France de l'ancien régime.* Paris, 1981.

————. *L'État et la mendicité dans la première moitié du XVIIIe siècle: Auvergne, Beaujolais, Forez, Lyonnais.* Lyon, 1973.

————. *La Société et les pauvres en Europe (XVIe–XVIIIe siècles).* Paris, 1974.

————. *La Société et les pauvres: L'Exemple de la généralité de Lyon.* Paris, 1971.

Hauser, Henri. *Recherches et documents sur l'histoire des prix en France de 1500 à 1800.* Paris, 1936.

Hay, Douglas; Linebaugh, Peter; Rule, John; Thompson, E. P.; Winslow, Cal. *Albion's Fatal Tree.* New York, 1975.

Hill, Christopher. *Society and Puritanism in Pre-revolutionary England.* New York, 1965.

Hoffman, Philip T. *Church and Community in the Diocese of Lyon 1500–1789.* New Haven, 1984.

Hufton, Olwen. *Bayeux in the Late Eighteenth Century: A Social Study.* London, 1967.

————. "Begging, Vagrancy, Vagabondage and the Law: An Aspect of the Problem of Poverty in Eighteenth-Century France." *European Studies Review* 2 (1972): 97–123.

————. "Le paysan et la loi en France au XVIIIe siècle." *Annales* 38 (1983): 679–701.

————. *The Poor of Eighteenth-Century France 1750–1789.* Oxford, 1974.

————. "Women in Revolution 1789–1796." *Past and Present* 53 (1971): 90–108.

Johnson, Douglas, ed. *French Society and the Revolution.* Cambridge, 1976.

Jones, Colin. *Charity and Bienfaisance: The Treatment of the Poor in the Montpellier Region 1740–1805.* Cambridge, 1983.

Jordan. T. K. *Philanthropy in England 1480–1660.* New York, 1958.

Joret, Charles. "Le Père Guévarre et les bureaux de charité." *Annales du Midi* 1 (1889): 340–393.

Kaplan, Steven L. *Bread, Politics and Political Economy in the Reign of Louis XV.* The Hague, 1976.

Kaplow, Jeffry. *The Names of Kings: The Parisian Laboring Poor in the Eighteenth Century.* New York, 1972.

Kingdon, Robert M. "Social Welfare in Calvin's Geneva." *American Historical Review* 76 (1971): 50–70.

Kousser, J. Morgan. "Ecological Regression and the Analysis of Post-Bellum Politics." *Journal of Interdisciplinary History* 4 (1973): 237–262.

Laborie, Louis de Lanzac de. *Jean-Joseph Mounier: Un Royaliste en 1789.* Paris, 1887.

La Croix, Antoine. "Claude Brosse et le procès des tailles." *Bulletin de la société archéologique et statistique de la Drôme* 31 (1887): 181–190, 388–396; 32(1888): 54–68, 142–160, 363–371; 33(1889): 75–80.

Ladurie, Emmanuel Le Roy. *The Carnival of Romans.* Translated by Mary Feeney. New York, 1981.

Lagier, Abbé. "La Compagnie du Saint-Sacrement de Grenoble." *Bulletin de la société d' archéologie et de statistique de la Drôme* 50–51 (1916).

Lallemand, Léon. *Histoire de la charité.* 3 vols. Paris, 1906.

———. *La Révolution et les pauvres.* Paris, 1898.

Laslett, Peter. *Family Life and Illicit Love in Earlier Generations.* Cambridge, 1977.

Le Bras, Gabriel. *Etudes de sociologie religieuse.* Paris, 1956.

Léon, Pierre. *Les Dolles et les Rabys: Marchands et spéculateurs dauphinois dans le monde antillais du XVIIIe.* Paris, 1963.

———. *La Naissance de la grande industrie en Dauphiné.* 2 vols. Paris, 1954.

Lougee, Carolyn. *Le Paradis des femmes: Women, Salons, and Social Stratification in Seventeenth-Century France.* Princeton, 1976.

Lottin, Allain. "Naissance illégitimes et filles mères à Lille au XVIIIe siècle." *Revue d'histoire moderne et contemporaine* 7 (1970): 1–25.

———. "Vie et mort du couple: Difficultés conjugales et divorces dans le nord de la France au XVIIe et XVIIIe siècles." *XVIIe siècle* 102–103 (1974): 65–80.

McCloy, Shelby T. *Government Assistance in Eighteenth-Century France.* Durham, N.C., 1946.

McManners, John. *Death and the Enlightenment: Changing Attitudes to Death among Christians and the Unbelievers in Eighteenth-Century France.* New York, 1981.

Moeller, Bendt. *Reichstadt und Reformation.* Gütersloh, 1962.

Mousnier, Roland. *Les Institutions de la monarchie absolue.* 2 vols. Paris, 1978.

———. "Recherches sur les soulèvements populaires en France avant la Fronde." *Revue d'histoire moderne et contemporaine* 5 (1958): 81–113.

Muchembled, Robert. *Culture populaire et culture des élites.* Paris, 1978.

Muston, Alexis. *Histoire populaire des Vaudois.* Paris, 1862.

Olson, Mancur. *The Logic of Collective Action.* Cambridge, Mass., 1956.

Orcibal, Jean. *Louis XIV et les protestants.* Paris, 1951.

Paturier, Louis. *L'Assistance publique à Paris sous l'ancien régime et pendant la Révolution.* Paris, 1897.

Payne, Harry C. *The Philosophes and the People.* New Haven, 1976.

Peristiany, J. G., ed. *Honor and Shame: The Values of Mediterranean Society.* London, 1965.

Pérouas, Louis. *Le Diocèse de La Rochelle de 1648–1724: Sociologie et pastorale.* Paris, 1964.

Peter, Jean-Pierre. "Disease and the Diseased." In *Man and Biology in History,* edited by Robert Forster and Orest Ranum. Baltimore, 1975. Pp. 81–124.

––––––. "Les Mots et les objects de la maladie." *Revue historique* 499 (1971): 21–38.

Phan, Marie-Claude. "Les Déclarations de grossesse en France (XVIe-XVIIIe siècles): Essai institutionel." *Revue d'histoire moderne et contemporaine* 7 (1975): 61–88.

Poisson, Jean-Paul. "La Pratique notariale au XVIIIe siècle." *Revue d'histoire économique et sociale* 50 (1980): 231–254.

Popkin, Samuel. *The Rational Peasant: The Political Economy of Rural Society in Vietnam.* Berkeley, 1979.

Porchnev, Boris. *Les Soulèvements populaires en France de 1623 à 1648.* Paris, 1963.

Poutet, Yves, "Les Ecoles de la rue Saint Laurent à Grenoble, 1707–1963." *Procès-verbaux mensuels de la société dauphinoise d'ethnologie et d'archéologie* 323–334 (1963–1964): 44–113.

––––––. "L'Enseignement des pauvres dans la France du XVIIe." *XVIIe siècle* 90–91 (1971): 33–48.

Prudhomme, Auguste. "Etudes historiques sur l'assistance publique à Grenoble." *Bulletin de l'académie delphinale* 9 (1985).

––––––. *Le Fédéralisme dans l'Isère et Francis de Nantes.* Grenoble, 1908.

––––––. *Histoire de Grenoble.* Grenoble, 1898.

Pugh, Wilma. "Protestant and Catholic Testamentary Charity in the Seventeenth Century." *French Historical Studies* 12 (1980): 1–24.

Pullan, Brian. *Rich and Poor in Venice.* Cambridge, 1971.

Rabb, T. K. *The Struggle for Stability in Early Modern Europe.* New York, 1975.

Rigault, Georges. *Histoire de l'Institut des Frères des Ecoles Chrétiennes.* 2 vols. Paris, 1937.

Rochas, Henri. *Bibliographie du Dauphiné.* 2 vols. Paris, 1856.

Roche, Daniel. "Les domestiques comme intermédiaires culturels." In *Les Intermédiaires culturels: Actes du colloque d'Aix-en-Provence.* Aix-en-Provence, 1981.

––––––. "La Mémoire de la mort: Recherches sur la place des arts de mourir dans la librairie et lecture en France aux XVIIe et XVIIIe siècles." *Annales* 31 (1976): 76–119.

––––––. *Le Peuple de Paris: Essai sur la culture populaire au XVIIIe siècle.* Paris, 1981.

––––––. *Le Siècle des lumières en province: Académies et académiciens provinciaux, 1670–1789.* Paris, 1908.

Rossiaud, Jacques. "Prostitution, Youth and Society in the Towns of Southeastern

France in the Fifteenth Century." In *Deviants and Abandoned,* edited by Robert Forster and Orest Ranum. Baltimore, 1978. Pp. 1–43.

Rudé, Georges. *The Crowd and the French Revolution.* Oxford, 1959.

Sauvan-Richou, Madeline. "La Révocation de l'édit de Nantes à Grenoble." *Cahiers d'histoire* 1 (1956): 147–171.

Sewell, William. *Work and Revolution.* Cambridge, 1981.

Shorter, Edward. "Illegitimacy, Sexual Revolution and Social Change in Modern Europe." *Journal of Interdisciplinary History* 2 (1971): 237–272.

_____. *The Making of the Modern Family.* New York, 1975.

Solé, Jacques. "Lectures et classes populaires à Grenoble au XVIIIe siècle: Le Temoignage des inventaires après décès." In *Images du peuple au XVIIIe siècle,* edited by Henri Coulet. Paris, 1973. Pp. 95–102.

_____. "Passion charnelle et société urbaine d'ancien régime: Amour vénal, amour libre et amour fou à Grenoble au milieu du règne Louis XIV." *Annales de la faculté des lettres et sciences humaines, Université de Nice* 9–10 (1969): 211–232.

Stearns, Peter. *Old Age in Pre-Industrial England and France.* New York, 1979.

Stone, Lawrence. *The Family, Sex and Marriage in England.* New York, 1978.

Taylor, Judith. "From Proselytizing to Social Reform: Three Generations of French Female Teaching Congregations." Ph.D. dissertation, Arizona State University, 1980.

Terrebasse, Henri. *Notes et documents pour servir à l'histoire des protestants du Dauphiné: Les Maisons de la Propagation de la Foi.* Lyon, 1890.

Thomas, Keith. *Religion and the Decline of Magic.* New York, 1971.

Tilly, Charles, ed. *Historical Studies in Changing Fertility.* Princeton, 1978.

Tilly, Louise; Scott, Joan W.; and Cohen, Miriam. "Women's Work and European Fertility Patterns." *Journal of Interdisciplinary History* 7 (1976): 447–476.

Tissot, Roger. *La Société populaire de Grenoble sous la Révolution.* Grenoble, 1910.

Tobin, James. "Estimates of Relationships for Limited Dependent Variables." *Econometrica* 26 (1958): 24–36.

Trénard, Louis. *Lyon de l'Encyclopédie au préromantisme.* 2 vols. Paris, 1958.

Trexler, Richard. *Public Life in Florence.* New York, 1980.

Vaillant, Pierre. "Intellectualité d'une société provinciale à la fin de l'ancien régime: La Fondation de la bibliothèque municipale de Grenoble." *Cahiers d'histoire* 8 (1963): 280–301.

Van Doren, Scott. "Revolt and Reaction in the City of Romans: 1580." *Sixteenth Century* 5 (1974): 70–100.

_____. "War, Taxes and Social Protest: The Challenge to Authority in Sixteenth Century Dauphiné." Ph.D. dissertation, Harvard University, 1970.

Van Gennep, Arnold. *Le Folklore du Dauphiné.* 2 vols. Paris, 1932.

Vermale, François. *Le pain à Grenoble (1793–1796).* Paris, 1945.

Viguerie, Jean de. *L'Institution des enfants: L'Education en France, XVIe–XVIIIe siècles.* Paris, 1978.

Virieux, Maurice. "Jansénisme et molinisme dans le clergé du diocèse de Grenoble au début du XVIIIe siècle." *Revue d'histoire de l'église de France* 60 (1974): 279–319.

_____. "Les Migrations en Dauphiné." *Evocations* 3 (1978): 97–114.

Vogler, Bernard. "Attitudes devant la mort et cérémonies funèbres dans les églises protestantes rhénanes vers 1600." *Archives des sciences sociales des religions* 33 (1975): 139–156.

Vovelle, Michel. *De la cave au grenier.* Paris, 1980.

———. "L'Elite ou le mensonge des mots." *Annales* 29 (1974): 33–55.

———. "From Beggary to Brigandage: The Wanderers in the Beauce during the French Revolution." In *New Perspectives on the French Revolution,* edited by Jeffry Kaplow. New York, 1965. Pp. 287–304.

———. *Mourir autrefois: Attitudes collectives devant la mort aux XVIIe et XVIIIe siècles.* Paris, 1974.

———. *Piété baroque et déchristianisation en Provence aux XVIIIe siècle.* Paris, 1973.

Wailly, Natalis de. *Mémoire sur les variations de la livre tournois depuis le règne de Saint Louis jusqu'à l'établissement de la monnaie décimale.* Mémoire de l'Institut impériale de France, Académie des inscriptions et belles lettres, vol. 21. Paris, 1857.

Weissman, Ronald. *Ritual Brotherhood in Renaissance Florence.* New York, 1982.

Index

Abortion, 38; methods of, 99; prevention of, 38, 56; recommended by unwed fathers, 99, 212

Absentee landlords, bequests by, 152–55

Académie Delphinale, 173; and Enlightenment ideas on poor relief, 258, 261

Académies de tabac, prostitutes in, 49, 52, 57

Achard de Germane, Antoine, 272, 295; on the causes and remedies for poverty, 261–65; Enlightenment views on poverty expressed by, 258, 261–66; on self-interest and poor relief, 263–64, 265, 302

Adolescents: begging by, 102; at the Hospital General, 178; in the labor force, 107; violent crime by, 45–46

Age: of beggars, 102; of bread recipients, 108, 185–86; of *dépôt de mendicité* inmates, 224, 225; of Hospital General inmates, 177–79, 277, 292, 293; and the propensity for poverty, 296

Agricultural labor, 103; and Enlightenment views on the causes of poverty, 261–62

Alcohol, crime induced by, 46, 237. *See also* Cabarets; Taverns

Allevard foundries, 15, 173

Almsgiving: for the confinement of the poor, 88; criteria for, 31; Enlightenment criticism of, 259, 260, 262, 263; to the Hospital General, 169; increase in, 84; opposition to, 33; during the Revolution, 270; in testamentary bequests, 149–51

Altruism: cultural and religious differences in, 123–37; indicators of, 118, 120–23

Apprentices, 42, 45

Archers, 101; compared with the *maréchaussée,* 220, 223; defined, 100

Aristocracy: Counter Reformation Catholicism supported by, 252–55; libertines among, 58–59, 253; reform by, 254; religious and social differences with the *basoche,* 254–57; seventeenth-century charity dominated by, 296–97. *See also* Judicial elite; Nobility

Artisans, 80; Jesuit associations of, 249; Protestant testamentary bequests by, 139, 140; religious giving by, 131–34; welfare for the legitimate children of, 196, 197–98

Ateliers de charité: defined, 217, 268; enlarged during the Revolution, 269; Enlightenment views on, 259, 260, 263, 265; and the genesis of national welfare, 217

Attitudes toward the poor, 2, 3; changes in, 4–5, 82, 91–92, 110–11; compassionate, 90–92, 104; crime and sin predominant in, 34–39, 58, 59, 68, 90, 92, 258; deserving vs. the undeserving poor in, 31; divergency between the aristocracy and the *basoche* in, 254–57; and elite personal relationships with individual paupers, 25, 62, 63, 77, 104, 192, 297; idleness and laziness of paupers prominent in, 34, 90, 259, 260, 261–65; indicated in the goals of charitable education, 160, 162, 164–65,

166; punitive vs. humane viewpoints in, 82, 86, 90–92; reduced role of crime and sin in, 92–100; reflected in the attempt to confine paupers, 31, 33–34, 62, 76–77, 90; in the seventeenth century, 58–64; in women's confraternities, 24–26

Bally de Montcarra, Sebastien Flodard de, 253, 255
Baptism, 35, 199; of illegitimate children, 52, 318n56
Barnave, Joseph, 174
Barnave the lawyer, 270; last will of, 254–55
Barral, Joseph Marie, marquis de Montferrat, 270; career of, 272, 279; political ostracism of, 295
Barral, Charles Gabriel Justin de, marquis de Rochechinard, 173; last will of, 254–57
Basoche, 23; charitable bequests by, 121, 241–42; conflicts with the aristocracy, 254–57; defined, 16; reduced pious bequests by, 245–48; religious bequests by, 130; secular social ethic of, 254–55, 257; seigneurial paternalism rejected by, 256. See also Lawyers
Bastards, 54; increased number of, 95–97. See also Illegitimate children
Beggars, 100–104; age of, 102; geographic origins of, 101–2; number of, 101; occupations of, 101, 103; recidivism rates of, 102; registers of, 82. See also Attitudes toward the poor; Confinement of the poor; Dépôt de mendicité; Paupers
Begging: attempted abolition of, 17, 28, 31–34, 86, 88, 91–92, 111; and eligibility for free bread, 105, 111, 191–92; Enlightenment views on the causes and remedies for, 258–60, 261–65; interaction with mobility, 219, 220–21, 222–25; and laws on the confinement of the poor, 86, 91–92, 100, 104, 217, 220, 259, 260. See also Poverty
Begue, Barbe, 110
Belay, Suzanne, 179–80
Benedict, Philip, 137
Benefactors, new types of, 85, 87, 92; for charitable education, 163–64; at the Hospital General, 171–74, 297; social status of, 297
Beneficence: social roots of, 65; violent methods for, 73–74, 76–77. See also Poor relief
Beyle, Henri (Stendhal), 11, 172
Bicêtre. See Dépôt de mendicité

Bishop of Grenoble, 12, 19; charitable institutions supported by, 83; and corruption among the clergy, 36; diocese of, 16; role at the Hospital General, 85. See also Le Camus, Etienne
Blasphemy: by the aristocracy, 59; by the common people, 42, 57–58
Bonne, François de. See Lesdiguières, duc de
Bonnets Rouges, 278–79, 289
Bourgeois: charitable bequests by, 121–22, 241–42, 243; and the emergence of new types of benefactors, 297; poverty among, 110; testamentary bequests to the rural poor by, 152
Bove, Caze de la, 218, 269; midwifery course established by, 292
Bovier, Gaspard, 172, 173, 174, 184
Bread distribution, 104–11, 182–92; cessation of, 285; to discourage begging, 111; eligibility requirements for, 105, 111, 191; by the Hospital General, 104–11, 182–92, 215, 276, 281, 284–85; Jacobin program for, 282, 284
Bread recipients: changes among the poor reflected by, 182–92; characteristics of, 104–10; increase of women among, 186–91; lists of, 82, 183; reduced number of, 183
Brothers of Charity, 32, 85, 292
Brothers of the Holy Sacrament. See Company of the Holy Sacrament
Bureaucratic poor relief, 82, 192; development of, 104, 297–98
Bureau de Bienfaisance, 284, 285
Bureau des Ecoles Charitables: Christian Brothers as the teachers for, 161–63; establishment of, 159, 160; social composition of, 160, 163–64
Bureau des Pauvres, 17
Bureaux de charité: Enlightenment views on, 259–60; in parishes, 110

Cabale des dévots, La (Raoul Allier), 28
Cabarets: closed during the Revolution, 283; violence in, 227–28. See also Taverns
Cachots, 175
Caisse des Pauvres, 270, 271
Canel, Claude, canon of Saint André: career of, 85, 88, 160, 317n13; will of, 129, 130
Capitation tax, 189–90, 273
Card-making, 104, 107
Carpenters, 228, 294
Catholicism, 3; and bequests for Catholic

masses, 113, 127–29, 135, 322n30, 323n33; charity inspired by, 28, 30–31, 64, 301–2; conflicting types of spirituality in, 250–51, 254; and the decline of religious giving, 247–52; vs. Protestantism, 12, 28, 68–77. *See also* Counter Reformation Catholicism

Catholic testamentary bequests, compared with Protestant bequests, 137–49

Celibacy, violations of, 36, 57

Ceramic workers, 214

Chambre de l'Edit: described, 15, 309n17; suppression of, 66

Chambre des Comptes, 12; charity financed by, 18; Company of the Holy Sacrament members in, 30; described, 15, 309n18

Chanrion, Joseph, 279, 284

Charitable bequests in the eighteenth century, 239–66 passim; compared with the decline of pious bequests, 244–55; compared with family bequests, 239, 240, 244; decline in, 242–44; by social groups, 241–43. *See also* Religious bequests

Charitable bequests in the seventeenth century, 113–56 passim; compared with family bequests, 114, 118, 120, 135, 144, 146; compared with the growth of religious giving, 123–37; increase in, 117–23; influence of social status and occupation on, 120–23, 131–37, 138–44

Charity: confinement of the poor as the focus of, 3, 17–18, 28, 31–34, 62, 75, 76, 81, 82, 91–92, 100; evolution of, 4, 6, 18–19, 20, 31–34, 82, 91–92, 164, 215; increased during the age of transition, 82–92; by the judicial elite, 18–19, 67, 84–85, 296–97 (*see also* Magistrates); misery as the focus of, 90–91; vs. popular culture, 60–62, 70, 72–73, 78–79, 133–35, 163, 164, 296; religious motivations for, 19, 23–26, 34–35, 74–76, 89, 147, 160, 162–63; seventeenth century social roots of, 65; by women's confraternities, 20–26. *See also* Confraternities; Paternalism

Children: abandonment of, 38–39, 177, 195, 199; as beggars, 102; labor by, 107, 165–66; legitimate, 177–78; of paupers, 107; petitions for the welfare of, 195–98. *See also* Foundling children; Illegitimate children; Orphans, illegitimate children by

Children, Protestant: abduction and

incarceration of, 65, 76; and the rationale of paternalistic charity, 78

Christian Brothers, 137; charitable education by, 161–63

Church: corruption of, 35–36, 57; Enlightenment views on the redistribution of the wealth of, 259–60; reform of, 260; testamentary bequests to, 135–36; wealth of, 16–17. *See also* Catholicism; Clergy; Religious bequests

Civil Constitution of the Clergy, 271

Clergy, 12; bequests to, 113, 253; in the Company of the Holy Sacrament, 29–30; corruption among, 35–36, 57; on the governing board of the Hospital General, 85, 173; as intermediaries for welfare petitioners, 194–95; medical care by, 85–86; and the "revolt of the curés," 173, 258; wealth of, 16–17. *See also* Parish priests

Clothing: bequested to the poor, 150–51, 325n77; distributed to the poor, 31

Cobblers, 57–58

Committee of Public Safety, 279

Committee on Mendicity, 269; principles of, 282

Community: and individual religious salvation, 78, 135, 302; solidarity of, strengthened by bequests to the poor, 149–56 passim

Company of the Holy Sacrament, 6, 26, 27–64, 111; attitudes of, toward crime and sin, 33–39 passim, 40, 41, 45, 52, 58, 59, 95; compared with Congregation for the Propagation of the Faith, 68, 75, 76, 78–79; on concubinage, 38, 53, 54; confinement of the poor pursued by, 31–34, 62, 89–90; demise of, 28; elite social composition of, 29–30; militant charity by, 60–61; on prostitution, 34, 37–38, 48, 49, 59–60, 63; Protestantism opposed by, 64 (*see also* Congregation for the Propagation of the Faith); relationships with individual paupers, 62, 63; religious instruction and moral reform by, 35–39, 60–61; secrecy of, 27, 28, 32, 64

Concubinage, 38; and social attitudes on illicit sex, 53–55

Confinement of the poor, 3, 28; alternative solutions to, 82, 91–92; demise of, 182; in *dépôts de mendicité*, 216–26 passim; generated by spiritual paternalism, 89; genesis of, 17–18; legal support for, 86, 91–92, 100, 104, 217, 220, 259, 260; motivations for, 62, 76–77, 88–89; as a panacea for social problems, 75, 76–

77; pursued by the Company of the
Holy Sacrament, 31–34, 62, 89–90;
realization of, 81, 88–89

Confraternities, 4, 6, 20–80, 297;
bequests by laborers to, 133–35,
248–49; bequests by women to, 251;
Congregation for the Propagation of
the Faith viewed as, 66, 67; defined, 4,
20, 67; hospices for orphans and
prostitutes established by, 21–26; of
women, 21–26. See also Company of
the Holy Sacrament

Congregation for the Propagation of the
Faith, 6, 24, 65–80, 299; chapters of,
66, 315n3; considered as a charitable
organization, 66–69, 74–76;
conversion of Protestant "heretics" by,
68, 72, 74, 76; demise of, 79; elite
membership of, 67–68, 80; excessive
generosity of, 74, 77; female members
of, 67, 315n13, 316n39; genesis and
goals of, 64, 66, 74, 76; money
distributed by, 71–72; paternalistic
charity by, 77–78; rural Protestant
poverty as the focus of, 69–74;
testamentary bequests to, 113, 137,
156; violent methods of, 73–74, 76–77

Congregation of the Artisans, 133, 134

Constituent Assembly, 269, 274

Conversion of souls: by charitable
education, 160, 162–63; as the goal of
Catholic charity, 25–26, 35, 74–75,
89, 147; of Protestant "heretics,"
68–77; reduced emphasis on, 164, 166;
by women's confraternities, 24

Counter Reformation Catholicism, 2, 3,
5, 156; aristocratic support of, 252–55;
charitable confraternities formed
during, 66–69; charity by the clergy
generated by, 19; conflicting views of
poor relief during, 61–62, 254–57;
religious bequests influenced by,
123–37, 247–51; renewed piety and
social change during, 79–80; social
ethic generated by, 302

Courts: increased use of, 229 232;
organizational structure of, 15–16. See
also Judiciary

Créqui, duc de, 11, 14; poor relief
promoted by, 18

Crime, 92–100; associated by the elite
with poverty, 34, 39, 58, 59, 258;
described in judicial records, 6, 40–58,
59, 93, 226–38 passim; increase in,
92–95; relationship with mobility,
93–94, 224–25; by vagabonds
and transients, 44, 286

Crime in the eighteenth century, 226–38;
among families, 230–31; judicial
attitudes toward, 236, 237–38;
increased theft in, 231–34; motivated
by passion and jealousy, 230–31;
punishment for, 237–38; reduced
violence in, 227–30

Crime in the seventeenth century, 40–58;
minimal incidence of theft in, 41–44,
59; and personal or familial honor, 46–
47; popular strictures against, 43, 44;
role of gossip and neighbors' observations in, 47–48, 50; in taverns, 36, 46,
49; violence in, 45–47; by young men,
45–46

Criminals, new types of, 226–27, 236–37

Culture of the poor, 3, 46–48. See also
Popular culture

Dauphiné: absorbed into the kingdom of
France, 12–13; rural Protestantism in,
69–74

Day laborers: pious bequests by, 133–34;
unwed mothers among, 203, 204; and
vagrancy, 224

Day of the Tiles, 235

Death, attitudes toward, 115, 128; effect
on religious bequests, 124–26, 245–47;
in Protestant theology, 146

"Dechristianization," 129, 247, 337n13

Déclarations de grossesse: cessation of,
286; defined, 6–7, 52; functions of, 38,
56; and illegitimate children at the
Hospital General, 198, 200–201; and
paternal responsibility for illegitimate
children, 56, 97–98, 213; and petitions
for poor relief, 193; social attitudes
toward illicit and premarital sex
indicated by, 52–57, 58, 96–99;
on unwed fathers, 96–98

"Deinstitutionalization" of poor relief,
197, 299

de la Croix de Chevrières, François, 137;
testamentary bequest by, 113–15

Delhors, Jean-Baptiste, role in Revolutionary poor relief, 273, 274, 279

"Demoiselles," at the Hospital General,
175, 294

Dépôt de mendicité, 216–26; confinement
of beggars in, 165, 216; criminals in,
286; defined, 7, 165; Enlightenment
criticism of, 259, 262; functions of,
216, 218; rehabilitation by, 218; during
the Revolution, 269, 283; royal
establishment and support of, 216–18;
venereal disease treated at, 219,
222, 269

Dépôt de mendicité inmates, 219–26; gender of, 221; geographical origins of, 222–23; number of, 220–21; occupations of, 224–26

Deviance, spiritual corruption as the cause of, 75. *See also* Crime

Disability: among beggars, 102–3; among the laboring poor, 108

Discipline: and acculturation by the laboring poor, 296; in the goals of charity by the elite, 60, 75, 90, 162; not maintained at the Hospital General, 176

Disease: among bread recipients, 185, 191–92; of *dépôt de mendicité* inmates, 221–22; of Hospital General inmates, 179–82, 277, 292, 293; among the laboring poor, 108; of prostitutes, 48. *See also* Venereal disease

"Disorder," in the elite views on poverty and poor relief, 60, 78–79, 160

Doctors, 172, 294. *See also* Medical care for the poor

Domestic servants: conflicting religious attitudes among, 250; hospices for, 83; illegitimate children of, 96, 202; and the incidence of theft, 41, 42, 233, 235; Protestant, 140–41; in Protestant households, 68; religious bequests by, 132, 134, 139, 250, 337n15; sexual encounters of, with their employers, 53–54, 58; in testamentary bequests, 114; unemployed, 82

Donations, 18; for the confinement of the poor, 88; increase in, 84; by magistrates, 18, 84; by new types of benefactors, 85. *See also* Charitable bequests in the eighteenth century; Charitable bequests in the seventeenth century

Dowries, 144, 149; in bequests to the poor, 153, 156; bestowed by lawyers and judges, 244, 336n5; consequences of the absence of, 210; in last wills and testaments, 117, 118, 240, 244

Drinking establishments, 36, 46. *See also* Cabarets; Taverns

Economy: crises in, 82, 93, 109, 117, 118, 171, 301; and the education of the female labor force, 167; in the Enlightenment approach to poor relief, 261–65; of the family, 295–96; growth of, 14–15; Jacobin experiments in, 282–83; in views on the nature of poverty, 91, 166, 295–96. *See also* Wages

Edict of Nantes, revocation of, 65, 79, 129, 132, 145

Education, charitable: by the Congregation for the Propagation of the Faith, 74–75; conversion of souls as the goal of, 160, 162–63; and the evolution of free public schools, 283–84; for girls, 161, 164, 165–66, 167; and "little" schools of the eighteenth century, 159–68; in medical fields, 292; new types of benefactors for, 163–64, 165–66; for prostitutes, 25–26; and schools for work, 165–66; secular pedagogy in, 162, 164, 165–66; social goals of, 160, 164–67; testamentary bequests for, 136–37. *See also* Vocational training

Elderly, the: family of, 178–79; petitions for the welfare of, 194–95

Eligibility requirements for poor relief: for bread recipients, 105, 111, 191–92; national legislation on, 275–76, 278; during the Revolution, 274

Elite, the, 160; personal interaction with individual paupers, 25, 62, 63, 77, 104, 192, 297; ties with tenants and the rural poor, 152–55. *See also* Aristocracy; Attitudes toward the poor; Judicial elite; Nobility

Employment, state responsibility for, 262–63, 265

Enlightenment, 7, 129, 239–66; care for children emphasized in, 197; charitable schools established during, 159–68 passim, 327n3; compared with poor relief during the Revolution, 269; decline of charitable giving in, 242–44; decline of pious requests in, 244–55; emergence of a secular social ethic in, 254–55, 257; evaluation of poor relief in, 300; ideas on poor relief developed during, 81, 257–66; new types of hospital directors in, 171–74; wills and testamentary bequests in, 239–57.

Eucharist, 136; profanation of, 35

Family: of beggars and paupers, 102, 105, 107; conflicting types of religiosity in, 251; economy of, 295–96; of elderly welfare recipients, 178–79; honor of, 46–47; of ill welfare recipients, 181; inheritance of, compared with testamentary charitable bequests, 114, 118, 120, 135, 144, 146, 239, 240; minimal violence within, during the seventeenth century, 45, 313n66;

violent disputes within, during the
    eighteenth century, 230–31
Famine, 17, 82; during the Revolution,
    278, 280, 281
Feudalism, abolition of, 271
Filles de Service hospice, 83, 89
Finances for poor relief, 169–72; during
    the Revolution, 270, 273–75, 285,
    290; by taxation, 17, 18, 32–33,
    170–71, 273, 284; by voluntary
    donations, 18, 88, 184, 185. See also
    Hospital General
Flax-workers, 103, 105
Food, in testamentary bequests, 149–50.
Foundling children, 177, 274; increased
    number of, 198, 199
"Free" poor, testamentary bequests to,
    149–56
"Free rider problem," 301
Funerals: food distributed to the poor
    during, 149; of nobles, 12, 130;
    testamentary bequests for, 128;
    traditional rituals for, 150–51

Gagnon, Doctor, career of, 172, 173, 174,
    190, 279, 295
Garde bourgeoise, increased efficiency of,
    229, 232
Gender: and attitudes toward illicit sex,
    99; and the changed nature of the poor,
    186–91; of dépôt de mendicité inmates,
    221; of Hospital General inmates and
    welfare recipients, 177, 276, 277; and
    the predominance of poverty among
    women, 106–8, 186–90, 206, 276–78;
    role in testamentary bequests, 120, 121,
    138, 139, 142, 250–52. See also Women
Girls: charitable education for, 161,
    165–66; hospices for, 83; vocational
    training for, 91, 218
Giroud, Jean-Louis-Antoine, printer,
    269–70, 271
Glove industry, 15, 295
Glove-workers, 46, 104, 228; and the
    education of the female labor force,
    167; female, 187, 188, 203, 204, 207;
    mobility of, 214; mutual aid society
    established by, 294; poverty of, 190;
    Protestant, 141; unwed mothers
    among, 203, 204, 207; and
    vagrancy, 225
Gossip, and crime reporting, 47–48, 50
Grain: prices of, 281, 296; taxation on,
    170–71
Grenoble: growth of, 14–15; as a
    research site, 5–6
Grésivaudan valley, 287–88

Guévarre, Père: on the characteristics and
    types of paupers, 90; confinement of the
    poor promoted by, 88–89; ideas of,
    compared with Enlightenment
    concepts, 258–59
Guilds, and theft prevention, 44

Heresy, and charitable organizations,
    66–69, 74, 76, 79
Historians of poor relief, 1–2, 3–4, 115,
    299; on confraternities, 21, 310n3; on
    politics, 303
Homeless people, 82
Homicide, 44, 59
Honor, and the incidence of violent crime,
    46–48
Hospices, 20–26, 83
Hospital General, 6, 21, 76, 114,
    169–215, 299–300; administered by
    doctors, 172, 294; admission policies
    of, 192–98, 274, 284, 291–92, 297,
    298, 299; bread distributed by;
    104–10, 111, 182–92, 215, 276, 281,
    284–85, 301; characteristics of beggars
    confined in, 100–104; compared with
    the dépôt de mendicité, 221–22;
    compared with the Maison de la
    Propagation, 75; completion of, 79;
    decline of poor relief services by, 285,
    288, 291; discipline and work
    cultivated in, 75, 90, 176; effect of the
    Revolution on, 271–94 passim; efforts
    to confine the poor at, 32–33, 34, 79;
    employees at, 175, 294; establishment
    of, 18–19, 79; evolution of the medical
    purposes of, 181–82, 274–75, 280–81,
    291–94; finances of, 18, 32–33,
    169–72, 175, 198, 267, 271, 272–75,
    280, 285, 290, 291; governing bureau
    and directors of, 32, 64, 68, 85, 86–88,
    169, 171–74, 272, 279, 284; illegitimate
    children supported by, 95, 97,
    198–201, 215, 286-88; innovations at,
    83–84, 92, 181–82; new attitudes
    toward the poor reflected by, 92, 100,
    104, 110–11, 177, 182, 192, 215, 274;
    new types of administrators at,
    171–74, 272, 279, 294, 297; Orphans
    hospice at, 20, 22; policies toward
    Protestants, 137–38; realization of
    pauper confinement in, 81, 89–90;
    rebellions at, 176; registers at, 176–77,
    276; role of the municipal government
    in, 18, 32–33, 271–73, 275; royal
    support and intervention in, 86–87,
    198, 217; testamentary bequests to,
    113, 120, 156, 171, 241, 254, 306

Hospital General inmates and welfare
  recipients, 175–82; age of, 177–79,
  277, 292, 293; compared between 1793
  and the 1771–74 period, 276–78;
  disease among, 179–82, 277, 292, 293;
  gender ratio in, 177, 276, 277; marital
  status of, 292, 293; medical care for,
  291–93; mortality rates of, 181,
  329n30, 330n31; number of, 177,
  280–81; single women among, 276–78
Hospital Notre Dame, 17–18
Hospitals: Enlightenment views on, 259,
  263; military, 274–75; nationalized
  estates of, 285; Providence, established
  by women, 83, 84, 85, 89
Huissiers, 12, 16; charitable bequests
  by, 122
Humanitarian approach to poor relief, 85,
  91–92

Illegitimacy, 4, 5; causes for the increase
  of, 199–201, 205–15; rate of, 52;
  during the Revolution, 286–87; and
  social attitudes toward illicit sex,
  52–54; among urban workers and wage
  laborers, 205–6, 209, 214
Illegitimate children: and charity by the
  Company of the Holy Sacrament,
  38–39; inadequate care of, 286–88;
  increased number of, 95–97; paternal
  responsibility for, 54, 55–56, 97–98,
  213; Protestant children viewed as, 78;
  supported by the Hospital General, 95,
  97, 198–201, 215, 286–88
Illicit sex, 52–57; changed attitudes of the
  elite toward, 95–100; comparison of
  elite and popular attitudes toward,
  59–60; prostitution generated by, 55;
  social stratification in, 54–55, 208. *See
  also* Unwed fathers; Unwed mothers
Illness. *See* Disease
Imbeciles, 180
Immigration, 106
Impiety, 60–61; by the aristocracy,
  58–59; by the clergy, 35–36, 57; by the
  poor, 35; social attitudes toward,
  57–58
Incest, 58
Individual salvation, 25, 301–2; and
  bequests for Catholic masses, 113,
  127–29, 135, 322n30, 323n33;
  changed attitudes toward, 246–47; in
  eighteenth-century testamentary
  bequests, 239–40, 246–47, 253; in
  seventeenth-century testamentary
  bequests, 113, 127–29

Industrialists, 163
Infanticide, 56, 332n74
Infant mortality, 56, 107–8
Insanity, 221
Institutions for poor relief, 4, 21;
  development of, 79, 83. *See also*
  Hospital General
Intellectual elite, 173; during the
  Enlightenment, 257–66; libertines
  among, 58–59, 253
Intendants, 86

Jacobin Club, 279, 283
Jacobins, 279; demise of, 284, 288;
  economic principles of, 282–83; free
  public schools promoted by, 283–84
Jansenism, 28, 129–30; decline of, 92
Jesuits: artisan associations of, 249;
  pedagogy of, 162
Journeymen, 42
Judicial elite: ascension of, 13; charity
  financed and administered by, 18–19,
  67, 84–85, 296–97; in the Company of
  the Holy Sacrament, 30; in the
  Congregation for the Propagation of
  the Faith, 67; social status and wealth
  of, 15–16. *See also* Magistrates
Judicial records: changed attitudes toward
  crime and sin indicated by, 93–100
  passim; compared with elite perceptions
  of criminality among the poor, 39,
  40–58; eighteenth-century deviance
  reflected by, 226–38; research value
  of, 3, 4
Judiciary: attitudes of, toward eighteenth-
  century criminality, 237–38; biconfessional court of, 15, 66; costs and
  monetary motivations of, 40, 313n49;
  organizational structure of, 15–16; on
  the paternal responsibility for
  illegitimate children, 56, 97–99,
  212–14; and the reduction of violent
  crime, 229
Jurieu, Pierre, 69, 72
Justice de Grenoble municipal court, 15,
  93–100 passim; and the evaluation of
  crime and sin among the seventeenth-
  century poor, 40–58; jurisdiction of,
  40; legal fees of, 40, 313n49

Laboring poor, 104–10; causes of the
  impoverishment of, 109–10; cultural
  change among, 167–68, 296; disease
  among, 108; and eligibility requirements
  for poor relief, 191–92; illegitimate

children by, 203–6; inadequate wages of, 196, 265, 276, 296; occupations of, 107, 108–9; single, unmarried women among, 186–90, 276–78; transformed into the working class, 295; welfare for the children of, 195–98. *See also* Workers

Lace manufacture, 218

Laclos, Choderlos de, *Les Liaisons dangereuses* by, 253

Lagardette, Reynaud de, 264

La Salle, Jean-Baptiste de, 159; role in charitable education, 160–61, 162

Laundresses, 187, 203, 204

Laws, 109; on the confinement of the poor, 86, 91–92, 100, 104, 217, 220, 259, 260; on national welfare, 275, 278, 284, 290

Lawyers, 16; and abortion, 99; in the administration of the Hospital General, 172, 272; attitudes of, compared with the views of the aristocracy, 254–57; bequests to family members, 244; charitable bequests by, 122–23, 241, 242, 254, 257; poor relief financed and administered by, 85, 87; poverty among, 110; religious bequests by, 130, 245, 246–47, 257. See also *Basoche*

Le Camus, Etienne (Bishop of Grenoble), 69, 72, 126, 133, 140; on Protestant converts, 73–74; role at the Hospital General, 85

Legal counsel for the needy, 83

Lent, 111, 136; alms collected during, 169, 170; impious behavior during, 36, 37

Les Affiches du Dauphiné, 269–70

Lesdiguières, duc de (François de Bonne), 88; career of, 12, 13–14; castle of, 172; funeral of, 11–12; municipal poor relief promoted by, 17–18

Letourneau, Pierre-François, 236

Libertines, aristocratic, 58–59, 253

Libraries, public, 173

Lieutenants de police, 87, 334n11

Ligues, 13. *See also* Popular uprisings

Literacy: charitable bequests influenced by, 120, 126; and charitable education, 168; vs. eligibility requirements for welfare, 275–76; and petitions for poor relief, 193

Litigation, increased use of, 229

Loans for the poor, 83, 91

Local government, autonomous poor relief by, 269

Louis XIV, 66; role in poor relief, 86–87; widespread poverty during the reign of, 110

Madeline confraternity, 24, 59; compared with the Congregation for the Propagation of the Faith, 67–68, 76; hospices for prostitutes established by, 20, 21–22, 25; religious motivations of, 25–26

Magistrates: bequests to the Hospital General by, 84, 241, 306; bequests for masses made by, 127–29, 322n30, 323n33; bequests to the rural poor by, 152, 154–55; charitable bequests by, 121, 241–42, 243; donations by, 18, 84–85; minimal theft experienced by, 235; Protestant, 138, 139; reduced role in charity, 171–72; religious bequests by, 126–29, 252–54; social status and wealth of, 15–16. *See also* Judicial elite

Maison de la Propagation, 67, 68, 80; confinement of children at, 76; degeneration of, 79; described, 65; educational functions of, 75

Maréchaussée: activities of, 219, 220–21; defined, 217; and rural thievery, 232

Marital status: of Hospital General welfare recipients, 292, 293; and the increase of impoverished single women, 186–91; of petitioners for poor relief, 331n50

Marriage: abuse of, 35; false proposals for, 207–11; vs. premarital sex, 53–54; prevented by poverty, 206; of prostitutes, 38. *See also* Dowries

Meat tax, 170–71. *See also* Octrois tax

Medical care for the poor: development of, 85, 181–82, 291–94; professionalization of, 86. *See also* Disease; Hospitals

Mental illness, 180, 221

Merchants, 80; and administrators of the Hospital General, 87–88, 172, 272; charitable bequests by, 241–42, 243; charitable education sponsored by, 163–64, 165–66; economic category of, 249; impiety among, 57; Protestant testamentary bequests by, 139, 140, 142, 143; religious bequests by, 249–50

Middle Ages, poor relief in, 17

Midwives, 195; instructional classes for, 292; as intermediaries for welfare petitioners, 193, 303

Migrant women, 203. *See also* Mobility

Mobility: among beggars, 101; illegitimacy generated by, 96–97, 214; interaction with begging and vagrancy, 219, 220–21, 222–25; of Protestants, 141; of thieves, 93–94, 235, 236; of urban workers, 225–26; of wage laborers, 214

Monarchy, 12–13; attitudes toward

Counter Reformation charity, 72–73; beggars' prisons established by, 216–18; demise of the Congregation for the Propagation of the Faith accelerated by, 79; laws on begging and the confinement of the poor issued by, 86, 91–92, 100, 217, 220, 259, 260. *See also* National welfare system

Money: allocated in bequests to the poor, 150, 152; conversion of figures for, 8, 321n9; distributed for religious conversion, 71–72; increased visibility of, 234; loaned to the poor, 83, 91

Mounier, Jean-Joseph, 174, 270

Municipal court. *See* Justice de Grenoble municipal court

Municipal poor relief: compared with charity by confraternities, 20; decline of, 285; development of, 17–18; guided by Jacobinism, 282–84; in the Revolution, 267, 270; role at the Hospital General, 18, 32–33, 271–75

Mutual aid societies, 295; formation of, 294

National welfare system: eligibility requirements in, 275–76; genesis of, 217; legislation for, 275, 278, 284. *See also* State, the

National workshops, 286

Navizet, merchant, 273, 279, 284

Neighbors: compared with the police, 229; role in crime reporting, 47–48, 50

"New converts," 74, 129; incarceration of, 77

Nobility, 18–19, 296–97; bequests to the rural poor by, 152–55; charitable bequests by, 121–22, 242, 243; in the Company of the Holy Sacrament, 29–30; concubinage and illicit sex among, 38, 58; old and new, 30; poverty among, 110; Protestants among, 138–39; religious bequests by, 130–31, 252–54; vs. the third estate, 13. *See also* Aristocracy; Judicial elite

Noblewomen, role in poor relief, 21, 311n10. *See also* Women: confraternities formed by

Notaries, 138; and the growth of religious giving, 123–24; pious bequests by, 130, 245

Nouveau riche, 190; and the increase of theft, 234

Occupations: of beggars and vagrants, 101, 103, 224–26; of bread recipients, 187, 188; of *dépôt de mendicité*

inmates, 224–26; of elderly welfare recipients, 179; of paupers and the laboring poor, 104, 106, 107, 108–9; of petitioners for poor relief, 194, 331n50; of Protestants, 140–42; of testators making charitable bequests, 120–23; of thieves, 236; of unwed fathers, 205–6; of unwed mothers, 202, 203–4; of women, 187

Octrois tax, 170–71; abolition of, 271, 273; origins of, 32–33

Orphans confraternities of, 20–26; compared with the Congregation for the Propagation of the Faith, 67–68, 76; female membership of, 21, 23, 311n10; genesis of, 22; hospice established by, 20, 21, 22–25 passim; religious motivations of, 23–25. *See also* Foundling children

Orphans, illegitimate children by, 202, 209, 210

Paris: asylum for prostitutes in, 21; Company of the Holy Sacrament in, 27–28; Congregation for the Propagation of the Faith in, 66

Parish priests, 85; bequests by workers to, 133; *déclarations de grossesse* written by, 201; Enlightenment views on the charitable functions of, 259–60; as intermediaries for welfare petitioners, 193–94, 303

Parlement of Dauphiné, 12, 13; charity financed by, 18; described, 15, 309n16; representatives in the Company of the Holy Sacrament, 30.

Paternalism, 297; in bequests to the rural poor and peasants, 152–55, 255–57; by the Company of the Holy Sacrament, 64; confinement of the poor based on, 89; demise of, 215, 256–57, 298–99; rejected by the *basoche*, 256; replaced by a new social ethic, 257; as the source of seventeenth-century charity, 26, 65. *See also* Seigneurialism

Patron saints, 57–58, 249

Paul, Vincent de, 66

Paupers, 104–11; charitable primary education of, 159–68, 283–84; female, 106–7; in funeral processions, 12, 150–51; geographic origins of, 106; individual relationships with the elite, 62, 63, 77, 104, 192; occupations of, 104, 106, 107, 108–9; residential patterns of, 105, 183–84

Pawnshops, charitable, 83, 91

Peasants: debts of, 154; paternalistic

testamentary bequests to, 152–55, 240, 255–57; Protestant bequests to, 139–40; reduced size of bequests to, 256–57

Pellison, Paul, 72

Penitents, 134; pious bequests to, 249, 251

Périer, Claude (Périer-Milord), 172, 174, 245; career of, 163–64, 166, 172, 174, 245, 279

Petitions for poor relief, 192–98, 298; for children, 195–98; intermediaries for, 193–94; marital status of the petitioners, 331n55; occupations of the petitioners, 331n50

Pimps, 50; clerics as, 57. See also Prostitutes

Plagues, 17, 82, 109; and the growth of religious bequests, 124

Plowmen, religious bequests by, 132, 134–35

Police, 41; increased efficiency of, 229; local equivalent of, 194. See also Lieutenants de police; Maréchaussée

Politics: and free public schools established during the Revolution, 283–84; neglect of, 303; poor relief during the Revolution influenced by, 270–71, 278–80, 304

Poor relief: in an age of transition, 81–112; decline in, 285, 288, 291, 302–3; in the eighteenth century, 113–297; historians of, 1–2, 3–4, 21, 115, 299, 303; fluctuations in, 300–304; in the seventeenth century, 11–80; in the sixteenth century, 17–19

Poor relief during the Revolution, 267–94; compared with Enlightenment charity, 269; education in, 283–84; financial problems of, 273–75, 280, 285; at the Hospital General, 271–94 passim; innovations in, 269–70, 278, 282, 283–84; national legislation on, 275, 278; political influences on, 270–71, 278–80, 282, 289; social ethic of, 283, 289; social value of, 267–68, 289–94

Poor tax rate, 17, 18. See also Taxation

Popular culture, 3, 46–48; acculturation in, 296; changed sexual morality in, 99; Counter Reformation Catholicism opposed by, 133; elite Catholicism altered by, 133–35; Jacobin attack on the morality of, 283; vs. elite charity, 62, 70, 72–73, 78–89, 133–35, 163, 164

Popular uprisings, 13, 166

Population of Grenoble, 14

Poverty: among the bourgeois and nobility, 110, 301; conflicting responses to, 239–57; Enlightenment theories on, 258–66, 300; in rural Protestant areas, 69–74; spiritual remedies for, 24–25, 34–35, 89, 297; of thieves, 236–37

Poverty, causes of, 295–96; analyzed by the Company of the Holy Sacrament, 34; economic and secular analysis of, 34, 91, 295–96; Enlightenment views on, 258, 261–62; and the failure of poor relief, 300; insufficient wages in, 196, 265, 276, 296; among the laboring poor, 109–10

Pragelas valley, 69; charity vs. popular culture in, 73, 78–79; religious conversions in, 71, 73–74

Pregnancies of unwed mothers, 38–39; social attitudes toward, 52–57, 96–99. See also Déclarations de grossesse

Presentation hospice for girls, 83, 91

Prêt Charitable, 83, 159, 160; new approach to poverty relief by, 91

Prié, Claire, 54; prostitution by, 48, 49, 57, 58

Procès des tailles, 154; and the defeat of the third estate, 13

Prostitutes, 48–52, 83; attitudes and responses of the Company of the Holy Sacrament toward, 34, 37–38, 48, 49, 59–60, 63; clients of, 51–52, 57; educational conversion of, 25–26; eviction of, 51; at the Hospital General, 83, 84; legal evidence for the conviction of, 47, 48; Madeline hospice for, sponsored by a women's confraternity, 20, 21–22, 25–26, 310n8; procuresses for, 37, 48–49, 50, 57

Prostitution: promoted by illicit sexual unions, 55; as a consequence of war, 95; generated by the poverty of single women, 206–7; Jacobin campaign against, 283; punishment for, 51, 57; social abhorrence of, 50–51

Protestant Consistory: bequests to, 145; role in Protestant charity, 138, 141, 146

Protestantism: Catholic charitable bequests as a tactic against, 125; Catholic opposition to, 65–80; in rural areas, 69–74

Protestant poor relief, 137–49; compared with Catholic charity, 61, 146–49; underlying social vision in, 147–48

Protestants: court for, 15, 66; persecution of, 70–79, 147; vs. Catholic charitable schools, 162–63

Protestant testamentary bequests: compared with Catholic testamentary bequests, 137–49; social composition of seventeenth-century Protestantism indicated by, 138–44

Providence hospital, 159, 279; administration of, 85; alms and donations received by, 84; demise of, 280; established by women, 83; religious observances in, 89; testamentary bequests to, 114

Public works projects. See Ateliers de charité

Punitive poor relief: demise of, 82; Enlightenment views on, 261–62; replaced by a compassionate approach to charity, 90–92

Queyras valley, 69–70

Rape, 40, 93, 194; decline of, 207

Ratafia, 233–34

Recollets, 36, 37; pious bequests by workers to, 133–34; testamentary bequests to, 113, 127

Rehabilitation of the poor, 218. See also Work as the remedy for poverty

Religion, 2, 3; and conversion of Protestants by Catholic charitable confraternities, 65–80; replaced by a secular approach to poor relief, 91–92, 166; and spiritual instruction of the poor, 23–26, 35, 74–75, 297. See also Counter Reformation Catholicism

Religious bequests: by the aristocracy and the nobility, 130–31, 252–55; by the basoche, 130, 245–48; by domestics, 132, 134, 250, 337n15; effect of Counter Reformation Catholicism on, 247–51; increased during the seventeenth century, 123–37; by magistrates, 126–30, 252–54, 322n30, 323n33, 337n19; by merchants, 249–50; reduced in the eighteenth century, 244–55; by rural nobles, 131, 323n40; by women, 250–52; by workers, 131–35, 247–49

Rentiers, 121–22

Residential patterns of the poor, 105; changes in, 183–84

Revolution, 5, 267–97; charitable benefactors during, 173–74; and the decline of seigneurial paternalism, 257; evaluation of, 267–68, 289–91, 294; new forms of poverty created during, 286, 289; political influences on charity

in, 270–71, 275-80, 283; revolt of the clergy during, 173, 258. See also Poor relief during the Revolution

Reymond, abbé: Enlightenment views on poor relief expressed by, 258–61; writings of, 258

Rich, the, 15–16; increased wealth of, 295; self-interest of, 263–64, 265, 301–2. See also Attitudes toward the poor; Judicial elite

Ritual "washing of the feet," 24

Rosary sodalities, 249, 251

Rousseau, Jean-Jacques, 173, 261

Rural areas: charitable and religious bequests in, 120, 126, 136; charitable education in, 136; community solidarity strengthened by paternalism in, 149–55; illegitimate children in, 200; paternalistic bequests in, 152–55, 255–57; Protestant nobility in, 138–39; Protestant poverty in, 69–74; theft in, 232

Sadin, curé of Saint Laurent parish, 174; role in charitable education, 164–65, 166

Saint André Church, 36, 127–28

Saint Claire convent, bequests to, 134, 251, 253

Saint François de Sales seminary, 161

Saint Hugues parish church, 16–17, 85, 161; alms collected in the vicinity of, 270; cemetery of, 239, 240

Saint Jean–Saint Joseph parish church, 17; bequests to, 133, 136

Saint Laurent parish, 16–17, 85, 161, 193; poverty in, 183, 184

Saint Louis parish, 85; charitable education in, 164–65

Sampling techniques, 116

Sans-culotte movement, 278–79, 289

Savoyard war, 82–83, 117

Scarron, Etienne (Bishop of Grenoble), 32

Schools: in the eighteenth century, 159–68; established by the Congregation for the Propagation of the Faith, 74–75; evolution of free public schools, 283–84; for midwifery, 292; for surgery, 292. See also Education, charitable; Vocational training

Seamstresses, poverty of, 106, 108

Secular social ethic: and economics in the approach to poor relief, 259, 261–65; emergence of, 254–55, 257; Enlightenment views on, 260, 261–65

Seigneurialism, 64, 65; abduction of

Protestant children justified by, 78;
evaluation of, 298–99; and the
evolution of seigneurial bequests,
153–55, 326*n*90; maintained by the
eighteenth-century aristocracy, 255;
opposition to, 70, 256; Protestant and
Catholic charity influenced by, 149,
156; replaced by a new social ethic,
257; in rural areas, 152–55; in urban
areas, 155–56. *See also* Paternalism
Sexual behavior: comparison of elite and
popular attitudes toward, 59–60; effect
of social status on, 54–55, 208; and
honor, 46–47; revolution in, 209–10;
and social attitudes toward illicit sex,
52–57, 95–100. *See also* Unwed
fathers; Unwed mothers
Sin: among the aristocratic rich, 58–59,
68; equated with poverty, 34–39, 68,
90; reduced role in elite attitudes
toward the poor, 95–100; and social
attitudes toward illicit sex, 52–57,
98–100
Sisters of Saint Joseph, 25, 85
Sisters of Saint Martha, 85, 279
Sisters of the Madeline, 21–22, 25, 26
Smith, Adam, 261
Social groups, 305–7; boundaries crossed
by women, 227; categories for the old
regime, 321*n*16; charitable bequests by,
120–23, 241–43; conflicting types of
religiosity and social views among, 250,
254–57; and confraternities supported
by the laboring poor, 133–35, 248–49;
and the persecution of Protestants,
68–71; and popular culture vs. elite
charity, 62, 70, 72–73, 78–79,
133–35, 163, 164; poverty among all
echelons of, 110; religious bequests by,
245–57; sexual interaction in, 53–56,
99–100, 208
Social reform, 254. *See also* Revolution
Social relations, 2; modernization of, 73,
298–99
Social status: compared between unwed
mothers and unwed fathers, 208; and
the emergence of a new type of benefactor, 85, 87, 92, 163–64, 171–74,
297; judicial decisions influenced by,
56; of seventeenth-century Protestants,
138–44; of sponsors for charitable
education, 160, 163–64; of unwed
fathers, 53, 54–55, 208, 212, 214
Société Philanthropique, 269–70
Société Populaire, 174, 270–71;
establishment of, 270; free public
education promoted by, 283; popular

morality attacked by, 283; renamed
the Jacobin Club, 279
Soldiers: crime induced by, 94–95;
illegitimate children fathered by,
96–97, 204–5, 207–8, 214
Soup kitchens, 288
Spinners, poverty of, 106
Starvation, 74; among welfare recipients,
280
State, the, 4; Enlightenment views on the
charitable functions of, 262–63, 265;
and Revolutionary poor relief, 282–83.
See also National welfare system
Statistical techniques, 4; regression and
tobit analysis in, 116, 118, 119, 124,
126, 127, 155, 243, 245
Stendhal. *See* Beyle, Henri
Stevedores, 233
Syphilis, 222, 224. *See also* Venereal
disease

Tailors, 57–58; poverty of, 107; and
vagrancy, 225
Taverns: clergymen in, 57; conflicts
among workers in, 57–58, 228; crime
and blasphemy in, 36, 46, 57–58, 93,
94, 111; prostitutes in, 49, 52. *See also*
Cabarets
Taxation: capitation rolls, 189–90, 273;
for the confinement of the poor, 32–33;
for poor relief and the Hospital
General, 17, 18, 170–71, 273, 284;
social conflicts induced by, 13
Testamentary bequests: to the Hospital
General, 113, 114, 120, 156, 171, 241,
254, 306; research value of, 4, 115–16.
See also Charitable bequests in the
eighteenth century; Charitable bequests
in the seventeenth century; Religious
bequests
Testamentary bequests in the eighteenth
century, 239–57, 307; by the *basoche,*
245–48; conflicting social and religious
views reflected in, 254–57; decline of
charitable giving in, 242–44; decline
of religious giving in, 244–55; family
inheritance in, 239, 240, 244; by
laborers, 248–49; to peasants, 240,
255–57; by social groups, 307
Testamentary bequests in the seventeenth
century, 113–56, 305; for Catholic
masses, 113, 127–29, 135, 322*n*30,
323*n*33; comparison of Protestant and
Catholic, 137–49; for education, 136–
37; to the "free" poor, 149–56; and the
growth of religious giving, 123–37; and

the increase in charitable giving, 117–23; by magistrates, 126–29, 152, 154–55; paternalism in, 152–55; social and religious influences on, 118, 120–23, 131–37; by various social groups, 120–37 passim, 307, 321n16

Textile industry, 14; and the vocational training of women, 167

Teysseire, liquor merchant, 233–34, 237, 245, 272

Theaters, 227

Theft, 232; by domestics, 41, 42, 233, 235; increase of, 93, 231–34; minimal incidence of, 41–44; popular strictures against, 43, 44; punishment for, 42, 43–44, 237–38; social condemnation of, 234; by transients, 94; vigilante approach to, 42, 43

Thieves: mobility of, 94, 235, 236; poverty of, 236–37; social background of, 236

Third estate: defeat of, 13; hegemony of the magistrates opposed by, 18–19; during the Revolution, 174. See also Popular culture

Three Orders of Grenoble, 173–74

Tour Dauphine, 55, 57

"Traffic in souls," 72, 74

Très Cloîtres, 14; paupers in, 105, 133

Unskilled laborers, 103, 107; disease and poverty of, 108–10; religious bequests by, 132–33. See also Laboring poor; Wages

Unwed fathers, 96–99; and efforts to conceal illicit paternity, 98–99; flight of, 211–14; legal responsibility of, 56, 97–98, 201, 212–14; marital promise as a tactic of, 207–9; in the military, 96–97, 204–5, 207–8, 214; mobility of, 96–97, 211–14; occupations of, 205–6; social status of, 53, 54–55, 208, 212, 214. See also Illicit sex

Unwed mothers, 7, 38, 52–57; baptism of the children of, 52; and charity by elite confraternities, 38–39; at the dépôt de mendicité, 222; and the increase of illegitimate children, 200–215 passim; as migrants, 203; motivations of, 207–11; occupations of, 96, 202, 203–4, 205–6; petitions for the welfare of, 193–94; social disapproval of, 99, 319n60; social status of, 208. See also Abortion; Déclarations de grossesse; Domestic servants; Illicit sex

Urban workers, mobility vs. vagrancy of, 225–26

Vagabonds, 59; distinguished from beggars, 102, 103, 104; in eighteenth-century charitable institutions, 218–26; fear of, 40, 44, 226; gender ratio among, 221; increased number of thieves and criminals among, 286, 289

Vaudois valleys, 69, 70–73

Venereal disease, 48; treatment for, 222, 269

Ventôse decrees, 267, 268

Vigilantism, 42, 43; decline of, 232

Violence: among families, 45, 230–31, 313n66; increased during the age of transition, 93, 94; perceived by the rich, 39; in the pursuit of charity, 73–74, 76–77; reduced in the late eighteenth-century, 227–30, 296; in the seventeenth century, 45–47; by young men, 45–46

Vocational training: and charitable schools for work, 165–66, 167; by confraternities, 75; for girls, 91, 218; testamentary bequests for, 137; for women, 91, 167. See also Work as the remedy for poverty

Voluntary charity, origins of, 18. See also Charitable bequests in the eighteenth century; Charitable bequests in the seventeenth century; Donations

Wage laborers: illegitimate children of, 205–6, 209, 214–15; and the increase of theft, 233; mobility of, 214, 225–26; and vagrancy, 225–26

Wages: chronic poverty induced by, 296; inadequacy of, 196, 265, 276, 296; and payment in kind, 233; vs. work as a remedy for poverty, 265

War: crime intensified during, 94–95; illegitimacy increased during, 96–97, 204–5, 207–8, 214; institutions for poor relief influenced by, 274–75, 281–82, 289; new types of poverty generated by, 286; between Savoy and France, 82–83, 117

Wars of Religion, 13, 17, 131; end of, 12

Weavers, poverty of, 103, 109

Wet nurses: for the children of wage laborers, 195–96; for illegitimate children, 54, 55–56; for infants of paupers, 107; wages of, 198, 212

Widows: poverty of, 106, 108, 110, 184–85, 286; as procuresses for prostitutes, 50

Wigmakers, 225, 228

Wills, 4, 115, 305. See also Testamentary bequests

Witches, 22

Women: charitable bequests by, 120; confraternities formed by, 20–26; in the Congregation for the Propagation of the Faith, 67, 315n13, 316n39; education of, 75, 316n39; history of, xi; impoverishment of single women, 186–90, 206, 276–78; and the incidence of violent crime, 45; in the labor force, 167; neglected in Revolutionary poor relief, 276–78; occupations of, 108, 187; poverty of, 106–7; Providence hospital established by, 83; religious bequests and attitudes of, 250–52, 337n19; sexual abuse of, 54–55; social attitudes on illicit sexual behavior by, 53–56, 99; vocational training for, 91, 167, 218. See also Gender; Prostitutes; Widows

Work as the remedy for poverty, 34; Enlightenment views on, 259, 260, 261–65; in the goals of charitable education, 160, 165–66; by incarcerated paupers, 34, 89–90, 218; in the Revolutionary poor relief ethic, 283

Workers: cabaret conflicts among, 57–58, 228; illegitimate children by, 205–6, 212; mutual aid societies established by, 294; religious bequests by, 132–34, 140–41, 247–49. See also Laboring poor

Workhouses, imprisonment of paupers in, 3, 17, 31–34, 62. See also Confinement of the poor

Workshops: for children, 166; national, 286

Young men: prostitutes evicted by, 51; violent crime by, 45–46

Designer: Mark Ong
Compositor: Innovative Media, Inc.
Text: Sabon
Display: Sabon
Printer: Braun-Brumfield, Inc.
Binder: Braun-Brumfield, Inc.